# The Periplus of the Erythraean Sea

# The Periplus of the Erythraean Sea

## Travel and Trade in the Indian Ocean by a Merchant of the First Century

TRANSLATED FROM THE GREEK AND ANNOTATED

BY

WILFRED H. SCHOFF, A.M.

GYAN

*Published by*

Gyan Publishing House
5, Ansari Road
Daryaganj, New Delhi-110002
Phone: 011-47034999, 9811692060
E-mail: books@gyanbooks.com

*Distribution Network*
gyanbooks.com
India, USA, Canada, UK, Australia, France



ISBN : 978-81-212-2989-0 (PB)
First Published, 1912

2nd Impression 2021

*Printed at:* Gyan Press, Delhi.



**The Periplus of the Erythraean Sea**
Translated: Wilfred H. Schoff

# THE PERIPLUS OF THE ERYTHRÆAN SEA

## TRAVEL AND TRADE IN THE INDIAN OCEAN BY A MERCHANT OF THE FIRST CENTURY

TRANSLATED FROM THE GREEK AND ANNOTATED
BY
WILFRED H. SCHOFF, A. M.
*Secretary of the Commercial Museum, Philadelphia*

LONGMANS, GREEN, AND CO.
FOURTH AVENUE & 30TH STREET, NEW YORK
LONDON, BOMBAY AND CALCUTTA
1912

# TABLE OF CONTENTS

# FOREWORD

The Philadelphia Museums came into existence some fifteen years ago with the avowed purpose of aiding the manufacturer in taking a larger share in the world's commerce.

They have lost no opportunity in presenting to the inquirer the trade conditions of all parts of the world.

More than four years ago the Museums undertook the work of making a graphic history of commerce from the earliest dawn of trade and barter down to the present time. The author of this translation was entrusted with the study and preparation of the exhibit, which in its early stages of development was shown at the Jamestown exposition. It was in the preparation of this exhibit that attention was directed to the Periplus, and its interest in the early history of commerce appreciated. The Periplus of the Erythræan Sea is the first record of organized trading with the nations of the East, in vessels built and commanded by subjects of the Western world. The notes add great interest, giving as they do an exhaustive survey of the international trade between the great empires of Rome, Parthia, India and China, together with a collection of facts touching the early trade of a number of other countries of much interest.

The whole trade of the world is every day coming more and more under exact laws of demand and supply. When the history of commerce from its earliest dawn to its present tremendous international proportions shall be carefully written, the Periplus will furnish a most interesting part of such early history, and the Commercial Museum will not have to apologize for rescuing this work from obscurity and presenting it to the general public.

W. P. WILSON, Sc.D.,
Director.

The Philadelphia Museums
September, 1911

# INTRODUCTION

The *Periplus of the Erythræan Sea* is one of those human documents, like the journals of Marco Polo and Columbus and Vespucci, which express not only individual enterprise, but the awakening of a whole race toward new fields of geographical discovery and commercial achievement. It is the first record of organized trading with the nations of the East, in vessels built and commanded by subjects of the Western World. It marks the turning of a tide of commerce which had set in one direction, without interruption, from the dawn of history. For thousands of years before the emergence of the Greeks from savagery, or before the exploits of the Phœnicians in the Mediterranean and Atlantic, human culture and commerce had centered in the countries bordering on the Persian Gulf; in Elam and Babylonia, and in the "whole land of Havilah, where there is gold: and the gold of that land is good; there is bdellium and the onyx stone." With the spread of culture in both directions, Egypt and the nations of Ancient India came into being, and a commercial system was developed for the interchange of products within those limits, having its center of exchanges near the head of the Persian Gulf. The peoples of that region, the various Arab tribes and more especially those ancestors of the Phœnicians, the mysterious *Red Men*, were the active carriers or intermediaries. The growth of civilization in India created an active merchant marine, trading to the Euphrates and Africa, and eastward we know not whither. The Arab merchants, apparently, tolerated the presence of Indian traders in Africa, but reserved for themselves the commerce within the Red Sea; that lucrative commerce which supplied precious stones and spices and incense to the ever-increasing service of the gods of Egypt. This was their prerogative, jealously guarded, and upon this they lived and prospered according to the prosperity of the Pharaohs. The muslins and spices of India they fetched themselves or received from the Indian traders in their ports on either side of the Gulf of Aden; carrying them in turn over the highlands to the upper Nile, or through the Red Sea and across the desert to Thebes or Memphis. In the rare intervals when the eyes of Egypt were turned eastward, and voyages of commerce and conquest were despatched to the Eastern Ocean, the officers of the Pharaohs found the treasures of all its shores gathered in the nearest ports, and sought no further to trace them to their sources.

As the current of trade gradually flowed beyond the Nile and Euphrates to the peoples of the north, and their curiosity began to trace the better things toward their source in India, new trade-routes were gradually opened. The story of the world for many centuries was that of the struggles of the nations upon the Nile and Euphrates to win all the territory through which the new routes passed, and so to prevent the northern barbarians from trading with others than themselves. It was early in this struggle that one branch of the people known as Phœnicians left their home on the Persian Gulf and settled on the Mediterranean, there to win in the West commercial glories which competition in the East was beginning to deny them. The Greek colonies, planted at the terminus of every trade-route, gained for themselves a measure of commercial independence; but never until the overthrow of the East by the great Alexander was the control of the great overland caravan-routes threatened by a western people, and his early death led to no more than a readjustment of conditions as they had always existed.

Meantime the brethren of the Phœnicians and their kinsfolk in Arabia continued in control of the carrying trade of the East, subject to their agreements and alliances with the merchants of India. One Arab kingdom after another retained the great eastern coast of Africa, with its trade in gold and ivory, ostrich feathers and oil; the shores of the Arabian Gulf produced an ever-rising value in frankincense and myrrh; while the cloths and precious stones, the timbers and spices—particularly cinnamon—brought from India largely by Indian vessels, were redistributed at Socotra or Guardafui, and carried to the Nile and the Mediterranean. Gerrha and Obollah, Palmyra and Petra, Sabbatha and Mariaba were all partners in this commercial system. The Egyptian nation in its later struggles made no effort to oppose or control it. The trade came and the price was paid. And the infusion of Greek energy after Alexander's day, when the Ptolemies had made Egypt once more mistress of the nations, led to nothing more than the conquest of a few outposts on the Red Sea and at the head of the Gulf of Aden; while the accounts of Agatharchides are sufficient proof of the opulence which came to Southern Arabia with the increase of prosperity in Egypt. Here, indeed, the trade control was more complete than ever; for changes in the topography of India, the westward shifting of the Indus delta, the shoaling of the harbors in the Cutch region, and the disorder incident to great invasions of Asiatic peoples, had sapped the vigor of the Indian sea-trade.

But in Arabia itself there were struggles for the control of all this wealth and power, and in the days of the later Ptolemies kingdoms rose and fell and passed into oblivion with bewildering frequency. The African coast was left to its own people and to the remnants of the Indian trade, and one Arab tribe maintained itself at the Straits, while its defeated adversary, establishing itself in the old "land of Cush," was building up the kingdom of Abyssinia, whose ambitions were bitterly opposed to the state which possessed its former home in the "Frankincense Country" of Arabia.

It was at this juncture that the rule of the Ptolemies came to an end under Cleopatra, and the new ruler of the Western World, the Empire of Rome, came into possession of Egypt, and thus added to its control of the caravan-routes previously won in Asia Minor and Syria, that of a direct sea-route to the East, by way of the Ptolemies' outposts on the Red Sea.

The prize thus within reach of the Roman people was a rich one. Successive conquests and spoliation of all the Mediterranean peoples had brought to Rome treasures as yet unexampled, and a taste for the precious things of the East was developed almost over-night. The public triumphs of the conquerors of Asia Minor and Syria glittered with new treasures, for which the people clamored. Money was plentiful and merchants flocked thither from all quarters. Within a generation the center of exchanges of the Mediterranean was moved from Alexandria to Rome. But a wise decision of the Emperor Augustus, only once departed from and that disastrously, limited the Roman dominion to the bank of the Euphrates; so that all this rich trade that flowed to Rome paid its tolls to the Empire of Parthia and to the Arab kingdoms, unless Rome could develop and control a sea-borne trade to India.

Against such an enterprise all the energy and subtlety of the Arab was called into action. No information was allowed to reach the merchants in Egypt, and every device the imagination could create was directed toward discouraging the least disturbance of the channels of trade that had existed since human memory began. And in an unknown ocean, with only the vaguest ideas of the sources of the products they sought, and the routes that led to them, it might have been many years before a Roman vessel, coasting along hostile shores, could reach the goal. But accidents favored Roman ambition. The new kingdom at Axum, smarting under the treatment of its former neighbors in Arabia, was courting the Roman alliance.

The old trading-posts at Guardafui, formerly under Arab control, were now free, through the quarrels of their overlords, and their markets were open to who might seek. And then a Roman subject, perhaps in the Abyssinian service, was driven to sea and carried in an open boat to India, whence he returned in a few months with a favorable wind and much information. Then Hippalus, a venturesome navigator whose name deserved as much honor in Roman annals as that of Columbus in modern history, observed the periodic change of the Indian monsoon (doubtless long known to Arab and Hindu), and boldly setting sail at the proper season made a successful trading voyage and returned with a cargo of all those things for which Rome was paying so generously: gems and pearls, ebony and sandalwood, balms and spices, but especially pepper. The old channels of trade were paralleled but not conquered; so strong was the age-long understanding between Arab and Hindu, that cinnamon, which had made the fortune of traders to Egypt in earlier times, was still found by the Romans only at Guardafui and was scrupulously kept from their knowledge in the markets of India, where it was gathered and distributed; while the leaf of the same tree producing that precious bark was freely offered to the Roman merchants throughout the Malabar coast, and as *malabathrum* formed the basis of one of their most valued ointments.

Great shiftings of national power followed this entry of Roman shipping into the Indian Ocean. One by one Petra and Gerrha, Palmyra and Parthia itself, their revenues sapped by the diversion of accustomed trade, fell into Roman hands. The Homerite Kingdom in South Arabia fell upon hard times, its capital into ruin, and some of its best men migrated northward and as the Ghassanids bowed the neck to Rome. Abyssinia flourished in proportion as its old enemy declined. If this state of things had continued, the whole course of later events might have been changed. Islam might never have appeared, and a greater Rome might have left its system of law and government from the Thames to the Ganges. But the logic of history was too strong. Gradually the treasure that fell to the Roman arms was expended in suppressing insurrections in the conquered provinces, in civil wars at home, and in a constant drain of specie to the east in settlement of adverse trade balances; a drain which was very real and menacing to a nation which made no notable advance in production or industry by means of which new wealth could be created. As the resources of the West diminished the center of exchange shifted to Constantinople. The trade-routes leading to that center were the old routes through Mesopotamia, where a revivified power under the

Sassanids was able to conquer every passage to the East, including even the proud Arab states which had not yielded submission to Hammurabi or Esarhaddon, Nebuchadrezzar or Darius the Great. Egypt, no longer in the highway of commerce, became a mere granary for Constantinople, and Abyssinia, driven from its hard-won footholds east of the Red Sea, could offer the Byzantine emperors no effective aid in checking the revival of Eastern power. And the whirlwind of activity let loose by Mohammed welded the Eastern World as no force had yet done, and brought the West for another millennium to its feet. Not until the coming of those vast changes in industry and transportation which marked the nineteenth century did the Western nations find commodities of which the East stood in need, and laying them down in Eastern markets on their own terms, turn back the channels of trade from their ancient direction.

The records of the pioneers, who strove during the ages to stem this irresistible current, are of enduring interest in the story of human endeavor; and among them all, one of the most fascinating is this *Periplus of the Erythræan Sea*—this plain and painstaking log of a Greek in Egypt, a Roman subject, who steered his vessel into the waters of the great ocean and brought back the first detailed record of the imports and exports of its markets, and of the conditions and alliances of its peoples. It is the only record for centuries that speaks with authority on this trade in its entirety, and the gloom which it briefly lighted was not lifted until the wider activities of Islam broke the time-honored custom of Arab secrecy in trading, and by grafting Arab discovery on Greek theory, laid the foundations of modern geography. Not Strabo or Pliny or Ptolemy, however great the store of knowledge they gathered together, can equal in human interest this unknown merchant who wrote merely of the things he dealt in and the peoples he met—those peoples of whom our civilization still knows so little and to whom it owes so much; who brought to the restless West the surplus from the ordered and industrious East, and in so doing ruled the waters of the "Erythræan Sea."

## THE DATE AND AUTHORSHIP OF THE PERIPLUS

The manuscript copies of the Periplus at Heidelberg and London do not enable us to fix either date or authorship. The Heidelberg manuscript attributes the work to Arrian, apparently because in that manuscript this Periplus follows a report of a voyage around the Black Sea made by the historian Arrian, who was governor of Cappadocia about 131 A. D. This is manifestly a mistake, and the London manuscript does not contain that reference.

The only guidance to date or authorship must be found in the Periplus itself.

Hippalus' discovery of the sea-route to India, described in § 57, is fixed by Vincent at about 47 A. D.

Vincent reasons from Pliny's account (VI, 24) of the accidental journey of a freedman of Annius Plocamus who had farmed from the Treasury the revenues arising from the Red Sea. This freedman was carried away by a gale and in fifteen days drifted to Ceylon, where he was hospitably received and after a stay of six months returned home; after which the Ceylonese kings sent an embassy to Rome. Pliny says that this occurred during the reign of Emperor Claudius, which began in the year 41. The discovery of Hippalus must have come very soon after. (The first question suggested by this story is, what the freedman was doing outside the Straits of Bab-el-Mandeb and from whom Annius Plocamus farmed the revenues. As to this Pliny is silent. Can it have been the friendly Abyssinians, or were the Greek colonies in Arabia still in existence?)

The discovery of Hippalus, described in § 57, seems to have occurred not long before the author of the Periplus made his voyage. He evidently feels a deep respect for the discoverer, and goes on to say that "from that time until now" voyages could be made directly across the ocean by the monsoon.

Pliny has but a passing reference to Hippalus, suggesting that between 73 and 77 A. D. when he was writing, the memory of the discoverer had faded somewhat from view.

Assuming 50 A. D. as a date earlier than which this Periplus can not have been written, we must look next for a limit on the other side.

In § 38 is mentioned "the sea-coast of Scythia" around the mouth of the Indus, and the metropolis of Scythia, Minnagara, which was "subject to Parthian princes at war among themselves."

In § 41 is mentioned another city Minnagara, which, as indicated in the notes, is simply the Hindu name for "city of the invaders."

In § 47 is mentioned the "very war-like inland nation of the Bactrians."

As explained in the notes, the Scythians of the Periplus are the Saka tribe, who had been driven from Eastern Turkestan by the Yueh-chi, and overran Beluchistan, the lower Indus valley, and adjacent parts of the coast of India itself. They submitted to the Parthian Kingdom, of which they formed an important part. Their southern extension under Sandares, the ruler mentioned in § 52, indicates a growing pressure from the Kushan kingdom on the north, but prior to the conquest of this whole country by the Kushans, which occurred soon after 95 A. D. The "war-like nation of the Bactrians" is the tribe of Yueh-chi or Kushans, formerly subject to China, who, after being driven westward by the Huns, overran the Greek kingdom of Bactria and set up there a powerful kingdom which, early in the second century A. D., conquered most of northern India. The conditions in the text indicate a time before this nation had commenced its conquests in the valleys of the Indus and Ganges, and probably before the great defeat of its king Kadphises by the Chinese general Panchao near Khotan, which occurred in 90 A. D. A defeat of this magnitude must certainly have been reported throughout India and would not have led our author to refer to the nation as "very warlike." Thus we arrive at two dates, 90 and 95 A. D., later than which this Periplus can not have been written.

In §§ 4 and 5 our author mentions the city of the Axumites, and the territory, coast and inland, ruled over by Zoscales; whom Henry Salt identified with the name "Za Hakale" found by him in the *Tarik Negusti* or Chronicles of the kings of Abyssinia. The duration of this Za Hakale's reign, according to the Chronicle, was thirteen years, and his dates Salt fixes at 76 to 89 A. D., following a note in the Chronicle that the birth of Christ took place in the eighth year of one of Za Hakale's predecessors, Zabaesi Bazen. The date of the accession of this Zabaesi Bazen was 84 years prior to that of Za Hakale. Salt's identification of the name is probably correct, but the dates as they stand in the Chronicles were written some centuries after the events, and can hardly be accepted as safe authority in the absence of other evidence. The fact that nearly all the reigns are given as lasting an even number of years, or else as so many years and six months, shows that the chroniclers were only estimating the time. Salt himself was obliged to rearrange their chronology in order to fit it to known facts, and it is quite possible that his rearrangement has slipped in a whole reign before that of Za Hakale. Obviously Salt's names are worth more than his dates. South Arabian inscriptions discovered by Glaser indicate the separation of Axum from its mother-land, the Habash or Ethiopia of South Arabia, not long before the date of the Periplus; and the fact that there is no mention of Axum in any work earlier than the Periplus, and not even in Pliny, suggests the same conclusion; namely, that the Abyssinian Chronicles are unreliable, at any rate in their earlier portions. They count as independent kings a number of rulers who must have been subject to the Arabian mother-land; the order of events they relate is uncertain, and their dates are merely approximations.

Even if the dates in the Chronicle, and Salt's identification of Zoscales with Zá Hakale were strictly correct, the date generally accepted for the birth of Christ, 5 B. C., would bring Za Hakale's accession down to 71 A. D. and his death to 84.

Nearly all the commentators think that the Periplus is earlier than Pliny's *Natural History*, which is known to have been published between 73 and 77 A. D. The principal indication is their similarity in the description of Arabia Felix, where Pliny seems to condense the Periplus; but, on the other hand, there are many statements in Pliny's sixth book which describe facts in disagreement with, and probably earlier than, the Periplus. Of course Pliny was a compiler and copyist, and usually not very discriminating, and he may have chosen to follow the Periplus only where it did not contradict the earlier accounts of King Juba II of Mauretania, for whose knowledge he repeatedly expressed respect. Pliny has much more information about Meroe than appears in the Periplus, but he does not mention Axum. He ends the African coast at the Promontory of Mosyllum and says that the Atlantic Sea begins there. In this he follows King Juba; but had he known the Periplus he ought to have included the African coast as far as Zanzibar. He has an account of Mariaba, the royal city of Arabia Felix, which the Periplus has not. He quotes Aelius Gallus, writing in 24 B. C., as stating that the Sabaeans are the richest tribe in southern Arabia. The Periplus, however, has them subject to the Homerites, who receive only passing mention from Aelius Gallus.

One is tempted to imagine that Pliny's account of the voyage to India (VI, 26) in which he refers to "information on which reliance may be placed, here published for the first time," refers to the Periplus, then existing merely as a merchant's diary; and Glaser has based much of his argument as to the authorship of the Periplus on that passage; but Pliny goes on to describe a voyage different in many ways from that of the Periplus, and giving quite a different account of the coast of India. At the time Pliny wrote, the sea-route to India had been opened for nearly thirty years, and he might have had this information from any sea-captain, as indeed he might have had the facts concerning Arabia Felix which seem to be in such close agreement with the Periplus. The argument that Pliny, whose work was dedicated in 77 A. D., borrowed from the Periplus is, then, suggestive and even plausible, but by no means conclusive.

Returning to § 41, the reference to the anarchy in the Indo-Parthian or Saka region does not suggest the consolidated power of that King of Kathiawar and Ujjain who founded the so-called Saka era of 78 A. D.; indicating for the Periplus a date earlier than that era.

Mention of the "land of This" in § 64, is helpful. This seems evidently to be the state of Ts'in in northwest China, at the date of the Periplus the most powerful of the states of China, and actively engaged in pushing Chinese boundaries and influence westward across Turkestan. The capital city is supposed to be the modern Singanfu. The text says that "silk is brought overland from that country to Bactria and India," but that "few men come from there and seldom." This suggests a time when the trade-routes across Turkestan were still in turmoil and before the conquests of the Chinese general Panchao. The route north of the desert of Turkestan was finally opened by him in 94 A. D., while the route south of the desert was opened as early as 73 A. D., indicating that the Periplus must be fixed before that date.

In § 19 is mentioned Malichas, king of the Nabataeans. As Fabricius has pointed out, this is one of the most important indications of date contained in the text. Josephus in his *Wars of the Jews* mentions a Malchus, king of Arabia, under which name he always refers to the Nabataean kingdom, as having assisted Titus in his expedition against Jerusalem, which he destroyed in the year 70 A. D. (*Bell. Jud.*, III, 4, § 2); and Vogüé in his *Syrie Centrale*, Semitic Inscriptions, p. 107, confirms that a Nabataean king Aretas (Hareth), contemporary with the Emperors Tiberius and Caligula, had a son Malik, or Malchus III, who reigned about 40 to 70 A. D. It was a sister of this Malchus who married Herod Antipas, tetrarch of Galilee, and was abandoned by Herod for his brother Philip's wife, Herodias, mother of Salome. (Josephus, *Ant. Jud.* XVIII, 8). This action of Herod brought him to war with his father-in-law, Aretas, and doubtless explains to some extent the policy of Malichas in assisting Rome against Judea. This must have been the same as the Malichas of the text, and his action against Jerusalem must have been near the end of his reign. It is fair to infer that if the Periplus had been written after that expedition, Malichas also would have been called, like Charibael in § 23, a "friend of the Emperor," and therefore that the Periplus was written before Titus' campaign of the year 70.

In §§ 23 and 27 we have the names of Charibael, king of the two tribes, the Homerites and the Sabaites, and of Eleazus, king of the Frankincense Country. It was the opinion of Glaser, based on inscriptions discovered by him in South Arabia, that both these names were titles rather than personal names, and that they were borne by several rulers during the first century A. D. His incription No. 1619 mentions a king Eleazus who was ruler in 29 A. D., and a king Charibael whose reign was from about 40 to 70 A. D. The mention of Charibael as "a friend of the Emperors" might answer for a date under Vespasian after the succession of short reigns that followed Nero; but the years of turmoil throughout the Roman Empire, for several years after the death of Nero, were not years of prosperous trade such as the Periplus describes. This reference indicates a date early in the reign of Nero, before the memory of his predecessor Claudius had faded; roughly, any time between 54 and 60 A. D.

In § 23 is a reference to the recent destruction of Arabia Eudaemon. Our present knowledge of Arabian history does not give us any positive date for the war leading to the destruction of this Sabaean port, but the inscriptions discovered and commented on by Glaser point to a time after the middle of the first century.

In § 2 our author mentions the city of Meroe. This capital of the Nubian kingdom was severely treated by the Romans soon after their occupation of Egypt. The Nubian queen Candace had attacked Egypt; and an expedition sent out against her under Petronius annihilated her army and destroyed many of her cities, including that of Napata. This was in B. C. 22. That another queen Candace of Nubia retained considerable power in the first half of the first century A. D. is shown in Acts VIII, 27. After this, Pliny relates, the savage tribes of the neighboring deserts came down and plundered what was left of the Nubian Kingdom, so that an expedition of inquiry sent by the emperor Nero (Pliny, VI, 35) when he was contemplating a campaign in the South, ventured as far as Meroe and reported that they had met with nothing but deserts on their routes; that the buildings in Meroe itself were but few in number and were still ruled over by a queen named Candace, that name having passed from queen to queen for many years. This state of things can be fixed at about 67 A. D. It is obviously later than the account in the Periplus.

Very soon after Pliny's time Meroe must have been destroyed, as the name does not appear again for several centuries.

A suggestive fact is that the Periplus tells only of the great increase in trade with India, and has no mention of a cessation or decline of that trade consequent upon the burning of Rome, July 19-25 in the year 64. Ten out of the fourteen districts of the city were destroyed. The loss was not equalized; fire insurance did not exist. It is true that this great calamity hardly receives mention in Pliny's work. He refers to the baseless story of Nero's having started the fire, and in several passages to the destruction of buildings, temples and the like, always with some reticence. In many places, however, once in so many words, he mentions the crisis through which Rome passed in the later years of Nero and his short-lived successors, and of the "rest brought to an exhausted empire" by the strong hand of Vespasian. But in a work distinctly of a commercial nature, written far from Rome but relating to a commerce whose sudden expansion was due entirely to Roman demand, some mention of the trade depression that must have followed such a destruction of capital and the ensuing political disorder, would have been most probable. The facts of this conflagration and of its effects upon trade are thought to be stated in Revelation, c. XVIII, and, notwithstanding the different point of view of the writer of that book, the circumstances he describes are of importance here.

"And the kings of the earth . . . shall bewail her, and lament for her, when they shall see the smoke of her burning, . . . and the merchants of the earth shall weep and mourn over her; for no man buyeth their merchandise any more: the merchandise of gold, and silver, and precious stones, and of pearls, and fine linen, and purple, and silk, and scarlet, and all sweet wood, and all manner vessels of ivory, and all manner vessels of most precious wood, and of brass, and iron, and marble, and cinnamon, and odours, and ointments, and frankincense, and wine, and oil, and fine flour, and wheat, and beasts, and sheep, and horses, and chariots, and slaves, and souls of men . . . . The merchants of these things, which were made rich by her, shall stand afar off for the fear of her torment, weeping and wailing, and saying, Alas, alas, that great city, that was clothed in fine linen, and purple, and scarlet, and decked with gold, and precious stones, and pearls! For in one hour so great riches is come to nought. And every shipmaster, and all the company in ships, and sailors, and as many as trade by sea, stood afar off, and cried when they saw the smoke of her burning, saying, What city is like unto this great city! And they cast dust on their heads and cried, weeping and wailing, saying, Alas, alas, that great city, wherein were made rich all that had ships in the sea by reason of her costliness! . . . . For thy merchants were the great men of the earth."

Now our author was one of those same shipmasters trading by sea; but in his account there is no suggestion of standing afar off, weeping and wailing, such as would probably have appeared if he were writing after that great disaster.

Following the discovery of Hippalus there seems to have been a sudden and enormous increase in the Roman trade with India, and particularly in the importation of Indian products. The Periplus, in § 10, refers to the "larger ships" now needed for the cinnamon trade. This increase, particularly in the importation of luxuries, can be ascribed to the fashion of extravagance set by Nero's court, during the ascendancy of his favorite Sabina Poppæa, whose influence lasted from 58 until her death in 65 A. D. Pliny's reference to the enormous quantity of spices used at Poppæa's funeral (XII, 41) indicates such an increased trade; which he further confirms (VI, 26) by stating that specie amounting to about $22,000,000 per year was required to balance the trade, and that these Indian imports sold in Rome at one hundred times their cost. Pliny's figures are untrustworthy, as in XII, 41, he estimates a little over $4,000,000 as the balance of specie required for the entire trade with India, Arabia and China; but a sudden increase in commerce is none the less evident.

The absence of any description in the Periplus of trade with the coasts of the Persian Gulf, then subject to Parthia, suggests that it was written at a time when Rome and Parthia were at war. Our author's descriptions, even of the southern coast of Arabia, stop at the Frankincense Country and its dependency, the island of Masira; and he explains that the coast beyond the islands of Kuria Muria was "subject to Persia" and thus closed to him. According to the account given by Rawlinson, (*Sixth Monarchy*, XVI,) conflicting claims as to the Armenian succession led Rome to make war on Parthia in 55 A. D., the second year of Nero's reign. The Parthians, at the time occupied with civil war in the South (possibly even in their newly-acquired South Arabian possessions), gave hostages and abandoned their Armenian pretensions; which, however, they reasserted in 58, when war broke out anew. Hostilities continued in a desultory way until 62, when the two powers agreed upon a mutual evacuation of Armenia and a settlement of the dispute by a Parthian embassy which was to visit Rome. This truce occurred in the summer of 62. The embassy made its visit in the autumn and returned without a treaty. The truce was broken the same winter by a Roman invasion of Armenia, which was repulsed and the truce renewed. A second Parthian embassy to Rome in the spring of 63 settled the matter by placing a Parthian prince on the Armenian throne and requiring him to receive investiture from the Roman Emperor. This ceremony occurred in 65 A. D.

Hostilities between the two countries certainly ceased in the winter of 62 and probably, as far as commercial interests were concerned, in the summer of that year. Therefore, the date of the Periplus, or at any rate the date of the voyage on which it was based, can probably be fixed at not later than the summer of 62 and not earlier than the summer of 58.

The possibilities are rather in favor of the second or third year of the renewed Roman-Parthian war, when the Parthian power had fully recovered from the disorders in the South.

The nearest single year that suggests itself as the date of the Periplus is, therefore, 60 A. D.

As to the authorship, it is best to admit that nothing is known. Fabricius in his first edition of the Periplus attributed it to an Alexandrian merchant named Arrian, but other editions, and Fabricius' own second edition, remove the name altogether.

Glaser, in an article published in *Ausland*, 1891, pp. 45-46, presents an argument that seems too tempting to be true. He assumes that the sixth book of Pliny quotes from the Periplus; that the "heretofore unpublished account," which Pliny mentions, was that of our author; that his work could have been quoted in no other book of Pliny, and therefore that by comparison of the indices of authorities which Pliny puts at the end of each book, any name appearing in the sixth book only would be the name of our author. By such means Glaser arrives at the name *Basilis*, and in all his references to the Periplus after the date of that article, he is careful to cite—"Basilis, author of the Periplus, 56 to 67 A. D." But Pliny himself in that same book (VI, 35) refers to Basilis as the author of an account of Meroe and the upper Nile, apparently considerably earlier than the expedition of Petronius against Nubia in 24 to 22 B. C.; and a work on India, also by Basilis, is quoted by Agatharchides (*Ap. Phot.* p. 454 b. 34, ed. Bekker), whose work on the Erythræan Sea was written about 113 B. C., a century and a half before the Periplus. It seems to be this same Basilis, rather than a later writer of like name, whose *Indica* is quoted by Athenaeus (*Deipnos.* IX, 390, b), who wrote about 230 A. D. Unless, therefore, Glaser assumes that the Basilis of Pliny's text is a different man from the Basilis of his index, his argument falls.

Then, too, a man of Pliny's standing would have been apt to refrain from mentioning by name a writer with no literary reputation in Roman society. His index would omit an obscure sea-captain, just as his text omits him, referring merely to "information on which reliance can be placed." For the aristocracy of letters was very real in imperial Rome, and the writer of the Periplus did not "belong." The possibility that Pliny may have used his account does not imply the use of his name. Altogether, Glaser's argument is more ingenious than probable.

That the author was an Egyptian Greek, and a merchant in active trade who personally made the voyage to India, is evident by the text itself; that he lived in Berenice rather than Alexandria is indicated by the absence of any account of the journey up the Nile and across the desert from Coptos, which Strabo and Pliny describe at length. It is possible that he made the voyage from Cape Guardafui to Zanzibar, but the text is so vague and uncertain that he seems rather to be quoting from someone else, unless indeed much of this part of the work has been lost in copying. The coast of Arabia east of the Frankincense Country, the entire Persian Gulf and the coasts of Persia and Beluchistan as far as the Indus river, seem to have been known to him only by hearsay. They were subject to Parthia, an enemy of Rome.

That he was not a highly educated man is evident from his frequent confusion of Greek and Latin words and his clumsy and sometimes ungrammatical constructions. The value of his work consists, not in its literary merits, but in its trustworthy account of the trade of the Indian Ocean and of the settlements around its shores; concerning which, until his time, we possess almost nothing of an intelligent and comprehensive nature.

# BIBLIOGRAPHY OF THE PERIPLUS

CODEX PAL. GRÆC., 398. A parchment of the Tenth Century, in the Library of the University of Heidelberg. It was taken to Rome during the Thirty Years' War, and to Paris under Napoleon; and was restored to Heidelberg in 1816.

This manuscript contains twenty different titles, of which the first six are as follows:

I. Argumentum a Leone Allatio. (Allazi, who packed and shipped the Heidelberg Library to Rome.)
II. Fragmentum de Palude Mæotide et de Ponto Euxino.
III. Arrianus de venatione.
IV. Ejusdem epistola ad Trajanum qua periplus Ponti Euxini continetur.
V. Ejusdem Periplus Maris Rubri.
VI. Hannonis periplus.

MANUSCRIPT 19,391. A parchment, supposed to be of the Fourteenth or Fifteenth Century, in the British Museum. A portion of it is supposed to have come from the monastery of Mount Athos. Such matter as it contains in common with the Heidelberg manuscript seems to have been copied therefrom, or from a common original.

In this the Periplus is anonymous.

ARRIANI ET HANNONIS PERIPLUS: PLUTARCHUS DE FLUMINIBUS ET MONTIBUS: STRABONIS EPITOME. *Froben. Basileæ Anno MDXXXIII. Sigismundus Gelenius Anselmo Ephorino Medico S.*

This first printed text, corrupt and full of errors due to lack of knowledge of the subject, served nevertheless for three centuries as the basis of later editions, because of the disappearance of the Heidelberg manuscript.

DELLE NAVIGATIONI ET VIAGGI RACCOLTA DA GIO. BATT. RAMUSIO. *In Venetia, nella Stamperia de Giunti, MDLXXXVIII.*

Vol. 1, pp. 281-283a has *Discorso di Gio. Battista Ramusio, sopra la navigatione del Mar Rosso, fino all' India Orientale scritta per Arriano* and p. 283a begins *Navigatione del mar Rosso fino Alle Indie Orientali scritta per Arriano in Lingua Greca, & di quella poi Tradotta nella Italiana.*

There were editions of Ramusio's Collection at Venice in 1550, 1554, 1563 and 1588.

ARRIANI HISTORICI ET PHILOSOPHI PONTI EUXINI & MARIS ERYTHRÆI PERIPLUS, AD ADRIANUM CÆSAREM. *Nunc primum e Græco sermone in Latinum versus, plurimusque mendis repurgatus. Jo. Guilielmo Stuckio Tigurino authore. Genevæ, apud Eustathium Vignon, 1577.*

This text is based on that of Gelenius, with few material emendations.

ARRIANI ARS TACTICA, ACIES CONTRA ALANOS, PERIPLUS PONTI EUXINI, PERIPLUS MARIS ERYTHRÆI, LIBER DE VENATIONE, etc., etc. *Cum Interpretibus Latinis, & Notis. Ex Recensione & Museo. Nicolai Blancardi, Amstelodami, Janssonio-Waesbergii, 1683.*

This text is professedly based on that of Stuck.

GEOGRAPHIÆ VETERIS SCRIPTORES GRÆCI MINORES. *Cum Interpretatione Latina, Dissertationibus, ac Annotationibus. Oxoniæ. E Theatro Sheldoniano, MDCXCVIII.* (Præstitit Joannes Hudsonus. Dissertationes Henrici Dodwelli.)

This contains as its fifth title, *Periplus Maris Erythræi eidem (Arriano) vulgo adscriptus. Interprete Jo. Guilielmo Stuckio Tigurino.* The text is based on Gelenius and Stuck.

SYLLOGÊS TÔN EN EPITOMÊI TOIS PALAI GEÔGRAPHETHENTON *typois ekdothentôn philotimôi dapanêi tôn ex Iôanninôn philogenestatôn adelphôn* ZOSIMIADÔN *charin tôn tês Hellênikês paideias ephiemenôn Hellênôn. En Biennêi tês Austrias ek tês Schraimblikês Typographias, 1807.*

It contains, pp. 295-333 *Arrianou Periplous tês Erythras Thalassês*, with notes translated from Hudson.

FLAVII ARRIANI NICOMEDIENSIS OPERA GRÆCE *ad optimas editiones collata. Studio Augusti Christiani Borheck. Lemgoviæ, Meyer, 1809.*

This contains, pp. 91-121, *Arrianou Periplous tês Erythras Thalassês.* The text is from Hudson.

THE PERIPLUS OF THE ERYTHREAN SEA. Part the first, containing: *An Account of the Navigation of the Ancients, from the Sea of Suez to the Coast of Zanguebar.* With Dissertations. By William Vincent. *London: Cadell, Jun., & Davies, 1800.*

THE COMMERCE AND NAVIGATION OF THE ANCIENTS IN THE INDIAN OCEAN. *By William Vincent, D.D., Dean of Westminster.* In two volumes. *London: Cadell & Davies, 1807.* Vol. I, *The Voyage of Nearchus.* Vol. II, *The Periplus of the Erythrean Sea.* Part the first containing, *An Account of the Navigation of the Ancients from the Sea of Suez to the coast of Zanguebar.* With Dissertations. Part the second containing, *An Account of the*

*Navigation of the Ancients from the Gulph of Elana, in the Red Sea, to the Island of Ceylon.*

These two beautiful volumes, presenting the Greek text and English translation in parallel columns, preceded by dissertations that denote exhaustive geographical and historical research, are still of deep interest and importance to the student of the Periplus.

The text is that of Blancard: "His edition I was obliged to adopt, because I could obtain no other to use as copy." (Vol. II, part II, preface, p. xi). Vincent's textual emendations are generally less useful than his geographical and commercial notes, which are still, in large part, illuminating and trustworthy, and were, when written, the first intelligent presentation of the subject.

THE VOYAGE OF NEARCHUS AND THE PERIPLUS OF THE ERYTHREAN SEA (ascribed to Arrian), translated by W. Vincent, Oxford, 1809.

UNTERSUCHUNGEN UEBER EINZELNE GEGENSTAENDE DER ALTEN GESCHICHTE, GEOGRAPHIE, UND CHRONOLOGIE. *G. G. Bredow, Altona, Hammerich, 1802.*

This includes Vincent's Periplus, translated into German, pp. 715-797.

SAMMLUNG KLEINER SCHRIFTEN AUS DEM GEBIETE DER MATHEMATISCHEN UND ALTEN GEOGRAPHIE. C. G. Reichard. *Güns, Reichard, 1836.*

This includes Vincent's work, pp. 374-425 and 438-496.

ARRIANO OPUSCOLI, TRADOTTI DA VARI. *Milano, Sonzogno, 1826-7, S. Blandi.*

DES PSEUDO-ARRIANS UMSCHIFFUNG DES ERYTHRAEISCHEN MEERES—*die Ersten neun Kapitel vollständig, die übrigen im Auszuge. Uebersetzt von Streubel* in *Jahres-Bericht über die Stralauer höhere Bürger-Schule* für das Schuljahr von Michaelis 1860 bis Michaelis 1861, womit—einladet C. Hartung. Berlin, Druck von Hickethier, 1861.

This partial translation is based on the texts of Stuck, Hudson and Borheck, and is of little value.

ARRIANI ALEXANDRINI PERIPLUS MARIS ERYTHRÆI. *Recensuit et brevi annotatione instruxit B. Fabricius. Dresdæ, in commissis Gottschalcki, MDCCCXLIX.*

Geographi Græci Minores. *E codicibus recognovit, prolegomenis, annotatione, indicibusque instruxit, tabulis æri incisis illustravit Carolus Müllerus. Parisiis, Didot, MDCCCLV.*

Vol. I, pp. xcv–cxi has *Prolegomena Anonymi Periplus Maris Erythræi*, and pp. 257–305 *Anonymi (Arriani, ut fertur) Periplus Maris Erythræi*, being the eighth title included in that volume. Vol. III contains four maps, xi–xiv, especially drawn to illustrate the Periplus, and four more, vi–viii and xv, drawn for other titles but presenting details that further elucidate this work.

This edition is a vast improvement over all its predecessors, presenting a text which is still the standard, admitting of modification only in minor details. The Greek text, carefully corrected from the Heidelberg manuscript, and critically revised and improved, is presented side by side with a Latin translation. The notes, which are in Latin, reflect almost everything of importance to the subject which had been written up to that time.

The Commerce and Navigation of the Erythræan Sea. *By J. W. McCrindle, M.A., LL.D., Calcutta, 1879. This volume contains a translation (with commentary) of the* Periplus Erythræi Maris, *by an unknown writer of the first Christian century, and of the second part of the* Indika *of Arrian.*

The translation of the *Periplus* was also printed in the *Indian Antiquary* of Bombay, Vol. VIII, pp. 108-151.

This excellent translation, while based professedly on Müller's text, is often reminiscent rather of Vincent's, and thus repeats various errors which Müller's notes had corrected.

The notes are valuable for the original material they contain concerning Hindu names, places and commodities, but show lack of acquaintance with German writers.

Der Periplus des Erythraeischen Meeres von Einem Unbekannten. *Griechisch und deutsch mit kritischen und erkärenden Anmerkungen nebst vollständigem Wörterverzeichnisse von B. Fabricius. Leipzig, Verlag von Veit & Comp., 1883.*

A most scholarly presentation of Greek text and German translation on opposite pages, with clear and exhaustive notes. The Greek text, which has been revised with extreme care, contains many verbal corrections of Müller's standard text, and leaves little to be desired. The historical and commercial notes call for revision where they omit conclusions previously reached by English writers, and in so far as they are affected by later research.

The present translation is based on Müller's text, adopting most of Fabricius' verbal emendations, but conforming as far as possible with the results of later research. Vincent's text and translation have also been consulted frequently. References in the text to articles of commerce have been carefully collated with Pliny and other contemporary writers, as well as with modern authorities.

# The Voyage around the Erythræan Sea

1. Of the designated ports on the Erythræan Sea, and the market-towns around it, the first is the Egyptian port of Mussel Harbor. To those sailing down from that place, on the right hand, after eighteen hundred stadia, there is Berenice. The harbors of both are at the boundary of Egypt, and are bays opening from the Erythræan Sea.

2. On the right-hand coast next below Berenice is the country of the Berbers. Along the shore are the Fish-Eaters, living in scattered caves in the narrow valleys. Further inland are the Berbers, and beyond them the Wild-flesh-Eaters and Calf-Eaters, each tribe governed by its chief; and behind them, further inland, in the country toward the west, there lies a city called Meroe.

3. Below the Calf-Eaters there is a little market-town on the shore after sailing about four thousand stadia from Berenice, called Ptolemais of the Hunts, from which the hunters started for the interior under the dynasty of the Ptolemies. This market-town has the true land-tortoise in small quantity; it is white and smaller in the shells. And here also is found a little ivory, like that of Adulis. But the place has no harbor and is reached only by small boats.

4. Below Ptolemais of the Hunts, at a distance of about three thousand stadia, there is Adulis, a port established by law, lying at the inner end of a bay that runs in toward the south. Before the harbor lies the

so-called Mountain Island, about two hundred stadia seaward from the very head of the bay, with the shores of the mainland close to it on both sides. Ships bound for this port now anchor here because of attacks from the land. They used formerly to anchor at the very head of the bay, by an island called Diodorus, close to the shore, which could be reached on foot from the land; by which means the barbarous natives attacked the island. Opposite Mountain Island, on the mainland twenty stadia from shore, lies Adulis, a fair-sized village, from which there is a three-days' journey to Coloe, an inland town and the first market for ivory. From that place to the city of the people called Auxumites there is a five days' journey more; to that place all the ivory is brought from the country beyond the Nile through the district called Cyeneum, and thence to Adulis. Practically the whole number of elephants and rhinoceros that are killed live in the places inland, although at rare intervals they are hunted on the seacoast even near Adulis. Before the harbor of that market-town, out at sea on the right hand, there lie a great many little sandy islands called Alalæi, yielding tortoise-shell, which is brought to market there by the Fish-Eaters.

5. And about eight hundred stadia beyond there is another very deep bay, with a great mound of sand piled up at the right of the entrance; at the bottom of which the opsian stone is found, and this is the only place where it is produced. These places, from the Calf-Eaters to the other Berber country, are governed by Zoscales; who is miserly in his ways and always striving for more, but otherwise upright, and acquainted with Greek literature.

6. There are imported into these places, undressed cloth made in Egypt for the Berbers; robes from Arsinoe; cloaks of poor quality dyed in colors; double-fringed linen mantles; many articles of flint glass, and others of murrhine, made in Diospolis; and brass, which is used for ornament and in cut pieces instead of coin; sheets of soft copper, used for cooking-utensils and cut up for bracelets and anklets for the women; iron, which is made into spears used against the elephants and other wild beasts, and in their wars. Besides these, small axes are imported, and adzes and swords; copper drinking-cups, round and large; a little coin for those coming to the market; wine of Laodicea and Italy, not much; olive oil, not much; for the king, gold and silver plate made after the fashion of the country, and for clothing, military cloaks, and thin coats of skin, of no great value. Likewise from the district of Ariaca across this sea, there are imported Indian iron, and steel, and Indian cotton cloth; the broad cloth called *monachê* and that called *sagmatogênê*, and girdles, and coats of skin and mallow-colored cloth, and a few muslins, and colored lac. There are exported from these places ivory, and tortoise-shell and rhinoceros-horn. The most from Egypt is brought to this market from the month of January to September, that is, from Tybi to Thoth; but seasonably they put to sea about the month of September.

7. From this place the Arabian Gulf trends toward the east and becomes narrowest just before the Gulf of Avalites. After about four thousand stadia, for those sailing eastward along the same coast, there are other Berber market-towns, known as the "far-side" ports; lying at intervals one after the other, without harbors

but having roadsteads where ships can anchor and lie in good weather. The first is called Avalites; to this place the voyage from Arabia to the far-side coast is the shortest. Here there is a small market-town called Avalites, which must be reached by boats and rafts. There are imported into this place, flint glass, assorted; juice of sour grapes from Diospolis; dressed cloth, assorted, made for the Berbers; wheat, wine, and a little tin. There are exported from the same place, and sometimes by the Berbers themselves crossing on rafts to Ocelis and Muza on the opposite shore, spices, a little ivory, tortoise-shell, and a very little myrrh, but better than the rest. And the Berbers who live in the place are very unruly.

8. After Avalites there is another market-town, better than this, called Malao, distant a sail of about eight hundred stadia. The anchorage is an open roadstead, sheltered by a spit running out from the east. Here the natives are more peaceable. There are imported into this place the things already mentioned, and many tunics, cloaks from Arsinoe, dressed and dyed; drinking-cups, sheets of soft copper in small quantity, iron, and gold and silver coin, not much. There are exported from these places myrrh, a little frankincense, (that known as far-side), the harder cinnamon, *duaca*, Indian copal and *macir*, which are imported into Arabia; and slaves, but rarely.

9. Two days' sail, or three, beyond Malao is the market-town of Mundus, where the ships lie at anchor more safely behind a projecting island close to the shore. There are imported into this place the things previously set forth, and from it likewise are exported the mer-

chandise already stated, and the incense called *mocrotu.* And the traders living here are more quarrelsome.

10. Beyond Mundus, sailing toward the east, after another two days' sail, or three, you reach Mosyllum, on a beach, with a bad anchorage. There are imported here the same things already mentioned, also silver plate, a very little iron, and glass. There are shipped from the place a great quantity of cinnamon, (so that this market-town requires ships of larger size), and fragrant gums, spices, a little tortoise shell, and *mocrotu*, (poorer than that of Mundus), frankincense, (the far-side), ivory and myrrh in small quantities.

11. Sailing along the coast beyond Mosyllum, after a two days' course you come to the so-called Little Nile River, and a fine spring, and a small laurel-grove, and Cape Elephant. Then the shore recedes into a bay, and has a river, called Elephant, and a large laurel-grove called Acannæ; where alone is produced the far-side frankincense, in great quantity and of the best grade.

12. Beyond this place, the coast trending toward the south, there is the Market and Cape of Spices, an abrupt promontory, at the very end of the Berber coast toward the east. The anchorage is dangerous at times from the ground-swell, because the place is exposed to the north. A sign of an approaching storm which is peculiar to the place, is that the deep water becomes more turbid and changes its color. When this happens they all run to a large promontory called Tabæ, which offers safe shelter. There are imported into this market-town the things already mentioned; and there are produced in it cinnamon (and its different varieties, *gizir*, *asypha*, *arebo*, *magla*, and *moto*) and frankincense.

13. Beyond Tabæ, after four hundred stadia, there is the village of Pano. And then, after sailing four hundred stadia along a promontory, toward which place the current also draws you, there is another market-town called Opone, into which the same things are imported as those already mentioned, and in it the greatest quantity of cinnamon is produced, (the *arebo* and *moto*), and slaves of the better sort, which are brought to Egypt in increasing numbers; and a great quantity of tortoise-shell, better than that found elsewhere.

14. The voyage to all these far-side market-towns is made from Egypt about the month of July, that is Epiphi. And ships are also customarily fitted out from the places across this sea, from Ariaca and Barygaza, bringing to these far-side market-towns the products of their own places; wheat, rice, clarified butter, sesame oil, cotton cloth, (the *monachê* and the *sagmatogênê*), and girdles, and honey from the reed called *sacchari*. Some make the voyage especially to these market-towns, and others exchange their cargoes while sailing along the coast. This country is not subject to a King, but each market-town is ruled by its separate chief.

15. Beyond Opone, the shore trending more toward the south, first there are the small and great bluffs of Azania; this coast is destitute of harbors, but there are places where ships can lie at anchor, the shore being abrupt; and this course is of six days, the direction being south-west. Then come the small and great beach for another six days' course and after that in order, the Courses of Azania, the first being called Sarapion and the next Nicon; and after that several rivers and other anchorages, one after the other, separately a rest and a

run for each day, seven in all, until the Pyralaæ islands and what is called the channel; beyond which, a little to the south of south-west, after two courses of a day and night along the Ausanitic coast, is the island Menuthias, about three hundred stadia from the mainland, low and and wooded, in which there are rivers and many kinds of birds and the mountain-tortoise. There are no wild beasts except the crocodiles; but there they do not attack men. In this place there are sewed boats, and canoes hollowed from single logs, which they use for fishing and catching tortoise. In this island they also catch them in a peculiar way, in wicker baskets, which they fasten across the channel-opening between the breakers.

16. Two days' sail beyond, there lies the very last market-town of the continent of Azania, which is called Rhapta; which has its name from the sewed boats (*rhaptôn ploiariôn*) already mentioned; in which there is ivory in great quantity, and tortoise-shell. Along this coast live men of piratical habits, very great in stature, and under separate chiefs for each place. The Mapharitic chief governs it under some ancient right that subjects it to the sovereignty of the state that is become first in Arabia. And the people of Muza now hold it under his authority, and send thither many large ships; using Arab captains and agents, who are familiar with the natives and intermarry with them, and who know the whole coast and understand the language.

17. There are imported into these markets the lances made at Muza especially for this trade, and hatchets and daggers and awls, and various kinds of glass; and at some places a little wine, and wheat, not for trade, but

to serve for getting the good-will of the savages. There are exported from these places a great quantity of ivory, but inferior to that of Adulis, and rhinoceros-horn and tortoise-shell (which is in best demand after that from India), and a little palm-oil.

18. And these markets of Azania are the very last of the continent that stretches down on the right hand from Berenice; for beyond these places the unexplored ocean curves around toward the west, and running along by the regions to the south of Aethiopia and Libya and Africa, it mingles with the western sea.

19. Now to the left of Berenice, sailing for two or three days from Mussel Harbor eastward across the adjacent gulf, there is another harbor and fortified place, which is called White Village, from which there is a road to Petra, which is subject to Malichas, King of the Nabatæans. It holds the position of a market-town for the small vessels sent there from Arabia; and so a centurion is stationed there as a collector of one-fourth of the merchandise imported, with an armed force, as a garrison.

20. Directly below this place is the adjoining country of Arabia, in its length bordering a great distance on the Erythræan Sea. Different tribes inhabit the country, differing in their speech, some partially, and some altogether. The land next the sea is similarly dotted here and there with caves of the Fish-Eaters, but the country inland is peopled by rascally men speaking two languages, who live in villages and nomadic camps, by whom those sailing off the middle course are plundered, and those surviving shipwrecks are taken for slaves. And so they too are continually taken prisoners

by the chiefs and kings of Arabia; and they are called Carnaites. Navigation is dangerous along this whole coast of Arabia, which is without harbors, with bad anchorages, foul, inaccessible because of breakers and rocks, and terrible in every way. Therefore we hold our course down the middle of the gulf and pass on as fast as possible by the country of Arabia until we come to the Burnt Island; directly below which there are regions of peaceful people, nomadic, pasturers of cattle, sheep and camels.

21. Beyond these places, in a bay at the foot of the left side of this gulf, there is a place by the shore called Muza, a market-town established by law, distant altogether from Berenice for those sailing southward, about twelve thousand stadia. And the whole place is crowded with Arab shipowners and seafaring men, and is busy with the affairs of commerce; for they carry on a trade with the far-side coast and with Barygaza, sending their own ships there.

22. Three days inland from this port there is a city called Saua, in the midst of the region called Mapharitis; and there is a vassal-chief named Cholæbus who lives in that city.

23. And after nine days more there is Saphar, the metropolis, in which lives Charibael, lawful king of two tribes, the Homerites and those living next to them, called the Sabaites; through continual embassies and gifts, he is a friend of the Emperors.

24. The market-town of Muza is without a harbor, but has a good roadstead and anchorage because of the sandy bottom thereabouts, where the anchors hold safely. The merchandise imported there consists

of purple cloths, both fine and coarse; clothing in the Arabian style, with sleeves; plain, ordinary, embroidered, or interwoven with gold; saffron, sweet rush, muslins, cloaks, blankets (not many), some plain and others made in the local fashion; sashes of different colors, fragrant ointments in moderate quantity, wine and wheat, not much. For the country produces grain in moderate amount, and a great deal of wine. And to the King and the Chief are given horses and sumpter-mules, vessels of gold and polished silver, finely woven clothing and copper vessels. There are exported from the same place the things produced in the country: selected myrrh, and the Gebanite-Minæan *stacte*, alabaster and all the things already mentioned from Avalites and the far-side coast. The voyage to this place is made best about the month of September, that is Thoth; but there is nothing to prevent it even earlier.

25. After sailing beyond this place about three hundred stadia, the coast of Arabia and the Berber country about the Avalitic gulf now coming close together, there is a channel, not long in extent, which forces the sea together and shuts it into a narrow strait, the passage through which, sixty stadia in length, the island Diodorus divides. Therefore the course through it is beset with rushing currents and with strong winds blowing down from the adjacent ridge of mountains. Directly on this strait by the shore there is a village of Arabs, subject to the same chief, called Ocelis; which is not so much a market-town as it is an anchorage and watering-place and the first landing for those sailing into the gulf.

26. Beyond Ocelis, the sea widening again toward

the east and soon giving a view of the open ocean, after about twelve hundred stadia there is Eudæmon Arabia, a village by the shore, also of the Kingdom of Charibael, and having convenient anchorages, and watering-places, sweeter and better than those at Ocelis; it lies at the entrance of a bay, and the land recedes from it. It was called Eudæmon, because in the early days of the city when the voyage was not yet made from India to Egypt, and when they did not dare to sail from Egypt to the ports across this ocean, but all came together at this place, it received the cargoes from both countries, just as Alexandria now receives the things brought both from abroad and from Egypt. But not long before our own time Charibael destroyed the place.

27. After Eudæmon Arabia there is a continuous length of coast, and a bay extending two thousand stadia or more, along which there are Nomads and Fish-Eaters living in villages; just beyond the cape projecting from this bay there is another market-town by the shore, Cana, of the Kingdom of Eleazus, the Frankincense Country; and facing it there are two desert islands, one called Island of Birds, the other Dome Island, one hundred and twenty stadia from Cana. Inland from this place lies the metropolis Sabbatha, in which the King lives. All the frankincense produced in the country is brought by camels to that place to be stored, and to Cana on rafts held up by inflated skins after the manner of the country, and in boats. And this place has a trade also with the far-side ports, with Barygaza and Scythia and Ommana and the neighboring coast of Persia.

28. There are imported into this place from Egypt a little wheat and wine, as at Muza; clothing in the Arabian style, plain and common and most of it spurious; and copper and tin and coral and storax and other things such as go to Muza; and for the King usually wrought gold and silver plate, also horses, images, and thin clothing of fine quality. And there are exported from this place, native produce, frankincense and aloes, and the rest of the things that enter into the trade of the other ports. The voyage to this place is best made at the same time as that to Muza, or rather earlier.

29. Beyond Cana, the land receding greatly, there follows a very deep bay stretching a great way across, which is called Sachalites; and the Frankincense Country, mountainous and forbidding, wrapped in thick clouds and fog, and yielding frankincense from the trees. These incense-bearing trees are not of great height or thickness; they bear the frankincense sticking in drops on the bark, just as the trees among us in Egypt weep their gum. The frankincense is gathered by the King's slaves and those who are sent to this service for punishment. For these places are very unhealthy, and pestilential even to those sailing along the coast; but almost always fatal to those working there, who also perish often from want of food.

30. On this bay there is a very great promontory facing the east, called Syagrus; on which is a fort for the defence of the country, and a harbor and storehouse for the frankincense that is collected; and opposite this cape, well out at sea, there is an island, lying between it and the Cape of Spices opposite, but nearer Syagrus: it is called Dioscorida, and is very large but desert and

marshy, having rivers in it and crocodiles and many snakes and great lizards, of which the flesh is eaten and the fat melted and used instead of olive oil. The island yields no fruit, neither vine nor grain. The inhabitants are few and they live on the coast toward the north, which from this side faces the continent. They are foreigners, a mixture of Arabs and Indians and Greeks, who have emigrated to carry on trade there. The island produces the true sea-tortoise, and the land-tortoise, and the white tortoise which is very numerous and preferred for its large shells; and the mountain-tortoise, which is largest of all and has the thickest shell; of which the worthless specimens cannot be cut apart on the under side, because they are even too hard; but those of value are cut apart and the shells made whole into caskets and small plates and cake-dishes and that sort of ware. There is also produced in this island cinnabar, that called Indian, which is collected in drops from the trees.

31. It happens that just as Azania is subject to Charibael and the Chief of Mapharitis, this island is subject to the King of the Frankincense Country. Trade is also carried on there by some people from Muza and by those who chance to call there on the voyage from Damirica and Barygaza; they bring in rice and wheat and Indian cloth, and a few female slaves; and they take for their exchange cargoes, a great quantity of tortoise-shell. Now the island is farmed out under the Kings and is garrisoned.

32. Immediately beyond Syagrus the bay of Omana cuts deep into the coast-line, the width of it being six hundred stadia; and beyond this there are mountains,

high and rocky and steep, inhabited by cave-dwellers for five hundred stadia more; and beyond this is a port established for receiving the Sachalitic frankincense; the harbor is called Moscha, and ships from Cana call there regularly; and ships returning from Damirica and Barygaza, if the season is late, winter there, and trade with the King's officers, exchanging their cloth and wheat and sesame oil for frankincense, which lies in heaps all over the Sachalitic country, open and unguarded, as if the place were under the protection of the gods; for neither openly nor by stealth can it be loaded on board ship without the King's permission; if a single grain were loaded without this, the ship could not clear from the harbor.

33. Beyond the harbor of Moscha for about fifteen hundred stadia as far as Asich, a mountain range runs along the shore; at the end of which, in a row, lie seven islands, called Zenobian. Beyond these there is a barbarous region which is no longer of the same Kingdom, but now belongs to Persia. Sailing along this coast well out at sea for two thousand stadia from the Zenobian Islands, there meets you an island called Sarapis, about one hundred and twenty stadia from the mainland. It is about two hundred stadia wide and six hundred long, inhabited by three settlements of Fish-Eaters, a villainous lot, who use the Arabian language and wear girdles of palm-leaves. The island produces considerable tortoise-shell of fine quality, and small sail-boats and cargo-ships are sent there regularly from Cana.

34. Sailing along the coast, which trends northward toward the entrance of the Persian Sea, there are

many islands known as the Calæi, after about two thousand stadia, extending along the shore. The inhabitants are a treacherous lot, very little civilized.

35. At the upper end of these Calæi islands is a range of mountains called Calon, and there follows not far beyond, the mouth of the Persian Gulf, where there is much diving for the pearl-mussel. To the left of the straits are great mountains called Asabon, and to the right there rises in full view another round and high mountain called Semiramis; between them the passage across the strait is about six hundred stadia; beyond which that very great and broad sea, the Persian Gulf, reaches far into the interior. At the upper end of this Gulf there is a market-town designated by law, called Apologus, situated near Charax Spasini and the River Euphrates.

36. Sailing through the mouth of the Gulf, after a six-days' course there is another market-town of Persia called Ommana. To both of these market-towns large vessels are regularly sent from Barygaza, loaded with copper and sandalwood and timbers of teakwood and logs of blackwood and ebony. To Ommana frankincense is also brought from Cana, and from Ommana to Arabia boats sewed together after the fashion of the place; these are known as *madarata*. From each of these market-towns, there are exported to Barygaza and also to Arabia, many pearls, but inferior to those of India; purple, clothing after the fashion of the place, wine, a great quantity of dates, gold and slaves.

37. Beyond the Ommanitic region there is a country also of the Parsidæ, of another Kingdom, and the bay of Gedrosia, from the middle of which a cape juts

out into the bay. Here there is a river affording an entrance for ships, with a little market-town at the mouth, called Oræa; and back from the place an inland city, distant a seven days' journey from the sea, in which also is the King's court; it is called —— (probably Rhambacia). This country yields much wheat, wine, rice and dates; but along the coast there is nothing but bdellium.

38. Beyond this region, the continent making a wide curve from the east across the depths of the bays, there follows the coast district of Scythia, which lies above toward the north; the whole marshy; from which flows down the river Sinthus, the greatest of all the rivers that flow into the Erythræan Sea, bringing down an enormous volume of water; so that a long way out at sea, before reaching this country, the water of the ocean is fresh from it. Now as a sign of approach to this country to those coming from the sea, there are serpents coming forth from the depths to meet you; and a sign of the places just mentioned and in Persia, are those called *graæ*. This river has seven mouths, very shallow and marshy, so that they are not navigable, except the one in the middle; at which by the shore, is the market-town, Barbaricum. Before it there lies a small island, and inland behind it is the metropolis of Scythia, Minnagara; it is subject to Parthian princes who are constantly driving each other out.

39. The ships lie at anchor at Barbaricum, but all their cargoes are carried up to the metropolis by the river, to the King. There are imported into this market a great deal of thin clothing, and a little spurious; figured linens, topaz, coral, storax, frankincense, vessels

of glass, silver and gold plate, and a little wine. On the other hand there are exported costus, bdellium, lycium, nard, turquoise, lapis lazuli, Seric skins, cotton cloth, silk yarn, and indigo. And sailors set out thither with the Indian Etesian winds, about the month of July, that is Epiphi: it is more dangerous then, but through these winds the voyage is more direct, and sooner completed.

40. Beyond the river Sinthus there is another gulf, not navigable, running in toward the north; it is called Eirinon; its parts are called separately the small gulf and the great; in both parts the water is shallow, with shifting sandbanks occurring continually and a great way from shore; so that very often when the shore is not even in sight, ships run aground, and if they attempt to hold their course they are wrecked. A promontory stands out from this gulf, curving around from Eirinon toward the East, then South, then West, and enclosing the gulf called Baraca, which contains seven islands. Those who come to the entrance of this bay escape it by putting about a little and standing further out to sea; but those who are drawn inside into the gulf of Baraca are lost; for the waves are high and very violent, and the sea is tumultuous and foul, and has eddies and rushing whirlpools. The bottom is in some places abrupt, and in others rocky and sharp, so that the anchors lying there are parted, some being quickly cut off, and others chafing on the bottom. As a sign of these places to those approaching from the sea there are serpents, very large and black; for at the other places on this coast and around Barygaza, they are smaller, and in color bright green, running into gold.

41. Beyond the gulf of Baraca is that of Barygaza and the coast of the country of Ariaca, which is the beginning of the Kingdom of Nambanus and of all India. That part of it lying inland and adjoining Scythia is called Abiria, but the coast is called Syrastrene. It is a fertile country, yielding wheat and rice and sesame oil and clarified butter, cotton and the Indian cloths made therefrom, of the coarser sorts. Very many cattle are pastured there, and the men are of great stature and black in color. The metropolis of this country is Minnagara, from which much cotton cloth is brought down to Barygaza. In these places there remain even to the present time signs of the expedition of Alexander, such as ancient shrines, walls of forts and great wells. The sailing course along this coast, from Barbaricum to the promontory called Papica, opposite Barygaza, and before Astacampra, is of three thousand stadia.

42. Beyond this there is another gulf exposed to the sea-waves, running up toward the north, at the mouth of which there is an island called Bæones; at its innermost part there is a great river called Mais. Those sailing to Barygaza pass across this gulf, which is three hundred stadia in width, leaving behind to their left the island just visible from their tops toward the east, straight to the very mouth of the river of Barygaza; and this river is called Nammadus.

43. This gulf is very narrow to Barygaza and very hard to navigate for those coming from the ocean; this is the case with both the right and left passages, but there is a better passage through the left. For on the right at the very mouth of the gulf there lies a shoal, long and narrow, and full of rocks, called Herone,

facing the village of Cammoni; and opposite this on the left projects the promontory that lies before Astacampra, which is called Papica, and is a bad anchorage because of the strong current setting in around it and because the anchors are cut off, the bottom being rough and rocky. And even if the entrance to the gulf is made safely, the mouth of the river at Barygaza is found with difficulty, because the shore is very low and cannot be made out until you are close upon it. And when you have found it the passage is difficult because of the shoals at the mouth of the river.

44. Because of this, native fishermen in the King's service, stationed at the very entrance in well-manned large boats called *trappaga* and *cotymba*, go up the coast as far as Syrastrene, from which they pilot vessels to Barygaza. And they steer them straight from the mouth of the bay between the shoals with their crews; and they tow them to fixed stations, going up with the beginning of the flood, and lying through the ebb at anchorages and in basins. These basins are deeper places in the river as far as Barygaza; which lies by the river, about three hundred stadia up from the mouth.

45. Now the whole country of India has very many rivers, and very great ebb and flow of the tides; increasing at the new moon, and at the full moon for three days, and falling off during the intervening days of the moon. But about Barygaza it is much greater, so that the bottom is suddenly seen, and now parts of the dry land are sea, and now it is dry where ships were sailing just before; and the rivers, under the inrush of the flood tide, when the whole force of the sea is

directed against them, are driven upwards more strongly against their natural current, for many stadia.

46. For this reason entrance and departure of vessels is very dangerous to those who are inexperienced or who come to this market-town for the first time. For the rush of waters at the incoming tide is irresistible, and the anchors cannot hold against it; so that large ships are caught up by the force of it, turned broadside on through the speed of the current, and so driven on the shoals and wrecked; and smaller boats are overturned; and those that have been turned aside among the channels by the receding waters at the ebb, are left on their sides, and if not held on an even keel by props, the flood tide comes upon them suddenly and under the first head of the current they are filled with water. For there is so great force in the rush of the sea at the new moon, especially during the flood tide at night, that if you begin the entrance at the moment when the waters are still, on the instant there is borne to you at the mouth of the river, a noise like the cries of an army heard from afar; and very soon the sea itself comes rushing in over the shoals with a hoarse roar.

47. The country inland from Barygaza is inhabited by numerous tribes, such as the Arattii, the Arachosii, the Gandaræi and the people of Poclais, in which is Bucephalus Alexandria. Above these is the very warlike nation of the Bactrians, who are under their own king. And Alexander, setting out from these parts, penetrated to the Ganges, leaving aside Damirica and the southern part of India; and to the present day ancient drachmæ are current in Barygaza, coming from this country, bearing inscriptions in Greek letters, and

the devices of those who reigned after Alexander, Apollodotus and Menander.

48. Inland from this place and to the east, is the city called Ozene, formerly a royal capital; from this place are brought down all things needed for the welfare of the country about Barygaza, and many things for our trade: agate and carnelian, Indian muslins and mallow cloth, and much ordinary cloth. Through this same region and from the upper country is brought the spikenard that comes through Poclais; that is, the Caspapyrene and Paropanisene and Cabolitic and that brought through the adjoining country of Scythia; also costus and bdellium.

49. There are imported into this market-town, wine, Italian preferred, also Laodicean and Arabian; copper, tin, and lead; coral and topaz; thin clothing and inferior sorts of all kinds; bright-colored girdles a cubit wide; storax, sweet clover, flint glass, realgar, antimony, gold and silver coin, on which there is a profit when exchanged for the money of the country; and ointment, but not very costly and not much. And for the King there are brought into those places very costly vessels of silver, singing boys, beautiful maidens for the harem, fine wines, thin clothing of the finest weaves, and the choicest ointments. There are exported from these places spikenard, costus, bdellium, ivory, agate and carnelian, lycium, cotton cloth of all kinds, silk cloth, mallow cloth, yarn, long pepper and such other things as are brought here from the various market-towns. Those bound for this market-town from Egypt make the voyage favorably about the month of July, that is Epiphi.

50. Beyond Barygaza the adjoining coast extends in a straight line from north to south; and so this region is called Dachinabades, for *dachanos* in the language of the natives means "south." The inland country back from the coast toward the east comprises many desert regions and great mountains; and all kinds of wild beasts—leopards, tigers, elephants, enormous serpents, hyenas, and baboons of many sorts; and many populous nations, as far as the Ganges.

51. Among the market-towns of Dachinabades there are two of special importance; Pæthana, distant about twenty days' journey south from Barygaza; beyond which, about ten days' journey east, there is another very great city, Tagara. There are brought down to Barygaza from these places by wagons and through great tracts without roads, from Pæthana carnelian in great quantity, and from Tagara much common cloth, all kinds of muslins and mallow cloth, and other merchandise brought there locally from the regions along the sea-coast. And the whole course to the end of Damirica is seven thousand stadia; but the distance is greater to the Coast Country.

52. The market-towns of this region are, in order, after Barygaza: Suppara, and the city of Calliena, which in the time of the elder Saraganus became a lawful market-town; but since it came into the possession of Sandares the port is much obstructed, and Greek ships landing there may chance to be taken to Barygaza under guard.

53. Beyond Calliena there are other market-towns of this region; Semylla, Mandagora, Palæpatmæ, Melizigara, Byzantium, Togarum and Aurannoboas. Then

there are the islands called Sesecrienæ and that of the Aegidii, and that of the Cænitæ, opposite the place called Chersonesus (and in these places there are pirates), and after this the White Island. Then come Naura and Tyndis, the first markets of Damirica, and then Muziris and Nelcynda, which are now of leading importance.

54. Tyndis is of the Kingdom of Cerobothra; it is a village in plain sight by the sea. Muziris, of the same Kingdom, abounds in ships sent there with cargoes from Arabia, and by the Greeks; it is located on a river, distant from Tyndis by river and sea five hundred stadia, and up the river from the shore twenty stadia. Nelcynda is distant from Muziris by river and sea about five hundred stadia, and is of another Kingdom, the Pandian. This place also is situated on a river, about one hundred and twenty stadia from the sea.

55. There is another place at the mouth of this river, the village of Bacare; to which ships drop down on the outward voyage from Nelcynda, and anchor in the roadstead to take on their cargoes; because the river is full of shoals and the channels are not clear. The kings of both these market-towns live in the interior. And as a sign to those approaching these places from the sea there are serpents coming forth to meet you, black in color, but shorter, like snakes in the head, and with blood-red eyes.

56. They send large ships to these market-towns on account of the great quantity and bulk of pepper and malabathrum. There are imported here, in the first place, a great quantity of coin; topaz, thin clothing, not

much; figured linens, antimony, coral, crude glass, copper, tin, lead; wine, not much, but as much as at Barygaza; realgar and orpiment; and wheat enough for the sailors, for this is not dealt in by the merchants there. There is exported pepper, which is produced in quantity in only one region near these markets, a district called Cottonara. Besides this there are exported great quantities of fine pearls, ivory, silk cloth, spikenard from the Ganges, malabathrum from the places in the interior, transparent stones of all kinds, diamonds and sapphires, and tortoise-shell; that from Chryse Island, and that taken among the islands along the coast of Damirica. They make the voyage to this place in a favorable season who set out from Egypt about the month of July, that is Epiphi.

57. This whole voyage as above described, from Cana and Eudæmon Arabia, they used to make in small vessels, sailing close around the shores of the gulfs; and Hippalus was the pilot who by observing the location of the ports and the conditions of the sea, first discovered how to lay his course straight across the ocean. For at the same time when with us the Etesian winds are blowing, on the shores of India the wind sets in from the ocean, and this southwest wind is called Hippalus, from the name of him who first discovered the passage across. From that time to the present day ships start, some direct from Cana, and some from the Cape of Spices; and those bound for Damirica throw the ship's head considerably off the wind; while those bound for Barygaza and Scythia keep along shore not more than three days and for the rest of the time hold the same course straight out to sea from that region,

with a favorable wind, quite away from the land, and so sail outside past the aforesaid gulfs.

58. Beyond Bacare there is the Dark Red Mountain, and another district stretching along the coast toward the south, called Paralia. The first place is called Balita; it has a fine harbor and a village by the shore. Beyond this there is another place called Comari, at which are the Cape of Comari and a harbor; hither come those men who wish to consecrate themselves for the rest of their lives, and bathe and dwell in celibacy; and women also do the same; for it is told that a goddess once dwelt here and bathed.

59. From Comari toward the south this region extends to Colchi, where the pearl-fisheries are; (they are worked by condemned criminals); and it belongs to the Pandian Kingdom. Beyond Colchi there follows another district called the Coast Country, which lies on a bay, and has a region inland called Argaru. At this place, and nowhere else, are bought the pearls gathered on the coast thereabouts; and from there are exported muslins, those called Argaritic.

60. Among the market-towns of these countries, and the harbors where the ships put in from Damirica and from the north, the most important are, in order as they lie, first Camara, then Poduca, then Sopatma; in which there are ships of the country coasting along the shore as far as Damirica; and other very large vessels made of single logs bound together, called *sangara;* but those which make the voyage to Chryse and to the Ganges are called *colandia,* and are very large. There are imported into these places everything made in Damirica, and the greatest part of what is brought at any

time from Egypt comes here, together with most kinds of all the things that are brought from Damirica and of those that are carried through Paralia.

61. About the following region, the course trending toward the east, lying out at sea toward the west is the island Palæsimundu, called by the ancients Taprobane. The northern part is a day's journey distant, and the southern part trends gradually toward the west, and almost touches the opposite shore of Azania. It produces pearls, transparent stones, muslins, and tortoise-shell.

62. About these places is the region of Masalia stretching a great way along the coast before the inland country; a great quantity of muslins is made there. Beyond this region, sailing toward the east and crossing the adjacent bay, there is the region of Dosarene, yielding the ivory known as Dosarenic. Beyond this, the course trending toward the north, there are many barbarous tribes, among whom are the Cirrhadæ, a race of men with flattened noses, very savage; another tribe, the Bargysi; and the Horse-faces and the Long-faces, who are said to be cannibals.

63. After these, the course turns toward the east again, and sailing with the ocean to the right and the shore remaining beyond to the left, Ganges comes into view, and near it the very last land toward the east, Chryse. There is a river near it called the Ganges, and it rises and falls in the same way as the Nile. On its bank is a market-town which has the same name as the river, Ganges. Through this place are brought malabathrum and Gangetic spikenard and pearls, and muslins of the finest sorts, which are called Gangetic.

It is said that there are gold-mines near these places, and there is a gold coin which is called *caltis*. And just opposite this river there is an island in the ocean, the last part of the inhabited world toward the east, under the rising sun itself; it is called Chryse; and it has the best tortoise-shell of all the places on the Erythræan Sea.

64. After this region under the very north, the sea outside ending in a land called This, there is a very great inland city called Thinæ, from which raw silk and silk yarn and silk cloth are brought on foot through Bactria to Barygaza, and are also exported to Damirica by way of the river Ganges. But the land of This is not easy of access; few men come from there, and seldom. The country lies under the Lesser Bear, and is said to border on the farthest parts of Pontus and the Caspian Sea, next to which lies Lake Mæotis; all of which empty into the ocean.

65. Every year on the borders of the land of This there comes together a tribe of men with short bodies and broad, flat faces, and by nature peaceable; they are called Besatæ, and are almost entirely uncivilized. They come with their wives and children, carrying great packs and plaited baskets of what looks like green grape-leaves. They meet in a place between their own country and the land of This. There they hold a feast for several days, spreading out the baskets under themselves as mats, and then return to their own places in the interior. And then the natives watching them come into that place and gather up their mats; and they pick out from the braids the fibers which they call *petri*. They lay the leaves closely together in several

layers and make them into balls, which they pierce with the fibers from the mats. And there are three sorts; those made of the largest leaves are called the large-ball malabathrum; those of the smaller, the medium-ball; and those of the smallest, the small-ball. Thus there exist three sorts of malabathrum, and it is brought into India by those who prepare it.

66. The regions beyond these places are either difficult of access because of their excessive winters and great cold, or else cannot be sought out because of some divine influence of the gods.

# NOTES

(Numerals refer to paragraphs similarly numbered in the text.)

Title. **Periplus** was the name applied to a numerous class of writings in Roman times, which answered for sailing-chart and traveler's hand-book. The title might be rendered as "Guide-Book to the Erythræan Sea."

Title. **Erythræan Sea** was the term applied by Greek and Roman geographers to the Indian Ocean, including its adjuncts, the Red Sea and the Persian Gulf. *Erythra* means *Red*, so that the modern name perpetuates the ancient; but we are assured by Agatharchides that it means, not Red Sea, but Sea of King Erythras, following a Persian legend.

The following is the account given by Agatharchides of the origin of the name: (*De Mari Erythræo*, § 5.)

"The Persian account is after this manner. There was a man famous for his valor and wealth, by name Erythras, a Persian by birth, son of Myozæus. His home was by the sea, facing toward islands which are not now desert, but were so at the time of the empire of the Medes, when Erythras lived. In the winter-time he used to go to Pasargadæ, making the journey at his own cost; and he indulged in these changes of scene now for profit, and now for some pleasure of his own life. On a time the lions charged into a large flock of his mares, and some were slain; while the rest, unharmed but terror-stricken at what they had seen, fled to the sea. A strong wind was blowing from the land, and as they plunged into the waves in their terror, they were carried beyond their footing; and their fear continuing, they swam through the sea and came out on the shore of the island opposite. With them went one of the herdsmen, a youth of marked bravery, who thus reached the shore by clinging to the shoulders of a mare. Now Erythras looked for his mares, and not seeing them, first put together a raft of small size, but secure in the strength of its building; and happening on a favorable wind, he pushed off into the strait, across which he was swiftly carried by the waves, and so found his mares and found their keeper also. And then, being pleased with the island, he built a stronghold at a place well chosen by the shore, and brought hither from the main-land opposite such as were dissatisfied with their life there, and subsequently settled all the other uninhabited islands with a numerous population; and such was the glory ascribed to him by the popular voice because of these his deeds, that even down to our own time they have called that sea, infinite in extent, *Erythræan*. And so, for the reason here set forth, it is to be well distinguished (for to say *Erýthra thálatta*, Sea of Erythras, is a very different thing from *Thálatta erythrâ*, Red Sea); for the one commemorates the most illustrious *man* of that sea, while the other refers to the color of the *water*. Now the one explanation of the name, as due to the color, is false (for the sea is not red), but the other, ascribing it to the man who ruled there, is the true one, as the Persian story testifies."

Here is manifestly a kernel of truth, referring, however, to a much earlier time than the Empire of the Medes and their capital Pasargadæ. It suggests the theory of a Cushite-Elamite migration around Arabia, as set forth by Glaser and Hommel: the story of a people from Elam, who settled in the Bahrein Islands and then spread along South Arabia, leaving their epithet of "Red" or "ruddy" in many places, including the sea that washed their shores and floated their vessels: "Sea of the Red People," or, according to Agatharchides, "of the Red King." See under §§ 4, 23 and 27.

1. **Designated ports.**—Trade was limited to ports of entry established, or, as the text has it, "designated" by law, and supervised by government officials who levied duties. There were many such ports on the Red Sea under the Ptolemies. There were also ports of entry maintained by the NabatæanKingdom, by the Homerite Kingdom in Yemen, and by the newly-established Kingdom of the Axumites; the latter, possibly, farmed to Egyptian Greeks, now Roman subjects.

Fabricius objects to "designated," and translates "frequented," thereby straining the meaning of the word and losing its obvious description of historical facts.

Under the early Ptolemies, who succeeded Alexander the Great, Egypt went far toward recovering her former wealth and glory. Under Ptolemy II, called Philadelphus (B. C. 285-246) the canal between the Nile and the Red Sea (originally dug by one of the Sesostrises, about the 20th century B. C., reopened under the Empire in the 15th century, and partly reopened by the Persians under Darius in the 5th century), was once more open to commerce; various caravan-routes, carefully provided with wells and stopping-places, were opened between the river and the sea, and where they terminated ports of entry were established and colonized. Egyptian shipping on the Red Sea was encouraged, and regular trade was opened with the Sabæans of

South Arabia, and the tribes of the Somali coast. The names of all these ports, and a description of this newly-created commerce, in terms of romantic enthusiasm, are given by Agatharchides in his work on the Erythræan Sea. At the time of this Periplus, the remaining settlements seem to be Arsinoe, Myos-hormus, Berenice, Ptolemais and Adulis. The other places mentioned by Agatharchides had probably lost their importance as the Egyptian ships ventured farther beyond the straits and frequented the richer markets that fringed the Gulf of Aden.

1. **Mussel Harbor** (Myos-hormus), is identified with the bay within the headland now known as Ras Abu Somer, 27° 12′ N., 35° 55′ E. It was founded by Ptolemy Philadelphus B. C. 274. He selected it as the principal port of Egyptian trade with India, in preference to Arsinoe (near the modern Suez), which was closer to the Egyptian capital, but difficult of access because of the bad passage through the upper waters of the Red Sea. Myos-hormus was distant six or seven days from Coptos on the Nile, along a road opened through the desert by Ptolemy Philadelphus. Strabo (XVII, I, 45) says "at present Coptos and Myos-hormus are in repute, and they are frequented. Formerly the camel-merchants traveled in the night, directing their course by observing the stars, and, like mariners, carried with them a supply of water. But now watering-places are provided; water is also obtained by digging to a great depth, and rain-water is found although rain rarely falls, which is also collected in reservoirs." Coptos is the modern Koft, in the bend of the Nile.

Vessels bound for Africa and Southern Arabia left Myos-hormus about the autumnal equinox, when the N. W. wind then prevailing carried them quickly down the gulf. Those bound for India or Ceylon left in July, and if they cleared the Red Sea before the first of September they had the monsoon to assist their passage across the ocean.

1. **Sailing.**—The ship used by the author of the Periplus probably did not differ very materially from the types created in Egypt long before, as depicted in the reliefs of the Punt Expedition in the Der-el-Bahri temple at Thebes, and elsewhere. By the first century A. D. the single square sail, with two yards, each much longer than the height of the sail, which distinguished the shipping of the 15th century B. C., had been modified by omitting the lower yard and by increasing the height of the mast; while a triangular topsail had come into general use. The *artimon* or sloping foremast, later developed into a bowsprit, was not generally used, even in the Mediterranean, until the 2d century. The accompanying illustration of a modern Burmah

*(From a sketch by R. T. Pritchett.)*

trader, which perpetuates in many ways the shipbuilding ideas of ancient Egypt, probably gives a better idea of our author's ship than any of the Greek or Roman coins or reliefs, which were all of Mediterranean shipping, built for different conditions and purposes.

In the Indian Ocean navigation depended on the trade-winds, and voyages were timed so that the ship could run before the wind in either direction, without calling the rudder into much use. This was at the quarter, the steersman plying the tiller from his station high in stern, overlooking the whole vessel.

Hippalus' discovery of the periodicity of the trade-winds, described in § 57, carried with it a knowledge of steering the boat somewhat off the wind, to reach a destination farther south than the straight course would make possible. This was done partly by the rudder, but largely by shifting the yard.

The lateen sail, as exemplified in the Arab *dhow*, the Bombay *kotia*, and so on, came into use about the 4th century B. C., but was used by Arab and Hindu, rather than Egyptian or Greek.

---

See Chatterton: *Sailing Ships and their Story:* Torr: *Ancient Ships*; Holmes: *Ancient and Modern Ships*; Pritchett: *Sketches of Shipping and Craft*; Lindsay: *History of Merchant Shipping and Ancient Commerce*; Charnock: *History of Marine Architecture*; Jal: *Archéologie Navale.*

1. **Stadia.**—Three stadia were in use in the Roman world at this time,—the Phileterian of 525 to the degree, the Olympic of 600, and that of Eratosthenes, of 700. Reduced to English measure this would make the Phileterian stadium equivalent to about 650 feet, the Olympic about 600 feet, and that of Eratosthenes about 520 feet. The stadium of the Periplus seems to be that of Eratosthenes. Generally speaking, ten stadia of the Periplus to the English statute mile would be a fair calculation. But it must not be forgotten that all distances named in this text are approximations, based principally on the length of time consumed in going from place to place, which naturally varied according to direction of the wind and current, of sailing-course, and other factors as well. The distance is generally given in round numbers; and without any means of arriving at an exact calculation, the figures in the text can be considered only as approximations.

According to the system of measurement laid down by Ptolemy, the circumference of the earth was estimated at 180,000 stadia, with 500 stadia to the degree.

The true length of the degree is 600 stadia.

The Olympic or standard Greek stadium (being the length of the race-course at Olympia), was 600 Greek feet, or 8 to the Roman mile. There was a later stadium of which 7½ went to the Roman mile (1000 paces, 4854 English feet). This, the Phileterian stadium, survived in Arabic science, and thence in the calculations of mediæval Europe; being very nearly the English furlong.

According to Col. Leake's calculations,

| | | | | |
|---|---|---|---|---|
| 1 Olympic stadium | = | 606.75 | English | feet. |
| 10 " " | = | 6067.50 | " | " |
| 1 Nautical mile | = | 6075.50 | " | " |
| 1 Admiralty knot | = | 6086.50 | " | " |
| or, by Clarke's measurement, | | 6087.11 | " | " |

Therefore,

| | | |
|---|---|---|
| 10 Olympic stadia | = | 1 minute of the equator. |
| 600 " " | = | 1 degree " " |

| | | | |
|---|---|---|---|
| 1 Roman mile | = 1000 *passus* = | 4854 English feet. | |
| 1 Old English mile | = 1000 paces = | 5090 " | " |
| 1 Modern Statute " | = | 5280 " | " |
| 75 Roman miles | = | 1 degree. | |

(or 75.09 to be exact).

4 Roman miles = 19,416 ft., English = 1 marine league.

The earth's circumference = 21,600 nautical miles, or
= 24,874 to 25,020 statute miles.

A degree on the equator = 69.1 to 69.5 statute miles.

The Tordesillas geographers, in 1494, gave 21.625 leagues to the equatorial degree. They were wrong, but followed Eratosthenes, who made the globe 1-16th larger than it really is.

Vespucci, following Ptolemy and Alfragan, figured 6000 leagues, or 24,000 Roman miles, as the measure of the earth's circumference; so that dividing by 360, 16⅔ leagues made a degree.

Columbus, following various Arabian geographers, made the degree 56⅔ miles, or 14⅙ leagues.

All this confusion goes back to some deduction based on Ptolemy.

By 1517, according to Navarrete, the valuation of 17½ leagues to the degree had become general. At the treaty of Zaragoza, in 1529, that ratio was admitted on both sides.

The correct figure is very close to 17½ leagues.

All ancient calculations were based on dead reckoning. The log-line did come into use until 1521.

---

See Vivien de Saint-Martin, *Le Nord de l'Afrique dans l'Antiquité grecque et romaine.* Paris, 1863: p. 197.

Samuel Edward Dawson: *The Line of Demarcation of Pope Alexander VI, and that of the Treaty of Tordesillas,* in Transactions of the Royal Society of Canada, 1899: Vol. V. § 2, pp. 467 ff.

1. **Berenice** (named for the mother of Ptolemy Philadelphus), is identified with Umm-el-Ketef Bay, below Ras Benas, 23° 55′ N. and about 35° 34′ E. It is 258 Roman miles, or 11 days, from Coptos, by a road across the desert. There are ruins still visible, even the arrangement of streets being clear; in the center is a small Egyptian temple with hieroglyphics and bas-reliefs of Greek workmanship. There is a fine natural harbor, but the bar is now impassable at low water; and Strabo (XVI, IV, 6) mentions dangerous rocks and violent winds from the sea.

At the time of this Periplus, Berenice seems to have been the leading port of Egypt for the Eastern trade, and was probably the home of the author.

2. **Berber Country.**—This word means more than the "land of the barbarians," and seems, like our modern "Barbary States," to refer to the Berber race, as representing the ancient Hamitic stock of North Africa.

The name itself seems to be foreign to the people, and is probably related to the Arabic *bar*, a desert; and its application to North Africa recalls that ancient race-opposition about the Gulf of Aden, when the *Red Men*, or ruddy people, overcame the "children of the desert"; who spread over all North Africa and carried the name with them, submitting time after time to similar Semitic conquests, Phœnician, Carthaginian or Saracen.

The occurrence of the name throughout North Africa is remarkable. We have the modern Somali port of Berbera, the Nile town and district of Berber (and its inhabitants, the Barbara, Barberins or Barbarins, who appear in the ancient Theban inscriptions as Beraberata); the Barbary States, the modern Berbers or Kabyles; and at the western extremity, on the Atlantic coast of Morocco, still another tribe calling themselves Berabra.

The ancient Egyptians extended the word to include the meanings of *savage* and *outlander*, or public enemies in general; and from them the Greeks took the word into their own language, with like meanings.

The Berbers of the Periplus probably included the ancestors of the Bejas between the Nile and Red Sea, the Danakils between the Upper Nile, Abyssinia and the Gulf of Aden, and the Somals and Gallas.

2. **Cave-Dwelling Fish-Eaters, Wild-Flesh-Eaters, Calf-Eaters.**—The original names, *Ichthyophagi* (Troglodytæ), *Agriophagi*, *Moschophagi*, add nothing to our ethnic knowledge, being merely appellations given by the Greeks; and they are therefore translated. These tribes are represented by the modern Bisharins. "Calf-Eaters" seems to mean eaters after the style of calves, i. e. of green things, rather than eaters of calves. Some commentators would replace *Agriophagi* by *Acridophagi*, locust-eaters.

2. **Meroe** was the final capital of the Kingdom of Nubia. It became the royal seat about 560 B. C. and continued as such until a few years after this Periplus, when the kingdom, worn out by continued attacks by the tribes of the desert and the negroes of the Sudan, fell to pieces. It was located on the Nile, below the 6th cataract, but just within the fertile region that begins above the confluence of the Atbara; and is identified with the modern Begerawiyeh, about 16° 55′ N.

The early Kingdom of Egypt comprised the Nile delta and the fertile valley of the river as far as the 1st cataract, the modern Assuan. Here a narrow gorge made the stream impassable for boats, and formed a natural barrier. Above Assuan the desert hugs the river close until above the 5th cataract, when it gives place to open fertile country. Between the island of Elephantine and Assuan, and the site of Meroe, the distance is about 480 miles in a direct line, and by the river about 1000 miles. This narrow strip of river-bed was Nubia proper. The Atbara, flowing into the Nile some 40 miles below Meroe, rises in northern Abyssinia or Tigre; at Khartum, about 150 miles above Meroe, the river branches again; the Blue Nile flowing down from the mountains of Central Abyssinia or Amhara, and the White Nile from the Nyanza lakes. These regions were more or less subject to Nubia at different periods, but their population varied greatly. The Abyssinian highlands were peopled by a Hamitic stock originally related to the Egyptians as well as to the still uncivilized tribes of the eastern and western desert, but with a mixture of negro blood and a strong strain of Arabian origin. The upper reaches of the Nile were peopled by various negro tribes, entirely distinct from Egyptian or Berber. From the mouth of the Red Sea there was a regular trade-route across the Tigre highlands to the Atbara River and so to the Nile; and other routes reached Meroe from the Sudan and Uganda. Thence the products of trade found their way down-stream to Elephantine, beyond which no negro was permitted to go. Here was the market for all Egypt, and the modern town, Assuan, repeats its history, as the very name means "market." From the Sudan came gold, ebony and ivory, panther skins and ostrich feathers; from the Nubian desert east of the Nile, gold; from the Red Sea across the Tigre, myrrh, frankincense, and various fragrant woods and resins: all of which were in constant demand for the Egyptian treasury and the service of the temples, and provided a constant reason for Egyptian control of this important avenue of commerce.

In the early period of the Egyptian nation the power centered in the Delta, but a loose control seems to have been maintained between the 1st and 2d cataracts over tribes appearing in the inscriptions as "Wa-wat," probably negroes. During the prosperous period of the Old Kingdom, between the 30th and 25th centuries B. C., the river-routes were kept in order, and Egyptian ships sailed the Red Sea as far as the myrrh-country. Then came a period of disorder and the fall of the Delta dynasties, followed in the 22d century by the rise of the Theban or Middle Kingdom, the dynasties of the Amenemhets and Sesostrises. These kings fully conquered the river tribes to the

2d cataract, as well as the "Nubian troglodytes" of the eastern desert, where they developed the gold-mines that added so much to their wealth and power. In this period, from the 22d to the 18th centuries B. C., the name "Cush" first appears in the inscriptions, indicating, as Glaser thought, a migration overland to the Nile by the wandering Cushite-Elamite tribes who had left their home at the head of the Persian Gulf some 300 years previously, and who, after settling in the incense-producing regions of Southern Arabia and Somaliland, whence they had opened trade with Mesopotamia, had now traced the same trade to its other great market in Egypt. The name "Cush" seems to have included not only the Nile valley between the 3d and and 6th cataracts, but much of the highlands. These people, apparently a mongrel race, were held in great contempt by the Egyptians, whose annals contain numerous references such as the following: "Impost of the wretched Cush: gold, negro slaves, male and female; oxen, and calves; bulls; vessels laden with ivory, ebony, all the good products of this country, together with the harvests of this country."

After the fall of the XIIth dynasty, 1788 B. C., came a period of feudal disorder, followed by an invasion from Arabia and a foreign dynasty, the Hyksos, probably Minæan Beduins. This was ended by the expulsion of the Arabs and the establishment of the Empire under the XVIIIth dynasty (1580-1350 B. C.). These great Pharaohs carried the Egyptian arms to their widest extent, from Asia Minor to the 4th cataract and possibly even farther south. The collapse of the Empire at the death of Rameses III (1167 B. C.) left Nubia still Egyptian. Invasions from the west resulted in a series of Libyan dynasties, which began, under Sheshonk or Shishak I, by reasserting sovereignty over Syria and by plundering the temple of Solomon and the treasures of the newly-established Kingdom of Israel; but the latter part of this administration was so inefficient that Theban princes established in Nubia separated from Egypt and formed a new kingdom, now called Ethiopia (indicating a growing Arabian settlement), with capital at Napata, below the 4th cataract (the modern Gebel Barkal), subsequently invading Egypt and establishing their power over the whole valley, from 722 to 663 B. C. Then came the Assyrian invasions, first by Esarhaddon and then the definite conquest of Egypt proper by Assurbanipal in 661 B. C. The ruin of Thebes is vividly described by the prophet Nahum (III, 8-10). The Nubians withdrew to Napata. There they were attacked by the restored power of Egypt under Psammetichus II, and about 560 B. C., transferred their capital to Meroe; a much better location, less open to attack from the north, in a fertile region instead of a narrow gorge in the desert, and in the direct path of the rapidly-growing immigration and trade from the south and east. Here they checked the army of Cambyses, which made Egypt a Persian province in 525 B. C. The capital fell into his hands for a time, but the country was not subdued. The conquest of Egypt by Alexander the Great, 332 B. C., left them undisturbed; and with his successors, the Ptolemies, they maintained an increasing commerce, notwithstanding the active policy then pursued to assert Egyptian supremacy in the Red Sea.

(See Breasted: *A History of Egypt.* N. Y., 1905.)

In 30 B. C. Egypt became a Roman province and the Nubians met a different foe. Their queen, Candace, attacked the Egyptians, and a punitive expedition by Petronius destroyed their power. (Strabo, XVII, 1, 54.) Gradually the enfeebled kingdom was engulfed by the tribes of the desert; and Pliny, whose *Natural History* was completed in 77 A. D., notes that of a long list of cities and towns above Philæ, described a century before, Nero's embassy in 67 A. D. could find hardly a trace, and that the capital itself, Meroe, was but a collection of a few wretched huts. National decay had done its work; and the few remnants left from the attacks of the Berbers had joined the new "Kingdom of the Axumites" in the highlands to the southeast.

In later times, under the Byzantine Empire, Nubia again became a center of culture and prosperity. Its new capital, the modern Khartum, became a leader in Christian thought, and maintained its influence even after the Saracens had overrun Egypt; only finally to repeat history by being utterly destroyed by a new irruption from the desert, under the spur of Islam, and to leave again to the Abyssinian highlands the defence of what remained of its Monophysite Christianity.

Josephus (*Antiquities of the Jews*, II, 9) has an account of a war of the Egyptians against the Ethiopians, under the command of Moses. The Ethiopians were finally driven back into their capital, Saba, "to which city Cambyses afterwards gave the name of Meroe, in compliment to his sister . . . . it being situated at the conflux of the rivers Astaphus and Astabora with the Nile." The city was finally delivered up to the Egyptians as the condition of Moses' marriage with the Ethiopian King's daughter Tharbis, who had fallen in love with him.

Aside from the obvious anachronisms in this story, one fact is of interest: the name of the capital, Saba, indicates that Nubia was ruled, if not mainly peopled, by Arabs, who had followed the ancient trade-routes from the mouth of the Red Sea.

Glaser (*Punt und die südarabischen Reiche*, 42-3) notes that Napata also is a Semitic name, probably Nabat, allied to Nabatu of the Assyrian inscriptions, to Nebaioth (son of Ishmael), and to the later Nabatæans of § 19.

Herodotus (II, 8) refers to the "mountain of Arabia" extending from north to south along the Nile, stretching up to the Erythræan Sea, and says that at its greatest width from east to west it is a two-months' journey; and that "eastward its confines produce frankincense." Here also is an indication of the connection of Nubia with Somaliland, confirmed by the pompous titles of the later Cushite kings in Meroe (Ed. Meyer: *Geschichte Aegyptens*, 359): "Kings of the four quarters of the world and of the nine distant peoples."

3. **Ptolemais.**—This is identified with Er-rih island, 18° 9′ N., 38° 27′ E., the southern portion of the Tokar delta. It was fortified by Ptolemy Philadelphus (B. C. 285-246), and became the center of the elephant-trade. Being situated near the Nubian forest, where elephants abounded, its location was very favorable. The Egyptians had formerly imported their elephants from Asia; but the cost was high and the supply uncertain, and Ptolemy sent his own hunters to Nubia, against the will of the inhabitants, to obtain a nearer supply.

From very early times there was a trade-route from the Red Sea to the Nile at this point, terminating near Meroe, and corresponding closely to the railway recently built between Berber on the Nile and Port Sudan on the Red Sea.

3. **Adulis.**—The present port is Massowa, center of the Italian colony of Eritrea, which lies near the mouth of the bay of Adulis. The ancient name is preserved in the modern village of Zula. The location has been described by J. Theodore Bent, (*Sacred City of the Ethiopians*, London, 1896: pp. 228-230). It is on the west side of Annesley Bay, and numerous black basalt ruins are still visible there. Adulis was one of the colonies of Ptolemy Philadelphus, and was always of commercial importance because it was the natural port for Abyssinia and the Sudan. It seems to have been built by Syrian Greeks. Here was the famous inscription reciting the conquests of Ptolemy Euergetes (B. C. 247-223) with an addition by Aizanas, or El Abreha, King of Abyssinia about 330 A. D., for a copy of which we are indebted to the *Christian Topography* of Cosmas Indicopleustes.

4. **Coloe.**—The ruins of Coloe were found by Bent at Kohaito, (*Sacred City of the Ethiopians*, Chap. XII). It is a large flat plateau many miles in extent, high above the surrounding country (7000 feet) and thus cool and comfortable. It seems to have been the main settlement, and Adulis the trading-post, which was inhabited no more

than necessary because of its hot climate. There is a fine dam, 219 feet long, and in one place 74 feet 4 inches above bed-rock, with sluice-gates 5 feet 3 inches wide; the whole built of large cut stones without mortar. When in use a large lake would have formed. There are numerous ruins of stone temples and dwellings; the architecture resembling that at Adulis, apparently Ptolemaic Greek. The town covered many acres.

Glaser thinks Kohaito is too near Adulis to be the ancient Coloe; but he seems to overlook the stiff climb up the mountain, which would naturally take longer in proportion than the subsequent road over the table-land.

The name Coloe, Glaser notes (*Punt und die südarabischen Reiche*, 23) is the same as the Arabic Kala'a, (which appears in the Adulis inscription of King Aizanas), and is derived from the same source as the Calæi Islands and Calon mountains in southeastern Arabia (in §§ 34-5). He derives the Alalæi Islands in this § 4 from the same tribal name, Kalhat, *via* Halâhila.

4. **Ivory.**—In the inscriptions of Harkhuf, an Assuan noble under King Mernere of the VIth Dynasty (B. C. 2600) occurs the first definite record of ivory as a commercial article in Egypt.

"I descended (from the country of Yam, southern Nubia) with 300 asses laden with incense, ebony, grain, panthers, ivory, throw-sticks, and every good product. I was more vigilant than any caravan-conductor who had been sent to Yam before." (Breasted: *Ancient Records of Egypt*, I, 336.)

There are numerous records of the receipt of ivory, in commerce and as tribute, under the XVIIIth Dynasty; coming from Tehenu (Libya, but *cf.* the Tenessis of Strabo); Punt (Somaliland), God's Land (S. W. Arabia), Gnbti (vicinity of Kuria Muria Islands), Cush (Nubia), the South Countries, Retenu (Syria) and Isy (Cyprus). Also articles made of ivory: chairs, tables, chests, statues, and whips.

Similar records occur under the XIXth and XXth dynasties; the latter, in the *Papyrus Harris*, being an item in a list of gifts of Rameses III to the god Ptah.

King Solomon's throne was of ivory, overlaid with gold; and his "navy of Tharshish" brought him the ivory every three years, together with gold and silver, apes and peacocks (I Kings X, 18-22).

4. **Cyeneum** is the modern Sennaar—Eastern Sudan.

4. **City of the people called Auxumites.**—This is the first known reference to the city of Axum, and serves very nearly to fix the date of its foundation. Pliny and other writers of this period mention the Asachæ living south of Meroe and known as elephant-

hunters; and their stronghold, *Oppidum Sacæ*, probably the same settlement as Axum. Bion speaks of Asachæ five days from the sea, and Ptolemy locates a "city of the Sacæ" in the Tigre highlands, but has no knowledge of Axum. Pliny (VI, 34) also speaks of the Ascitæ who brought myrrh and frankincense to South Arabia on their rafts supported on inflated skins, and suggests a derivation of the name from *askos*, bladder; but both names reproduce rather the mountainous coast of South Arabia, east of Hadramaut, called Hasik (Asich in § 33 of the Periplus), and there is evidently an ethnic and geographic connection between Hasik, the Asachæ or Ascitæ, and Axum.

Axum, the ancient capital and sacred city of the kingdom we call Abyssinia, is still the place of coronation for its kings. Abyssinia is the Latinized form of Habash, while its people call themselves *Itiopyavan*, Hellenized into Aethiopians. Habash is translated by modern Arabs as "mixture," while Herodotus explained Aethiopia as "land of the sunburned faces;" each explanation being, probably, incorrect. The Habashat appear likewise along the eastern terraces of South Arabia (Mahra) where they were the dominant race for several centuries before the Christian era. Pausanias (*de Situ Græciæ*, VI, 26-9), speaks of a "deep bay of the Erythræan Sea, having islands, Abasa and Sacæa" (probably Kuria Muria, Masira, and Socotra); the Roman writers mention an Abissa Polis in this region, and Stephanus of Byzantium says "beyond the Sabæans are the Chatramotitæ (Hadramaut) and the Abaseni." From the Egyptian inscriptions we learn that one of the Punt-people visited in their trading voyages was called *Hbsti*, and dwelt, apparently, not only in Mahra, but also in Socotra and Eastern Somaliland.

Glaser derives the name Habash from a Mahri word, meaning "gatherers." Synonymous with this is Aethiopian or *Itiopyavan*, which he derives from *atyôb*, "incense;" and it is significant that even in the time of the Periplus their ancient home in Mahra was still the "Frankincense Country." As "gatherers of incense," then, we have the mission of the Asachæ or Axumites. This people, like their predecessors from the same region, the Cushites who traded with Babylon and Thebes, a branch of whom, "intermarrying with the natives" (Periplus, § 16), helped found the Nubian Kingdom, and like the Punt or Poen-people of the Theban inscriptions, left their settlements in Mahra, Socotra and Somaliland (the true frankincense country) and migrated westward, settling finally in the Tigre highlands, where for the first time they established an enduring power. But their migration was different from the others, in that it was due to warfare and oppression rather than trade.

In the 3d century B. C. the Habashat or "gatherers" were supreme in their "incense-lands," and their allies and, perhaps, relatives, the Sabæans, worked with them in the spice and incense trade to Egypt, then at the height of its power under the Ptolemies. The prosperity of the trade is attested by Agatharchides. The Habashat held Socotra and Cape Guardafui, and much of the East African coast. But the succeeding centuries were turbulent. In order along the south Arabian coast, from west to east, were the Homerites (Himyar), the Sabæans, Hadramaut, Kataban, and the Habashat. Beyond were tribes under Persian influence. With the establishment of the Parthian, or Arsacid, empire, came a wave of conquest by the Parthians throughout eastern Arabia. Almost simultaneously came the African campaigns of Ptolemy Euergetes, said to have reached Mosyllum on the Somali coast (Periplus, § 10). The two incense-lands were hard hit. Then came the conquest of Kataban by Hadramaut and a threatening policy by Himyar against the Sabæans. Glaser has edited an inscription telling of an alliance of Djadarot, King of the Habashat, with three successive kings of Saba, for mutual protection against Hadramaut and Himyar. This dates from about 75 B. C. Isidorus of Charax Spasini, writing in the time of Augustus, mentions a chief of the Omanites in the Incense-Country, named Goaisos (*cf.* the language of the Habashat, *Geez*) who was apparently of the same race. But very soon afterward the Parthians renewed their attack from the East; Himyar overthrew Saba and demolished its port, and Hadramaut moved on Habash. Egypt was in a bad way, and the Romans who were taking over its government were encouraging a direct sea-trade from India, receiving Indian embassies, and breaking up the system which had so long closed the Arabian gulf to Indian shipping. Despoiled of their incense-terraces in Arabia and of their commercial activities at Guardafui, the Habashat sought a new home; and in the Tigre highlands built their stronghold, the *Oppidum Sacæ*, which soon became the city of Axum. It lay across the natural trade-route from India to Egypt; from Adulis, the seaport, to the Atbara River, was no great journey, and through a fertile country instead of the desert to the north. Here, then, so long as the "Berbers" of the lowlands could be dominated, a state could flourish; and hence the picture of its King Zoscales in § 5, "miserly in his ways and always striving for more." For six centuries the new kingdom of Abyssinia kept up its alliance with Rome and Constantinople against its ancient enemies the Homerites, and their allies the Parthians and Persians. The kingdom grew apace, and twice it overran southern Arabia; and not until the later Mohammedan conquests was its power broken and its people shut up in their mountains, there to preserve, for hundreds of years unknown to the outside world, their Monophysite Christianity.

The Abyssinian Chronicles make Zoscales at the time of the Periplus, the successor of a long line of kings at Axum. It is probable that Habashat had frequented the country for a century before, as the power of Egypt receded, but as colonists rather than state-builders, until driven from Arabia; and that most of Zoscales' predecessors were local chiefs and not tribal kings. The final migration Glaser places not far from the Christian era.

The Abyssinians were converted to Christianity about 330 A. D. Before that time their strongest outside influence may have been Buddhism. James Fergusson (*History of Architecture*, I, 142-3) notes

Monoliths at Axum

that the great monolith at Axum is of Indian inspiration; "the idea Egyptian, but the details Indian. An Indian nine-storied pagoda, translated in Egyptian in the first century of the Christian era!" He notes its likeness to such Indian temples as Bodh-Gaya, and says it represents "that curious marriage of Indian with Egyptian art which we would expect to find in the spot where the two people came in contact, and enlisted architecture to symbolize their commercial union." Such an alliance was to the advantage of the Hindu traders. The Homerites stopped their vessels at Ocelis on the Arabian shore (Periplus, § 25), taking their cargoes thence to Egypt by caravan; here was a new power that allowed them to trade to Avalites and Adulis, and even to march overland and take their wares to Egypt themselves. Ujjeni and Bharukacha, Axum and Alexandria were in close connection during the first and second Christian centuries, and

Temple of Bodh-Gaya, India, dating from early in the 6th century

the ooserver of the early relations between Buddhism and Christianity may find along this frequented route greater evidence of mutual influence than along the relatively obstructed overland routes through Parthia to Antioch and Ephesus. By the third century, with the decline of Rome, the growth of Antioch and Byzantium, and the fall of the Arsacid dynasty, the tendency would be the other way.

See Glaser: *Die Abessinier in Arabien und Afrika*, Munich, 1895. (A masterly marshaling of inscriptions in support of his thesis, above summarized.) *Punt und die südarabischen Reiche*, Berlin, 1899; *Skizze der Geschichte und Geographie Arabiens*, Berlin, 1890; Dillmann: *Geschichte des Axumitischen Reiches*, in Kön. Preuss. Akad. d. Wissenchaften, Berlin, 1880. For the interrelation between Buddhism and early Christianity, and the historical causes leading thereto, see Edmunds: *Buddhist and Christian Gospels now first compared from the originals*, Philadelphia (4th edition), 1908.

---

4. **Alalæi Islands.**—These preserve the name, being called Dahalak. They lie at the entrance to Annesley Bay.

5. **Bay of the Opsian stone.**—This is identified with Hauakil Bay, north of Ras Hanfilah, 14° 44′ N., 40° 49′ E. "Hanfilah" is Amphila, the *Antiphili Portus* of Artemidorus.

Pliny (*op. cit.* XXXVI, 67) says the obsian stone (as he spells it) of Aethiopia was very dark, sometimes transparent, but dull to the sight, and reflected the shadow rather than the image. It was used in his day for jewelry and for statues and votive offerings.

It was used by the Emperor Domitian to face a portico, so that from the reflections on the polished surface he might detect any one approaching from behind.

It seems to have been a volcanic glass, feldspar in a more or less pure state, and the same as our obsidian.

It was found also, according to Pliny, in India, at Samnium in Italy, and in Portugal; and it was extensively imitated in glass.

Henry Salt (*A Voyage into Abyssinia*, pp. 190-4), describes his visit to the Bay of the Opsian stone, which was marked by a hill, near which he "was delighted with the sight of a great many pieces of a black substance, bearing a very high polish, much resembling glass, that lay scattered about on the ground at a short distance from the sea; and I collected nearly a hundred specimens of it, most of which were two, three, or four inches in diameter. One of the natives told me that a few miles farther in the interior, pieces are found of much larger dimensions. This substance has been analyzed since my return to England and found to be true obsidian."

5. **Coast subject to Zoscales.**—Col. Henry Yule in his *Marco Polo*, II, 434, says "To the 10th century at least, the whole coast-country of the Red Sea, from near Berbera probably to Suakin, was still subject to Abyssinia. At this time we hear only of 'Musalman families' residing in Zeila and the other ports and tributary to the Christians." (See also Mas' udi, III, 34.)

5. **Zoscales.**—Salt (*op. cit.* 460-5) identifies this name with Za Hakale, which appears in the Abyssinian Chronicles. The reign is said to have lasted 13 years, and Salt fixes the dates as 76 to 89 A. D.

But he admits (p. 460) that "no great dependence can be placed" upon the Chronicles.

The list begins with "Arwe, the serpent," who reigned 400 years; Za Beesi Angaba, 200; Zagdur, 100; Zazebass Besedo, 50; Zakawasya b'Axum, 1; Za Makeda, 50; "in her 4th year she went to Jerusalem, and after her return reigned 25 years." Then comes Menilek, 29; followed by 15 others, 91 years 2 months; then Za Baesi Bazen, 16 years, "and in the eighth year of his reign Christ was born." Then follow 7 names, 68 years, and Za Hakale, 13; then 15 more names, 227 years 4 months, and Aizanas (el Abreha), and Saizanas (el Atzbeha), 26 years 6 months, "and in the 13th year of this reign Christianity was introduced," and so on.

If Za Makeda was the Queen of Sheba who visited King Solomon in the 10th century B. C., there are evidently great omissions before Za Baesi Bazen, whose reign is said to have begun in 8 B. C. And Salt was obliged to move Aizanas and Saizanas from their places in the Chronicle, and to advance them 130 years, in order to make them tally with their Axum and Adulis inscriptions, and the correspondence known to have been carried on between them and the Roman Emperors Constantine and Constantius. Therefore Za Hakale's place in the list, in the absence of confirming evidence, can hardly fix the date of the Periplus, as proposed by Müller. More probable is it that, like Salt's Aizanas, he must be advanced in the Chronicle to meet known facts. By moving him up three places in the line his accession is brought to 59 A. D., a very probable date.

The Abyssinian Chronicle was composed some time after the conversion of the people to Christianity. Its earlier portions are, therefore, mere tradition; and two versions of it which Salt examined during his visit to that country were found to differ materially.

The reigns in the first Christian century, as given by Salt, are as follows:

| | | | | |
|---|---|---|---|---|
| Za Baesi Bazen, | 16 | years, | 0 | months |
| Za Senatu, | 26 | " | 0 | " |
| Za Les, | 10 | " | 0 | " |
| Za Masenh, | 6 | " | 0 | " |
| Za Sutuwa, | 9 | " | 0 | " |
| Za Adgaba, | 10 | " | 6 | " |
| Za Agba, | 0 | " | 6 | " |
| Za Malis, | 6 | " | 0 | " |
| Za Hakale, | 13 | " | 0 | " |
| Za Demahé, | 10 | " | 0 | " |
| Za Awtet, | 2 | " | 0 | " |

The *Za* prefix, recalling the *Dja* of Glaser's Arabian inscriptions, gives way in the 3d century to a long list beginning with *El*, indicating perhaps a change of dynasty from the Habash stock to the Sabæan.

6. **Egyptian cloth.**—This was linen, made from flax.

6. **Arsinoe** was at the head of the Heroopolite Gulf, corresponding to the modern Suez, but now some distance inland owing to the recedence of the Gulf. It was named for the favorite wife of Ptolemy Philadelphus. At one time it was important commercially, as an entrepôt for the Eastern trade; and while it soon lost that position, it continued for centuries to be a leading industrial center, particularly in textiles.

6. **Glass.**—Pliny (*op. cit.* XXXVI, 65) says that glass-making originated in Phœnicia, and that the sand of the river Belus was long the only known material suitable for the industry. He attributes the discovery for the process to the wreck of a ship laden with nitre on this shore, and the accidental subjection of nitre and sand to heat as the merchants set caldrons on the beach to cook their food. Later the Phœnicians applied themselves to the industry; and their experiments led to the use of manganese and other substances, and to an advanced stage of perfection in the product.

In Pliny's time a white sand at the mouth of the river Volturnus was much used in glass-making. It was mixed with three parts of nitre and fused into a mass called *hammo-nitrum;* which was subjected to fusion a second time, and then became pure white glass. Throughout Gaul and Spain a similar process was used, and this was doubtless the process used in Egypt, as mentioned in the Periplus.

The color was added in the second fusion, after which the glass was either blown, turned or engraved.

6. **Murrhine.**—See the note to § 49. It was probably agate and carnelian from the Gulf of Cambay; but was extensively imitated in glass by the Phœnicians and Egyptians. The murrhine mentioned here was evidently a cheap trading product, probably colored glass.

6. **Diospolis** (City of God) was probably Thebes, the metropolis of the Egyptian Empire—the modern Karnak. This was its name under the Ptolemies and Romans. There was another Diospolis in Egypt, mentioned by Strabo; it was in the Nile delta, above the Sebennytic mouth; but it was not of great importance. Still another, known as Diospolis Parva, was on the Nile some distance below Coptos. The greater Diospolis—Diospolis Magna—was a center of commerce and industry, being no great way above Coptos, from which the caravans started for Berenice.

As illustrating the fame of that city, Strabo quotes Homer (*Iliad* IX, 383) "with her hundred gates, through each of which issues two hundred men with horses and chariots." The prophet Nahum (III, 8-10) draws another picture of the city after its capture by the Assyrians: "populous No (or No-Amon, City of God) that was situate among the rivers, that had the waters round about it . . . . Ethiopia and Egypt were her strength, and it was infinite; Put and Lubim (Cyrene and Libya) were thy helpers. Yet was she carried away, she went into captivity; her young children also were dashed in pieces at the top of all the streets; and they cast lots for her honourable men, and all her great men were bound in chains."

6. **Brass.**—The Greek word is *oreichalcos*, "mountain-copper," which Pliny (*op. cit.* XXXIV, 2) makes into a hybrid, as *aurichalcum*, golden copper; brass, a yellow alloy, as distinguished from pure copper or the darker alloys. Pliny describes it as an ore of copper long in high request, but says none had been found for a long time, the earth having been quite exhausted. It was used for the sestertium and double as, the Cyprian copper being thought good enough for the as.

Oreichalch seems to have been a native brass obtained by smelting ores abundant in zinc; the Roman metallurgy did not distinguish zinc as a separate metal.

Mines yielding such ores were held in the highest estimation, and their exhaustion was deeply regretted, as in the case of the "Corinthian brass." But later it was found by accident that the native earth, calamine, an impure oxide of zinc, added to molten copper, would imitate the true oreichalch; and this the Romans did without understanding what the earth was, just as they used native oxide of cobalt in coloring glass without knowing the metal cobalt.

(See Pliny XXXVII, 44, and Beckmann, *History of Inventions*, II, 32-3.)

Philostratus of Lemnos, about 230 A. D., mentions a shrine in Taxila in which were hung pictures on copper tablets representing the feats of Alexander and Porus. "The various figures were portrayed in a mosaic of orichalcum, silver, gold, and oxidized copper, but the weapons in iron. The metals were so ingeniously worked into one another that the pictures which they formed were comparable to the productions of the most famous Greek artists" (McCrindle: *Ancient India*, 192).

The Greek word is effectively used by Oscar Wilde in his poem *The Sphinx:*

—the God of the Assyrian,
Whose wings, like strange transparent talc, rose high above his hawk-faced head,
Painted with silver and with red and ribbed with rods of oreichalch.

6. **Sheets of soft copper.**—The text is "honey-copper." That the metallurgy of Roman days included a fusion with honey or other organic substances, such as cow's blood, to produce greater ductility, has been asserted, but not proven. Müller makes a more plausible suggestion, that this was ductile copper in thin sheets, and was called "honey-copper" because the sheets were shaped like honey-cakes. Ductile copper in Roman times generally meant an alloy with 5 to 10 per cent of lead.

6. **Iron.**—Pliny (*op. cit.* XXXIV, 39-46) speaks of iron as "the most useful and most fatal instrument in the hand of man." The ore, he says, is found almost everywhere; "even in the Isle of Elba." It is worked like copper, and its quality depends somewhat on the water into which the red-hot metal is plunged. Bilbilis and Turiasso in Spain, and Comum in Italy, are distinguished for the use of their waters in smelting. The best iron is that made by the Seres, "who send it to us with their tissues and skins." Next to this in quality is the Parthian iron. In all other kinds the metal is alloyed, that is, apparently, the ore is impure.

·6. **Coats of skin.** The text is *kaunakai.*—Originally these were of rough skins with the hair left on; later they were imitated in Mesopotamia by a heavy woolen fabric, suggesting the modern frieze overcoat, which was largely exported. It is not known which is meant here.

6. **Ariaca.**—This is the northwest coast of India, especially around the Gulf of Cambay; the modern Cutch, Kathiawar and Gujarat. As the name indicates, it was at the time of the Periplus one of the strongholds of the Indo-Aryan races, and incidentally of Buddhism, the religion then dominant among them.

6. **Indian iron and steel.**—Marco Polo (Yule ed. I, 93) Book I, chap. XVII, mentions iron and *ondanique* in the markets of Kerman. Yule interprets this as the *andanic* of Persian merchants visiting Venice, an especially fine steel for swords and mirrors, and derives it from *hundwániy* "Indian" steel.

Kenrick suggests that the "bright iron" of Ezekiel XXVII, 19, must have been the same.

Ctesias mentions two wonderful swords of such material which he had from the King of Persia.

Probably this was also the *ferrum candidum* of which the Malli and Oxydracæ sent 100 talents' weight as a present to Alexander.

*Ferrum indicum* also appears in the lists of dutiable articles under Marcus Aurelius and Commodus.

Salmasius notes a Greek chemical treatise "On the tempering of Indian steel."

Edrisi says "The Hindus excel in the manufacture of iron. They have also workshops wherein are forged the most famous sabres in the world. It is impossible to find anything to surpass the edge that you get from Indian steel."

6. **Cotton.**—Sanscrit, *karpāsa;* Hebrew, *carpas;* Greek, *karpasos;* Latin, *carbasus*—the seed-fibers of *Gossypium herbaceum* and *G. arboreum* (order, *Malvaceæ*) native in India, and woven into cloth by the natives of that country before the dawn of history. The facts concerning it have been admirably stated by Mr. R. B. Handy in *The Cotton Plant*, a report of the U. S. Department of Agriculture, issued in 1896. Cotton thread and cloth are repeatedly mentioned in the laws of Manu, 800 B. C. Professor A. H. Sayce in his Hibbert Lectures shows ground for the belief that it was exported by sea to the head of the Persian Gulf in the 4th millennium B. C.; and it found its way very early to Egypt. Herodotus describes it as a wool, better than that of sheep, the fruit of trees growing wild in India.

The manufacture of cotton cloth was at its best in India until very recent times, and the fine Indian muslins were in great demand and commanded high prices, both in the Roman Empire and in Mediæval Europe. The industry was one of the main factors in the wealth of ancient India, and the transfer of that industry to England and the United States, and the cheapening of the process by mechanical ginning, spinning and weaving, is perhaps the greatest single factor in the economic history of our own time.

Pliny and Pollux state that cotton was grown in Egypt in their time (1st and 2nd centuries A. D.), how extensively is unknown. It was also grown in the island of Tylos in the Persian Gulf, and according to Theophrastus, in Arabia; and the Periplus confirms this by mentioning it as an article of export from Ommana.

Cotton seems also to have been grown in Syria, Cilicia and Palestine; and the fiber known to Josephus as *chedôn*, Hebrew, *ketonet*; Arabic, *kut'n*, (the same sound appears in Phœnician, Syrian and Chaldee), was perhaps cotton. Movers states that the inhabitants of Palestine before the Hebrew migration made use of cotton, and that the Phœnicians exported Syrian cotton cloth to Sabæa.

Pausanias describes cotton as growing in Elis, in Achæa, and says that it was made into cloth by the women of Patræ; but this could not have been an extensive industry. It was quite certainly not produced or woven in Italy during Roman days.

Any generalizations based on the Arabic *kut'n* or the Greek *karpasos* are uncertain, because those words were applied also to flax, which was in very general use in all the Mediterranean countries.

It is noteworthy that the word used in the Periplus is uniformly *othonion*, meaning simply "cloth," but usually cotton cloth; while the *himatismos*, translated as "clothing," was very likely cloth in suitable lengths to be worn as tobe or toga.

6. **Monachê cloth.**—Vincent says cloth "singularly fine," and for *sagmatogênê* would read "the sort used for stuffing" (from *sasso*, to stuff; *sagma*, a saddle) being the down from the tree-cotton, *Gossypium arboreum*. But these words may be Greek corruptions of some Indian trade-names for different grades or dyes of cloth, as to the particulars of which we cannot determine.

Fabricius alters *monachê* to *molochinê* because of the occurrence of the same word in the following line, and makes a similar alteration wherever the word appears in the text, but it is difficult to see just what is gained.

This "broad cloth" was no doubt used for garments such as the modern Somali "tobe," described by Burton (*First Footsteps*, p. 29): "It is a cotton sheet eight cubits long, and two breadths sewn together. It is worn in many ways; sometimes the right arm is bared; in cold weather the whole person is muffled up, and in summer it is allowed to fall below the waist. Generally it is passed behind the back, rests upon the left shoulder, is carried forward over the breast, surrounds the body, and ends hanging on the left shoulder, where it displays a gaudy silk fringe of red and yellow. This is the man's Tobe. The woman's dress is of similar material, but differently worn; the edges are knotted generally over the right, sometimes over the left shoulder; it is girdled round the waist, below which hangs a lappet, which in cold weather can be brought like a hood over the head. Though highly becoming and picturesque as the Roman toga, the Somali Tobe is by no means the most decorous of dresses; women in the towns often prefer the Arab costume—a short-sleeved robe extending to the knee, and a Futah or loin-cloth underneath."

McCrindle, *Ancient India*, p. 26, notes that India has two distinct species of cotton, *Gossypium herbaceum*, and *Gossypium arboreum* or tree-cotton. The former only is made into cloth, while the latter yields a soft and silky texture, which is used for padding cushions, pillows, etc. Pliny says (XIX, 1) that Upper Egypt also produces "a shrub bearing a nut from the inside of which wool is got, white and soft."

6. **Molochinê,** or **mallow cloth,** was a coarse cotton cloth dyed with a preparation of a variety of the hibiscus native in India. This purplish cloth must have corresponded closely to the coarse blue drills still in demand on this coast.

6. **Lac.**—McCrindle notes that the Sanscrit is *lâkshâ*, a later form of *râkshâ*, connected with the root *ranj*, to dye. The Prakrit form is *lakkha*. It was used by women for dyeing the nails and feet, also as a dye for cloth.

The lac insect (*Tachardia Lacca*, Kerr) is native in India and still practically confined to that country.

According to Watt (*Commercial Products of India*, pp. 1053 ff.), it yields two distinct products: a dye and a resin. The dye competed on favorable terms with the Mexican cochineal until both were displaced by manufactured aniline, when the resin *shellac* again became more important.

The resin is formed around the young swarms as they adhere to the trees; the lac being a minute hemipterous insect living on the plant-juices sucked up by a proboscis.

The dye is taken from the bodies of the females, which assume a bright red color during the process of reproduction. For a complete account of the product and its uses see Watt.

Of somewhat similar nature to lac was the "kermes-berry" produced on the Mediterranean holm-oak; whence the dye known as carmesin, cramoisi, crimson or carmine; or, by another derivation, scarlet; or, referring to the pupa-stage of the insect, vermiculum or vermilion.

These insect dyes were used separately, or, associated with murex, as an element in the so-called "Tyrian purple."

6. **Tortoise-shell.**—This was a great article of commerce in the Roman world, being used for small receptacles, ornaments, and for inlaying furniture and woodwork. It is one of the most frequently-mentioned commodities in the Periplus. The antiquity of the trade is uncertain, but this seems to be the "shell" brought from the Land of Punt by Queen Hatshepsut's expedition in the 15th century B. C.

6. **Rhinoceros.**—The horns and the teeth, and probably the skin, were exported from the coast of Abyssinia, where Bruce found the hunting of this animal still a trade and described it (*Travels*, Vol. IV).

7. **Avalites** is identified with the modern Zeila, 11° 20′ N., 43° 28′ E. It is 79 miles from the straits of Bab-el-Mandeb. The ancient name is preserved by the village Abalit, on the north shore of

the bay. The Somali tribes call the place Ausal, apparently perpetuating the Ausan of the South Arabian coast; which also at one time possessed much of the coast of East Africa (called the "Ausanitic coast" in § 15 of the Periplus). Avalites is thought by Forster (*Historical Geography of Arabia*, Vol. I) to perpetuate the name of Obal, son of Joktan (Gen. IV) whose name is almost unknown in Arabia; thus indicating a very early migration of this tribe to the Somali coast. This name seems also to survive in Obollah at the Euphrates mouth on the Persian Gulf; which was the Ubulu of the Assyrian inscriptions, and the Apologus of § 35.

Of Zeila, Ibn Batuta, writing in the 14th century, said: "I then went from Aden by sea, and after four days came to the city of Zeila. This is a settlement of the Berbers, a people of Sudan, of the Shafia sect. Their country is a desert of two months' extent; the first part is termed Zeila, the last Makdashu. The greatest number of the inhabitants, however, are of the Rafizah sect. Their food is mostly camel's flesh and fish. The stench of the country is extreme, as is also its filth, from the stink of the fish and the blood of the camels which are slaughtered in its streets."

Zeila is described by Burton (*First Footsteps in East Africa*, p. 14) as "the normal African port—a strip of sulphur-yellow sand, with a deep blue dome above, and a foreground of the darkest indigo. The buildings, raised by refraction, rise high, and apparently from the bosom of the deep. . . . No craft larger than a canoe can ride near Zeila. After bumping once or twice against the coral reefs, it was considered advisable for our ship to anchor. My companions put me into a cockboat, and wading through the water, shoved it to shore. The situation is a low and level spit of sand, which high tides make almost an island. There is no harbor; a vessel of 250 tons cannot approach within a mile of the landing-place; the open roadstead is exposed to the terrible north wind, and when gales blow from the west and south it is almost unapproachable. Every ebb leaves a sandy flat, extending half a mile seaward from the town; the reefy anchorage is difficult of entrance after sunset, and the coraline bottom renders wading painful."

Zeila, the nearest port to Harrar in the interior, had, when Burton wrote, lost the caravan trade to Berbera, owing to the feuds of its rulers; so that the characteristics of its people had not changed from the account given in § 7 of the Periplus.

At that time the exports from Zeila were slaves, ivory, hides, honey, antelope horns, clarified butter, and gums. The coast abounded in sponge, coral, and small pearls. In the harbor were about twenty native craft, large and small; they traded with Berbera, Arabia, and Western India, and were navigated by "Rajput" or Hindu pilots.

Burton (*op. cit.*, pp. 330-1) says again:

"I repeatedly heard at Zeila and at Harrar that traders had visited the far West, traversing for seven months a country of pagans wearing golden bracelets, till they reached the Salt Sea upon which Franks sail in ships. I once saw a traveler descending the Nile with a store of nuggets, bracelets and gold rings similar to those used as money by the ancient Egyptians. Mr. Krapf relates a tale current in Abyssinia, namely: that there is a remnant of the slave trade between Guineh (the Guinea coast) and Shoa. Connection between the east and west formerly existed; in the time of João I, the Portuguese on the river Zaire in Congo learned the existence of the Abyssinian church. Travelers in Western Africa assert that Fakihs or priests, when performing the pilgrimage, pass from the Fellatah country through Abyssinia to the coast of the Red Sea. And it has lately been proved that a caravan line is open from the Zanzibar coast to Benguela."

The foregoing, written before modern discovery had altered the trade of Africa, indicates the same condition as that existing in ancient history: a well-established trade to Egypt and South Arabia, coming from tribe to tribe through the heart of Africa, from great distances West and South.

7. **The "Far-side" coast.**—According to Burton (*op. cit.* p. 12) the Somali tribes called their country the *Barr el Ajam*, which he translates as "barbarian land," but goes on to explain that *Ajam* means all nations not Arab, just as among Egyptians and Greeks "barbarian" meant all nations not of their country.

The name seems to apply to the migration and trade from South Arabia, the tribes who had crossed the gulf at Aden at various periods of history being referred to by their countrymen as those "of the farther side," which our author has rendered into Greek as *peratikos* (*pera*, beyond).

7. **Juice of sour grapes.**—The text is *omphakion*. Pliny says (XII, 60): "Omphacium is a kind of oil obtained from the olive and the vine—the former is produced by pressing the olive while still white; the latter from the Aminæan grape, when the size of a chick-pea, just before the rising of the Dog-star. The verjuice is put into earthen vessels, and then stored in vessels of Cyprian copper. The best is reddish, acrid, and dry to the taste. Also the unripe grape is pounded in a mortar, dried in the sun, and then divided into lozenges."

The Aminæan grape he describes in XIV, 4: also a *lanata* or woolly grape—"so that we not be surprised at the wool-bearing trees of the Seres or the Indians." These latter were cotton; the former were mulberry trees with silkworm cocoons bred on them. *cf.* Virgil, (*Georgics*, II, 121.)

"Velleraque ut foliis depectant tenuia Seres."

Pliny (XXIII, 4) says again: "Omphacium heals ulcerations of the humid parts of the body, such as the mouth, tonsillary glands, etc. The powerful action of omphacium is modified by the admixture of honey or raisin wine. It is very useful, too, for dysentery, spitting of blood, and quinsy."

And in XXIII, 39: "The most useful of all kinds of oil (other than olive) is omphacium. It is good for the gums, and if kept from time to time in the mouth, there is nothing better as a preservative of the whiteness of the teeth. It checks profuse perspiration."

7. **Wheat.**—*Triticum vulgare*, Villars, order *Gramineæ*. The cultivation of wheat, says De Candolle, is prehistoric. It is older than the most ancient languages, each of which has independent and definite names for the grain. The Chinese grew it 2700 B. C. It was grown by the Swiss lake-dwellers about 1500 B. C., and has been found in a brick of one of the Egyptian pyramids dating from about 3350 B. C.

Originally it was doubtless a wild grass which under cultivation assumed varying forms. In the early Roman Empire vast quantities of wheat were raised in Sicily, Gaul, North Africa, and particularly Egypt, for shipment to Rome. Later a great wheat area was opened up in what is now Southern Russia, which finally supplanted Egypt in the markets of Constantinople, after Alexandria and Antioch fell into Saracen hands. The trade in wheat as described in the Periplus is interesting. It shows that South Arabia, Socotra and East Africa had wheat not only from Egypt but also from India, which has not usually been considered as a wheat country at that time. Watt (*op., cit.* p. 1082) thinks wild rice (*Oryza coarctata*) may have been intended, but the Periplus distinguishes between wheat and rice as coming from India. The Hindus might certainly have had the seed from Egypt and cultivated it, but Watt notes the complete absence, so far as known, of wild wheat in modern India.

7. **Wine.**—The fermented juice of *Vitis vinifera*, Linn., order *Vitaceæ*. The culture of the vine seems to have begun in Asia Minor and Syria, but within the period of written history it is almost universal. It introduction was ascribed to the gods: by the Greeks to Dionysos, the Romans to Bacchus, the Egyptians to Osiris; or in the case of the Hebrews, to the patriarch Noah. The vine and the

olive, requiring continued cultivation from year to year, almost distinguish settled civilization from nomadic conditions, and the product of both industries appears in commerce from the earliest times.

The wine of the Damacus valley was an important export in the time of Ezekiel (XXVII, 18); of the Greek wines the best were from the Aegean islands and the Asiatic coast near Ephesus (Strabo, XIV, 1, 15). The Phœnicians carried the vine to Spain, and the Greeks to southern Gaul. It was unknown in early Italy, but was fostered by the Roman republic, which restricted imports of foreign growths, and stimulated exports by restricting viticulture in the provinces. In the valleys of the Seine and Moselle wine was not produced until the later days of the Roman Empire.

At the time of the Periplus, the popular taste demanded a wine highly flavored with extraneous substances, such as myrrh and other gums, cinnamon and salt.

The Periplus tells us that Italian and Laodicean wines were imported into Abyssinia, the Somali Coast, East Africa, South Arabia, and India. Arabian wine was also carried to India; this may have included grape-wine from Yemen (§ 24) but was principally date-wine from the Persian Gulf (§36). Italian wine was preferred to all others (§ 49). This was from the plain of Campania, in the vicinity of the modern Naples, whence Strabo tells us (V, VI, 13), "the Romans procured their finest wines, the Falernian, the Statanian, and the Calenian. That of Surrentum is now esteemed equal to these, it having been lately discovered that it can be kept to ripen." Petronius (*Cena Trimalchionis*) mentions a Falernian wine which had been ripened 100 years.

The Laodicean wine was from Laodicea on the Syrian coast, some 60 miles south of Antioch, the modern Latakia. Strabo (XVI, II, 9) says: "it is a very well-built city, with a good harbor; the territory, besides its fertility in other respects, abounds with wine, of which the greater part is exported to Alexandria. The whole mountain overhanging the city is planted almost to its summit with vines."

7. **Tin.**—Hebrew, *bedil;* Greek, *kassiteros;* Sanscrit, *kasthira;* Latin, *stannum.* This metal, the product of Galicia and Cornwall, was utilized industrially at a comparatively late period, having been introduced after gold, silver, copper, iron, lead, and mercury. It made its appearance in the Mediterranean world soon after the migration of the Phœnicians to Syria. The Phœnician traders may have found it first on the Black Sea coast, coming overland from tribe to tribe; very soon they discovered the Spanish tin and traced it to its source, and finally that of Cornwall. The value of tin in hardening

copper was soon understood, and the trade was monopolized for centuries by the Phœnicians and their descendants, the Carthaginians. How carefully they guarded the secret of its production appears in Strabo's story (III, V, 11) of the Phœnician captain who, finding himself followed by a Roman vessel on the Atlantic coast of Spain, ran his ship ashore rather than divulge his destination, and collected the damage from his government on returning home.

There is much confusion in the early references to this metal, because the Hebrew *bedil* (meaning "the departed") was also applied to the metallic residue from silver-smelting—a mixture of silver, lead, and occasionally copper and mercury. The same comparison applies to *kassiteros* and *stannum*. Pliny, for example, distinguishes *plumbum nigrum*, lead, and *plumbum candidum*, stannum. Without any definite basis for determining metals, appearance was often the only guide.

Suetonius (*Vitell.* VI, 192) says that the Emperor Vitellius took away all the gold and silver from the temples, (69 A. D.) and substituted *aurichalcum* and *stannum*. This *stannum* could not have been pure tin, but rather an alloy of lead, like pewter.

The letters from the King of Alashia (Cyprus), in the Tell-el-Amarna tablets, indicate the possibility of the use of tin there in the 15th century B. C., and of the shipment of the resultant bronze to Egypt; and tin, as a separate metal, is thrice mentioned in the *Papyrus Harris*, under Rameses III (1198-1167 B. C.). This confirms the mention of tin in Numbers XXXI, 22. By the time of Ezekiel (XXVII, 12) it was, of course, well known; here it appears with silver, iron, and lead, as coming from Spain. The stela of Tanutamon describes a hall for the god Amon, build by the Pharaoh Taharka at Napata (688-663 B. C.), of stone ornamented with gold, with a tablet of cedar incensed with myrrh of Punt, and double doors of electrum with bolts of tin. (Breasted, *Ancient Records of Egypt*, Vol. IV).

By the Greeks the true tin was understood and extensively used, and the establishment of their colony of Massilia was largely due to the discovery of the British metal coming overland to the mouth of the Rhône. The Romans ultimately conquered both Galicia and Cornwall, and then controlled the trade; but to judge from Pliny's account, their understanding of it was vague.

According to the Periplus, tin was shipped from Egypt to both Somaliland and India.

Lassen (*Indische Alterthumskunde*, I, 249) and Oppert, arguing from the similarity between the Sanscrit *kasthira* and the Greek *kassiteros*, would transfer the earliest tin trade to India and Malacca; but it seems probable that the Sanscrit word was a late addition to the language, borrowed from the Greek with the metal itself; which, as stated by the Periplus in §§ 49 and 56, came to India from the west.

See also Movers, *Phönizier*, Vol. III; Beckmann, *op. cit.*, II, 206-230.

8. **Malao** is the modern Berbera, 10° 25′ N., 45° 5′ E. It is now the leading port of this coast, the capital of British Somaliland, and the center of the caravan trade to the interior. Glaser (*Skizze*,

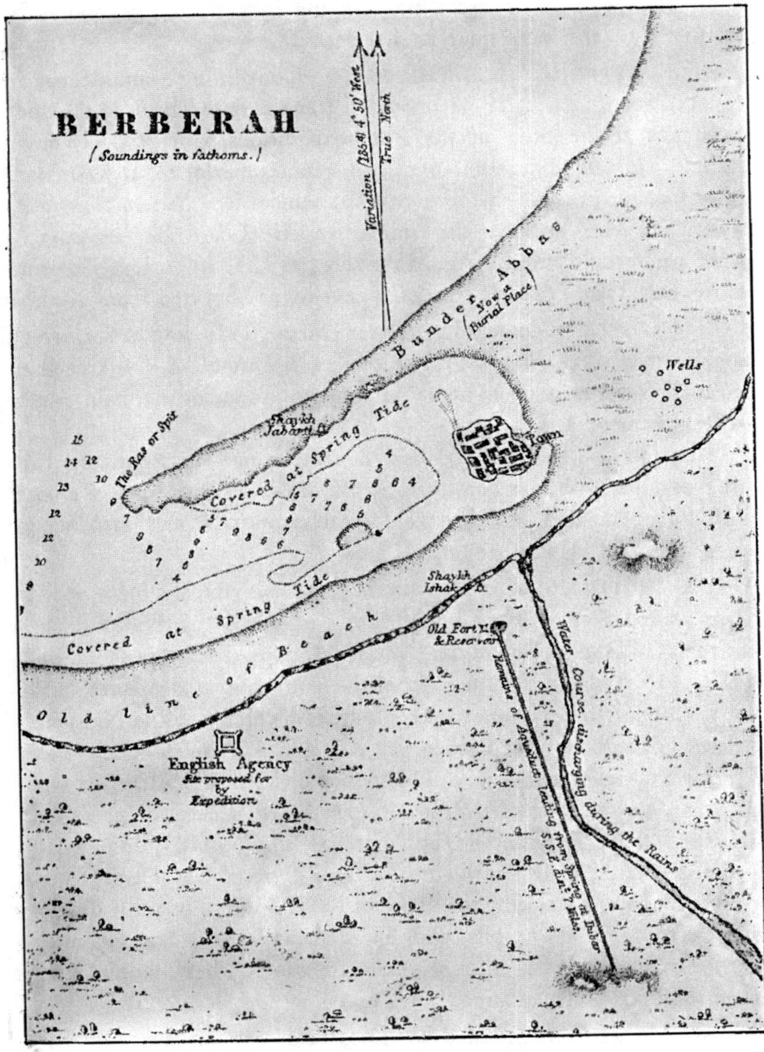


From Burton: *First Footsteps in East Africa.*

p. 196) would identify it with Bulhar, about 30 miles farther west; but the description of the "sheltering spit running out from the east" in § 8, places it beyond doubt at Berbera, which has just such a spit, while Bulhar is on the open beach.

Burton (*op. cit.*, pp. 407-418) gives a detailed description of the town and harbor, of the stream of sweet water flowing into it, and of the interior trade and the great periodical fair, frequented by caravans from the interior and by sailing vessels from Yemen, the South Arabian coast, Muscat, Bahrein and Bassora, and beyond as far as Bombay; the same trade as that described in § 14.

8. **"Far-side" frankincense.**—Concerning frankincense in general, see under §§ 29-32. Somali frankincense figures in the trade of Egypt at the time of the Punt expeditions, and probably much earlier. It was different from, and often superior to, the Arabian. It is, indeed, possible that the true frankincense (*Boswellia neglecta*) was native here, and that the Arabian varieties (*Boswellia serrata*, etc.) were a later cultivation. Yet Fabricius (p. 124) in curious disregard of the text, thinks the Malao frankincense was imported from Arabia!

8. **Duaca** is identified by Glaser (*Skizze*, 197) with *duakh*, which appears in several Arabic inscriptions as a variety of frankincense; *duka*, he says, is a trade-name in modern Aden for a certain quality of frankincense.

Burton (*op. cit.*, p. 416) describes the range of mountains running parallel with this coast, some 30 miles inland from Berbera, "4000 to 6000 feet, thickly covered with gum-arabic and frankincense trees, the wild fig and the Somali pine."

8. **Indian copal.**—The text is *kankamon*, which is mentioned by Pliny as a dye (probably in confusion with lac); by Dioscorides as the exudation of a wood like myrrh, and used for incense. Pliny (XII, 44) says that it came "from the country that produces cinnamon, through the Nabatæan Troglodytæ, a colony of the Nabatæi." Glaser (*Skizze*, 196) is positive that it is no Arabian product. Col. Henry Yule identifies it with Indian copal, Malabar tallow, or white dammar, the gum exuded from *Vateria Indica*, Linn., order *Dipterocarpeæ;* which is described by Watt (*op. cit.*, p. 1105,) as a "large evergreen of the forests at the foot of the Western Ghāts from Kanara to Travancore, ascending to 4000 feet." This gum or resin dissolves in turpentine or drying oils, and, like copal, is chiefly used for making varnishes. The bark is also very astringent, rich in tannin, and is used to control fermentation.

8. **Macir** is mentioned by Dioscorides as an aromatic bark. Pliny (XII, 16) says that it was brought from India, being a red bark

growing upon a large root, bearing the name of the tree that produced it. He was ignorant of the tree itself. A decoction of this bark, mixed with honey, was used in medicine as a specific for dysentery.

Lassen (*op. cit.*, III, 31) identifies it with *makara*, a remedy for dysentery, consisting of the root-bark of a tree native on the Malabar coast; but he does not identify the tree.

This *macir* was doubtless the root-bark of *Holarrhena antidysenterica*, Wall., order *Apocynaceæ*, described by Watt (*op. cit.* p. 640) as "a small deciduous tree, found throughout India and Burma, ascending the lower Himalaya to 3500 feet, and to a similar altitude on the hills of Southern India. . . . Both bark and seed of this plant are among the most important medicines in the Hindu *materia medica*. By the Portuguese this was called *herba malabarica*, owing to its great merit in the treatment of dysentery, they having found it on the Malabar coast. The preparation, generally in the form of a solid or liquid extract, or of a decoction, is astringent, antidysenteric and anthelmintic. The seeds yield a fixed oil, and the wood-ash is used in dyeing. The wood is much used for carving, furniture and turnery."

9. **Mundus** is probably the modern Bandar Hais, 10° 52′ N., 46° 50′ E. Glaser (*Skizze*, 197) would identify it with Berbera. But the text gives "two or three days' sail" between Malao and Mundus, altogether too much for the 30 miles, more or less, between Bulhar and Berbera. And just as the "sheltering spit" identifies Berbera as Malao, so does the "island close to shore" identify Hais as Mundus. Vivien de Saint-Martin (*Le Nord de l'Afrique dans l'antiquité grecque et romaine*, p. 285) describes a small island protecting this little harbor, and says it was much frequented by Arab and Somali tribes.

Müller's identification with Burnt Island (11° 15′ N., 47° 15′ E.) is less probable because that island is too far from shore to afford protection to small vessels.

9. **Mocrotu** was probably a high grade of frankincense. Glaser (*Skizze*, 199-201) notes that the Arabic name for the best variety is *mghairot*, or in Mahri, *mghâr*; and that the same word appears in Somaliland as *mokhr*. From this to the Greek of the text the change is negligible.

10. **Mosyllum** is placed by most commentators at Ras Hantara, (11° 28′ N., 49° 35′ E.) Glaser prefers Ras Khamzir (10° 55′ N., 45° 50′ E.) many miles farther west. The text gives no help in the way of local description. It is noteworthy that Pliny says the Atlantic Ocean begins here; ignoring not only the coast of Azania, as

described in § 15, but the Cape of Spices itself. Mosyllum was probably, therefore, rather a prominent headland on the coast, altogether such as Ras Hantara.

This, by the way, was reputed to have been the eastward limit of the conquests of Ptolemy Euergetes, King of Egypt, in the 3d century B. C.

10. **Cinnamon.**—The text is *kasía*, from Hebrew *kezia* (Ps. XLV, 8; Ezek. XXVII, 19, XXX, 24), the modern *cassia*. This meant usually, in Roman times, the wood split lengthwise, as distinguished from the flower-tips and tender bark, which rolled up into small pipes and was called *kinnamomon*, from Hebrew *kheneh*, a pipe; *khinemon* (Exod. XXX, 23, Prov. VII, 17, Cant. IV, 14); Latin *canna*, French *cannelle.*

Cinnamon and cassia are the flower-tips, bark, and wood of several varieties of laurel native in India, Tibet, Burma and China. Engler and Prantl, *Die Natürlichen Pflanzenfamilien*, classify them as follows:

*Lauraceæ*
- Persoideæ:
  - Cinnamomeæ:
    1. Cinnamomum
       - Sect. 1. Malabathrum
         - including C. javaneum
         - C. cassia
         - C. zeylanicum
         - C. culilawan
         - C. tamala
         - C. iners
       - Sect. 2. Camphora
         - including C. camphora
         - C. parthenoxylon

Cinnamon is mentioned as one of the ingredients of the sacred anointing oil of the Hebrew priests (Exod. XXX). The Egyptian inscriptions of Queen Hatshepsut's expedition, in the 15th century B. C., mention cinnamon wood as one of the "marvels of the country of Punt" which were brought back to Egypt.

Cinnamon was familiar to both the Greeks and Romans, and was used as an incense, and as a flavor in oils and salves. It is mentioned by Hippocrates, Theophrastus, and Pliny. Dioscorides gives a long description of it. He says it "grows in Arabia; the best sort is red, of a fine color, almost like coral; straight, long, and pipy, and it bites on the palate with a slight sensation of heat. The best sort is that called *zigir*, with a scent like a rose. . . . The cinnamon has many names, from the different places where it grows. But the best sort is that which is like the *casia* of Mosyllum, and this cinnamon is called Mosyllitic, as well as the cassia." And this cinnamon, he says, "when fresh, in its greatest perfection, is of a dark color, something between the color of wine and a dark ash, like a small twig or spray full of knots, and very fragrant."

Roman writers distinguish between true cinnamon and cassia; the former was valued at 1500 denarii (about $325) the pound; the latter at 50 denarii. The Periplus makes no distinction; "cassia" it mentions at Mosyllum and Opone, and the "harder cassia" at Malao. Cinnamon, under the Empire, probably meant the tender shoots and flower-tips of the tree, which were reserved for the emperors and patricians, and distributed by them on solemn occasions. Cassia was the commercial article, and included the bark, the split wood, and the root. The Romans could not distinguish between species, and their classification was according to the appearance of the product as it came to them.

As to the country of origin, Herodotus (book III) states that cassia was from Arabia; naturally so, as the Phœnicians brought it thence. He distinguishes cinnamon, and gives a fabulous story of its recovery from the nests of great birds "in those countries in which Bacchus was nursed," which in Greek legend meant India. The Periplus says that it was produced in Somaliland, to which Strabo and other Roman writers refer as the *regio cinnamomifera* in the same belief. But there is no sign of a cinnamon tree in that region at present, where the requisite conditions of soil and climate do not exist. Pliny (VI, 29) indicates that it was merely trans-shipped there. Strabo (XVI, IV, 14) says that it came from the "far interior" of this region, and that nearer the coast only the "false cassia" grew. Pliny (XXI, 42) says that it came from Aethiopia and was brought "over vast tracts of sea" to Ocelis by the Troglodytes, who took five years in making the round trip. Here are indications that the true cinnamon was brought from India and the Far East to the Somali coast, and there mixed with bark from the laurel-groves mentioned in § 11 and by Strabo, and taken thence to Arabia and Egypt. The Periplus notes also (§ 10) the "larger ships" required at Mosyllum for the cinnamon trade. This was probably the very midst of the "Land of Punt" whence the Egyptian fleet brought cinnamon 15 centuries before.

In India various barks and twigs are sold as cassia and cinnamon, and according to Watt (*op. cit.*, p. 313) it is still almost impossible to distinguish them. Cassia bark (*C. cassia*, or *Cassia lignea*) was historically the first to be known, and the best qualities came from China, where it is recorded first about 2700 B. C. The Malabar bark was less valuable. Persian records invariably refer to cinnamon as *Dar Chini*, "Chinese bark;" and between the 3d and 6th centuries A. D. there was an active sea-trade in this article, in Chinese ships, from China to Persia.

Marco Polo describes cinnamon as growing in Malabar, Ceylon, and Tibet. The British East India Company's records show that it came usually from China; and Millburn (*Or. Comm.* 1813, II, 500) describes both bark and buds, and warns traders against the "coarse, dark and badly packed" product of Malabar.

Since the later years of the 18th century the variety *C. zeylanicum* has been extensively cultivated in Ceylon; but the best quality is still shipped from Canton, being from *C. Cassia*, native throughout Assam, Burma, and Southern China. It seems altogether probable that the true cinnamon of the ancient Egyptian and Hebrew records, of Herodotus and Pliny, reached the Mediterranean nations from no nearer place than Burma, and perhaps through the Straits of Malacca from China itself. Many, indeed, must have been the hands through which it passed on its long journey to Rome.

The *malabathrum* of the Romans, which they bought in India while still unable to obtain cinnamon there, was the leaves of three varieties: that of the Malabar mountains from *C. zeylanicum*, and that of the Himalayas from *C. tamala*, with a little from *C. iners*.

These trees are all of fairly large growth, evergreen, rising to about 6000 feet altitude. The tree flowers in January, the fruit ripens in April, and the bark is full of sap in May and June, when it is stripped off and forms the best grade of cinnamon. The strippings of later months are not so delicate and are less valued.

See Watt, *op. cit.*, pp. 310-313; Lassen, *op. cit.*, I, 279-285, II, 555-561; Vincent, II, 130, 701-16; Flückiger and Hanbury, *Pharmacographia*, 519-527; *Marco Polo*, Yule Ed., II, 49, 56, 315, 389; and for *malabathrum* or *folium indicum*, see Garcia de Orta, Coll., XXIII; also comment by Ball in Roy. Ir. Acad., 3d ser., I, 409; also Linschoten, Voy. E. Ind. (Ed. Hakl. Soc.), II, 131.

11. **Little Nile River.**—The text is *Neilopotamion*, perhaps a reflection of Egyptian Greek settlement. Another reading is *Neiloptolemaion*, which might also suggest a connection with one of the Ptolemies. But in Egyptian records there is no mention of settlement or conquest so far east.

Müller identifies this river with the Tokwina (11° 30′ N., 49°

55′ E.) which empties below a mountain, Jebel Haima, 3800 feet high; there are ancient ruins here. The "small laurel grove" he places at Bandar Muriyeh (11° 40′ N., 50° 25′ E.), below the Jebel Muriyeh, 4000 feet high.

11. **Cape Elephant** seems to be the modern Ras el Fil, or Filuk, 12° 0′ N., 50° 32′ E. It is a promontory 800 feet high, about 40 miles west of Cape Guardafui. The word *fil* is said also to mean "elephant," and the shape of the headland suggests the name. A river empties into the gulf just east of the promontory. Glaser (*Skizze*, 199) thinks this is too far east, and prefers Ras Hadadeh (48° 45′ E.). Elephant River he identifies with the Dagaan (49° E.) or the Tokwina (49° 55′ E.), from which the modern *fusus* frankincense is brought to Aden. But by placing Mosyllum at Ras Khamzir, Glaser is entirely too far west to admit of covering the remainder of this coast in two days' journey, as stated in § 11. And the "southerly trend" of the coast just before Guardafui, mentioned in § 12, fixes Cape Elephant at Ras el Fil.

Glaser objects to the relatively short two days' sail between Ras Hantara and Guardafui; but he fails to take into account the prevailing calms north of the cape, which would justify a shorter day's sail in that vicinity than farther west, where the winds are steadier.

Salt (*op. cit.*, 97-8) says: "Scarcely had we got round the cape (Guardafui) when the wind deadened. At daylight we found that we had made scarcely any progress. The same marks on the shore remained the whole day abreast of us."

11. **Acannae** is identified with Bandar Ululah, 12° 0′ N., 50° 42′ E. McCrindle notes that Captain Saris, an English navigator, called here in 1611, and reported a river, emptying into a bay, offering safe anchorage for three ships abreast. Several sorts of gums, very sweet in burning, were still purchased by Indian ships from the Gulf of Cambay, which touched here for that purpose on their voyage to Mocha.

12. **The Cape of Spices** is, of course, the modern Cape Guardafui, or Ras Asir, 11° 50′ N., 51° 16′ E. McCrindle describes it as "a bluff point, 2500 feet high, as perpendicular as if it were scarped. The current comes round it out of the Gulf (of Aden) with such violence that it is not to be stemmed without a brisk wind, and during the S. W. monsoon the moment you are past the Cape to the north there is a stark calm with insufferable heat."

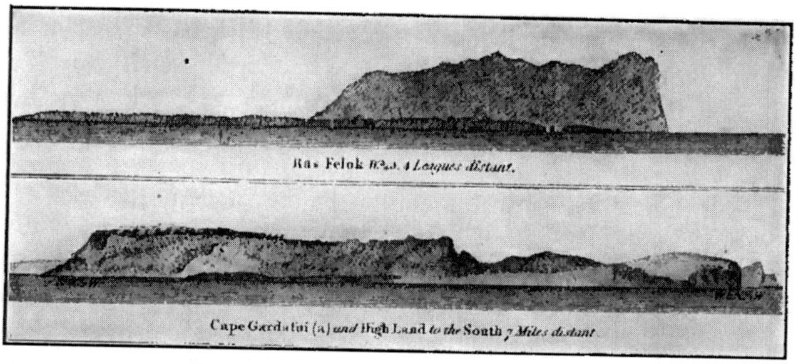


From Salt: *A Voyage into Abyssinia.*

This is the "Southern Horn" of Strabo, who says (XVI, IV, 14) "after doubling this cape toward the south, we have no more descriptions of harbors or places, because nothing is known of the seacoast beyond this point."

Pliny prefers the account of King Juba of Mauretania, compiled from earlier information, in which the end of the continent is placed at Mosyllum; so that if he had before him this Periplus, he ignored completely the account it gives of this coast.

The **Market of Spices** is identified by Glaser (*Skizze*, II, 20) with the modern Olok, on the N. W. side of the Cape.

Strabo's description is as follows (XVI, IV, 14): "Next is the country which produces frankincense; it has a promontory and a temple with a grove of poplars. In the inland parts is a tract along the banks of a river bearing the name of Isis, and another that of Nilus, both of which produce myrrh and frankincense. Also a lagoon filled with water from the mountains; next the watchpost of the Lion, and the port of Pythangelus. The next tract bears the false cassia. There are many tracts in succession on the sides of rivers on which frankincense grows, and rivers extending to the cinnamon country. The river which bounds this tract produces rushes in abundance. Then follows another river, and the port of Daphnus, and a valley called Apollo's, which bears, besides frankincense, myrrh and cinnamon. The latter is more abundant in places far in the interior. Next is the mountain Elephas projecting into the sea, and a creek; then the large harbor of Psygmus, a watering-place called that of the Cynocephali, and the last promontory of this coast, Notu Ceras (the Southern Horn)."

12. **Tabae** is placed by Müller at the Ras Chenarif, 11° 5′ N. Glaser (*Skizze*, 201) thinks the distance from Olok too great, and places Tabæ just behind the eastern point of the cape.

13. **Pano** is probably Ras Binna, 11° 12′ N., 51° 7′ E. There is a modern village on the north side, a little west of the point, which affords shelter from the S. W. monsoon.

13. **Opone** is the remarkable headland now known as Ras Hafun, 10° 25′ N., 51° 25′ E., about 90 miles below Cape Guardafui.

Glaser finds a connection between these names, Pano and Opone, the Egyptian "Land of Punt" or *Poen-at*, the island *Pa-anch* of the Egyptians (Socotra), the incense-land *Panchaia* of Virgil (*Georgics*, II, 139; "Totaque turiferis Panchaia pinguis arenis,") and the Puni or Phœnicians; who, he thinks, divided as they left their home in the Persian Gulf (the islands of King Erythras in the story quoted by Agatharchides); one branch going to the coasts of Syria, the other to those of South Arabia and East Africa.

13. **Cinnamon produced.**—A letter from Mr. R. E. Drake-Brockman, F. Z. S., F. R. G. S., (author of *The Mammals of Somaliland*, and now at work on *Somali Flora*) dated Berbera, January 7, 1910, says:

"The 'Horn of Africa' was known to the Romans as the *regio aromatifera* on account of the large quantities of myrrh that were exported. The country abounds in the various species of the acacias, which produce gums of varying commercial value, also certain trees producing resins.

"I have so far not come across any trees of the cinnamon group, nor have I heard of their existence.

"The tree producing myrrh, or *malmal* as it is known to the Somalis, is called *garron;* but owing to the activities of the Mullah I have never been able to penetrate the southern Dholbanta and Mijertain countries where it grows."

And again, March 3: "I have never heard of the exportation of cinnamon from this part of Africa. . . . It is just possible that there might be some species of laurels in the Dholbanta country and south of it, but it is not possible to venture so far owing to the hostility of the Mullah."

If there was any aromatic bark produced near Cape Guardafui and not merely trans-shipped there, it seems almost certain that it was an adulterant added there to the true cinnamon, that came from India.

14. **Ships from Ariaca.**—The antiquity of Hindu trade in East Africa is asserted by Speke (*Discovery of the Source of the Nile*, Chaps. I, V, X). The Purānas described the Mountains of the Moon and the Nyanza lakes, and mentioned as the source of the Nile the "country of Amara," which is the native name of the district north of Victoria Nyanza. A map based on this description,

drawn by Lieut. Wilford, was printed in the *Asiatic Researches*, Vol. III, 1801.

"Nothing was ever written concerning their Country of the Moon, as far as we know, until the Hindus, who traded with the east coast of Africa, opened commercial dealings with its people in slaves and ivory, possibly some time prior to the birth of our Saviour, when, associated with their name, Men of the Moon, sprang into existence the Mountains of the Moon. These Men of the Moon are hereditarily the greatest traders in Africa, and are the only people, who, for love of barter and change, will leave their own country as porters and go to the coast, and they do so with as much zest as our country-folk go to a fair. As far back as we can trace they have done this, and they still do it as heretofore.

"The Hindu traders had a firm basis to stand upon, from their intercourse with the Abyssinians—through whom they must have heard of the country of Amara, which they applied to the Nyanza—and with the *Wanyamuezi* or Men of the Moon, from whom they heard of the Tanganyika and Karague mountains. Two church missionaries, Rebmann and Erhardt, without the smallest knowledge of the Hindus' map, constructed a map of their own, deduced from the Zanzibar traders, something on the same scale, by blending the Victoria Nyanza, Tanganyika, and Nyassa into one; whilst to their triuned lake they gave the name of Moon, because the Men of the Moon happened to live in front of the central lake."

This trading-voyage of the first century by Indian vessels, although less extended, was in other respects similar to that of the Arab traders of a century ago as described by Salt (*op. cit.*, p. 103):

"The common track pursued by the Arab traders is as follows: they depart from the Red Sea in August (before which it is dangerous to venture out of the gulf), then proceed to Muscat, and thence to the coast of Malabar. In December they cross over to the coast of Africa, visit Mogdishu, Merka, Barawa, Lamu, Malindi, and the Querimbo Islands; they then direct their course to the Comoro Islands, and the northern ports of Madagascar, or sometimes stretch down southward as far as Sofala; this occupies them until after April, when they run up into the Red Sea, where they arrive in time to refit and prepare a fresh cargo for the following year."

14. **The products of their own places.**—For a discussion of the products of India imported into the Somali ports, see later, under § 41. The important thing to be noted here is that these agricultural products were regularly shipped, in Indian vessels, from the Gulf of Cambay; that these vessels exchanged their cargoes at Cape

Guardafui and proceeded along the coast, some southward, but most westward; and that, according to § 25, Ocelis, at the entrance to the Red Sea, was their terminus, the Arabs forbidding them to trade beyond. Between India and Cape Guardafui they apparently enjoyed the bulk of the trade, shared to some extent by Arabian shipping and quite recently by Greek ships from Egypt; on the Somali coast they shared the trade in an incidental way; and they received their return cargoes at Ocelis and shared none of the Red Sea trade, which in former times the Arabs of Yemen had monopolized, but in the days of the Ptolemies the Egyptians had largely taken over. .

At the time of the Periplus, owing to the conquest of Egypt by the Romans, the establishment of the Axumite Kingdom, and a settled policy in Rome of cultivating direct communication with India, this commercial understanding, or alliance, between Arabia and India (which had existed certainly for 2000 years and probably much longer), is shown to be at the point of extinction; but still to be strong enough for the Romans to know the cinnamon-bark only as a product of the Arabian tributary, Somaliland, while the cinnamon-leaf, a later article of commerce, they knew (§§ 56, 65) under the name of *malabathrum*, as a product of India and Tibet.

14. **Clarified butter.**—The text is *boutyron*. Some of the commentators object to the word (Lassen and Fabricius especially) and Fabricius, in his notes (p. 130) thinks it would be "very wrong to suppose that butter could have been brought from India, in this hot climate, to the eastern coast of Africa." Therefore they propose substitutes, as noted under § 41.

The voyage from India to Africa by the N. E. monsoon may have averaged 30 to 40 days. As shown under § 41, clarified butter will keep in the tropics not only for years, but for centuries; but the account given by Burton (*First Footsteps*, pp. 136 and 247) shows that modern caravans take it for trips of six weeks or more, under the same hot climate of Somaliland; and Lieut. Cruttenden, in his description of the Berbera Fair, tells of modern Cambay ships laden with ghee in jars, bought in Somaliland for trade elsewhere; probably along the Arabian coast. That is, the Somali had learned the art of clarifying butter, and exported it in the 19th century by the same class of ships that had brought it to them from India in the 1st century.

Mungo Park found the same product entering into the commerce of the much more humid Senegal coast of West Africa:

"The Foulahs use the milk chiefly as an article of diet, and that not until it is sour. The cream which it affords is very thick, and is converted into butter by stirring it violently in a large calabash. This butter, when melted over a gentle fire, and freed from impurities, is preserved in small earthen pots, and forms a part in most of their dishes; it serves likewise to anoint their heads, and is bestowed very liberally on their faces and arms." (*Travels of Mungo Park*, London: 1799. Chap. IV.)

14. **Honey from the reed called sacchari** is the first mention in the history of the European world of sugar as an article of commerce. It was known to Pliny as a medicine. *Sacchari* is the Prakrit form of the Sanscrit *sarkara*, Arabic *sukkar*, Latin *saccharum*.

Grinding sugar, in Western India

The modern languages reflect the Arabic form—Portuguese, *assucar*, Spanish *azucar*, French *sucre*, German *zucker*, English *sugar*. The sugar is derived from *Saccharum officinarum*, Linn., order *Gramineæ*. It was produced in India, Burma, Anam and Southern China, long before it found its way to Rome, and seems to have been cultivated and crushed first in India.

14. **Exchange their cargoes.**—This trade of the Indian ships at Opone and elsewhere, is so like that described on the same

coast by Lieut. Cruttenden in 1848, that his account deserves to be quoted in full:

"From April to early October," (the quotation is from Burton, *First Footsteps*, 408-10), "the place is deserted. No sooner does the season change than the inland tribes move down toward the coast, and prepare their huts for their expected visitors. Small craft from the ports of Yemen, anxious to have an opportunity of purchasing before vessels from the gulf could arrive, hastened across, followed two or three weeks later by their larger brethren from Muscat, Sur, and Ras el Khyma, and the valuably freighted *bagalas* from Bahrein, Bassora, and Graen. Lastly, the fat and wealthy Banian traders from Porebandar, Mandavi and Bombay, rolled across in their clumsy *kotias*, and with a formidable row of empty ghee-jars slung over the quarters of their vessels, elbowed themselves into a permanent position in the front tier of craft in the harbor, and by their superior capital, cunning, and influence soon distanced all competitors.

"During the height of the fair there is a perfect Babel, in confusion as in languages; no chief is acknowledged, and the customs of bygone days are the laws of the place. Disputes between the inland tribes daily arise, and are settled by the spear and dagger, the combatants retiring to the beach at a short distance from the town, in order that they may not disturb the trade. Long strings of camels are arriving and departing day and night, escorted generally by women alone, until at a distance from town; and an occasional group of dusty and travel-worn children marks the arrival of the slave-caravan from the interior.

"Here the Somali or Galla slave merchant meets his correspondent from Bassora, Bagdad or Bandar Abbas; and the savage Gudabirsi, with his head tastefully ornamented with a scarlet sheepskin in lieu of a wig, is seen peacefully bartering his ostrich feathers and gums with the smooth-spoken Banian from Porebandar, who, prudently living on board his ark, and locking up his puggaree, which would infallibly be knocked off the instant he was seen wearing it, exhibits but a small portion of his wares at a time, under a miserable mat spread on the beach.

"By the end of March the fair is nearly at an end, and craft of all kinds, deeply laden, and sailing generally in parties of three or four, commence their homeward journey. By the first week in April the place is again deserted, and nothing is left to mark the site of a town lately containing 20,000 inhabitants, beyond bones of slaughtered camels and sheep, and the framework of a few huts, which is carefully piled on the beach in readiness for the ensuing year."

15. The **Bluffs of Azania** are the rugged coast known as El Hazin, ending at Ras el Kyl, 7° 44′ N., 49° 40′ E.

15. The **Small and great beach** is the Sif el Tauil or "low coast," ending at Ras Aswad, 4° 30′ N., 47° 55′ E.; but this is actually a longer course than the bluffs, whereas the Periplus rates them both as six days' journey.

15. The **Courses of Azania** are the strips of desert coast extending below the equator. The Arabs divide this coast into two sections, the first called *Barr Ajjan* (preserving the ancient name), the second *Benadir*, or "coast of harbors." Sarapion may be the modern Mogdishu, 2° 5′ N., 45° 25′ E. Nicon is, perhaps, the modern Barawa, 1° 10′ N., 44° 5′ E. The "rivers and anchorages" are along the modern *El Djesair* or "coast of islands."

Concerning the name Azania, R. N. Lyne, in his *Zanzibar in Contemporary Times*, and Col. Henry Yule, in his edition of Marco Polo, have much of interest. The name survives in the modern Zanzibar (the Portuguese form of Zanghibar), which Marco Polo applied not only to the island, but to the whole coast; and it is popularly derived from *bar*, coast, and *zang*, black: "land of the blacks." But the name seems to be older, and to refer to the ancient Arabic and Persian division of the world into three sections, Hind, Sind and Zinj, wherefrom even European geographers in mediæval times classified East Africa as one of the Indies, and Marco Polo located Abyssinia in "Middle India." Cosmas Indicopleustes, writing in the 6th century A. D., indicates that the whole "Zingi" coast, to a point certainly below Mogdishu, was subject to the Abyssinian Kingdom. Yule notes that the Japanese Encyclopædia describes a "country of the Tsengu in the S. W. ocean, where there is a bird called *pheng*, which in its flight eclipses the sun. It can swallow a camel, and its quills are used for water casks." This is doubtless the Zanghibar coast, the name and legend reaching Japan through the Arabs.

The lack of distinction in ancient geography between Asia and Africa goes back to the dawn of letters. Hecatæus in the 6th century B. C. divided the world into two equal continents—Europe, north of the Mediterranean; Asia, south of it. Around them ran the ocean stream. The distinction is supposed to have been based on temperature. Tozer (*History of Ancient Geography*, p. 69) refers it to ancient Assyria, *açu* (sunrise) and *irib* (darkness) frequently occurring in inscriptions there.

15. "In this place there are canoes hollowed from single logs."

15. The **Pyralaæ Islands** are evidently Patta, Manda, and Lamu, back of which there is a thoroughfare, the only protected waterway on the whole coast. This is the "channel;" several rivers empty into it, and there is a passage to the ocean between Manda and Lamu, 2° 18′ S., 40° 50′ E. Vincent's identification of the "channel" with Mombasa, on account of a canal now known to have been dug there much later, is impossible.

15. **Ausanitic Coast.**—Ausan was a district of Kataban in South Arabia, which had been absorbed by Himyar shortly before the time of the Periplus; hence the natural result, that a dependency of the conquered state should be exploited for the advantage of the Homerite port, Muza.

15. **Menuthias.**—This whole passage is corrupt, and there are probably material omissions. The first island south of Manda is Pemba (at about 5° S.). But the topographic description is perhaps truer to Zanzibar (about 6° S.), and the name seems perpetuated in the modern Monfiyeh (about 8° S.). Our author was possibly unacquainted with this coast, and included in his work hearsay reports from some seafaring acquaintance, in which he may have lumped the three islands into one; or if he is describing places he has visited (which is suggested by the mention of the local fishing-baskets and the like), some scribe may have omitted a whole section of the text.

16. **Rhapta.**—This location depends on the condition of the preceding text regarding the island Menuthías. If that be Pemba, Rhapta would be the modern Pangani (5° 25′ S., 38° 59′ E.), at the mouth of the river of the same name; if Zanzibar, it would be at or near Bagamoyo (6° 31′ S., 38° 50′ E.); if Monfiyeh, the modern Kilwa (8° 57′ S., 39° 38′ E.). Vincent's insistence upon Kilwa is very likely well grounded, from the suggestion of the ancient name; that is, if the text is a mutilated description of three islands known to exist in close proximity, the "last market-town of the continent" would naturally be below the southernmost island, Monfiyeh. But the distances given by Ptolemy between Rhapta and Prasum suggest for the former a location near Bagamoyo, perhaps Dar-es-Salaam, (6° 42′ S., 39° 5′ E.). The Prasum of Ptolemy, the farthest point in Africa known to him, is evidently Cape Delgado (10° 30′ S., 40° 30′ E.). The later identification of Menuthías with Madagascar was due to the discoveries of the Saracens, and is impossible for Roman times.

Rhapta, Glaser notes, has its name from an Arabian word *rabta*, to bind.

15. "They catch them in a peculiar way, in wicker baskets, which they fasten across the channel-opening between the breakers"

16. **Great in stature.**—"The whole system of slaveholding by the Arabs in Africa, or rather on the coast or at Zanzibar, is exceedingly strange; for the slaves, both in individual strength and in numbers, are so superior to the Arab foreigners, that if they chose to rebel, they might send the Arabs flying out of the land. It happens, however, that they are spell-bound, not knowing their strength any more than domestic animals, and they seem to consider that they would be dishonest if they ran away after being purchased, and so brought pecuniary loss on their owners." (Speke, *op. cit.*, introduction.)

16. **Sovereignty of the state that is become first in Arabia.**—A vivid picture is here given us of the early policies of the Arabs. Prevented by superior force from expanding northward, but useful commercially to their stronger neighbors, they were free to exploit Africa. The early Egyptian records bear testimony to their activities in the second millennium B. C., if not earlier. The "Ausanitic Coast" mentioned in § 15 was probably a possession of Ausan when that state was independent, which was not later than the 7th century B. C. Later the coast became Katabanic, then Sabæan, then Homerite. From the 3d to the 6th centuries A. D., according to the Adulis inscription and Cosmas Indicopleustes, it was Abyssinian. In Mohammedan times it returned to the Arab allegiance, and until Zanzibar and the adjacent coast accepted the English protectorate they were dependencies of the Sultan of Muscat.

Glaser has well expressed this undoubted fact of Arab dominion (*Skizze*, II, 209): "We must finally abandon the idea that Mohammed was the first to bring Arabia into a leading position in the world's history. So long as Rome and Persia (and Egypt and Babylon before them) retained their power, the Arabs could expand in Africa only. But as soon as these states became exhausted, then Arabia burst forth irresistibly and overflowed the northern world." (See also *Punt und die Südarabischen Reiche*, 20-23.)

Previous translators of the Periplus have much misunderstood the meaning of this passage in the text.

16. **Arab captains who know the whole coast.**—The discovery by Carl Mauch in 1871, of strange temple-like structures in northern Rhodesia, led to a great deal of wild assumption as to their history. The ruins are loosely-built stone enclosures, some of them irregularly elliptical in form, having conical pillars within, and apparently facing North, East and West. The largest of them were situated somewhat South of the present Salisbury-Beira railway line, near the upper waters of the Sabi River and within reach of the trade

of Sofala, known to have been frequented by Arab traders in mediæval times. It was at once assumed that they were of Sabæan or Phœnician origin and of great antiquity. The subject was voluminously but uncritically written up. See for instance *Ancient Ruins of Rhodesia*, by Hall and Neal, London, 1894; *Monomotapa*, by A. Wilmot, London, 1896, and *The Ruined Cities of Mashonaland*, by J. T. Bent, London, 1902.

The appearance of the structures suggested the form of ancient Arabian temples, and the locality was at once identified with the ubiquitous "land of Ophir" of King Solomon's voyages. Professor Müller (*Burgen und Schlösser*, II, 20), noted a resemblance between the Zimbabwe enclosure (20° 30′ S , 31° 10′ E.) and the temple at Marib, the capital of the ancient Sabæan kingdom of Southern Arabia. The whole argument was of course pure assumption, as there is no reference in ancient literature to any knowledge of the African coast within six hundred miles of the port of Sofala. Dr. David Randall-Maciver made a careful investigation of the ruins in 1905, and proved conclusively in his account of that work, *Mediæval Rhodesia*, London, 1906, that the structures were the work of negroes, probably Kaffirs, of the so-called kingdom of Monomotapa. A piece of Nankin china of the late mediæval period, found in the cement at the bottom of one of the structures, showed that they could not date earlier than the 14th or 15th century. They were enclosures for defence, rudely built of loose stone, and their supposed orientation was found to be inexact and probably accidental.

The service done by Dr. Maciver in disproving the antiquity of this Kaffir kraal did not, however, need to be supplemented by his denial (pp. 1-2) of the probability of Arabian trade far down this coast at a very early age. The Periplus mentions Rhapta, some distance south of the Zanzibar islands, as the last settlement on the coast; and Ptolemy describes Cape Delgado. Dr. Maciver may have known the Periplus only through the account given by Guillain in 1856 (*Documents sur l'histoire, la géographie et le commerce de l'Afrique Orientale*), but at all events he ignores the detailed account given in both those works, and in the Periplus the statement is definitely made that this whole coast (to about 10° S.) was "subject under some ancient right to the sovereignty of the power which held the primacy in Arabia;" that is, in the 1st century A. D. the right was still so ancient as to be beyond the explanation of the merchant who described it. The coast was frequented by Arab ships in command of Arab captains who knew the harbors, spoke the language of the natives and intermarried with them.

This condition is corroborated by the known Arab infusion in the negro peoples on the whole coast, which is of far earlier origin than the Mohammedan colonization.

Who were the natives and what was their language, as mentioned in the Periplus? Rev. J. Torrend, S. J., in a paper read before the Rhodesia Scientific Association, included in its Proceedings (V, 2, Buluwayo, 1905), analyzes the languages of the coast and finds a striking similarity between the speech of the Tana River, which empties below the island of Lamu about 2° 40′ S., and that of the lower Zambesi (18°-19° S.). He gives a long comparative list of words in these so-called Pokomo and Cizimba tongues, evidently identical. He quotes Dr. Krapf and other German philologists as saying that the Pokomo is the aboriginal language of the coast, and that the modern Swahili is derived from it; and he himself believes that the Cizimba is even more primitive, and that it gives the key to most of the modern dialects of the southern coast. Father Torrend, full of the Sofala-Ophir theory, argues that the language was brought from the Tana River to the Zambesi, not by land because the modern tribes are of peaceful disposition, but rather by sea, and particularly by sea-traders, assuming such to have come from Arabia. The assumption is certainly far-fetched, as it is hardly likely that any traffic, however busy, would have brought this negro language and transplanted it 1500 miles down the coast to a different tribe. The suggestion is rather that this branch of the Bantu race migrated southward within historical times, through the African rift-valley, and that the modern tribes of the lower Zambesi, said to be speaking to-day the most primitive language, are their descendants, while those who remained on the Tana have had their speech modified more notably by later contact with the outside world.

The name *Cizimba*, borne by the modern dialect, suggests the *Agisymba* of the Roman geographers; which was known to them through the report of an adventurous youth, Julius Maternus, who marched for four months southward from the Garamantes (Fezzan), and brought back word of a region abounding in rhinoceros, inhabited by negroes and bearing that name (Ptolemy, I, 8, 5). It seems not an unreasonable assumption that he did reach the head-waters of the Nile and found somewhere in that great rift-valley the ancestors of this Bantu tribe which later migrated southward and formed, among other confederations, the so-called *Monomotapa* of the mediæval geographers.

This rift-valley of East Africa is a striking feature of its topography, and must have had a great bearing on its early trade. A good description is given by Prof. J. M. Gregory, (*The Great Rift Valley*, London, 1896). It is a natural depression beginning at the lower shore of the Red Sea between Massowa and the straits, taking a south-westerly direction through Abyssinia to the British and German East African possessions, including lakes Rudolf, Nyanza, Tanganyika and Nyassa, and running almost to the Zambesi. While it is unlikely that this valley was ever at one time under the control of any Arabian power, it is probable that the tribes inhabiting it were in more or less regular commercial relations with the North, and that it was a more important avenue of trade than the sea-coast with its broad unhealthy swamps. It is indeed quite possible that the Mashonaland gold, which lay at no great distance south of the valley, might to some extent have found its way along this natural trade-route by exchange from tribe to tribe; and it is entirely unnecessary, in disproving the antiquity of the Mashonaland ruins, to attempt to disprove the manifest fact of early Arab influence and infusion along the East African coast. Neither is it necessary to deny the general infiltration of early Arabian culture in two directions from the head-waters of the Nile, southward down the rift-valley, and westward through the Sudan toward the Gulf of Guinea. In fact this general spread of culture, folk-lore and religious beliefs and practices, is too well attested to admit of denial.

17. **Palm oil.**—The word in the text, *nauplios*, is corrected to *nargilios*, a word which appears in modified forms in other Greek geographers. This is the Sanscrit *narikela*, *narikera*, Prakrit *nargil*, "cocoañut," and the appearance of the word on the Zanzibar coast is of course a confirmation of Indian trade there. (See Lassen, *op. cit.*, I, 267.) The Greek word was *koix*, whence the adjective *koukiophoros*, Latin *cucifera*, from which the Periplus, § 19, coins the Greek adjective *koukinos*.

This palm oil was from *Cocos nucifera*, Linn., order *Palmeæ*; probably native in the Indian archipelago, and carried by natural causes as well as Hindu activity to most of the tropical world. It is one of the most useful plants known, providing timber for houses and ships, leaves for thatch and fiber for binding and weaving, aside from the food value of the nut, fresh and dried, and the oil. As a medicine also it was of importance to the Hindus, the pulp of the ripe fruit being mixed with clarified butter, coriander, cumin, cardamoms, etc., to form their *narikela-khanda*, a specific for dyspepsia and consumption. The nut was described by Cosmas Indicopleustes in the 6th century as *argellion:* and by Marco Polo in the 13th century (I, 102; II, 236, 248) as *Indian nut.* (See also Watt, *op. cit.*, 349-363.)

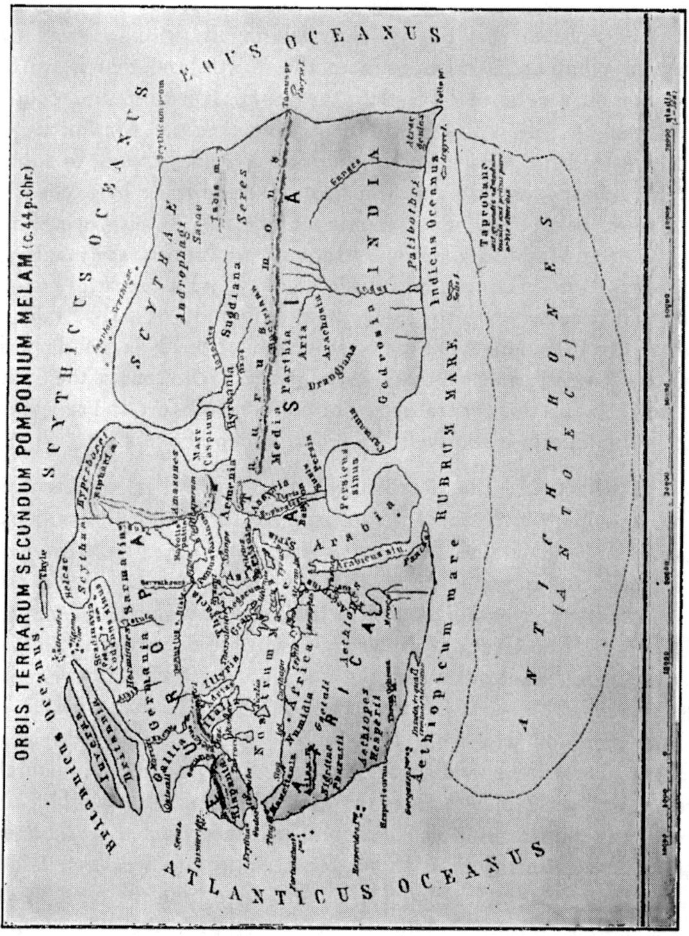


From Justus Perthes, *Atlas Antiquus*

18. **Unexplored ocean.**—This reflects the settled belief of the Greeks that Africa was surrounded by the ocean and could be circumnavigated. Herodotus gives an account, by no means impossible (IV, 42) of a Phœnician expedition, under the Pharaoh Necho, which did so about 600 B. C., returning to Egypt in the third year of their journey. Eratosthenes and Strabo placed the southern ocean immediately below Cape Guardafui; Pliny thought it began even at "Mossylum" west of Guardafui; our author shifts it to the Zanzibar Channel, and Ptolemy carried it as far as the Madagascar Channel. The actual southern extension of Africa was not known to Europeans until the Portuguese discoveries in the 15th century. The Saracens seem to have discovered it in the 9th or 10th century, but their knowledge did not reach Europe. The Guinea coast was known in part to the Carthaginians and Romans, and they supposed that it continued due eastward and thus joined the Indian Ocean, or "Erythræan Sea."

The current ideas of geography at this time are reflected by the accompanying map according to Pomponius Mela, about 44 A. D. The contribution of the author of the Periplus was to establish the southern extension of both Africa and India, to a distance never before understood by his civilization.

19. **To the left.**—This section begins the account of a second voyage, from Berenice to India.

19. **White Village** (*Leukê Komê*) is placed by most commentators at El Haura, 25° 7′ N., 37° 13′ E., which lies in a bay protected by Hasani island. The name *Haura* also means "white," and the Arab name itself appears as *Auara*, in Ptolemy. The place is on the regular caravan route that led, and still leads, from Aden to the Mediterranean.

The words "from Mussel Harbor," in the text, are probably there only through an error in copying. The distance and direction are more nearly right from Berenice, which is the starting-point named at the beginning of this paragraph.

19. **Petra** (30° 19′ N., 35° 31′ E.) lay in the Wady Musa, east of the Wädy-el-Araba, the great valley connecting the Dead Sea with the Gulf of Akaba. It was the great trading center of the northern Arabs, and the junction of numerous important caravan-routes, running from Yemen northward, and from the Persian Gulf eastward. Thus it controlled the Eastern trade from both directions, and held its advantage until the results of Trajan's conquests transferred the overland trade to Palmyra; the sea-trade having been already diverted to Alexandria.

The district of Arabia Petræa has its name from this city. The native name, according to Josephus (*Ant. Jud.* IV, 7, 1) was *Rekem*, referring to the variegated color of the rocks in the Wady Musa. The Biblical name was *Sela*, "a city of Edom" (2 Kings, XIV, 7; Isaiah, XVI, 1; Judges, I, 36). *Sela* (Arabic *Sal*) means a "hollow between rocks," and Obadiah, 3, apostrophizes Edom as "thou that dwellest in the clefts of the rocks, whose habitation is on high." Strabo (XVI, IV, 21) says "Petra is situated on a spot which is surrounded and fortified by a smooth and level rock, which externally is abrupt and precipitous, but within there are abundant springs of water both for domestic purposes and for watering gardens. Beyond the enclosure the country is for the most part a desert, particularly toward Judæa. . . . Athenodorus, my friend, who had been at Petra, used to relate with surprise, that he found many Romans and also many other strangers residing there."

Ammianus Marcellinus (XIV, 8, 13) describes the place as "full of the most plenteous variety of merchandise, and studded with strong forts and castles, which the watchful solicitude of its ancient inhabitants has erected in suitable defiles, in order to repress the inroads of the neighboring nations."

The topography of Petra is well known through the descriptions of Flinders Petrie and others. It was a fertile bit of valley surrounded by precipitous cliffs, with a long, narrow and winding entrance, and almost impregnable. It seems to have been, first, a place of refuge and a safe storehouse for the myrrh, frankincense, silver, etc., coming from Yemen. The Biblical references show it as an Edomite stronghold; but, being abandoned when the Edomites entered Palestine after the Babylonian captivity, it was taken by the Nabatæans; whom Josephus makes the descendants of Nebaioth, son of Ishmael, while Glaser and others see rather Nabatu, an Aramaic tribe noted in an inscription of Tiglathpileser III (745-727 B. C.), who migrated to the valley of Edom probably in the 6th century B. C.

Here the Nabatæans were at first nomadic and predatory, inviting attack by land from Antigonus, and by sea on the Gulf of Akaba, from the Ptolemies (Agatharchides, 88; Strabo, XVI, IV, 18). Soon, however, they settled down to orderly commerce and prospered exceedingly, as the ruins of Petra testify. One may suppose that a part, at least, of their trouble with Syria and Egypt was due to their commercial aggressiveness rather than their predatory habits. They fought hard to maintain and control the caravan trade against the competition of Egyptian shipping. In their dealings with Rome they tried to carry water on both shoulders; helping Titus against Jerusalem, but supporting the Parthians against Rome as occasion offered. This conflict of interests was terminated in 105 A. D., when Trajan reduced them to subjection (Dio Cassius, LXVIII, 14). After that time Petra declined; the ship of the desert was blanketed by the ship of the sea; and when the overland trade revived, toward the end of the 2d century, it was Palmyra which reaped the advantage.

19. **Malichas.**—The mention of this king of the Nabatæans is important in fixing the date of the text. Ordinarily the name might be accepted as a transcription of the Arabic word *malik*—Hebrew *melech*, king, which appears in such Hebrew names as "Abimelech" and "Melchizedek;" but according to the writings of Josephus, who as a Jew would have been likely to distinguish between the name and the title, there were kings having that name in what he called the "country of Arabia," which was certainly the same as that of the Nabatæans. In his *Antiquities of the Jews* (XIV, 14, 1) he mentions Malchus, King of Arabia, who had befriended Herod and who had loaned him money just before his case was taken up by Mark Antony, and the Roman Senate agreed to make him King of the Jews. This occurred in the year 38 B. C. This same Malchus loaned cavalry to Julius Cæsar for his siege of Alexandria (Aulus Hirtius, *Bell. Alex.*, I, i); and subsequently sent auxiliaries to Pacorus, the Parthian emperor, for which Mark Antony compelled him to pay an indemnity.

This Malchus can not, of course, be the one mentioned in the Periplus. But Josephus (*Jewish War*, III, 4, 2) mentions a King of Arabia, Malchus, who sent a thousand horsemen and five thousand footmen to the assistance of Titus in his attack upon Jerusalem. These events were in the year 70 A. D., and this King Malchus can hardly be other than the Malichas mentioned in the text. See also Vogüé, *Syrie Centrale*, who quotes inscriptions of this Malichas or Malik, and of his father Aretas Philodemus, or Hareth, a contemporary of Tiberius and Caligula.

19. **Small vessels from Arabia.**—Strabo (XVI, IV, 24) has the following account of this trade:

"Merchandise is conveyed from Leuce Come to Petra, thence to Rhinocolura in Phœnicia near Egypt, and thence to other nations. But at present the greater part is transported by the Nile to Alexandria. It is brought from Arabia and India to Myos Hormus, and is then conveyed on camels to Coptus of the Thebais, situated on a canal of the Nile, and to Alexandria."

The policy of the Ptolemies, in seeking to free Egypt from commercial dependence on Yemen, and to encourage direct communication with India, had been continued by Rome at the expense of the Arabs. The "small vessels" of § 19 from Muza to the Nabatæan port are to be contrasted with the "large vessels" of § 10 that traded from Mosyllum to Egypt. The caravan trade could not be reached in the same way, and along the Red Sea the camel could always compete with the ship. This remained in Arabian hands for another half-century, when the Emperor Trajan reduced the Nabatæans to subjection to Rome.

19. **Centurion.**—Vincent assumes that this was a Roman officer, but the text does not indicate it. At this time the kingdom of the Nabatæans was independent, powerful and prosperous; as it might well have been, from the 25 per cent duty our author tells us it levied on the rich trade between Arabia and Rome.

20. **Arabia.**—Two meanings are attached to this word in the text; in this § 20 and in § 49 it refers to the entire peninsula; in every other instance it means Yemen, the Homerite-Sabaite kingdom as distinguished from the other kingdoms and political divisions of the peninsula.

20. **Differing in their speech.**—In the north the Nabatæans spoke a dialect of the Aramaic; along the coast the "Carnaites" spoke various Ishmaelite dialects, out of which has grown the modern Arabic; at the trading-posts of the true Minæans, their own language, allied to Hadramitic, was spoken; on reaching Yemen, the speech was Himyaritic.

20. **Similarly**, that is, to the opposite coast below Berenice, described at the beginning of the first voyage, in § 2.

20. **Rascally men.**—Compare the observations of other writers concerning these same Beduin robbers:

"The oxen were plowing, and the asses feeding beside them: and the Sabeans fell upon them, and took them away; yea, they have slain the servants with the edge of the sword." (Job I, 14-15. These are not the Sabæans of Yemen, but men of Saba in Central Arabia, the "nation tall and smooth" of Isaiah XVIII.)

"The Beduins have reduced robbery in all its branches to a complete and regular system, which offers many interesting details." (Burckhardt.)

"Before we lightly condemn the robber we must realize his sore need. According to Doughty and other travelers three-fourths of the Beduins of northwest Arabia suffer continual famine. In the long summer drought when pastures fail and the gaunt camel-herds give no milk they are in a very sorry plight; then it is that the housewife cooks her slender mess of rice secretly, lest some would-be guest should smell the pot. The hungry gnawing of the Arab's stomach is lessened by the coffee-cup and the ceaseless 'tobacco-drinking' from the nomad's precious pipe." (Zwemer, *Arabia the Cradle of Islam*, p. 157.)

"Thou shalt call his name *Ishmael;* because *the Lord hath heard* thy affliction. And he will be a wild man; his hand will be against every man, and every man's hand against him; and he shall dwell in the presence of all his brethren." (Gen. XVI, 11-12.)

20. **Carnaites.**—These wild tribes are called in the text *Canraites*, which cannot be identified with any other contemporary record. Some commentators would change the name to *Cassanites;* and Fabricius, following Sprenger, substitutes *Cananites*. Glaser's suggestion is certainly preferable (*Skizze*, 165-6). He thinks that the n and r should be reversed, making *Carnaites;* Karna being one of the northern settlements of the ancient kingdom of the Minæans, to which the neighboring Beduin tribes were nominally subject. Pliny (VI, 32) and Ptolemy both mention this place as a city of the Minæans; whom Pliny describes as the oldest commercial people in Arabia, having a monopoly in the trade in myrrh and frankincense, through their control of the caravan-routes from the producing regions. He refers doubtfully to their legend of the relationship of Minæans and Rhadamæans to Minos of Crete and his brother Rhadamanthus. Pliny need not have doubted, and is to be thanked for preserving this evidence of early Arabian trade in the Mediterranean. Ptolemy adds his testimony to the wide extent of this early Arabian trade, when he describes the "people called Rhamnæ who dwelt in the extreme east near the banks of the Purali, and who planted their capital at a place called Rhambacia." From Crete to the borders of India was no mean sphere of activity. Compare Ezekiel XXVII, 22: "The merchants of Sheba and Raamah, they were thy merchants: they occupied in thy fairs with chief of all spices, and with all precious stones, and gold."

Strabo also (XVI, III, 1) describes "the Minæi in the part toward the Red Sea, whose largest city is Carna; next to them are the Sabæans, whose chief city is Mariaba."

At the time of the Periplus the term "Minæan" was no longer limited to the southern traders, but had been extended to include the nomadic Ishmaelites over whom their settlements along the caravan-routes exerted a varying measure of authority.

The Minæan kingdom had long since lost its identity, having been conquered by the Sabæans. When Saba fell before Himyar its allegiance was transferred likewise; but we may assume that at the date of the Periplus it was almost independent. When the Homerite dynasty became powerful, it asserted its authority over most of the Hejaz; when the Abyssinians conquered Yemen their rule was not acknowledged so far north. The insurgence of the Ishmaelites under the spur of Islam was a logical consequence of centuries of civil war among their former overlords in Yemen.

20. **Burnt Island** is identified by Ritter and Müller with Jebel Tair, 15° 35′ N., 41° 50′ E.; a volcanic island in the direct course from Berenice to Muza. Fabricius prefers Disan, the most northerly of the Farsan group, 16° 45′ N., 41° 40′ E.; but this location is improbable, as being out of the course "straight down the middle of the gulf," and in the midst of "foul waters."

20. **Chiefs and Kings of Arabia.**—The turmoil in South Arabia at this time has already been mentioned. Within a few years the Habashat had been driven to Africa, Kataban and Saba had succumbed, and Hadramaut and Himyar remained. The Homerite dynasty was not yet firmly established, and the condition of the country was feudal, each tribe enjoying a large measure of independence. Such is the condition here described, where Mapharitis, nominally Homerite, levied its own taxes on commerce, and maintained its own colonial enterprise in Azania.

21. **Muza,** mentioned by our author as a seaport, is identified with the modern Mocha (13° 19′ N., 43° 20′ E.). According to Pliny and Ptolemy, the market-town was some miles inland, probably at the modern village of Mauza; and Pliny distinguishes the seaport as Masala. Both names still exist (Glaser, *Skizze*, 138-40; 168). In the Periplus the name of the city is, apparently, extended to include the port.

21. **Twelve thousand stadia.**—The actual distance is about 800 miles or 8000 stadia. It may be a mistake in the text (a very easy matter with Greek numerals), or, as Bunbury suggests (*History of Ancient Geography*, II, 455) our author may have calculated the distance as so many days' sail of 500 stadia each. No calls being made on the coast, contrary winds might readily cause such an error in calculation. Where no instruments existed for measuring distances, estimates would necessarily be rather general.

21. **Sending their own ships,**—to the Somali coast and India in competition with the Egyptian Greeks; down the east African coast to their own possessions (§ 16) where they doubtless enjoyed special privileges. Foreign shipping was unwelcome at Muza, which preferred to supply the north-bound caravans. Roman subjects, such as our author, had to pay dearly, in the form of gifts to the rulers,

for permission to trade there; Hindu shipping was stopped at Ocelis (§ 25).

22. **Saua** is identified by Sprenger with the Sa'b of Ibn Mogâwir, (13° N., 44° E.). Ritter and Müller, following Niebuhr, prefer the modern Ta'is (13° 35′ N., 43° 55′ E.), in the mountains about 40 miles above Mocha.

22. **Mapharitis** is the country of the Ma'âfir, a tribe belonging to the Himyaritic stock, whose chief or sheikh had, evidently, especial privileges from his "lawful king" (§ 23) Charibael. Their location was in the southern Tehama.

22. **Cholæbus** is the Arabic Kula'ib.

23. **Saphar,** mentioned by Arabian geographers as Zafar, is located by Niebuhr about 100 miles N. E. of Mocha on the road to Sanaa, near the modern town of Yerim, some miles southeast of which, on the summit of a circular hill, its ruins still exist. Zafar was the capital of the Homerite dynasty, displacing Marib, that of the Sabæan, Timna of the Gebanite, and Carna of the Minæan. Here, in the 4th century A. D., a Christian church was built, following negotiations between the Roman Emperor Constantius and the Homerite King Tubba ibn Hassan, who had embraced Judaism. In the 6th century it was the seat of a bishopric, one incumbent of which, St. Gregentius, resenting a profanation of the church at Sanaa by certain of the Koreish, inspired the Abyssinian government, then ruling in Yemen, to undertake a disastrous expedition against Mecca.

23. **Charibael.**—This is the Arabic Kariba-il, and means "God blessed (him)." (Hommel, *The Ancient Hebrew Tradition*, p. 84.) Glaser has shown this to be a royal title, rather than a name, and has edited numerous inscriptions of a king named Kariba-il Watar Juhan'im who ruled about 40-70 A. D., and whom he identifies with this Charibael. (*Die Abessinier in Arabien und Afrika*, pp. 37-8.)

23. **Homerites and Sabaites.**—Both were of the Joktanite race of South Arabia, the former being the younger branch. In the tribal genealogy in Genesis X, we are shown their relation to the Semites of the North. Three of the children of Shem are given as Elam, Asshur, and Arphaxad. Arphaxad's son was Salah, and his grandson Eber. These names are associated with Babylonia and Chaldæa. Eber's second son was Joktan, of which the Arabic form is Kahtan, which appears farther south along the Persian Gulf, in the peninsula of El Katan. Of the sons of Joktan, most are identified with the southern coast; two of them being Hazarmaveth (Hadramaut), and Jerah (*cf.* the *Jerakôn Komê* of Ptolemy, north of Dhofar). The last-named the Arabs call Yarab: his son was Yashhab (*cf.*

the Asabi in Oman, § 35), and his grandson "Saba the Great" (surnamed Abd-es-Shems) is said to have founded the city of Marib, and to have begun its great dam, on which the irrigation of the vicinity depended. The Sabæans are thus connected with this Saba, a descendant of Jerah, and not with Sheba, son of Joktan, who is referred rather to Central Arabia; whom Glaser and Hommel would make a colony from Yemen, while Weber would reverse the process, having the Sabæans migrate southward for the conquest of the Minæans.

According to Arab accounts the dam at Marib was finished by a certain King Zul Karnain, suggesting the primacy of the Minæan dynasty at that time; but from about the 7th century B. C. the Sabæans were supreme in all southern Arabia, controlling the caravan-routes, and forcing the wild tribes into caravan service. Colonies and resting-stations were established at intervals along the routes. We learn from the Koran (Chap. XXXIV) that the journey was easy between these cities, and travel secure by night or by day; the distances being so short that the heat of the day might be passed in one, and the night in the next, so that provisions need not be carried. The number of such settlements may be inferred from Strabo's statement that the caravans took seventy days between Minæa and Aelana; and all the Greek and Roman writers, from Eratosthenes to Pliny, testify to the value of the trade, the wealth of those who controlled it, and their jealous hindrance of all competition.

The entry of the fleets of the Ptolemies into the Red Sea, and their establishment of colonies along its shores, dealt a hard blow to the caravan-trade. If we sift fact from homily in the same chapter of the Koran, we find that the result was abandonment of many of the caravan-stations, and a consequent increase in the cost of camel-hire and of the provisions which now had to be carried; impoverishment, dispersion and rebellion of the dwellers in the stations, so that finally "most of the cities which were between Saba and Syria were ruined and abandoned," and a few years later than the Periplus, Marib itself, stripped of its revenues and unable to maintain its public works, was visited with an inundation which carried away its famous reservoir-dam, making the city uninhabitable and forcing the dispersion of its people. Many of them seem to have migrated northward and to have settled in the country southeast of Judæa, founding the kingdom of the Ghassanids, which was for generations a bulwark of the Roman Empire at its eastern boundary.

The great expedition against Sabæa by the Romans under Aelius Gallus, (Strabo, XVI, IV, 22-4; Pliny, VI, 32) never got beyond the valley of the Minæans; turning back thence, as Vincent surmised

(II, 306-311), and as Glaser proves (*Skizze*, 56-9), without reaching Marib, and probably without inflicting any lasting injury on the tribes along their route. It was the merchant-shipping of the Romans, and not their soldiery, that undermined the power of the Sabæans.

As the wealth of Marib declined, its power was resolved into its elements, and was reorganized by a neighbor of the same blood. The oldest son of Saba the Great, founder of Marib, was Himyar, whose descendants included most of the town-folk of the southwest corner of Arabia. Two sons of Himyar, Malik and Arib, had carried the Joktanite arms back toward the east again, subduing the earlier inhabitants of the frankincense region north of Dhofar. The center of the tribe was at Zafar, southwest of Marib, and some days' journey nearer the sea. Allied with the sheikh at Zafar was he of the Ma'âfir, controlling the port of Muza. This combination was able to overthrow the old order, Zafar supplanting Marib, and Muza stripping Aden of its trade and its privileges along the African coast. Thereafter the Himyarite dynasty—the Homerite kings—assumed the title "Kings of Saba and Raidan." This was during the first century B. C.

The subsequent policy of the Kariba-îls of Zafar was to expand both north and east, to regain the old supremacy over the "Carnaites" along the caravan-routes, and to control the shipping from the east.

(See Prof. D. H. Müller's article, *Yemen*, in the Encyclopædia Britannica, 9th Edition; Glaser, *Skizze* and *Die Abessinier*, etc.; Weber, *Arabien vor dem Islam* in *Der alte Orient*, III, Leipzig, 1901; Prof. Hommel's chapter, *Arabia*, in Hilprecht, *Explorations in Bible Lands*, Phila., 1903; Hogarth, *The Penetration of Arabia*, N. Y., 1904; and the reports of the Austrian South-Arabian Expedition.)

23. **Embassies and gifts.**—This wooing of Yemen by Rome was soon ended. It was no part of the Arab policy, whether Homerite, Minæan, or Nabatæan, to let Rome cultivate direct relations with India, and as the empire expanded stronger measures were necessary. Fifty years later than the Periplus, Trajan had captured Petra, and Abyssinia was being subsidized to attack Yemen.

23. **A friend of the Emperors.**—Some commentators suppose that this refers to a time when two Roman emperors ruled together, thus dating the Periplus well into the 2d century A. D., but there is nothing in the text to require it. The Homerite king, who began to rule, probably, in the last days of Claudius, was simply, (in the mind of our author, writing early in the reign of Nero), the friend of both those Roman Emperors, as he was also of several others whose short reigns coincided with his. A list of the Emperors of the 1st and 2d centuries confirms this:

| B.C. A.D. | Roman | Parthian | B.C. |
|---|---|---|---|
| 39- 14 | Augustus Cæsar | Phraates IV | 37- 2 |
| A.D. | | | B.C. A.D. |
| 14- 37 | Tiberius | Phraataces | 2- ? |
| 37- 41 | Caligula | Orodes II | ? |
| 41- 54 | Claudius | Vonones I | ?- 16 |
| 54- 68 | Nero | Artabanus III | 16- 42 |
| 68- 69 | Galba | Vardanes | 42- 46 |
| 69 | Otho | Gotarzes | 46- 51 |
| 69 | Vitellius | Vonones II | 51 |
| 69- 79 | Vespasian | Volagases I | 51- 78 |
| 79- 81 | Titus | Pacorus | 78-108 |
| 81- 96 | Domitian | Chosroes | 108-130 |
| 96- 98 | Nerva | Volagases II | 130-149 |
| 98-117 | Trajan | Volagases III | 149-191 |
| 117-138 | Hadrian | Volagases IV | 191-209 |
| 138-161 | Antoninus Pius | disputed succession: | |
| 161-169 | Marcus Aurelius<br>Lucius Verus | Volagases V<br>Artabanus III | 209-215 |
| 169-180 | Marcus Aurelius | Artabanus III | 215-226 |
| 180-192 | Commodus | (End of Parthian Empire) | |
| 193 | Pertinax | | |
| 193 | Didius Julianus | | |
| 193-211 | Septimius Severus | | |
| 211-212 | Caracalla<br>Geta | | |
| 212-217 | Caracalla | | |
| 217-218 | Macrinus | | |
| 218-222 | Heliogabalus | | |
| 222-235 | Alexander Severus | | |

Two Roman Emperors serving together:

Marcus Aurelius, Lucius Verus—161-169.

Caracalla, Geta—211-212.

Valerian, Gallienus—253-259.

Diocletian, Maximian—286-305, and through several succeeding reigns.

24. **Saffron** (*Crocus sativus*, Linn., order *Iridaceæ*).—The part that entered into trade was the stamens and pistils of the flower, which were used medicinally, as a paint or dye, a seasoning in cookery, and a perfume or ingredient of ointments.

As a perfume, halls, theatres and courts were strewed with the plant, and it entered into the composition of many spirituous extracts, which retained the same scent. (See Pliny, XIII, 2.)

Lucan (*Pharsalia*, IX, 809) refers to the "sweet-smelling essence of saffron that issues from the limbs of a statue."

Saffron also entered into many of the scented salves or balsams. It was much adulterated by adding the stigmata of other plants, such as the safflower (*Carthamus tinctorius*, order *Compositæ*), and the marigold (*Calendula officinalis*, order *Compositæ*).

Pliny (XXI, 81) says, "Saffron is blended with wine or water and is extremely useful in medicine. It is generally kept in horn boxes. Applied with egg it disperses all kinds of inflammations, those of the eyes in particular; it is employed also for hysterical suffocations, and for ulcerations of the stomach, chest, kidneys, liver, lungs, and bladder. It is particularly useful in cases of inflammation of those parts, and for cough and pleurisy. . . . . The flower is used locally with Cimolian chalk for erysipelas." (See also Beckmann, *op. cit.*, I, 175-7.)

24. **Sweet rush.**—The text is *kyperos*. There is much confusion among the Roman writers between various species of aromatic rush, some including the *calamus* of the Hebrew anointing oil (Exodus XXX), which was probably *Acorus calamus*, Linn., order *Aroideæ*; a semi-aquatic sub-tropical herb, useful medicinally and as a flavor. But Pliny (XIII, 2) distinguishes between "Syrian calamus" and "Syrian sweet-rush," both components of the Parthian "regal ointment;" so that sweet-rush may rather have been *Andropogon schœnanthus*, Linn., order *Gramineæ*. An account of its production is given by Pliny (XII, 48), and of its medicinal properties (XXI, 70). That most highly esteemed, he says, came from near the temple of Jupiter Ammon in Egypt; the next best from Rhodes. It had an odor resembling that of nard; and aside from its use in perfumes and ointments, it was employed as a diuretic, and with wine and vinegar for throat ulcers, or in liniments for ulcerous sores generally.

It is possible, also, that the *kyperos* of the text may have been the Egyptian papyrus (*Cyperus papyrus*, Linn., order *Cyperaceæ*); used, according to Pliny (XIII, 21-2) for boat-building, sails and mats, cloths, coverlets and ropes, and the roots for fuel. He notes it as a product of Syria, growing in conjunction with the sweet calamus, and much favored by King Antiochus for cordage for his navy, instead of spartum, which was preferred by the Romans. Again (XXXIII, 30) he says papyrus was used for smelting copper and iron, being favored next to pine wood.

The suggestion in the text is, however, for an aromatic rather than cordage or fuel, so that *Andropogon schœnanthus* is the more probable identification.

McCrindle's suggestions of turmeric (*Curcuma longa*, Linn., order *Zingiberaceæ*) and galangal (*Alpinia officinarum*, Hance, order *Zingiberaceæ*) are not borne out by Pliny's descriptions; and these are both products of the Far East, while the text indicates an Egyptian or Mediterranean product.

24. **Fragrant ointments.**—Pliny (XIII, 1) says that "luxury thought fit to mingle all known fragrant odors, and to make one single odor of the whole; hence the invention of ointments. The Persians use them extensively, and they quite soak themselves in it, and so, by an adventitious recommendation, counteract the bad odors which are produced by dirt."

His account of the manufacture of ointments (XIII, 2) throws light on numerous articles of trade in his time. There were two principal components. They consisted of oils or juices, and solids: the former known as *stymmata*, the latter as *hedysmata*. A third element was the coloring matter, usually cinnabar or alkanet. Resin and gum were added to fix the odor. Among the *stymmata* were oil of roses, sweet-rush, sweet calamus, xylo-balsamum, myrtle, cypress, mastich, pomegranate-rind, saffron oil, lilies, fenugreek, myrrh, cassia, nard, and cinnamon. The *hedysmata* included amomum, nard, myrrh, balsam, costus, and marjoram.

Myrrh used by itself, without oil, formed an ointment, but it was *stacte* only that must be used, for otherwise it would be too bitter.

The formula of the "regal ointment," made for the Parthian Kings, included myrobalanus, costus, amomum, cinnamon, comacum, cardamom, spikenard, marum, myrrh, cassia, storax, ladanum, opobalsamum, Syrian calamus and Syrian sweet-rush, œnanthe, malabathrum, serichatum, cypress, aspralathus, panax, saffron, cypirus, sweet marjoram, lotus, honey and wine.

The Mendesian ointment included resin and myrrh, oil of balanus, metopion (Egyptian oil of bitter almonds), omphacium, cardamom, sweet-rush, honey, wine, myrrh, seed of balsamum, galbanum, and resin of terebinth.

Another included oils (the common kinds), sampsuchum, lilies, fenugreek, myrrh, cassia, nard, sweet-rush, and cinnamon.

24. **Myrrh,**—a gum exuded from the bark of a small tree, native in South Arabia, and to some extent in Oman, and the Somali coast of Africa; classified as *Balsamodendron Myrrha* (Nees), or *Commiphora Abyssinica* (Engl.), order *Burseraceæ*. It forms the underwood of

forests of acacia, moringa, and euphorbia. From earliest times it has been, together with frankincense, a constituent of incense, perfumes, and ointments. It was an ingredient of the Hebrew anointing oil (Exod. XXX), and was also one of the numerous components of the celebrated *kyphi* of the Egyptians, a preparation used in fumigations, medicine, and embalming. It was the object of numerous trading expeditions of the Egyptian kings to the "Land of Punt." A monument of Sahure, 28th century B. C., records receipts of 80,000 measures of myrrh from Punt. The expedition of Hatshepsut (15th century B. C.) again records myrrh as the most important cargo; its list of the "marvels of the country of Punt" was as follows: All goodly fragrant woods of God's Land, heaps of myrrh-resin, fresh myrrh trees, ebony, pure ivory, green gold of Emu, cinnamon wood, khesyt wood, ihmut incense, sonter incense, eye cosmetic, apes, monkeys, dogs, skins of southern panther, natives and their children. The inscription adds: "Never was brought the like of this for any king who has been since the beginning." (Breasted, *Ancient Records of Egypt*, II, 109; Flückiger and Hanbury, *op. cit.*, 140-6.)

Pliny (XII, 35) gives a clear account of the gathering of the gum: "Incisions are made in the myrrh-tree twice a year, and at the same season as in the incense-tree; but in the case of the myrrh-tree they are made all the way up from the root as far as the branches which are able to bear it. The tree spontaneously exudes, before the incision is made, a liquid which bears the name of *stacte* (*stazo*, to drop) and to which there is no myrrh that is superior. Second only in quality to this is the cultivated myrrh; of the wild or forest kind, the best is that which is gathered in summer."

*Stacte*, he says, sold as high as 40 denarii the pound; cultivated myrrh, at a maximum of 11 denarii; Erythræan at 16, and *odoraria* at 14. And he continues: "They give no tithes of myrrh to the god, because it is the produce of other countries as well; but the growers pay the fourth part of it to the king of the Gebanitæ. Myrrh is bought up indiscriminately by the common people and then packed into bags; but our perfumers separate it without any difficulty, the principal tests of its goodness being its unctuousness and its aromatic smell.

"There are several kinds of myrrh: the first among the wild myrrhs is the Troglodytic; and the next are the Minæan, which includes the aromatic, and that of Ausaritis, in the kingdom of the Gebanitæ. A third kind is the Dianitic, and a fourth is the mixed myrrh, or *collatitia* . . . a fifth again is the Sambracenian, which is brought from a city in the kingdom of the Sabæi, near the sea; and a sixth is known by the name of Ausaritic. There is a white myrrh also which is produced in only one spot, and is carried for sale to the city of Messalum." (This is the same as the port of Masala or Muza. See Glaser, *Skizze*, 138.)

The name *myrrh* is from the Hebrew and Arabic *mur*, meaning "bitter." The ancient Egyptian word was *bola* or *bal*, and the Sanscrit was *vola*. The modern Persian and Indian call it *bol* or *bola*.

24. **Gebanite-Minæan stacte.**—The text is corrupt, having *gabeirminaia:* Müller and Fabricius alter this to "Abiræa and Minæa," which appear in Sprenger's map of Arabia, but not in the myrrh district. *Stacte* has already been described as the gum yielded by natural exudation from wild trees, as distinguished from that coming from incisions on trees either wild or cultivated; while the qualifying adjective can hardly be other than Gebanite-Minæan, which was among the best varieties in Pliny's classification. (See also Glaser, *Skizze*, 88-9.)

24. **Alabaster.**—Pliny (XIII, 3), says, "Ointments keep best in boxes of alabaster, and perfumes when mixed with oil, which conduces all the more to their durability the thicker it is, such as the oil of almonds, for instance. Ointments, too, improve with age; but the sun is apt to spoil them, for which reason they are usually stowed away in a shady place in vessels of lead." (See also Pliny, XXXVI, 12; Mark, XIV, 7; John, XII, 3.)

24. **Avalites and the far-side coast.**—The text is corrupt, having *Adulis;* Fabricius translates "aus dem gegenüber gelegenen Adulis." But Adulis was not opposite Muza, its exports were quite different, and it is not mentioned that they went to Muza. The relations of Habash and Himyar, at the date of the Periplus, were not those of friendly commerce, and Adulis was distinctly an Egyptian trading-station. On the other hand, the text describes, in § 7, the articles carried by the Berbers from *Avalites* to Ocelis and Muza for sale there; to which this passage refers as "already mentioned." We must conclude, therefore, that the scribe copied "Adulis" instead of "Avalites," which was what our author wrote.

25. **A narrow strait.**—This is, of course, the strait of Bab-el-Mandeb, or "Gate of Tears" (12° 35′ N., 43° 12′ E.), so called because of its treacherous winds and currents.

25. **The island Diodorus** is the modern Perim (12° 38′ N., 43° 18′ E.).

25. **Ocelis** is the *Acila* of Strabo, Artemidorus and Pliny; the name surviving in the modern Cella. Forster traces in this name the

tribe of Uzal, son of Joktan (Genesis X, 27) with whom he also connects Ausar (Ausal or Ausan) in the Frankincense Country—which survives in the modern Ras el Sair. This is the district which at one time held the "Ausanitic coast" near Zanzibar, as stated in §15. The ancient city of Uzal is the modern Sanaa.

Ocelis is identified by Glaser with a bay on the northern side of the promontory of Sheikh Sa'id (12° 48′ N., 43° 28′ E.), a volcanic formation which juts out from the Arabian shore and is separated by a narrow channel from the island of Perim. He notes the probability that Indian ships were permitted to go no further than this place, whence their cargoes went by land to Muza. The text says merely that it was "not a market-town, but the first landing for those sailing into the gulf;" but Pliny (VI, 104) states on the authority of Onesicritus, that Ocelis was the most convenient port for those coming from India. He mentions two other ports, Muza (Masala) and Cana, which were not frequented by Indian travellers, but were only for the merchants dealing in frankincense and Arabian spices.

26. **Eudæmon Arabia** is the modern Aden (12° 48′ N., 45° 0′ E.), from very early times an important trade center, where goods from the east were trans-shipped for the Mediterranean markets. It was, probably, the Eden of Ezekiel XXVII, 3, and the chief port of the Minæan and Sabæan dynasties. While temporarily in eclipse under the Homerite kings, it had regained its position by the 4th century A. D. when Constantius negotiated for a church to be built there; and the Arabian geographers and Marco Polo refer to its activities in terms almost as glowing as those of Agatharchides.

The Periplus gives the port the name of the entire district; *Eudæmon* like *Felix*, being an attempt at translating *Yemen*, "the country to the right hand" (as one faces the east); the Arabic, like the Greek and Latin, attaching the idea of good fortune to the right hand. *Eden* had the same significance, of good fortune.

26. **Charibael destroyed the place.**—The text is corrupt, having *Cæsar*. It is quite certain that no Roman emperor attacked this place during the 1st century, and the title is equally suspicious, our author having more correctly referred to his sovereign, in § 23, as *autokrator*. Müller and Fabricius substitute *Elisar*, retaining the second syllable of the word, and suppose him to have been a king of the Frankincense Country. But Schwanbeck (*Rheinischen Museum für Philologie*, VII. Jahrgang, 1850) prefers *Charibael*, and Glaser supports him by proving that *Eleazus*, and not Elisar, was the name of the king mentioned in § 27.

The indications are against a westward movement by the monarch at Sabbatha; his outlook was in the other direction. The Periplus indicates his control of the fertile frankincense valleys far beyond the account of Strabo, who knew Chatramotitis as a producer of myrrh only; this movement followed the Habash migration. The Chatramotitæ had, it is true, to cope with an alliance of Homerites and Persians which ultimately pressed them on either side and engulfed them; but this was in a later century. Saphar and Sabbatha were not yet beyond the period of expansion within their respective spheres. From the Red Sea to the summits of the Arabian Alps was that of the former; the Wadi Hadramaut, on the eastern slope, that of the latter. Between the two lay precipitous mountains. Topography and history alike discredit an attack upon Aden by the Chatramotitæ.

But in the alliance of Muza with Saphar we have the motive for the destruction of Aden. The foreign trade was centered at the Homerite port, and Cholæbus gained for his merchants the rights which those of Aden had enjoyed under the Sabæan kings. The loss was not great; Ibn Khaldun (Kay's edition, p. 158) tells us that the city was built mostly of reeds, so that conflagrations by night were common there. It involved hardly more than the discontinuance of an annual fair, as described in the account by Lieut. Cruttenden at Berbera, quoted under § 14.

27. **Cana** may be identified with Hisn Ghorab ( 14° 10′ N., 48° 20′ E.), a fine harbor, protected from all winds by projecting capes on either side and by islands in the offing, as described in the text. Here are numerous ruins and one famous Himyaritic inscription, of which a version is given by Forster. The "Island of Birds" is described by Müller as 450 feet high, covered with guano, and thus has its name from the same cause as the promontory Hisn Ghorab (Raven Castle). The modern town is called Bir Ali.

Fabricius (pp. 141-2), following Sprenger and Ritter, locates Cana slightly farther west, at Bâ-l-Haf. This seems not to accord with the text, which says the port was "just beyond the cape projecting from this bay," while Bâ-l-Haf would be "just before." The identification depends too literally on the stated distance of the islands and fails to take into account that they are described as "facing the port." This is true of Hisn Ghorab and not of Bâ-l-Haf.

Müller (p. 278) and Glaser (*Skizze*, pp. 174-5) support the Hisn Ghorab location by comparison of the distances given by Ptolemy (VI, 7, 10) between his *Kanê emporion* and the neighboring ports.

From Hisn Ghorab the way to the interior leads up the Wadi Maifa, which empties into the ocean a short distance to the east.

The Cana of the Periplus is probably the same as the Canneh of Ezekiel XXVII, 23.

The trade which it formerly enjoyed passes now through the port of Makalla, some distance to the east, and the capital of the country has shifted in like manner eastward to the modern city of Shibam.

27. **Eleazus, King of the Frankincense Country.**—This is the Arabic Ili-azzu, "my God is mighty," a name which Glaser shows to have belonged to several kings of the Hadramaut; and this Eleazus he identifies with Ili-azzu Jalît, of whose reign, dating about 25-65 A. D., he gives an inscription (*Die Abessinier*, 34, etc.).

The name given the kingdom, "Frankincense Country," is notable, being a translation of the "Incense-Land" of the Habashat, or Aethiopians, already mentioned. This ancient object of contention among the nations was now divided between Hadramaut and Parthia, and its name was, apparently, assumed by the king of the Hadramaut; perhaps officially, but certainly by the popular voice, and by merchants such as the author of the Periplus, interested in the product of the country and not in its politics.

A glance at the topography of this Incense-Land will help toward an understanding of its dealings with its neighbors. The southern coast of Arabia from Bab el Mandeb to Ras el Hadd has a length of about 1200 miles, divided almost equally in climatic conditions. The western half is largely sandstone bluff, sun-scorched and arid; cut, however, by occasional ravines which bring down scanty rains during the monsoon to fertilize a broad strip of coast plain. On the western edge the mountains of Yemen, rising above 10,000 feet, attract a good rainfall which waters the western slope toward the Red Sea. On the eastern slope the water-courses are soon lost in the sand, but on the upper levels the valleys are protected and fertile. Such were the Nejran, the Minæan Jauf, and the valley of the Sabæans, which last was made rich by the great dam that stored its waters for irrigation; and these three valleys, the centers of caravan-trade bound north toward the Nile and Euphrates, owed their prosperity mainly to their position above the greatest of all the east-flowing courses, the Valley of Hadramaut. This great cleft in the sandstone rock, (originally, Bent believes an arm of the sea, now silted up), which gathers the streams from the highest peaks, runs parallel with the coast for more than 200 miles, fertile and productive for nearly the entire distance; then it turns to the south and its waters are lost, the mouth of the valley being desert like the cliffs that line its course. This was one of the best frankincense districts.

Beyond the mouth of the Wadi Hadramaut is Ras Fartak, nearly north of Cape Guardafui. Here the climate changes; the monsoon, no longer checked by the African coast, leaves its effect on the coastal hills, which gradually rise above 4000 feet, clothed with tropical vegetation; while the coast plains are narrow and broken. The northern slopes of these mountains (known to our author as Asich, § 33) feed the water-course now known as the Wadi Rekot, about 100 miles long, which empties into the Kuria Muria Bay; beyond which are fertile coast plains as far as Ras el Hadd. These mountains, and the Dhofar and Jenaba districts, facing which lie the Kuria Muria islands, were the oldest and perhaps the most productive of the frankincense districts of Arabia; and it was always the ambition of the various powers of that region to extend their rule so as to include the Dhofar mountains, the Hadramaut valley, and the opposite Somali coast of Africa—thus controlling the production and commanding the price; in short, forming a "frankincense trust." The restricted area of the Arabian incense-lands, bordered as they were by the steppe and the desert, made them constantly subject to attack and control by different wandering tribes; while at the same time their local conditions, of intensive cultivation of a controlled product of great and constant value, made for a peculiarly ordered state of society—for a development of caste unusual in Semitic lands, and in which the cultivator, the warrior, and the privileged slave, had their place in the order given.

Of the age-long struggle for control of these sacred lands we know today little more than the Greek writers of two thousand years ago. The modern world takes its little supply of frankincense from the Arab vessels that carry it to Bombay or Aden; its armies are sent to the conquest or defence of lands in other lines of productivity—of a Kimberley, a Witwatersrand, a Manchuria. But to the ancient world the Incense-Land was a true Eldorado, sought by the great empires and fought for by every Arab tribe that managed to enrich itself by trading incense for temple-service on the Nile or Euphrates, on Mount Zion, or in Persia, India, or China. The archæological expedition that shall finally succeed in penetrating these forbidden regions, and recovering the records of their past, cannot fail to add greatly to our store of knowledge of the surrounding civilizations, by showing the complement to such records as those of Hatshepsut in Egypt and Tiglath-Pileser III in Assyria, and by giving the groundwork for the treasured scraps of information preserved by Herodotus, Theophrastus, Eratosthenes, Agatharchides, Strabo, Pliny, and Ptolemy. At present we must be satisfied with such knowledge of the Incense-Land as may be had from these, and from inscriptions found by

Halévy and Glaser in the homes of its neighbors, the Minæans and Sabæans.

During the 2d and 1st centuries B. C., the greater part of the Incense-Land was held by the Incense-People, the Aethiopians or Habashat. Pressure by the Parthians on the East forced an alliance, of which Glaser found the record at Marib, between the Habashat, Hadramaut and Saba on one hand, against Himyar and Raidan on the other. This was not far from 50 B. C. Soon afterwards we find the Habashat gone into their African outposts, and Marib ruled by "Kings of Saba and Raidan;" while after a couple of generations more the Periplus shows us a Homerite king who rules also over Saba and Raidan and the East African coast; and a king of the Hadramaut whose title is expanded to "King of the Frankincense Country," and whose rule extends over the islands of Kuria Muria, Socotra and Masira, all former dependencies of the Habashat.

By the 4th century A. D. the kings at Zafar had absorbed the whole, being known as "Kings of Saba, Raidan, Hadramaut and Yemen;" while the Abyssinian kings, who regained a foothold in Arabia during that century, were known as "Kings of Axum, Himyar, Raidan, Habashat, Saba," etc.

The name "Hadramaut," the Hazarmaveth of Genesis X, means "Enclosure of Death," referring probably to the crater of Bir Barhut, whose rumblings were held to be the groans of lost souls (W. Robertson Smith: *Religion of the Semites*, p. 134, and authorities there quoted).

(See Wellsted: *Narrative ot a Journey to the Ruins of Nakeb el Hajar*, Journal of the Royal Geographical Society, VII, 20; H. von Maltzan: *Reisen in Arabien*, Braunschweig, 1873; L. W. C. Van den Berg: *Le Hadramaut et les Colonies Arabes dans l'Archipel Indien*, Batavia, 1886; J. Theodore Bent: *The Hadramaut, a Journey*, Nineteenth Century, 1894; *Expedition to the Hadramaut*, Geographical Journal, IV, 313; L. Hirsch: *Reisen in Süd-Arabien, Mahra-Land und Hadhramut*, Leiden, 1897; the works already cited of Glaser, Hommel, Weber, Hogarth, and Zwemer; and the Austrian Expedition Reports.)

27. **Sabbatha.**—The native name of this capital of the Chatramotitæ was Shabwa. It lies in the Wadi Rakhiya, some distance above the Wadi Hadramaut, and about 60 miles west of the present capital, Shibam. According to Bent (*Geographical Journal*, IV, 413: 1894) it is now deserted, save for a few Beduins, who work the salt mines in the vicinity; while the natives are now all in the lower Hadramaut valley.

This is the Sabota of Pliny (VI, 32) "with sixty temples within its walls."

27. **Frankincense,** one of the most ancient and precious articles of commerce, is a resin exuded from various species of *Boswellia*, order *Burseraceæ*, native in Somaliland and South Arabia. Birdwood (*Trans. Linn. Soc.*, XXVII, 1871), distinguishes particularly *B. Frereana*, *B. Bhau-Dajiana* (the *mocrotu* of § 9), and *B. Carterii*, the last-named yielding the best incense. *B. thurifera*, native in India, yields a resin of less fragrance, much used as an adulterant. Frankincense is thus closely allied to myrrh, bdellium, and benzoin.

The Greek word is *libanos*, from Hebrew *lebonah*, Arabic *lubân*, meaning "white"; *cf. laben*, the Somali word for cream, and "milk-perfume," which is the Chinese term for frankincense. Marco Polo always calls it "white incense."

Another Hebrew name was *shekheleth*, Ethiopic *sekhin*, which Hommel would connect with the "Bay of Sachalites" of § 29.

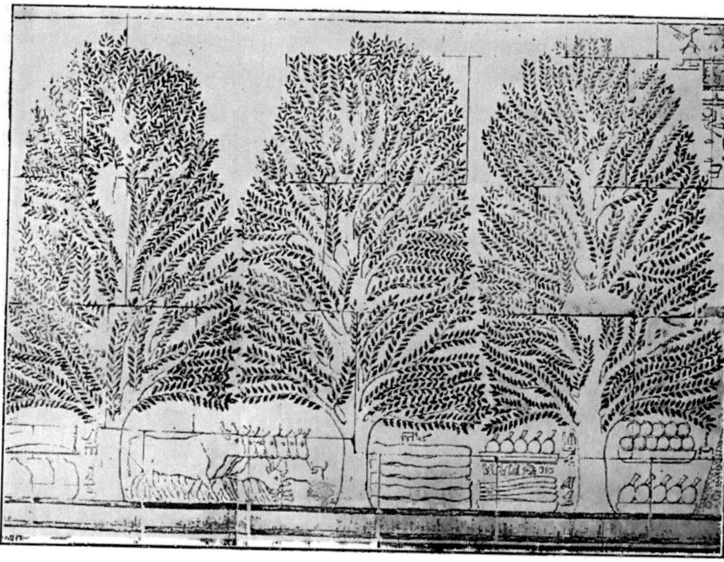

Frankincense trees, from the Punt Reliefs in the Deir el Bahri temple at Thebes; dating from the 15th century B. C. After Naville.

The inscriptions of the early Egyptian dynasties contain, as we might expect, few references to the trade in incense, which was brought overland to the upper Nile by the "people of Punt and God's Land" and not sought out by the Pharaohs. That incense was in use is sufficiently clear from the early ritual. The expedition to the

Incense-Land under Sahure, in the Vth dynasty (28th century B. C.) was a notable exception. In the VIth dynasty, under Pepi II (26th century B. C.), a royal officer Sebni, sent to the Tigre highlands, records how he "descended to Wawat and Uthek, and sent on the royal attendant Iri, with two others, bearing incense, clothing (probably cotton), one tusk, and one hide" (as specimens). In the XIth dynasty, under Mentuhotep IV (21st century B. C.), a record of the completion of a royal sarcophagus states that "Cattle were slaughtered, goats were slain, incense was put on the fire. Behold, an army of 3000 sailors of the nomes of the Northland (Delta of the Nile) followed it in safety to Egypt." And in the XIIth dynasty, under Amenemhet I (20th century B. C.), another royal officer named Intef was sent for stone to Hammamat along what was, in the time of the Periplus, the caravan-route from Coptos to Berenice. He sought for it eight days without success, then prostrated himself "to Min, to Mut, to —— Great-in-Magic, and all the gods of this highland, giving to them incense upon the fire. . . . Then all scattered in search, and I found it, and the entire army was praising, it rejoiced with obeisance; I gave praise to Montu."

Then followed a period of disorder and Arabian domination in Egypt, during which Arab merchants controlled the trade. This was the condition described in Genesis XXXVII, 25, when "a traveling company of Ishmaelites came from Gilead, with their camels bearing spicery and balm and myrrh, going to carry it down to Egypt." It was ended by a native reaction under the great Pharaohs of the XVIIIth or Theban dynasty, under whom the land increased in power in all directions. These monarchs were not content to remain in commercial dependence upon Arabia, but organized great fleets which went to the "Land of Punt" each season and brought back unprecedented treasure. This land in former times, according to the Deir el Bahri reliefs, "the people knew not; it was heard of from mouth to mouth by hearsay of the ancestors. The marvels brought thence under thy fathers, the kings of Lower Egypt, were brought from one to another, and since the time of the ancestors of the kings of Upper Egypt, who were of old, as a return for many payments; none reaching them except thy carriers." But Amon-Re, so the inscription continues, led the Egyptian army by land and sea, until it came to the Incense-Land, and brought back great store of myrrh, ebony and ivory, gold, cinnamon, incense, eye-paint, apes, monkeys, dogs, panther-skins, natives and their children. "Never was brought the like of this for any king who has been since the beginning." Incense-trees were planted in the court of the temple; "heaven and earth are flooded with incense; odors are in the Great House," and the heart of Amon was made glad.

Then followed a series of campaigns in Syria, resulting in the submission of that country, and annual remittances of great quantities of Arabian and Eastern treasure—incense, oil, grain, wine, gold and silver, precious stones—while even the "Chief of Shinar" at Babylon sent gifts of lapis lazuli, and the "Genabti" of the Incense-Land came direct, offering their tribute. The sudden opulence of the Theban dynasty made possible a great enrichment in the worship of Amon, and the setting aside of enormous endowments for the temples, as well as annual gifts of princely value. So Rameses II, of the XIXth dynasty (1292-1225 B. C.), "founded for his father offerings for his *ka*—wine, incense, all fruit, cultivated trees, growing for him;" while the court responded that Rameses himself was "the god of all people, that they may awake, to give to thee incense." His successor Merneptah was bidden by the All-Lord to "set free multitudes who are bound in every district, to give offerings to the temples, to send in incense before the god." And in the XXth dynasty, under Rameses III (1198-1167 B. C.), it seemed as if the resources of the nation were poured bodily into the lap of Amon. The god opened for the Pharaoh "the ways of Punt, with myrrh and incense for thy serpent diadem;" "the Sand-Dwellers came bowing down to thy name." And in the *Papyrus Harris*, that great record of his gifts and endowments to Amon, compiled for his tomb, there are such entries every year as "gold, silver, lapis lazuli, malachite, precious stones, copper, garments of royal linen, jars, fowl; myrrh, 21,140 *deben*, white incense 2,159 jars, cinnamon 246 measures, incense 304,093 various measures;" stored of necessity, in a special "Incense House."

(The quotations are from Breasted, *Ancient Records of Egypt.*)

At this time the Hebrews ended their servitude in Egypt and migrated to Palestine; and naturally among them also frankincense was counted holy. The sacred incense of the priests (Exod. XXX, 34-5) was composed of "sweet spices, stacte, onycha, galbanum, with pure frankincense; of each a like weight . . . a perfume . . . pure and holy." And "when any will offer a meat offering (Levit. II, 1-3) it shall be of fine flavor, and he shall pour oil upon it, and put frankincense thereon . . . and the priest shall burn the memorial upon the altar, to be an offering made by fire, of a sweet savour unto the Lord." There were special rooms in the temple at Jerusalem for storing it under priestly guard (I Chron. IX, 26-30); and later, when one of these rooms was occupied as a dwelling, it was considered a sacrilege (Nehemiah XIII, 4-9). The trade in the days of

Israel's prosperity was important: "Who is this that cometh out of the wilderness like pillars of smoke, perfumed with myrrh and frankincense, with all powders of the merchant?" (Song of Solomon III, 6.) "The multitude of camels shall cover thee, the dromedaries of Midian and Ephah: all they from Sheba shall come; they shall bring gold and incense; and they shall shew forth the praises of the Lord." (Isaiah LX, 6.) And the Queen of Sheba "gave the king an hundred and twenty talents of gold, and of spices a very great store, and precious stones; there came no more such abundance of spices as these which the Queen of Sheba gave to King Solomon." (1 Kings X, 10.)

The Nimrud Inscription of the great Assyrian monarch Tiglath-Pileser III, tells how "fear of the brilliance of Ashur, my lord, overcame Merodach-baladan, of Yakin, King of the Sea-Country," and how he came and made submission, bringing as tribute "gold—the dust of his land—in abundance, vessels of gold, necklaces of gold, precious stones, the product of the sea (pearls?), beams of *ushu*-wood, *ellutu*-wood, party-colored clothing, spices of all kinds."

In the Persian empire frankincense was equally treasured. Herodotus tells us that the Arabs brought a tribute of 1000 talents' weight every year to Darius (III, 97), and that a similar quantity was burnt every year by the Chaldæans on their great altar to Bel at Babylon (I, 183). From the spoils of Gaza in Syria, 500 talents' weight of frankincense was sent by Alexander the Great to his tutor Leonidas (Plutarch, *Lives*) who had rebuked him for loading the Macedonian altars too lavishly, remarking that he must be more economical until he had conquered the countries that produced the frankincense! (Pliny XII, 32.) The temple of Apollo in Miletus was presented with 10 talents' weight in 243 B. C., by Seleucus II, King of Syria, and his brother Antiochus Hierax, King of Cilicia. The temple of Venus at Paphos was fragrant with frankincense:

> "Ipsa Paphum sublimis abit, sedesque revisit
> Læta suas ubi templum illi, centumque Sabæo
> Ture calent aræ sertisque recentibus halant."
>
> —Virgil, *Aeneid*, I, 416.

And to the infant Saviour in Bethlehem came "three wise men from the east, with gifts,—gold, frankincense, and myrrh" (Matt. II, 11), signifying, according to a Persian legend quoted by Yule, "the gold the kingship, the frankincense the divinity, the myrrh the healing powers of the Child."

Likewise in funerals were its virtues required. The priests of Amon under the XVIIIth dynasty were instructed to "be vigilant concerning your duty, be ye not careless concerning any of your rules; be ye pure, be ye clean concerning divine things . . . bring ye up for me that which came forth before, put on the garments of my statues, consisting of linen; offer ye to me of all fruit, give ye me shoulders of beef, fill ye for me the altar with milk, let incense be heaped thereon." (Breasted, *op. cit.*, II, 571.) "They buried him in his own sepulchres . . . and laid him in the bed which was filled with sweet odours and divers kinds of spices prepared by the apothecaries' art; and they made a very great burning for him." (II Chron. XVI, 14). At the time of the Periplus this was particularly the fashion in Rome, as Pliny observes with disapproval (VII, 42):—

"It is the luxury which is displayed by man, even in the paraphernalia of death, that has rendered Arabia thus "happy;" and which prompts him to bury with the dead what was originally understood to have been produced for the service of the gods. Those who are likely to be the best acquainted with the matter, assert that this country does not produce, in a whole year, so large a quantity of perfumes as was burnt by the Emperor Nero at the funeral obsequies of his wife Poppæa. And then let us only take into account the vast number of funerals that are celebrated throughout the whole world each year, and the heaps of odors that are piled up in honor of the bodies of the dead; the vast quantities, too, that are offered to the gods in single grains; and yet, when men were in the habit of offering up to them the salted cake, they did not show themselves any the less propitious; nay, rather, as the facts themselves prove, they were even more favorable to us then than they are now. How large a portion, too, I should like to know, of all these perfumes really comes to the gods of heaven, and the deities of the shades below?"

The customs ruling the gathering and shipment of frankincense are carefully described by Pliny (XII, 30), as follows:

"There is no country in the world," (forgetting, however, the Somali peninsula), "that produces frankincense except Arabia, and indeed not the whole of that. Almost in the very center of that region are the Atramitæ, a community of the Sabæi, the capital of whose kingdom is Sabota, a place situate on a lofty mountain. At a distance of eight stations from this is the incense-bearing region, known by the name of Saba (*Abasa?*). This district is inaccessible because of rocks on every side, while it is bounded on the right by the sea, from which it is shut out by tremendously high cliffs. . . . .

The forests extend 20 schœni in length and 10 schœni in breadth. (A schœnus = 40 stadia = 4 English miles.)

"Adjoining are the Minæi, a people of another community, through whose country is the sole transit for the frankincense, along a single narrow road. The Minæi were the first people who carried on any traffic in frankincense. . . . It is the Sabæi alone, and no other people among the Arabians, that behold the incense-tree;* and not all of them, for not over 3000 families have a right to that privilege by hereditary succession; for this reason these persons are called sacred, and are not allowed, while pruning the trees or gathering the harvest, to receive any pollution, either by intercourse with women or coming in contact with the dead; by these religious observances it is that the price of the commodity is so enhanced.

"The natural vintage takes place about the rising of the Dog-star, a period when the heat is most intense; on which occasion they cut the tree where the bark appears to be the fullest of juice, and extremely thin, from being distended to the greatest extent. The incision thus made is gradually extended, but nothing is removed; the consequence of which is, that an unctuous foam oozes forth, which gradually coagulates and thickens. When the nature of the locality requires it, this juice is received upon mats of palm-leaves, though in some places the space around the tree is made hard by being well rammed down for the purpose. The frankincense that is gathered after the former method is in the purest state, though that which falls upon the ground is the heaviest in weight.

"The forest is allotted in certain portions, and such is the mutual probity of the owners, that it is quite safe from all depredation; indeed, there is no one left to watch the tree after the incisions are made, and yet no one is ever known to plunder his neighbor. But, by Hercules! at Alexandria, where the incense is dressed for sale, the workshops can never be guarded with sufficient care; a seal is even placed upon the workmen's aprons and a mask put upon the head, or else a net with very close meshes, while the people are stripped naked before they are allowed to leave work. So true it is that punishments afford less security among us than is to be found by these Arabians amid their woods and forests!

"The incense which has accumulated during the summer is gath-

---

**Cf.* Virgil, *Georgics* II, 116-117:

> Divisæ arboribus patriæ. Sola India nigrum
> Fert ebenum, solis est turea virga Sabæis.

And again, I, 57:

> India mittit ebur, molles sua tura Sabæi.

ered in the autumn; it is the purest of all, and is of a white color. The second gathering takes place in the spring, incisions being made in the bark for that purpose during the winter; this, however, is of a red color, and not to be compared with the other incense."

And of the storage of all the incense of the country in the capital, Pliny gives a further account (XII, 32):

"The incense after being collected, is carried on camels' backs to Sabota, of which place a single gate is left open for its admission. To deviate from the high road while carrying it, the laws have made a capital offense. At this place the priests take by measure, and not by weight, a tenth part in honor of their god, whom they call Sabis; indeed, it is not allowable to dispose of it before this has been done; out of this tenth the public expenses are defrayed, for the divinity generously entertains all those strangers who have made a certain number of days' journey in coming thither. The incense can only be exported through the country of the Gebanitæ, and for this reason it is that a certain tax is paid to their king as well.

"There are certain portions also of the frankincense which are given to the priests and king's secretaries: and in addition to these, the keepers of it, as well as the soldiers who guard it, the gate-keepers and various other employees, have their share as well. And then besides, all along the route, there is at one place water to pay for, at another fodder, lodging of the stations and various taxes and imposts besides; the consequence of which is, that the expense for each camel before it arrives at the shores of our sea (the Mediterranean) is 688 denarii; after all this, too, there are certain payments still to be made to the farmers of the revenue of our empire.

"Hence a pound of the best incense sells at 6 denarii, of the second quality at 5, and of the third quality at 3 denarii."

27. **To Cana on rafts.**—This was the Dhofar, or "Sachalitic" frankincense, as distinguished from that of the Hadramaut valley, which would naturally go by camel direct to Sabbatha. Pliny (VI, 34) doubts the story of the inflated rafts, derived, he thinks, from a fancied resemblance to the name given the African tribe tribe using them—*Ascitæ*; the Greek word *askos* meaning "bladder." But the Ascitæ, as already shown, were from Asich (§ 33) and were the founders of Axum. And the inflated raft is authentic, being the well-known *kelek*, a type still in general use on the Euphrates, whence the migrating Arabs no doubt brought it to the south coast. This is probably, also, the "cargo-ship" of § 33, sent from Cana to Masira Island for tortoise-shell.

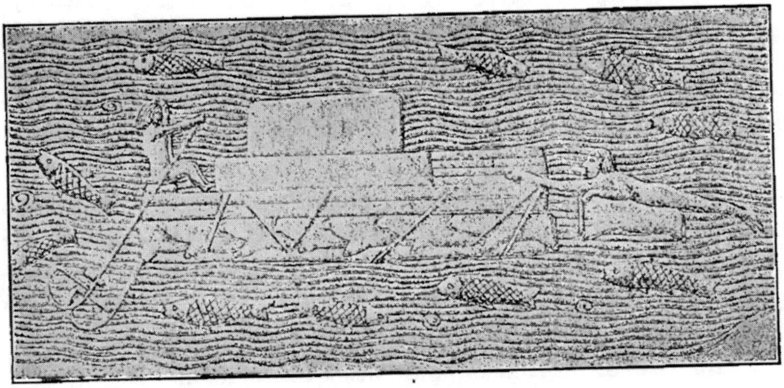

Inflated raft, from a relief at Nineveh. After Layard.

27. **The neighboring coast of Persia** means that part of the South Arabian coast between Kuria Muria Bay and Ras el Hadd, which had recently been conquered by the Parthian Empire. The word "Parthia" our author avoids, and it is likely that this coast did likewise, knowing rather the independent sphere of influence of the constituent Kingdom of Persia; which, while an integral part of the Arsacid possessions, maintained its local government to an extent never allowed the districts nearer Ctesiphon.

28. **Imported into this place.**—The list of imports indicates the nature of the trade: a little wheat, wine, and cheap clothing for the Hadramaut, and graven images for the household worship of its king; and the Mediterranean products, copper, tin, coral and storax, for re-shipment to India, where they were in demand (§ 49), and whither they went in Hadramaut shipping (§ 57), along with the frankincense produced in the country. The outlook of Hadramaut, then as now, was toward India by sea, and toward Egypt by land. Bent found the same conditions; the capital full of Parsee merchants, the natives going to India, the Straits and Java, and returning when they had amassed a competence; the English protectorate accepted because of England's domination of India, in the face of the religious convictions of rulers and people (*Geographical Journal*, IV, 322). Maltzan described the Hadrami traders in Cairo as the keenest of the lot, and spoke of their activities in the East; while the Dutch government, finding the islands of Java and Sumatra overrun with Hadramaut Arabs, stimulated inquiries of them in Batavia, which resulted in Van den Berg's book on their country, comprising more details than Bent could gather on the spot! An enterprising and uncompromising people, these Chatramotitæ, who may have been the

active power in the Minæan dynasty and the Sabæan that followed it, both of whom subsisted mainly on the carriage of frankincense to the north, in which they were the mediators between the profane world and the unpolluted caste of those who were able by propitiating the spirit of the sacred tree, to shed and gather its blood for the purification of mankind.

28. **Coral.**—This was the red coral of the Mediterranean, which commanded a high price in India and China, and was one of the principal Roman exports thither, being shipped to Barbaricum, Barygaza and Muziris. (See §§ 39, 49, and 56.) As an import at Cana it was intended for reshipment to India in Arab or Hindu bottoms.

28. **Storax** in Roman times meant two different things: one, a solid, was the resin of *Styrax officinalis*, order *Styracaceæ*, somewhat resembling benzoin, and used in incense. Liquid storax was the sap of *Liquidambar orientalis*, order *Hamamelidaceæ*, native in S. W. Asia Minor, and exported, according to Flückiger and Hanbury (*Pharmacographia*, pp. 271-6), as far as China. It was an expectorant and stimulant, useful in chronic bronchial affections. The Periplus does not distinguish between them, but Flückiger thinks that the storax dealt in at Cana was the liquid storax, destined for India and China; which would have had little use for an incense of less value than their own.

There was, however, a local use for storax in defending the frankincense gatherers from the "serpents" guarding the trees; see pp. 131-2.

Hirth in his *China and the Roman Orient* quotes Chinese annals covering this period, which state that the Syrians "collect all kinds of fragrant substances, the juice of which they boil into *su-ho*"—which he identifies with storax. Later annals, referring to the 6th century, are more complete. "Storax is made by mixing and boiling the juice of various fragrant trees; it is not a natural product. It is further said that the inhabitants of Ta-ts'in (Syria) gather the storax (plant, or parts of it), squeeze the juice out, and thus make a balsam (*hsiang-kao*); they then sell its dregs to the traders of other countries; it thus goes through many hands before reaching China, and, when arriving here, is not very fragrant."

These references indicate that the Chinese *su-ho* may not have been the product of one particular tree.

Glaser notes the name *su-ho*, which the Chinese annals further state to have been the name of the country producing the storax, and connect with the city *Li-kan*, supposed to be the same as *Rekam* or Petra, which was a point of shipment. He compares this with the *usu*-wood mentioned in several Assyrian inscriptions a tribute received from Arabia, and with a city called Usúu, placed by Delitzsch south of Akko on the sea—but Glaser thinks it may have been farther north, near Tyre.

28. **Aloes,** a bitter cathartic, being the dried juice exuded from *Aloe Perryi*, Baker, order *Liliaceæ*. This was from very early times an important article of commerce, and was produced almost entirely in Socotra. Another variety, less in demand, was from *Aloe hepatica*, native in South Arabia, particularly in the Hadramaut valley, but also as far as northern Oman. The failure of the Periplus to mention Socotrine aloes is surprising, unless the product of the island was monopolized in Cana. This is quite possible, as the island was subject to the Hadramaut.

In modern times these and many other varieties are in use, both wild and cultivated, throughout the tropics. Bent (*Southern Arabia*, p. 381) found very little aloes collected in Socotra, but many fields enclosed by walls, where it had formerly been produced. He describes the ancient method still used to prepare the gum; the thick leaves piled up until the juice exudes of their own weight, then allowed to dry in the sun for six weeks and finally packed in skins for shipment.

29. **The Bay of Sachalites.**—Until the Arabian coast was surveyed, there was an erroneous idea held by all the geographers, of a deep indentation in the coast-line between Ras el Kelb (14° 0′ N., 48° 45′ E.) and Ras Hasik (17° 23′ N., 55° 10′ E.), midway between which Ras Fartak, or Syagrus (14° 0′ N., 52° 12′ E.) bisected the supposed gulf. The error is very evident in Ptolemy's observations, which make Ras Fartak one of the most striking features of the coast, whereas its actual projection is unimportant, and its height less than that of the ranges farther east.

The name as applied in § 29 seems to apply to this whole strip of coast; in § 32 that part of it lying east of Ras Fartak is subdivided as the district of Omana; but in § 33 the name is resumed. This accords with the Arabian geographers, whose *Shehr* extended beyond Dhofar.

The word *Sachalites* is Hellenized from the Arabic *Sahil*, "coast," the same word that appears in East Africa as *Sawahil*, where the natives are called *Swahili*. This narrow strip of coast plain was different topographically and ethnologically from the Valley of Hadramaut.

The mediæval form of the word was Sheher or Shehr, and the mediæval port that replaced Cana was Es-shehr (the Escier of Marco Polo).

Ibn Khaldun (Kay's translation, p. 180) has the following account of this coast: "Ash-Shihr is, like Hijaz and Yaman, one of the kingdoms of the Arabian peninsula. It is separate from Hadramaut and Oman. There is no cultivation, neither are there palm-trees in the country. The wealth of the inhabitants consists of camels and goats. Their food is flesh, preparations of milk and small fish, with which they also feed their beasts. The country is also known as that of Mahra, and the camels called Mahriyah camels are reared in it. Ash-Shihr is sometimes conjoined with Oman, but it is contiguous to Hadramaut, and it has been described as constituting the *shores* of that country. It produces frankincense, and on the seashore the Shihrite ambergris is found. The Indian Ocean extends along the south and on the north Hadramaut, as if Shihr were the sea-shore of the latter. Both are under one king."

Hommel (in Hilprecht, *op. cit.* 700-1) argues for a derivation of this name from some word allied to the old Hebrew term for frankincense, *shekheleth;* which does not seem to have been in use on the south coast, while the evidence of the Arab writers is against him. (See also Glaser, *Skizze*, 178-9.) The Periplus in § 32 is against him, by using the adjective *Sachalitic* as qualifying "frankincense," which would be quite redundant.

Vaughn (*Pharm. Journ.* XII, 1853) speaks of the *Shaharree luban* from Arabia, as yielding higher prices than that produced in Africa; a term exactly corresponding to the "Sachalitic frankincense" of the Periplus.

29. **Always fatal.**—The reports of the unhealthy character of this coast, spread by the earliest traders, have been assumed to be their device to discourage competition. The fate of Niebuhr's party in Yemen, and the more recent tragic outcome of Bent's explorations, sufficiently confirm the dangers from malaria, dysentery and the scorching sun.

But aside from the question of physical health, the tapping of the frankincense tree was believed to be attended by special dangers, expressed in the faith of the people, and arising from the supposed divinity of the tree itself.

W. Robertson Smith (*Religion of the Semites*, p. 427) recounts this belief as follows:

"The religious value of incense was originally independent of animal sacrifice, for frankincense was the gum of a very holy species of tree, which was collected with religious precautions. Whether, therefore, the sacred odor was used in unguents or burned like an altar sacrifice, it appears to have owed its virtue, like the gum of the *samora* (acacia) tree, to the idea that it was the blood of an animate and divine plant."

And again (p. 133): "In Hadramaut it is still dangerous to touch the sensitive mimosa, because the spirit that resides in the plant will avenge the injury. The same idea appears in the story of Harb b. Omayya and Mirdas b. Abi Amir, historical persons who died a generation before Mohammed. When these two men set fire to an untrodden and tangled thicket, with the design to bring it under cultivation, the demons of the place flew away with doleful cries in the shape of white serpents, and the intruders died soon afterwards. The *jinn* it was believed slew them because they had set fire to their dwelling-place. Here the spirits of the trees take serpent form when they leave their natural seats, and similarly in Moslem superstition the *jinn* of the *ʻoshr* and *hamāta* are serpents which frequent trees of these species. But primarily supernatural life and power reside in the trees themselves, which are conceived as animate and even as rational . . Or again the value of the gum of the acacia as an amulet is connected with the idea that it is a clot of menstruous blood, *i. e.*, that the tree is a woman. And similarly the old Hebrew fables of trees that speak and act like human beings (Judg. IX, 8 ff., 2 Kings XIV, 9) have their original source in the savage personification of vegetable species."

The Romans and Greeks, it is well known, believed that the souls of the dead were incarnate in the bodies of serpents and revisited the earth in that form; hence, as Frazer has shown (*Golden Bough*, 3d ed., IV, 74), such practices as that described in the *Bacchæ* of Euripides, when nursing mothers entered the Dionysiac revels clad in deer-skins and girded with serpents, which they suckled. Hence, also, the Roman custom of keeping serpents in every household, and the serpent-worship connected with their god Aesculapius, to whose shrines, as well as to those of Adonis in Syria, childless women repaired that they might be quickened by a dead saint, a *jinn*, or by the god himself, in serpent form. Such was the belief concerning the births of Alexander of Macedon and the Emperor Augustus.

Herodotus refers to this same belief in two passages (III, 107 and II, 75) which have been laughed at as travellers' yarns. "The Arabians gather frankincense," he says, "by burning styrax, which the Phœnicians import into Greece; for winged serpents, small in size and various in form, guard the trees that bear frankincense, a great number round each tree. These are the same serpents that invade Egypt. They are driven from the trees by nothing else but the smoke of the styrax." That is, the wrath of the incense-spirit was appeased by the perfume provided by the styrax-spirit. And every spring, he says, these winged serpents flew into Egypt through a narrow pass near Buto, where they were met by the ibis and defeated; hence the veneration for the ibis in Egypt. Here is evidently a belief that the tree-spirit hovered over its blood as the traders carried it to market, and that the danger that threatened the Egyptians was averted by the defensive power of their own sacred bird. The location of this Buto is disputed, but it was probably along some ancient desert trade-route such as that between Coptos and Berenice at the time of the Periplus. Buto was also the name of an Egyptian deity, borrowed from "God's Land" (Yemen).

Theophrastus has the same story of the tree guarded by winged serpents, but refers it to cinnamon (*Hist. Plant.*, IX, 6).

According to Herodotus, all the fragrant gums of Arabia were similarly guarded, except myrrh; which may suggest that myrrh was from a more purely Joktanite district, less imbued with the animism of the earlier races of Arabia.

The same belief probably appears in the "fiery flying serpents" of Isaiah XXX, 60.

Medicinal waters were guarded by similar powers; a dragon sacred to Ares protected the sacred spring above Ismenian Apollo (Frazer, *Pausanias*, V, 43-5); while among the Arabs all medicinal waters were protected by *jinns* (W. Robertson Smith, *op. cit.*, 168).

The faith of the Incense-Land presents many features in common with that of the Greeks. While Frazer is no doubt right in warning against indiscriminate assimilation of deities Greek, Egyptian and Semitic, there is certainly some truth in the words of Euripides' Bacchus (son of Jove and Semele, daughter of the Phœnician Cadmus) who came to Greece "having left the wealthy lands of the Lydians and Phrygians and the sun-parched plains of the Persians, and the Bactrian walls; and having come over the stormy land of the Medes, and *the happy Arabia*, and all Asia which lies along the coast of the Salt Sea, . . . there having established my mysteries"—and "every one of these foreign nations celebrates these orgies."

According to Herodotus (III, 8 and I, 131), the only deities of the Incense-Land were Dionysus and Urania, whom they called Orotal and Alilat; while the Semitic people of Meroe (II, 29) worshipped Zeus (Ammon) and Bacchus (Osiris) whom Glaser assimilates with the Katabanic gods 'Am and Uthirat (*Punt und die Südaralischen Reiche*, 43). Now the invocations of Dionysus in the mysteries were "Evoe, *Sabai*, Bacchi, Hues, Attes, Attes, Hues!" and according to Cicero (*De natura deorum*, I, iii, 23) one of the names of Bacchus was *Sabazius;* in whose mysteries at Alexandria, we are told by Clement (*Protrept.* ii, 16) persons initiated had a serpent drawn through the bosom of their robes, and the reptile was identified with the god (Frazer, *Golden Bough*, IV, 76). Here seems to be some basis, at least, for identification of the god of the Incense-Land to whom Pliny gives the name *Sabis;* whom Glaser (*Punt*, etc., p. 46) thinks identical with Shams, the Sabæan sun-god, and whose name appears also in the capital city, Sabota or Sabbatha (Shabwa).

There is a suggestive similarity in the legions concerning the crater of Bir Barhut in the Hadramaut, and Aetna, on the top of which an ancient Latin poem describes the people offering incense to the celestial deities. Formerly, Frazer says, victims were sacrificed also, probably to appease the spirits who were supposed to dwell there.

The Abyssinian Chronicle, tracing the descent of the monarchs of that people who migrated from the Incense-Land, heads the list with "Arwê the Serpent" (Salt, *op. cit.*, p. 460) and Ludolfus in his *Commentaries* (III, 284) refers to the "great dragon who lived at Axum," said to have been burst asunder by the prayers of nine Christian saints. (See also James Fergusson, *Tree and Serpent Worship;* Plutarch, *De Iside et Osiride* and *De Defectu Oraculorum.*)

30. **Syagrus** is unquestionably Ras Fartak, 15° 36′ N., 52° 12′ E., a bluff headland rising to a height of about 2500 feet, visible for many miles along the coast. This name, meaning "wild boar" in Greek, is probably a corruption of the Arabic tribe-name *saukar*, plural *sawâkir*, appearing also in Saukira Bay, and in the modern village of Saghar. This was an incense-gathering folk, whose name Pliny assimilates to the Greek for "holy"—*sacros*, from *sakr*, the root-form of *saukar*. See Glaser, *Skizze*, 180.

Yet the modern name Fartak, according to Forster (*op. cit.* II, 171), has the same meaning, "Wild Boar's Snout," the mediæval Arabic geographers having possibly followed Ptolemy's nomenclature.

30. **Dioscorida,** (nearer the Arabian coast than the African in point of population and language, if not in location as our author asserts), continues its name in the modern Socotra (12° 30′ N., 54° 0′ E.). Both forms are corruptions of the Sanscrit *Dvipa Sukhâdâra*, meaning "Island abode of bliss." Agatharchides refers to it as "Island of the Blest," a stopping-place for the voyagers between India and Arabia. How ancient the Hindu name may be is unknown; the sense possibly antedates the language in which it is expressed. An Egyptian tale of the XIIth Egyptian dynasty (18th century B. C.), recounted by Golénischef (Report of the Vth Congress of Orientalists, Berlin, 1881), speaks of it as "Island of the Genius," *Pa-anch*, the home of the King of the Incense-Land; and in the "Genius" may be recognized the *jinn* or spirit of the sacred tree. There is good cause

for believing that this is also the "Isle of the Blest," the farthest point reached by the wandering hero of that Babylonian Odyssey, the narrative of Gilgamesh; which joins to the story of a search over the known world for the soul of a departed friend, found in the end by prayer offered to Nergal, god of the dead, the material record of an early migration around the shores of Arabia. The theory of this Cushite-Elamite migration, outlined by Glaser (*Skizze*, vol. II) is thus recounted by Hommel (*Ancient Hebrew Tradition*, p. 39):

"Egyptian records furnish us with an important piece of ethnological evidence. From the XIIth dynasty (2200 B. C.?) onwards a new race makes its appearance on the Egyptian horizon: the *Kashi* in Nubia. This name was originally applied to Elam (Babyl. *kashu: cf.* the *Kissioi* of Herodotus, the modern *Khuzistan; cf.* also *Cutch* and *Kachh* in India), and according to Hebrew translation, was afterwards given to various parts of central and southern Arabia; from this he argues that in very early times—prior to the 2d millennium B. C.—northeast Africa must have been colonized by the Elamites, who had to pass around Arabia on their way thither. This theory is supported by the fact that in the so-called Cushite languages of northeast Africa, such as the Galla, Somali, Beja, and other allied dialects, we find grammatical principles analogous to those of the early Egyptian and Semitic tongues combined with a totally dissimilar syntax presenting no analogy with that of the Semites or with any Negro tongue in Africa, but resembling closely the syntax of the Ural-altaic languages of Asia, to which . . . the Elamite language belongs. According to this view, the much-discussed Cushites (the Aethiopians of Homer and Herodotus) must originally have been Elamitic Kassites, who were scattered over Arabia and found their way to Africa. It is interesting to note that the Bible calls Nimrod a son of Cush, and that the name Gilgamesh has an Elamitic termination. What the Nimrod epic tells us of his wanderings around Arabia must therefore be regarded as a legendary version of the historical migration of the Kassites from Elam into East Africa. Nimrod is merely a personification of the Elamitic race-element of which traces are still to be found both in Arabia and in Nubia."

And in the same book, pp. 35-6, Hommel thus describes the references in the epic, which in its present form he dates at about 2000 B. C.:

"In the 9th canto we are told how he set out for the land of Mâshu (central Arabia), the gate of which (the rocky pass formed by the cliffs of Aga and Salma), was guarded by legendary scorpion-men. (Hence perhaps the name "land of darkness" applied to Arabia in early Hebrew annals.) For 12 miles the hero had to make his way through dense darkness; at length he came to an enclosed space by the sea-shore where dwelt the virgin goddess Sabitu; who tells him that "no one since eternal days has ever crossed the sea, save Shamash, the hero.

> "Difficult is the crossing, and extremely dangerous the way,
> And closed are the Waters of Death which bolt its entrance;
> How, then, Gilgamesh, wilt thou cross the sea?"

But Gilgamesh is directed to Arad-Ea, the sailor of Per-napishtim, who is in the forest felling a cedar. Him he asks to ferry him across to the "Isle of the Blest." After cutting 120 timbers 60 cubits long (surely not "oars," as the translation has it, but rather logs for an inflated raft) and smearing them with pitch,

> "Then Gilgamesh and Arad-Ea embarked;
> The ship tossed to and fro while they were on their way.
> A journey of forty and five days they accomplished in three days,
> And thus Arad-Ea arrived at the Waters of Death"—

which may have been Bab el Mandeb, and at the "Isle of the Blest" where dwelt Shamash-Napishtim, great-grandfather of Gilgamesh.

The island *Pa-anch* of the Egyptian tale is obviously the same as the incense-land *Panchaia* of Virgil (*Georgics* I, 213), and the tale itself indicates that Socotra was an important center of international trade not far from the time of Abraham. Here the occasional navies of Egypt met the peoples of Arabia and Africa and the traders of India, from the Gulf of Cambay and perhaps in greater numbers from the active ports in that ruined sea of past ages, the Rann of Cutch (the *Eirinon* of § 40); a condition not changed at the time of the Periplus, when the inhabitants were a "mixture of Arabs and Indians and Greeks," nor yet when Cosmas Indicopleustes visited the place, noting its conversion to Christianity, and observing that the Greek element was planted there by the Ptolemies. Marco Polo (III, 32) found still "a great deal of trade there, for many ships come from all quarters with goods to sell to the natives. A multitude of corsairs (called *Bawarij*, from Cutch and Gujarat) frequent the island; they come there and encamp and put up their plunder for sale; and this they do to good profit, for the Christians of the island purchase it knowing well that it is Saracen or Pagan gear."

The names *Pa-anch* and *Panchaia* Glaser would connect, as already noted, with such others as *Pano* and *Opone*, the land of *Punt* and the Puni or Phœnicians, whose sacred bird was likewise connected with Panchaia. Pliny gives the story (X, 2):

"The Phœnix, that famous bird of Arabia . . . the size of an eagle, and has a brilliant golden plumage around the neck, while the rest of the body is of a purple color; except the tail, which is azure, with long feathers intermingled of a roseate hue; the throat is adorned with a crest, and the head with a tuft of feathers. . . . It is sacred to the sun. . . . When old it builds a nest of cinnamon and sprigs of incense, which it fills with perfumes, and then lays its body upon them to die. From its bones and marrow there springs a small worm, which changes into a little bird; the first thing that it does is to perform the obsequies of its predecessor, and to carry the nest entire to the City of the Sun near Panchaia, and there deposit it upon the altar of that divinity. The revolution of the great year is completed with the life of this bird, and a new cycle comes round again with the same characteristics as the former one, in the seasons and appearance of the stars."

Seyffarth has supposed this to refer to the passage of Mercury every 625 years, and Glaser connects the legend with the hawk-faced Egyptian god Horus (*Khor*). Compare Job XXIX, 18: "Then I said, I shall die in my nest, and I shall multiply my days as the Phœnix" (*Khor* or *Khol*). The bird came from an Arabian land, hence his name from the people thereof; just as the Greeks gave the same name *phoinix* to the date-palm, native in that land; which may be assumed to have been the southern shore of the Persian Gulf, whence convulsions of nature, climatic or political changes, drove its inhabitants in opposite directions, carrying their culture with them and duplicating Persian Gulf place-names continuously in the Mediterranean and Erythræan Seas.

(See the introduction *Ueber die Völker und Sprachen Afrikas* in Lepsius' *Nubische Grammatik;* Glaser, *Punt und die Südarabischen Reiche*, and the reports of the Austrian South Arabian Expedition.)

30. **Great lizards, of which the flesh is eaten.**—These are probably *Varanus niloticus*, family *Varanidæ*, order *Lacertilia*, native throughout the African region, and attaining a length of more than five feet. Another species, *V. salvator*, while somewhat larger, seems to be native only in India and farther east. The flesh of all the *Varanidæ*, although offensive to the smell, is eaten by the natives, and considered equal to that of fowls. The name *Varanus* is from the Arabic *Ouaran*, lizard; which by a mistaken resemblance to the English "warn" has been rendered into a popular Latin name, *Monitor*. (*Cambridge Natural History*, VIII, 542-5.)

30. **Tortoise.**—It is uncertain what species are meant. The tortoise-shell of commerce is from *Chelone imbricata*, family *Chelonidæ*, the so-called "hawks-bill" turtle, found in all tropical waters, but seldom reaching a length of more than thirty inches. This is a "true

sea-tortoise," as our author puts it, but he goes on to describe a "mountain-tortoise, the largest and with the thickest shell," which may be *Chelone mydas*, the "green turtle" (also a sea-tortoise), but is more likely one of the gigantic land-tortoises (family *Testudinidæ*) which appear in many of the islands of the Western Indian Ocean; of which most are now extinct, (*Testudo grandidieri* only recently in Madagascar), while others, like *T. gigantea* and *T. daudini*, are still found in less frequented islands. The "land-tortoise" and the "white-tortoise" may include several species of *Cinyxis*, *Pyxis* and *Testudo*.

(See *Cambridge Natural History*, VIII, 364-387.)

30. **Cinnabar, that called Indian.**—(Dragon's blood.) The confusion between dragon's blood (the exudation of a dracæna) and our cinnabar (red sulphide of mercury) is of long standing, but less absurd than it seems at first sight. The story is given by Pliny (XXXIII, 38, and VIII, 12). The word *kinnabari*, he says, is properly the name given to the thick matter which issues from the dragon when crushed beneath the weight of the dying elephant, mixed with the blood of either animal. The occasions were the continual combats which were believed to take place between the two. The dragon was said to have a passion for elephant's blood; he twined himself around the elephant's trunk, fixed his teeth behind the ear, and drained all the blood at a draught; when the elephant fell dead to the ground, in his fall crushing the now intoxicated dragon. Any thick red earth was thus attributed to such combats, and given the name *kinnabari*. Originally red ochre (peroxide of iron), was probably the principal earth so named. Later the Spanish quicksilver earth (red sulphide of mercury), was given the same name and preferred as a pigment to the iron. Later, again, the exudations of *Dracæna cinnabari* in Socotra and *Dracæna schizantha* in Somaliland and Hadramaut (order *Dracæneæ*), and *Calamus draco* in India (order *Palmeæ*), were given the name *kinnabari*. Being of similar texture and appearance, the confusion is not surprising, as the Romans had no knowledge of chemistry.

Pliny noted errors made by physicians in his day, of prescribing the poisonous Spanish cinnabar instead of the Indian; and proposed a solution of the problem by calling the mercury earth *minium*, the ochre *miltos*, and the vegetable product *kinnabari*, but usage did not follow him. We now give the mercury earth the old Greek name for dragon's blood, and the dried juice we give the same name in English.

Wellsted (*Travels in Arabia*, 1838, II, 450-1) noted the two varieties of *Dracæna*, one of which had leaves the camels could eat, while the other was too bitter. Bent (*Southern Arabia*, 379, 381, 387) gives a good description of this peculiar tree, with its thick, twisted trunk and foliage resembling an umbrella turned inside out. He notes that very little is now exported from Socotra, the cultivated product from Sumatra and South America having superseded it. The method of gathering is the simplest possible, the dried juice deing knocked off the tree into bags, and the nicely-broken drops fetch the best price.

According to the Century Dictionary the word *cinnabar* is "of eastern origin: *cf.* Persian *zinjarf*, *zinjafr*, = Hindu *shangarf*, cinnabar."

The bit of folk-lore quoted by Pliny confirms the Indian connections of Socotra. Combats with a dragon or serpent for possession of a sacred place, or for the relief of a suffering people, appear in all the Mediterranean countries; such were related of Apollo at the oracle of Delphi, of Adonis in Syria (perpetuated in the modern faith in St. George in the same locality), to say nothing of Marduk and Tiamat in the Babylonian creation-story. But in all these legends, held by Semitic people or borrowed from them, the contender is a hero or a god; while in Socotra it is an elephant. Pliny offers a materialistic explanation, which is unconvincing because elephants are not found in Socotra or in the neighboring parts of Africa. It is evidently a local faith rather than a natural fact, and light may be thrown upon it by Bent's observation (*Southern Arabia*, 379) that dragon's blood is still called in Socotra "blood of two brothers."

In the Mediterranean world this gum was used medicinally and as a dye; in India it had also ceremonial uses. One must refer, not to the Buddhism of the Kushan dynasty, apparently dominant as far south as the modern Bombay at the time of the Periplus, but rather to the earlier faith—Brahmanism overlaid upon nature-worship, then prevalent among the Dravidian races farther south. The members of the Brahman triad were Brahma, Vishnu and Siva, the creator, preserver, and destroyer; they were worshipped especially at a shrine on an island in Bombay harbor, called Elephanta (in constant connection commercially with the Gulf of Aden), and an elephant's head was the visible emblem of the sacred syllable AUM, representing the triad, which was pronounced at the beginning and the end of any reading of the sacred books, and had many mystic properties. The elephant signified more particularly the first person of the triad, Brahma the creator, while the dragon or serpent, in the form of the cobra, represented Siva the destroyer; and these combats of Pliny, between an elephant and a dragon, the blood from which was called "blood of two brothers," seem to be a reflection of the perpetual conflict between the first and third persons of the Hindu triad.

It is notable that the Hindu name for Socotra appears likewise among the mysterious names of the seven manifestations of the power of AUM in their ritual: "Earth, Sky, Heaven, Middle Region, Place of Births, *Abode of the Blest,* Abode of Truth;" indicating that the island had its name from the Indian merchants who had "emigrated to carry on trade there" (§ 30), especially in this legendary gum of the dracæna, and suggesting that the name is as old as the XIIIth dynasty tale and the Gilgamesh epic.

Another survival of Hindu influence seems to be the *mateb* or blue silk neck-cord, the badge of baptism in modern Abyssinian Christianity, which suggests, more than any Arab custom, the *zennār* or sacred cord of the Brahman priest.

(See the references in J. G. Frazer's *Pausanias* and *Golden Bough;* Porphyry, *de Ant. Nymph.*, 268; *Asiatic Researches*, V, 348; Maurice, *Indian Antiquities.*)

30. **Yields no fruit.**—This must be understood as referring to agriculture; this island was particularly rich in natural products of commercial value. Aloes, dragon's blood and frankincense were all plentiful, also myrrh and other gums; but owing to the monopoly of the Chatramotitæ these went to market at Cana. Bent found many evidences of this early trade, but no present exploitation; the walled aloe-fields deserted, the frankincense, myrrh and dragon's blood uncollected, and the energies of the people employed in the production of clarified butter. The island seemed full of cattle, and the Sultan kept a special dhow to carry the skins and jars of clarified butter to the mainland, where it was in demand as far as Muscat and Zanzibar. (*Southern Arabia*, p. 346).

31. **Subject to the Frankincense Country.**—By speech, race and political allegiance Socotra has been joined to the Mahra district of South Arabia from time immemorial. La Roque's map of 1716 showed it "depending upon the Kingdom of Fartach" (Hogarth, *op. cit.*, p. 45); Wellsted, writing in 1838 (*op. cit.*, 450-3) found it jealously mentioned as a dependency of the Sheikh of Kissin, "formerly called King of Furtak;" and Bent found the same. (See also the numerous reports of the Austrian Expedition.)

31. **Garrisoned;** for defence against the two enemies of the Chatramotitæ, by whom they were hard pressed on either side: namely, the Homerites and the Parthians.

32. **The Bay of Omana,** being that portion of the Bay of Sachalites lying east of Syagrus, is the modern Kamar Bay. (16°

15′ N., 53° 30′ E.). The "mountains, high and rocky and steep, inhabited by cave-dwellers," are the modern Jebel Kamar and Jebel Gara, reaching altitudes of over 3,000 feet.

The name "Omana," the same as the modern Oman, seems to have extended at the time of the Periplus over a larger area, including much of the south shore of the Persian Gulf as well as the coast of South Arabia as far as Ras Hasik; all of which seems to have been subject to the Parthians, but recently—for Isidorus of Charax Spasini, writing in the time of Augustus, speaks of "Goæsus, King of the Omanitæ in the Frankincense Country." The coast between Ras Hasik and Ras Fartak, likewise associated with the name Omana in the Periplus, had fallen to the Chatramotitæ in the recent partition of the Incense-Land.

32. **The harbor called Moscha.**—This is identified with Khor Reiri (17° 2′ N., 54° 26′ E.), a protected inlet (now closed at low tide by a sand-bar); into which empties the Wadi Dirbat. It is a couple of miles east of the modern town of Taka, in the eastern part of the plain of Dhofar, a fertile strip of some 50 miles along the coast between Ras Risut and Ras Mirbat, surrounded by the Gara Mountains. Marco Polo describes it (III, xxxviii) as "a very good haven, so that there is a great traffic of shipping between this and India." It is, no doubt, the "harbor of the Abaseni" of Stephanus Byzantius. The ancient capital, Saphar (whence the modern name of Dhofar, confused by many mediæval geographers with Saphar or Zafar, the capital of the Homerites in Yemen) lay probably in the western part of the plain, near the modern Hafa.

Saphar seems to mean no more than "capital" or "royal residence," so that the true name of the ancient city is unknown. Ptolemy calls it *Abissa Polis*, "City of the Habashat."

The Plain of Dhofar, and the mountains behind it and for some distance beyond on either side, are the original, and perhaps always the most important, Incense-Land of Arabia. We are fortunate in having a vivid description of the whole region, by J. Theodore Bent (*Geographical Journal*, VI, 109-134, with a map facing page 204; reprinted in his *Southern Arabia*) with careful corrections by Glaser (*Die Abessinier in Arabien und Afrika*, 182-192). The plain is alluvial soil washed down from the mountains, which are of limestone, cavernous, and high enough to attract the rains; so that instead of the sandstone and volcanic rocks elsewhere on the south coast, here is "one large oasis by the sea," abundantly watered the year round, and producing crops of all kinds. The encircling mountains are the source of many streams, gathering in lakes on the upper levels and falling to the plain through densely wooded valleys. "Limes, cactus, aloes, and mimosa form on all sides a delightful forest, and the mountains above the lakes are clad almost to the summit with timber. Such a scene we never expected to witness in Arabia; it reminded us more of the rich valleys leading up to the tableland of Abyssinia. . . Sweet-scented white jessamine hung in garlands from the trees, and the air was fragrant with the odor of many flowers. . . It is probable that a knowledge of such valleys as these gained for Arabia its ancient reputation for floral wealth." And following up the stream leading to the ancient harbor, which falls over a remarkable limestone cliff, Bent found a broad grassy plain used for grazing, and in the midst a wooded lake, the center of the local faith of the Gara tribe; "they affirm that jinnies live in the water, and that whoever wets his feet here is sure to have fever. . . . Every November a fair is held here, to which all the Beduins of the Gara tribe come and make merry. The fair of Dirbat is considered by them the great festival of the year. A round rock was shown us on which the chief magician sits to exorcise the jinni of the lake, and around him the people dance."

A short way up the mountain-side just back of Hafa, the modern town, is "a great cave hung with stalactites, below which are the ruins of an ancient town, in the center of which is a natural hole 100 feet deep and about 50 in diameter; around this hole are the remains of walls, and the columns of a large entrance gate." This, the natives told Bent, was the "well of the Adites," no doubt an ancient oracle, mentioned as such by Ptolemy, Ibn Batuta and others.

Near Hafa are the ruins of the ancient capital, "by the sea, around an acropolis some 100 feet in height, encircled by a moat still full of water; and in the center, still connected with the sea, but almost silted up, is a tiny harbor. The ground is covered with the remains of ancient temples, the architecture of which at once connects them with that of the columns at Adulis, Coloe and Axum—after seeing which no doubt can be entertained that the same people built them all."

In Hafa the Bents found "a bazaar with frankincense in piles ready for shipment, just as depicted in the Deir el Bahri temple," while a large tract of country was still "covered with frankincense trees, with their bright green leaves like ash trees, their small green flowers, and their insignificant fruit." (See later, p. 218.)

This plain, with its ancient capital, Saphar, was the center of the ancient Cushite empire (or Adite, from Ad, grandson of Ham) which included most of Southern Arabia and much of East Africa; having a civilization and religion similar to and derived from the Chaldæan. About 1800 B. C., according to the Arab historians, Joktanite tribes entered and conquered South Arabia, but were largely absorbed by the Cushite stock; as a result of which the second, or Sabæan, empire of Ad was formed, in which the Joktanites became the sacred and land-owning caste, while the political and economic activities remained with the Cushites. This was probably the power that dealt with the Egyptians under the XVIIIth dynasty, as pictured at Deir-el-Bahri; concerning which the publication of the Egypt Exploration Fund seems a little too positive that the "Land of Punt" could not be in Arabia because the faces of the Punt people were not Semitic. The testimony of Arabia would be at fault if they were. Later the Sabæan Cushites, conquered by the Banu Ya'rub, a Joktanite stock from Yemen, migrated into Africa, and establishing themselves in Abyssinia, continued the ancient conflict for six centuries more.

The account of Ibn Khaldun (Kay's edition, pp. 179-80) gives a hint of the northern origin of the "Adites." Hadramaut, Ash-Shihr and Oman, he says, "originally belonged to Ad, from whose people it was conquered by the Banu Ya'rub, son of Kahtan (Joktan). It is said that the Banu Ad were led thither by Rukaym *son of Aram*, who had formerly visited the country in company with the Prophet Hud. He returned to the people of Ad and led them in ships to the country and to its invasion. They wrested it from the hands of its inhabitants, but they were themselves subsequently conquered by the Banu Ya'rub, son of Kahtan. Kahtan ruled over the country, and it was governed by his son Hadramaut, after whom it was named."

Makrizi varies the legend by making Ad son of Kahtan, by whom he was made ruler *over Babylonia*, and his brother Hadramaut over "Habassia;" and he preserves a memory of the trade of the Incense-Land with India, in the tale of a hero of that land who came by night to the land of the Indians in the form of a vulture, whence he returned bearing seeds of the green pepper, as proof of his journey.

It is regrettable that Bent could not have learned more of the local faith of the Gara tribe, exemplified at the annual reunion at the Dirbat lakes, which is probably an interesting survival of the ancient faith. For as the Mahri represent the Himyarite conquerors of the incense coast-land, so do the Gara represent to some extent the earlier inhabitants. Bent found a state of armed truce under the restraining influence of Muscat; Haines, Carter, and Cruttenden had found the villages of the plain fighting among themselves, and the mountain folk fighting with the plain, the gatherers with the overlords, as of old. Bent tells enough, however, to indicate the worship of the spirit of the lake, the waters of which might not be polluted by the foot of man; the propitiation of the spirit by the "chief magician" at the time of gathering the frankincense, and the celebration of the harvest by a "tribal dance" probably reminiscent of bacchanalian rites; after which the product is sent to Bombay for distribution, that the rest of the world, in the words of Pausanias (IX, 30) may "worship God with other people's incense."

The name *Moscha* is another of those place-names that are repeated along the coast from east to west, and survives in the modern Muscat, with which Müller mistakenly identifies this port. According to Forster (*op. cit.*, II, 174-5) this is an Arabic word meaning "inflated skin," from the Genaba "Fish-Eaters" or "floaters on skins." The word continues in the Greek *moschos,* calf. Glaser supposes the word to be the same as *Mocha,* and to signify a "commercial harbor," and to the author of the Periplus, and to Ptolemy, it is probable that *Moscha limên* meant "Incense Harbor;" *moschos* meaning also "musk," or in later Greek any perfume, even to that of strawberries; as indeed the same idea was uppermost with Camões (*Lusiad,* X, 201) and with Milton:—

> ——Now gentle gales,
> Fanning their odoriferous wings, dispense
> Native perfumes, and whisper whence they stole
> Those balmy spoils. As when to them who sail
> Beyond the Cape of Hope, and now are past
> Mozambic, off at sea northeast winds blow
> Sabean odors from the spicy shore
> Of Araby the Blest, with such delay
> Well pleased they slack their course, and many a league
> Cheered with the grateful smell old Ocean smiles:
>
> —*Paradise Lost,* IV, 156-165.

(See the works already cited of Bent, Wellsted, Glaser, Hommel, Zwemer, and Hogarth; Lenormant and Chevalier, *Manual of Ancient History of the East,* VII, 1-2; also J. B. Haines, in the *Journal of the Royal Geographical Society* for 1839 and 1845; H. J. Carter, in *Transactions of the Bombay Asiatic Society,* for 1845, 1847, and 1851; Makrizi *De Valle Hadramaut,* Bonn, 1866; Wellhausen, *Skizzen und Vorarbeiten,* III, 135-146.)

32. **The ship could not clear.**—Compare the trading of the Egyptian expeditions with the "chiefs of the land of Punt" over these "heaps of incense," and again Marco Polo's description (III, xxxvii): "'A great deal of white incense grows in this country, and brings in a great revenue to the Prince; for no one dares sell it to any one else; and whilst he takes it from the people at 10 livres of gold for the

hundredweight, he sells it to the merchants at 60 livres, so his profit is immense." And according to the *Marásid-al-Ittila'*, an Arab geographical dictionary of about the same period, "this incense is carefully watched, and can be taken only to Dhafár, where the Sultan keeps the best part for himself; the rest is made over to the people. But any one who should carry it elsewhere than to Dhafár would be put to death."

33. **Seven Islands called Zenobian.**—These are now called Kuria Muria, about 17° 20′ N., 56° E., and belong to England, which acquired them from the Sultan of Oman. In the time of the Periplus they belonged to their western neighbors, the Hadramaut.

The name *Zenobian* is Hellenized from the Arabic Zenâb or Genâb; the tribe of Beni Genâb having possessed the neighboring coast. This same tribal name, in the form of *Genabti*, appears in numerous Egyptian inscriptions as one of the peoples of the "Land of Punt." (See Glaser, *Punt und die Südarabischen Reiche*, p. 10.)

Concerning the relation of these islands to the early frankincense trade, a bit of folk-lore preserved by Marco Polo is particularly important. Pauthier in his French text rightly connects the story with the Kuria Muria group because of its geographical position; Yule and Cordier repudiate it as nonsense. Vincent, in his edition of the Periplus (II, 347) refers the "fable," without explanation, to these islands. Its actual source, so far as known, has not been observed.

About half-way between Makran and Socotra, Marco Polo says (III, xxxi), are the two islands "called Male and Female, lying about 30 miles distant from one another. . . . In the island called Male dwell the men alone, without their wives or any other women. Every year when the month of March arrives the men all set out for the other island, and tarry there for three months, to wit, March, April, May, dwelling with their wives for that space. At the end of these three months they return to their own island, and pursue their husbandry and trade for the other nine months. . . . As for the children which their wives bear to them, if they be girls they abide with their mothers; but if they be boys the mothers bring them up till they are fourteen, and then send them to the fathers. Such is the custom of these two islands. The wives do nothing but nurse their children and gather such fruits as their island produces; for their husbands do furnish them with all necessaries." (Yule's *Marco Polo*, Cordier's edition, II, 404-6.)

This story is a reflection of the belief, already noted from Pliny, that the ceremonial value of the incense depended on the personal purity of the gatherers, who were considered sacred. No man touching the tree, whether a proprietor according to the caste system of the Incense-Land, or a farmer or gatherer, slave or free, might undergo pollution through the presence of women or of the dead. The spirit of the tree was a woman, and the protecting serpents were the souls of the dead. If gathered without pollution, the incense constituted the most effective vehicle of prayer, and had also certain sovereign uses in purification after conjugal intercourse, availed of by both Arabians and Babylonians, as described by Herodotus (I, 198) and Strabo (XVI, i, 20).

Pliny's account of the Ascitæ, swimming to the mainland on inflated skins, has been noted. Stephanus Byzantius, writing in the 4th century A. D., says "beyond the Sabæi and the Chatramotitæ dwell the Abaseni, whose land yields myrrh, aloes, frankincense, cinnamon and the red plant which resembles the color of Tyrian purple (dragon's blood)." Pausanias in the 2d century (*de situ Græciæ*, VI, 269) mentions a "deep bay of the Erythræan Sea having islands, Abasa and Sacæa," which were the home of these same Ascitæ. Bent (*Southern Arabia*, p. 230) describes the "Jenefa" tribe on these Kuria Muria islands, pursuing sharks on inflated skins, and Wellsted (*op. cit.*, Chap. V) found the "Beni Geneba" spread all along the coasts of South Arabia and Oman, "shark-fishers swimming on inflated skins, and pastoral folk, living in skin tents, but under the S. W. monsoon retreating to caves," as noted in § 32. Lieut. Cruttenden (Trans. Bombay Geog. Soc., VII, 121; 1846) and General Miles (J. Geog. Soc., 1872) observe that the coast of South Arabia "is visited every season by parties of Somalis, who pay the Arabs for the privilege of collecting the frankincense."

Here is obviously the foundation for Marco Polo's tale. The wandering Beni Genâb, whose locality included the Kuria Muria islands and the coast north and east thereof, would act as fishermen and herdsmen during certain seasons, while during the remainder of the year they would engage in the more profitable occupation of incense gathering; in which they were subjected to the rigid rules maintained by the *Sayyid* or saintly caste of landed proprietors, themselves too dignified to do the work (Van den Berg, *op. cit.*, 40-44). When the first rush of sap occurred in the spring they left their wives perforce, to gather the best of the white gum, remaining on the incense-terraces for later gatherings until the trees became dormant again, when their work for that year was over and they returned home. And their sons would naturally remain with their mothers only during childhood; past which they would be under the same *tabu* as the grown men, and would begin work as gatherers.

Far from being a fairy tale, it is quite possible that at the time Marco Polo wrote—the caste-system of the Hadramaut being fully crystalized under the rule of Islam—this story of the Christian dwellers on the "Male and Female Islands" was literally true, as it was in the earlier times in the race-conflict between Joktanite overlords and Cushite gatherers.

The "Male Island" was, of course, the coast, and the Female included the entire group of islands; the Arabic dialects failing to distinguish between "coast" and "island."

33. **Beyond Moscha.**—The "mountain range along the shore" is the modern Jebel Samhan, and the name Asich is preserved in the modern Ras Hasik, 17° 23′ N., 55° 20′ E., as well as in the westernmost of the Kuria Muria Islands, which faces it.

33. **Sarapis** is the modern Masira Island, 20° 20′ N., 58° 40′ E., the first syllable only being from the native name, which our author assimilates to that of the Alexandrian Osiris of the bull-worship, Osor-Hapi, Sarapis, or in the Latin, Serapis. (Concerning this worship, in high favor at the time of the Periplus, see Strabo, book XVII, Plutarch, *de Iside et Osiride*, Maspéro, *Histoire Ancienne*, pp. 30 ff., Frazer's *Pausanias*, II, 175-6.)

The syllable *Sar*-apis or Ma-*sir*-a is probably the same as the tribe-name Au-*sar* or Ausan mentioned in § 15.

This island is curiously confused by Pausanias (VI, 26) with the Seres. After describing the Chinese silk culture, he observes: "the island of Seria is known to be situated in a recess of the Red Sea. But I have also heard that the island is formed, not by the Red Sea, but by a river named the Ser (this being Masira Channel), just as the Delta of Egypt is surrounded by the Nile and not by a sea; such also, it is said, is the island of Seria. Both the Seres and the inhabitants of the neighboring islands of Abasa and Sacæa are of the Aethiopian race; some say, however, that they are not Aethiopians, but a mixture of Scythians and Indians."

Here are confirmations of the Periplus, as to the possession of Masira and Kuria Muria by the Habashat, and as to the commercial activity of the Indo-Scythians, then in possession of the Indus valley.

The use of the "Arabian language" (Himyaritic or Hadramitic, represented by the modern Mahri), noted in § 33, confirms the accompanying statement that the island was then subject to Hadramaut, and its trade controlled from Cana. Ordinarily the connection would be rather with the "Fish-Eaters" of the adjoining Genaba coast, subject at that time to the Parthians, so that the language spoken would have been Aethiopic or Geez.

34. **A barbarous region which now belongs to Persia.** The Arabian coast beyond the Kuria Muria Islands, being now recently conquered by the Parthian Empire, at war with Rome, was inaccessible to the author of the Periplus and is described by him briefly and apparently from hearsay. His own sailing-course carried him "well out at sea" from Kuria Muria to Masira, and thence direct to the mouth of the Indus.

34. **Calæi Islands.**—These are the Daimaniyat Islands N. W. of Muscat (23° 48′ N., 58° 0′ E.), the distance being calculated from Masira. The name is obviously the same as the modern Kalhat, just north of Sur (22° 35′ N., 59° 29′ E.) an ancient trading port, mentioned by Pliny (VI, 32) as Acila (not to be confused with Ocelis in Yemen), "a city of the Sabæi (Asabi) a nation of tent dwellers, with numerous islands. This is their mart, from which persons embark for India."

On this coast, between Ras el Had and Muscat, are the modern ports of Kuryat and Sur, which, in the words of General Miles (*Journal of an Excursion in Oman*, Geographical Journal, VII, 335-6) "are the Karteia and Tsor, the Carthage and Tyre, of the race whom we know as Phœnicians, and who, earlier than the time of Solomon, had trading-stations along the southern coast of Arabia. Their convenient and important position just opposite India must have led to their early occupation by the merchants of those times who were engaged in exchanging the productions of the East and West."

An eastern migration of this tribe-name is strongly suggested in Kalat, city and district, in eastern Beluchistan.

34. **Very little civilized.**—This follows Fabricius' reading of a doubtful passage in the text; that offered by Müller, "who do not see well in the daytime," while less probable, recalls the fact noted by numerous observers in Oman, that a good proportion of the inhabitants suffer from ophthalmia or total blindness, due, largely, to the terrific heat of this coast; which was picturesquely described by Abd-er-Razzak, a 15th century Persian, as follows:

"The heat was so intense that it burned the marrow in the bones; the sword in its scabbard melted like wax, and the gems which adorned the handle of the dagger were reduced to coal. In the plains the chase became a matter of perfect ease, for the desert was filled with roasted gazelles." (Quoted from Curzon: *Persia and the Persian Question*. See also Hakluyt Society's ed., XXII, 9.)

35. **Calon mountain.**—While the name has a Greek form, and was supposed to mean "fair," it is the same as that of the islands and is probably a tribal name: "mountains of the Kalhat."

The range is the Jebel Akhdar, or "Green Mountains," behind Muscat, and about 10,000 feet in altitude. Good descriptions are given by Wellsted, Zwemer, and Hogarth, and of especial interest is the account of the fertile and populous Wadi Tyin, enclosed by these mountains, visited by General S. B. Miles (*op. cit.*).

35. **The pearl-mussel,** *Meleagrina margaritifera*, Ham., family *Aviculidæ*, is found in many parts of the Indian Ocean, but particularly on the southern shores of the Persian Gulf and in the shallow water between India and Ceylon. The pearl is a deposit formed around a foreign substance in the mantle of the mussel, generally a parasitic larva. Examination by Prof. Herdman at the Manaar fisheries indicated that the nucleus of the pearl was generally a Platyhelminthian parasite, which he identified as the larval condition of a cestode or tapeworm. This cestode passes from the body of the pearl mussel into that of a file-fish and thence into some larger animal, possibly the large Trygon or ray. (Watt, *op. cit.*, pp. 557-8; *Cambridge Natural History*, III, 100, 449.)

35. **Asabon mountains.**—This is another tribal name, "mountains of the Asabi," or Beni Assab, whom Wellsted described as still living there (*op. cit.*, I, 239-242), a people very different from the other tribes of Oman, living in exclusion in their mountains; and whom Zwemer (*Oman and Eastern Arabia*, in the Bulletin of the American Geographical Society, 1907; pp. 597-606) considers a remnant of the aboriginal race of South Arabia, their speech being allied to the Mahri and both to the ancient Himyaritic; who were probably not as Zwemer thinks, "driven northward by Semitic migration," but represent rather a relic of that pre-Joktanite southward migration around this very coast.

The mountain preserves the name, being now the Jebel Sibi, 2800 feet, 26° 20′ N., 56° 25′ E., continued at the end of the cape in the promontory of Ras Musandum.

35. **A round and high mountain called Semiramis.** Fabricius, following Sprenger and Ritter, identifies this with Kôh-i-mubârak, "Mountain of the Blest" (25° 50′ N., 57° 19′ E.), which, while not high, being only about 600 feet, is of the shape here described and directly on the strait.

Fabricius (p. 146) suggests that the name Semiramis is probably the Arabic *Shamarîda* "held precious." Ras Musandum has been a sacred spot to Arabian navigators from time immemorial. The classic geographers describe some of the practices of the ship-captains passing it, and Vincent tells of those in his time as follows (II, 354): "All the Arabian ships take their departure from it with some ceremonies of superstition, imploring a blessing on their voyage, and setting afloat a toy, like a vessel rigged and decorated, which, if it is dashed to pieces by the rocks, is to be accepted by the ocean as an offering for the escape of the vessel."

35. **Apologus.**—This was the city known as Obollah, which was an important port during Saracen times, and from which caravan-routes led in all directions. As "Ubulu, in the land of Bit-Yakin" it figures in many of the Babylonian and Assyrian inscriptions. It was among the conquered places named in the Nimrud Inscription of Tiglath-Pileser III (745-727 B. C.) whose arms were carried from Bit-Yakin "as far as the river Uknu (Cynos, Wadi ed Dawasir?) on the coast of the Lower Sea," and who received from Merodach-Baladan, of Yakin, king of the sea, a tribute of "gold—the dust of his land—precious stones, timber, striped clothing, spices of all kinds, cattle and sheep."

The location of Obollah seems always to have given it importance as a commercial center. Under the Seleucidæ, and in the time of Strabo, Teredon was the leading port; while in the time of the Periplus Obollah had regained its former position.

The name seems derived from Obal, son of Joktan (Gen. X, 28).

35. **Charax Spasini** is the modern Mohammarah (30° 24′ N., 48° 18′ E.), on the Shatt-el-Arab, at its confluence with the Karun. Pliny says (VI, 31) that it was founded by Alexander the Great, whose name it bore; destroyed by inundations of the rivers, rebuilt by Antiochus Epiphanes under the name of Antiochia, again overflowed, and again restored, protected by three miles of embankments, by Spasinus, "king of the neighboring Arabians, whom Juba has incorrectly described as a satrap of King Antiochus." Formerly, Pliny says, it stood near the shore and had a harbor of its own; "but now stands a considerable distance from the sea. In no part of the world have alluvial deposits been formed by the rivers more rapidly and to a greater extent than here." (At the present day it is about 40 miles from the gulf.)

Pliny's reference to the possession of the lower Tigris by an Arabian chieftain, the name of whose city he extends to the "Characene" district of Elymais, or Elam, indicates how large a part in the affairs of the Parthian Empire may have been played, at the date of the Periplus, by its subjects south of the Persian Gulf. Charax was an important stronghold of the Parthian Empire, protecting its shipping trade; and was the home of that Isidorus whose works, written in the time of the Roman Emperor Augustus, include the *Mansiones Parthicæ*, a detailed account of the overland caravan-route from Antioch in Syria to the borders of India; the same, probably, as the author of the "description of the world" mentioned by Pliny (VI, 31) who was commissioned by Augustus "to gather all necessary information in the east, when his eldest son was about to set out for Armenia to take the command against the Parthians and Arabians."

36. **A market-town of Persia called Ommana.**—The Roman geographers were much confused by similar statements concerning this port, and supposed that it was geographically, instead of politically, "of Persia," and that the "six days' sail" from the straits of Hormus mentioned in the Periplus, was eastward along the coast of Makran. But Pliny this time is better informed, and locates it on the Arabian side of the Persian Gulf, between the Peninsula of El Katar and Ras Musandum, then a Persian or Parthian dependency. Beyond the river Cynos (Wadi ed Dawâsir?) he says (VI, 32) "the navigation is impracticable on that side, according to Juba, on account of the rocks; and he has omitted all mention of Batrasave, a town of the Omani, and of the city of Omana, *which former writers have made out to be a famous port of Carmania*; as also of Homna and Attana, towns which at the present day, our merchants say, are by far the most famous ones in the Persian Sea."

The spelling "Ommana," as distinct from "Omana," is due to Ptolemy, and, while perhaps incorrect for the Periplus, it conveniently distinguishes between the two districts. Both are certainly the same as the modern Oman, which maintains a nominal, as a century ago a real, dominion over the whole coast-land from the bay of El Katan to that of Kuria Muria. This was no doubt the dominion of that Goæsus mentioned by Isidorus of Charax Spasini, "King of the Omanitæ in the Incense-Land," and had only recently come under the Parthian control. After numerous alternations between dependence and freedom the whole country submitted again to Persia in 1650, remaining under Persian control until 1741.

The exact location of the port of Ommana is uncertain owing to the limited knowledge yet at hand concerning this coast. Ptolemy confirms Pliny in locating it east of the peninsula, by a river Ommano, (possibly the Wadi Yabrin, an important trade-route) and Glaser argues strongly for the bay of El Katan. (*Skizze*, pp. 189-194.) Almost any location between Abu Thabi (24° 30′ N., 54° 21′ E.), and Khor ed Duan (24° 17′ N., 51° 27′ E.) might be possible, but the distance stated, six days, or 3000 stadia, from the straits, indicates Abu Thanni or Sabakha, at both of which there are fertile spots on the coast; El Mukabber on the Sabakha coast (24° N., 51° 45′ E.) being perhaps more closely in accord with Ptolemy.

Aside from the obvious linking of Apologus and Ommana as Persian Gulf ports, in §§ 35 and 36, the text gives two further proofs. The "sewed boats" are such as are still made along this coast, and the wine mentioned in § 36 as an export to India is referred to in § 49 as an import at Barygaza *from Arabia*. The "many pearls" exported, and in fact the whole list of imports and exports in § 36, suggest such a trade as now centers at Bahrein.

Müller, Fabricius, and McCrindle locate Ommana in the bay of Chahbar on the Makran coast (25° 15′ N., 60° 30′ E.), reckoning the six days' sail eastward from the Straits of Hormus; and Sir Thomas Holdich followed them in his *Notes on Ancient and Mediæval Makran* (Geographical Journal, 1896; VII, 393-6). It is notable that in his *Gates of India*, 1910, (pp. 299-300) he abandons this position and refers the activity of the Chahbar ports to the mediæval period. General S. B. Miles (Journal of the Royal Asiatic Society, N. S., X, pp. 164-5) argues for Sohar, on the Batineh coast of Oman, north of Muscat, the ocean terminus of an ancient and important caravan-route; but the location does not tally with the statement in the text, that Ommana was six days *through*, or *beyond*, the Straits.

Ommana was the center of an active and extensive shipping trade with India, conveniently located with reference to the trans-Arabian caravan-routes; and Glaser points out the probability that this coast of El Katan was also the "land of Ophir" of King Solomon's trading-voyages; a trading center where the products of the East were received and reshipped, or sent overland, to the Mediterranean.

36. **Copper** is here mentioned as an article of export from India to the Persian Gulf. It is no longer extensively produced in India, but was formerly smelted in considerable quantities in South India, Rajputana, and at various parts of the outer Himalaya, where a killas-like rock persists along the whole range and is known to be copper-bearing in Kullu, Garhwal, Nepal, Sikkim, and Bhutan. See the authorities cited in Watt, *Commercial Products of India*, p. 401.

But it is possible that this copper imported at Ommana included also European copper, exported from Cana (§ 28) to the Indus mouth and Barygaza (§§ 39 and 49) and thence reshipped to the Persian Gulf. During the suspension of trade between the Roman and Parthian Empires, owing to war, this would have been a natural trade arrangement.

Pliny (VI, 26) speaks of copper, iron, arsenic, and red lead, as exports of Carmania, whence they were shipped to Persian Gulf and Red Sea ports for distribution; indicating again that Ommana was no Carmanian port.

36. **Sandalwood.**—*Santalum album*, Linn., order *Santalaceæ*. A small evergreen tree native in the dry regions of South India (as the Western Ghats, Mysore, and Coimbatore); in North India chiefly as a cultivated plant. Sandalwood has been known in India from the most ancient times, the Sanskrit authors distinguishing various woods according to color. *Chandana* is the name for the series, *srikhanda* the tree, or white, sandal, and *pitachandana* the inferior, or yellow, sandal, both being derived from *Santalum album*. They distinguish two kinds of red sandal or *raktachandana*, namely, *Pterocarpus santalinus* and *Cæsalpinia sappan*.

This mention in the Periplus seems to be the earliest Roman reference to sandalwood. It is mentioned by Cosmas Indicopleustes (6th century A. D.) under the name *Tzandána;* and thereafter frequently by the early Arab traders who visited India and China. Cosmas and the Arabs attributed it to China, this mistake arising, as Watt points out (*op. cit.*, p. 976) from the fact that Chinese vessels at this time made the voyage between China and the Persian Gulf, stopping to trade in Ceylon and India, and disposing of their cargoes finally to the Bagdad merchants. The wood is not native of China.

According to experiments at the Royal Botanic Gardens at Calcutta, sandalwood is a root-parasite on many plants.

For further references see Lassen: *Indische Alterthumskunde*, I, 287.

36. **Teakwood.**—*Tectona grandis*, Linn., order *Verbenaceæ*. A large deciduous tree indigenous in both peninsulas of India. The wood is that chiefly exported from India at the present time, particularly from Burma, and is the most important building timber of the country.

Watt, (*op. cit.*, p. 1068), quoting Gamble, says that the western Indian teak region has for its northern limit the Narbada and Mahanadi rivers, although it is occasionally found farther north. Climatic changes since the date of the Periplus have probably restricted its area. It is plentiful in Bombay and Travancore.

The wood owes its value to its great durability, ascribed to the fact that it contains a large quantity of fluid resinous matter, which fills up the pores and resists the action of water. Watt mentions one structure known to be over 2000 years old, and the discovery of teak in the Mugheir ruins indicates its use there under Nabonidus (6th century B. C.), and possibly very much earlier.

36. **Blackwood.**—The text is *sasamin*, which Fabricius alters and translates "white mulberry," from conjecture only. McCrindle shows that the text refers to the wood still known in India as *sisam*,

which Watt describes (*op. cit.*, pp. 484-5) as one of the best hard-woods of the Panjab and Western India. It is very durable, does not warp or split, and is highly esteemed for all purposes where strength and elasticity are required—agricultural implements, carriage-frames and wheels, boat-building, etc.—as well as furniture and wood-carving. In Upper India the *sisam* takes the place of rosewood, to which it is closely related.

Watt distinguishes the true *sisam* or blackwood, *Dalbergia sissoo*, order *Leguminosæ*. The Indian rosewood, native somewhat farther south, is *Dalbergia latifolia*. *D. sissoo* is described as sub-Himalayan, gregarious on the banks of sandy, stony, torrential rivers, such as the Indus and Narbada, from which the Periplus says it was exported.

36. **Ebony.** — *Diospyros*, Linn., order *Ebenaceæ*. *Diospyros ebenum* and *D. melanoxylon* are the leading varieties producing ebony wood; India has also *D. embryopteris* and *D. tomentosa*.

This fine black heart-wood (from the date plum tree) has been in favor since the dawn of civilization. An Egyptian inscription of King Mernere, VIth dynasty (B. C. about 2500), mentions ebony as a product brought down from the "negro-land" on the Upper Nile; and the expedition of Queen Hatshepsut (XVIIIth dynasty, B. C. about 1500) brought it from the "Land of Punt," in this case probably from the Abyssinian highlands, although it might have come from India.

The earliest definite Old Testament reference is in Ezekiel XXVII, where it appears as a commodity in the trade of Tyre: "the men of Dedan were they merchants; many isles were the merchandise of thine hand; they brought thee for a present horns of ivory and ebony." If the Oxford editor's identification of Dedan with the south shore of the Persian Gulf be correct, this passage indicates a steady trade in ebony from India prior to the 7th century B. C., and exactly confirms the statement of the Periplus that it was shipped from Barygaza to Ommana and Apologus.

Pliny (XII, 8, 9) says that ebony came to Rome from both India and Egypt, and that the trade began after the victories of Pompey the Great in Asia. He notes two kinds, one precious, the other ordinary. Virgil (*Georgics* II, 116-117) speaks in glowing terms of the ebony tree, as peculiar to India. Herodotus, however, has preferred to ascribe it (III, 97) to Aethiopia, and states that the people of that country were in the habit of paying to the King of Persia, every third year, by way of tribute, 100 billets of ebony-wood, together with a certain quantity of gold and ivory.

36. **Sewed boats known as madarata.**—Glaser (*Skizze*, p. 190) shows this to be the Arabic *muddarra' at*, "fastened with palm fiber," which included, first, the fibers sheathing the base of the petioles of the date; and second, those taken from the husks of the cocoanut. This latter is what Marco Polo calls "Indian nut." It was a later cultivation in Arabia than the date, and the Periplus does not include it among Arabian exports, although noting it in § 33 as a product of Sarapis or Masira Island.

The text notes that these sewed boats were exported to "Arabia," meaning the South Coast, Yemen and Hadramaut.

Marco Polo (I, xix) gives a description of these craft, as follows: "Their ships are wretched affairs, and many of them get lost; for they have no iron fastenings, and are only stitched together with twine made from the husk of the Indian nut. They beat this nut until it becomes like horse-hair, and from that they spin twine, and with this stitch the planks of the ships together. It keeps well and is not corroded by the sea-water, but it will not stand well in a storm. The ships are not pitched, but are rubbed with fish-oil. They have one mast, one sail, and one rudder, and have no deck, but only a cover spread over the cargo when loaded. This cover consists of hides, and on the top of these hides they put the horses which they take to India for sale. They have no iron to make nails of, and for this reason they use only wooden trenails in their shipbuilding, and then stitch the planks with twine as I have told you. Hence 'tis a perilous business to go a voyage in one of those ships, and many of them are lost, for in that Sea of India the storms are often terrible."

Gemelli Carreri, who visited this coast in 1693-9, gives a similar description, quoted by Capt. A. W. Stiffe: *Former Trading Centers of the Persian Gulf*: Geographical Journal, XIII, 294:

"Instead of nails, which they are without, they use pegs of bamboo or cane, and further join the planks with strings made of rushes. For anchor, they have a large stone with a hole, and for oars, a stout stick with a little round plank attached to the end."

"Stitched vessels," Sir B. Frere writes (Yule's *Marco Polo*, Cordier's Ed., I, 117), "are still used. I have seen them of 200 tons burden, but they are being driven out by iron-fastened vessels, as iron gets cheaper, except where (as on the Malabar and Coromandel coasts) the pliancy of a stitched boat is useful in a surf." But the stitched build in the Gulf is now confined to fishing-boats.

The fish-oil used to rub the ships was whale-oil. The old Arab voyagers of the 9th century describe the fishermen of Siraf in the Gulf as cutting up the whale-blubber and drawing the oil from it, which was mixed with other stuff, and used to rub the joints of ships' planking. (Reinaud, *Relation des Voyages*, I, 146.)

Friar Odoric (*Journal*, Chap. II), writing of "Ormes," says "here also they use a kind of barque or ship called *Jase*, being compact together only with cords. And I went on board into one of them, wherein I could not find any iron at all, and in the space of twenty-eight days I arrived at the city of Thana" (on Salsette Island, a short distance north of Bombay), "wherein four of our friars were martyred for the faith of Christ."

*Jase*, Cordier observes, is the Arabic *Djehaz*.

"Sir John Mandeville" gives a legend arising from this method of construction (*Voyage and Travel*, Chap. LIII, p. 125, Ashton's edition.) "Near that isle (Hormus) there are ships without nails of iron or bonds, on account of the rocks of adamants (loadstones), for they are all-abundant there in that sea that it is marvellous to speak of, and if a ship passed there that had iron bonds or iron nails it would perish, for the adamant, by its nature, draws iron to it, and so it would draw the ship that it should never depart from it."

Theodore Bent (*Southern Arabia*, p. 8) describes these boats as having "very long-pointed bows, elegantly carved and decorated with shells. When the wind is contrary they are propelled by poles or paddles, consisting of boards of any shape, tied to the end of the poles with twine, and the oarsman always seats himself on the gunwales."

Zwemer, (*op. cit.*, p. 101), further confirms the Periplus:

"Even Sinbad the Sailor might recognize every rope and the odd spoon-shaped oars. All the boats have good lines and are well built by the natives of Indian timber. For the rest, all is of Bahrein manufacture except their pulley-blocks, which come from Bombay. Sail-cloth is woven at Menamah and ropes are twisted of date-fiber in rude ropewalks which have no machinery worth mentioning. Even the long soft iron nails are hammered out on the anvil one by one.

"Each boat has a sort of figurehead called the *kubait*, generally covered with the skin of a sheep or goat which was sacrificed when the boat was first launched. This blood-sacrifice Islam has never uprooted. The larger boats used in diving hold from twenty to forty men—less than half of whom are divers, while the others are rope-holders and oarsmen."

36. **Pearls inferior to those of India.**—This is said still to be the case, the Bahrein pearls being of a yellower tint than those of the Manaar fisheries, but holding their lustre better, particularly in tropical climates, and therefore always in demand in India.

36. **Purple.**—A dye derived from various species of *Murex*, family *Muricidæ*, and *Purpura*, family *Buccinidæ*. Pliny (IX, 60-63) tells of its use at the time of our author: "The purple has that exquisite juice which is so greatly sought after for the purpose of dyeing cloth. . . . This secretion consists of a tiny drop contained in a white vein, from which the precious liquid used for dyeing is distilled, being of the tint of a rose somewhat inclining to black. The rest of the body is entirely destitute of this juice. It is a great point to take the fish alive; for when it dies it spits out this juice. From the larger ones it is extracted after taking off the shell; but the smaller fish are crushed alive, together with the shells, upon which they eject this secretion.

"In Asia the best purple is that of Tyre, in Africa that of Meninx and Gætulia, and in Europe that of Laconia. . . .

"After it is taken the vein is extracted and salt is added. They are left to steep for three days, and are then boiled in vessels of tin, by moderate heat; while thus boiling the liquor is skimmed from time to time. About the tenth day the whole contents of the cauldron are in a liquid state; but until the color satisfies the liquor is still kept on the boil. The tint that inclines to red is looked upon as inferior to that which is of a blackish hue.

"The wool is left to lie in soak for five hours, and then, after carding it, it is thrown in again, until it has fully imbibed the color. The proper proportions for mixing are, for fifty pounds of wool, two hundred pounds of juice of the *buccinum* and one hundred and eleven of the juice of the *pelagiæ*. From this combination is produced the admirable tint known as amethyst color. To produce the Tyrian hue the wool is soaked in the juice of the *pelagiæ* while the mixture is in an uncooked and raw state; after which its tint is changed by being dipped in the juice of the *buccinum.* It is considered of the best quality when it has exactly the color of clotted blood, and is of a blackish hue to the sight, but of a shining appearance when held up to the light; hence it is that we find Homer speaking of purple blood. (*Iliad*, E. 83; P, 360.)

"Cornelius Nepos, who died in the reign of the late emperor Augustus, has left the following remarks: 'In the days of my youth the violet purple was in favor, a pound of which used to sell at 100 denarii; and not long after the Tarentine red was all the fashion. This last was succeeded by the Tyrian *dibapha* (double dyed) which could not be bought for even 1000 denarii per pound. Nowadays who is there who does not have purple hangings and coverings to his banqueting couches, even?' "

36. **Wine.**—This was probably date wine. Its destination, according to § 49, was India.

Sir B. Frere (*Amoen. Exot.*, 750, quoted in Yule's Marco Polo, Cordier's edition, I, 115) says "a spirit is still distilled from dates. It is mentioned by Strabo and Dioscorides, according to Kämpfer, who says it was in his time made under the name of a medicinal stomachic; the rich added *radix Chinæ* (rhubarb root), ambergris, and aromatic spices; the poor, licorice and Persian absinth."

This may, however, have included grape wine also, the mountain valleys of Oman having been the region originally producing the muscatel grape.

36. **Dates.**—*Phœnix dactylifera*, Linn., order *Palmeæ*. According to De Candolle (*L'Origine des Plantes Cultivées*, 240), it has existed from prehistoric times in the warm, dry zone which extends from Senegal to the Indus basin, principally between the parallels 15° and 20°. It was an important article of cultivation in Egypt, Arabia, Mesopotamia, and the Indus valley, for its wood, fiber, juice, and fruit.

Date-wine is mentioned as an Egyptian product shipped up the Nile to the "negro-land," in an inscription of the reign of Mernere, VIth dynasty, about 2600 B. C. (Breasted, *Ancient Records*, I, 336.) Dates appear as food, in an Abydos inscription of the reign of Khenzer, 17th century B. C. (I, 785). In the coronation inscription of Thothmes III and Queen Hatshepsut, XVIIIth dynasty, 15th century B. C., divine offerings to Amon-Re included wine, fowl, fruit, bread, vegetables, and dates (II, 159). Similar lists appear among the feasts and offerings from conquests during the same reign. Under Rameses III (IV, 244, 295, 299, 347) the *Papyrus Harris* notes as "offerings for new feasts," dates, 65,480 measures, 3,100 cut branches; again, 241,500 measures; and as "offerings to the Nile-god," dried dates, 11,871 measures, 1,396 jars; dates, 2,396 measures. Later, under Psamtik II, XXVIth dynasty, 6th century B. C. (IV, 944) the Adoption Stela of Nitocris says: "Sail was set; the great men took their weapons, and every noble had his provision, supplied with every good thing: bread, beer, oxen, dates, herbs."

The Greek name for the date, *phoinix,* was the same as that given the traders from Sidon and Tyre—Phœnicians—*Phoinikes,* whence numerous commentators, including Movers himself (*Die Phönizier*, II, i, 1) suppose the name of race and country to have been derived from the date, which was one of the leading exports to the northern Mediterranean; noting that the date-palm was a symbol of that race. But this in itself is better evidence that the tree received the name of the race, being truly, for Mediterranean peoples, the "tree of the Phœnicians." (So Lepsius in the introduction to his Nubian Grammar, *Ueber die Völker und Sprachen Afrikas*, and Glaser, *Punt und die Südarabischen Reiche*, 66-9).

Pliny (XIII, 7) has a long description of the date-palm and its numerous uses; he says the Arabian date was the best, and describes fully the different sexes of the trees, and the pollination of the flowers. A specially fine variety of dates comes from the "southern parts, called *Syagri*," which Pliny translates "wild boar," ascribing such a taste to the fruit; but as he connects it with the story of the phœnix, his account means no more, probably, than that the fruit came from the southern coast of Arabia. (See under § 30.)

The date-palm being diœcious, the flowers must be artificially fertilized in order to ripen the fruit, and this involves a knowledge of the habit of the tree, and regular cultivation, in favorable surroundings, including intense heat and drought during the fruiting season. These conditions are only partially fulfilled on the Syrian coast, and not at all on the Northern Mediterranean. They exist to perfection around the Persian Gulf, still the principal, and probably the earliest, source of supply. When the cultivation became important in Egypt is uncertain. The earliest inscription, in the VIth dynasty, refers not to the fruit, but to wine (made from the sap), and the time is centuries later than the first Egyptian Punt-voyages. Not until the 17th century does the Egyptian date-fruit appear as food, and not until the 15th as temple-offering. It is by no means impossible that Egypt owed this cultivation to its intercourse with Southern Arabia (the *Poen*-land) whence it had come in turn from the Persian Gulf, that original Phœnician, Erythræan, or in a larger sense Arabian, Sea.

Among the classical references to this home-land of the Phœnicians may be cited the Odyssey, IV, 81-5, where Sidonia and Aethiopia are conjoined, both clearly Arabian. (*cf.* Strabo, I, ii, 34-5; XVI, iii, 4, iv, 27.) The Old Testament gives numerous accounts of later migrations from that quarter to Palestine; *e. g.*, Zechariah IX, 6; Ezra IV, 9. The historian Justin (XVIII, 3, 2) gives the reason for the earlier migration: "the people of Tyre were sprung from the Phœnicians, who left their own land, being greatly distressed by earthquakes, and dwelt some time in the marsh-land of Babylonia, but later by the shores of the (Mediterranean) Sea, where they built a town which they called Sidon because of the abundance of the fish; for *sidôn* is the Phœnician word for fish." For the relation of this legend to the fish-god of Chaldæa, Oannes, see William Simpson, *The Jonah Legend.* The connection is noted by the poet Priscian, 843-7:

——sed litora iuxta
Phœnices vivunt, veteri cognomine dicti,
Quos misit quondam mare rubrum laudibus auctos,
Chaldæo nimium decoratam sanguine gentem,
Arcanisque Dei celebratam legibus unam.

According to Eiselen, *Sidon*, p. 12: (N. Y., 1907), the word *sidôn* means to *hunt* rather than to fish; but Simpson shows how readily the whole legend changed according to the surroundings of the people.

As to the race-origin of the Phœnicians, Syncellus derives them from "Iudadan," and Josephus (*Antiq. Jud.*, I, 6, 2) from Dedan, who was a son of Raamah, the son of Cush, according to the genealogy of Genesis X. A later account (*Chron. Pasch.*, I, 54) derives them from Jobab, whom that genealogy makes a son of Joktan. This would indicate for Phœnicia precisely the same experience as that of Southern Arabia: succeeding waves of migration, the later tending to become absorbed by the earlier.

It is significant that even the Greeks knew Phœnice as Canaan. Hecatæus refers to "Chna, as Phœnice was formerly called," and the name survived as late as an inscription of Antiochus Epiphanes, being connected with the legendary hero Chna, who can be no other than the Canaan of Genesis X, a brother to Cush, and who "begot Sidon, his first born." This word, according to Movers, means "lowland," particularly a strip of coast under the hills; and the same meaning is attached to Cush, Cutch, or in its Indian form, Kachh (Holdich, *Gates of India*, 35), and to the modern Sawahil of East Africa, and Shehr of South Arabia, the Sachalites of the Periplus.

Another derivation of "Phœnician" from *phonioi,* (bloody, murderous), rests on the activities of that people as sea-folk, traders and pirates. So do the habits of the race survive in the puns of the Greeks. The author of the Periplus (§ 33) found the dwellers on Sarapis Island *anthrôpois ponêrois*, and the Roman shipping out of Egypt had always to go armed or under convoy.

36. **Gold.**—The Periplus mentions gold coin as an export from Rome to India, but gold itself as an export from Ommana only, and as a product of the Ganges region.

Gold was an important product of Eastern Arabia, the best fields being in the middle courses of the Wadi er Rumma, the Wadi ed Dawasir, and the Wadi Yabrin. Glaser (*Skizze*, 347-9) locates altogether ten Arabian gold-fields. It was this production that led the Assyrian Tiglath-Pileser III to refer to gold as the "dust of the country" of Merodach-Baladan, king of Bit-Yakin, and to make the Persian Gulf ports centers also for the gold produced farther to the east, in Persia, Carmania, and the Himalayas. The watercourses of northeastern Arabia were probably the producing areas of the "land of Havilah" of Genesis II, 11-12, which could readily supply caravans for Chaldæa or Canaan; while El-Yemama and the southern fields, of richer yield, were probably the "land of Ophir" of Solomon's voyages (I Kings X); and according to the tribal genealogy (Genesis X, 29) Ophir was a son of Joktan and therefore purely Arabian. Into this voluminous controversy it is not necessary to go farther; the evidence is summed up by Glaser (*Skizze*, 357-388).

To the Greeks and Romans the "gold of Ophir" was known as *apyron*, which Diodorus Siculus (II, 50) assumes to be a Greek word, "without fire," and goes on to explain that it was not reduced by roasting the ores, but was found in the earth in shining lumps the size of chestnuts. Agatharchides and Pliny (XXI, 11) are both acquainted with this *apyron* gold, and Pliny (VI, 23) mentions also a river Apirus in Carmania, in a region previously described by Alexander's admiral, Onesicritus, as gold-producing.

To the mixed Cushite-Joktanite Havilah of Genesis, the Joktanite Ophir of I Kings, and the Cushite Raamah of Ezekiel XXVII, the cosmopolitan Ommana of the Periplus, under Parthian rule, was the lineal successor.

36. **Slaves.**—The Arabs were inveterate slave-traders then as now, and the ports of Oman were always active slave-markets. Arabian dominion along the African coast had this as one of its principal results, until checked by international agreement after European occupation.

37. **The Country of the Parsidæ, of another kingdom.** The author of the Periplus gives the name Persis, or Persia, to the whole Parthian Empire and refers to the recent conquests of that power in East and South Arabia. This "country of the Parsidæ" is Persia proper, including Carmania; a vassal state in the Arsacid following, which would not have shared, as a state, in the Arabian spoils of the empire. Ommana was subject to the Parthian monarchy, not to Persia proper.

Pliny (VI, 28) says "Persia is a country opulent even to luxury, but has long since changed its name for that of 'Parthia.'" Strabo (VI, iii, 24) observes more exactly, "at present the Persians are a separate people, governed by kings who are subject to other kings; to the kings of Macedon in former times, but now to those of Parthia."

37. **The Bay of Gedrosia,** while hardly a separate bay at all, may be assumed to be that bounded by the strip of coast between Ras Nuh (25° 7′ N., 62° 18′ E.) and Cape Monze (24° 45′ N., 66° 40′ E.), while the "jutting cape" is Ras Ormara (25° 6′ N., 64° 36′ E.).

37. **Oræa.**—The bay is the modern Sonmiani Bay (25° 0′ N., 66° 15′ E.), and the river is the Purali. According to Holdich, the Purali at the time of the Periplus emptied into a bay running some distance inland, and now silted up to the coast lines. These are the people described by Arrian (*Anabasis of Alexander*, VI, 21-2; *Indica*, XXI, XXIV, XXV) under the name of Oritæ or Oritians, their country being called Ora. The river was called Arabis, and on its eastern bank dwelt "an Indian nation called Arabians;" while the Oritæ on the western bank were "dressed like the Indians and equipped with similar weapons, but their language and customs were different." Their coast-line ran westward from the Arabis 160 miles; or, according to Pliny (VI, 25-6), 200 miles. They dwelt on the inland hills,

and along the shore, the latter being distinguished as Fish-Eaters. Alexander conquered the hill-folk and colonized their capital, Rhambacia, under his own name (Diodorus Siculus, XVI, 104); while Nearchus fought the coast-folk, reporting them "covered with hair on the body, their nails like wild birds' claws, used like iron for killing and splitting fish, and cutting soft wood; other things they cut with sharp stones, having no iron." Strabo (XV, ii, 2) describes their dwellings, made of the bones of whales and great shells; the ribs being used for beams and rafters, and the jawbones for doorways.

Here are more echoes of the early migrations that radiated outward from the Persian Gulf. The river Arabis and the Arabians are sufficiently reminiscent of Arabia, while the capital, Rhambacia, appears in Ptolemy as a city of the Rhamnæ, derived from the same source. The Oritæ are represented by the modern Brahui. Both names have the same meaning, "hill-folk," one in Greek and the other in Persian; but this is probably no more than a punning translation, like that of Makran into *Mahi Khuran*, Ichthyophagi, "fish-eaters."' The country of *Ora* is rather related to the *Uru* of Chaldæan place-names; being connected with the sun-worship that survived well into the Christian era. The Brahui are a Dravidian tribe left behind by their race on its way to Southern India; in earlier days the connection of both with the Persian Gulf was less broken. The name "Makran," as shown by Curzon (*Geographical Journal*, VII, 557) is Dravidian; while "Brahui" is thought to refer to the hero of the tribe, Braho, a name having the same root as Abraham (*Imperial Gazetteer of India*, IX, 15-17). These people are probably the same as those called by Herodotus (III, 94) "Asiatic Aethiopians," and again (VII, 70) as "Aethiopians from the sunrise," who were similar to the Aethiopians of Southern Arabia, both peoples being represented in the Persian army, and both having presumably sprung from the same stock; as witness the record in Genesis X, 7, "the sons of Cush: Seba, and Havilah, and Sabtah, and Raamah, and Sabteca; and the sons of Raamah: Sheba, and Dedan." The Cushite name seems to survive in Kej, in the valley of Makran; the "Kesmacoran" of Marco Polo.

The names of the Pharaohs of the XXVth or "Aethiopian" dynasty in Egypt, point to a like origin: Kashta, Shabaka, Piankhi (*cf.* Pa-anch, Poen, etc.), and Taharka (*cf.* Katar, Socotra).

Wellsted (I, ch. v) noted the strong racial similarity between the Beni Genâb in South Arabia and the people found on the Makran coast. Holdich (*Geographical Journal*, VII, 388) finds the island of Haftalu off the Makran coast—the Astola of Ptolemy, a center of the sun-worship—locally known as Serandip; a name which the Saracens gave to Ceylon, but which, apart from its last syllable, the Sanscrit *dvîpa*, island, seems to be related to the island of Sera, Sarapis, or Masira, off the Arabian coast.

The evident connection between both wings of this system is generalized by Götz (*Verkehrswege im Dienste des Welthandels*, 33-117) as "Turanian-Hamitic."

Holdich (*Gates of India*, 36) seems to have in mind a race resembling African negroes as the original of the "Asiatic Aethiopians" in Makran. But their descent should have been from the Persian Gulf. "Sir John Mandeville" (chap. xxiv) gives a legend which in some ways seems nearer the truth:

"Noah had three sons, Shem, Cham and Japhet . . . Cham, for his cruelty, took the greater and the best part, toward the east, that is clept Asia, and Shem took Africa, and Japhet took Europe . . . Cham was the greatest and the most mighty, and of him came more generations than of the other. And of his son Chuse was engendered Nimrod the giant, that began the foundation of the tower of Babylon . . . And of the generation of Cham be come the Paynims and divers folk that be in isles of the sea by all Ind."

See also Lassen, *op. cit.*, II, 187-191; Sir Thomas Holdich, *Gates of India*, pp. 146-161; and Gen. M. R. Haig, *Geographical Journal*, VII, 668-674.

37. **Rhambacia.**—The name of the capital is not given in the text, but Müller fills the lacuna with that mentioned by Arrian. Fabricius prefers Parsis, the capital of Gedrosia according to Ptolemy; but this place was probably much farther west.

Rhambacia was at no great distance from the modern Las Bela (26° 26′ N., 66° 20′ E.). According to Holdich (*Gates of India*, 320, 372), this whole neighborhood is full of evidences of early Arabian occupation; but the exact site is undetermined (150-1).

The tribe-name, Rhamnæ, Lassen connects with the Sanscrit *rāmana*, happy; which, while possibly a mere pun, may explain the Hindu name "blessed" for Socotra, which had been identified with Raamah, or Cushite stock generally. The root of So-*cotr*-a is evidently the same as El Katar peninsula, adjoining Bahrein.

*Shamarîda*, "precious," an Arabic name for the mountain at the Straits of Hormus; the "Island of the Blest" of the Babylonian Gilgamesh epic; may these reflect a Cushite race-appellation, like the "chosen people" of the Hebrews?

37. **Bdellium** is an aromatic gum exuded from *Balsamodendron mukul*, order *Burseraceæ*, a small tree native in northwestern India,

Beluchistan, Arabia, and East Africa; closely allied to myrrh and frankincense, and similarly employed from a very early date. According to Pliny (XII, 19) the best sort came from Bactria, and the inferior from India and Arabia, Media and Babylonia. The gum, he says, "ought to be transparent and the color of wax, odoriferous, unctuous when subjected to friction, and bitter to the taste, though without the slightest acidity. When used for sacred purposes it is steeped in wine, upon which it emits a still more powerful odor." The price in Rome he states as 3 denarii per pound, making it equal only to the poorest quality of myrrh.

Bdellium was particularly the product of the hills between the Hindu Kush and the Indian Ocean, and found its way westward through the Persian Gulf ports or overland through Babylonia. Arrian (*Anabasis*, VI, 22) tells how the army of Alexander, returning through the country of the Oritæ, came upon "many myrrh trees, larger than usual," from which the Phœnician traders accompanying the army gathered the gum and carried it away. It is probably the *bdolach* of Genesis II, 12, which reached the Hebrews from the "land of Havilah," the south shore of the Persian Gulf, the district of Ommana of § 36. *Bdolach*, however, is thought by some Hebrew authorities to be a crystalline gem; while the same word is used in the *Itinerary* of Benjamin of Tudela (Adler's edition, p. 98) for the *pearls* of the Bahrein fisheries, and with the same meaning in the *Meadows of Gold* of Mas'udi (Sprenger's translation, p. 544). See also Watt, *op. cit.*, p.400; Lassen, *op. cit.*, I, 290; Glaser, *Skizze*, 324-5, 364-7.

A passage in the Book of Numbers (XI, 7) is perhaps of interest as reflecting the ancient classification of fragrant gums by size and shape of the piece, rather than by distinguishing the tree. The manna of the Israelites is there said (in the R. V.) to have been "like coriander seed," and the "*appearance* thereof as the appearance of bdellium." The A. V. has the "*color* as the color of bdellium," in contradiction to Exodus XVI, 31, where the color was said to be white; bdellium being brown, like myrrh. The marginal note in the Revised Version, "Hebrew, *eye*," points to the true meaning. Glaser has already shown the *anti* incense of the Egyptian Punt Reliefs to be an Arabian word, *a-a-nete*, "tree-eyes" (*Punt und die Südarabischen Reiche*, p. 7), and to refer to the large lumps, exuded through cracks in the bark, or through substantial incisions, as distinguished from the small round drops, which were supposed to be tree-tears (§ 29) or the the tree-blood (as shown under § 29). The Hebrews after the Exodus would have had the same classification; so we may conclude that the author of Numbers meant to compare the small crystalline particles of the tamarisk-root syrup, which this manna probably was, to the "coriander seed, white," while the larger and coarser efflorescence was likened to the lumps of bdellium (or myrrh) with which he was familiar in the Levitical ritual.

38. **River Sinthus.**—The Sanscrit is *Sindhu*, and this form *Sinthus* is unusual in Greek, the river being generally known as *Indus*. Hindu names reaching the West generally drop the *s* and substitute *h* in Persian mouths. Sayce, in his *Hibbert Lectures* (pp. 136-138), argues on that basis for an ancient sea-trade between India and the Euphrates, from the word *sindhu*, or muslin, mentioned in an ancient Babylonian list of clothing. This is the *çadin* of the Old Testament, the *sindôn* of the Greeks.

38. **The greatest river.**—The Indus is exceeded by the Yangtse, Mekong, Irawadi, Brahmaputra, Ganges, and Shatt-el-Arab (none of which had been seen by the author of the Periplus). Its mean discharge is greater than that of the Hoang-ho. The sediment brought down is very great, forming in a single year an island 65 square miles in area and 1 yard deep. The delta projects little beyond the normal coast-line, owing to the distribution of silt along shore by the ocean currents, and to the deposit of the remainder in a vast submarine trough 1200 feet deep and upwards, due south of the river mouths. (Réclus, *Asia*, III, 139.)

38. **Graæ** is the Sanscrit *graha*. The presence of great water-snakes is still observed along these coasts, in the bays and at the mouths of rivers.

38. **Barbaricum.**—This name is evidently Hellenized from some Hindu word—one suspects *Bandar*, port, or possibly some name such as Bahardipur, which survives in the modern Delta. With the steady silting of the Delta, the remains of this port are probably yards deep in the soft alluvium, and very likely quite away from any of the present branches of the river.

Shah-bandar (Royal Port), formerly accessible to men-of-war, now lies far inland to the east of the present main channel of the Indus, while a similar fate has overtaken Ghora Bari or Vikkar, Keti, and other places. Since the opening of the Karachi railway most of these fever-stricken towns have been abandoned.

38. **Minnagara** was a name given temporarily to several cities of India during the period of the occupation by the Scyths (the Saka and Yueh-chi). After the collapse of the Indo-Scythian power these cities resumed their former names with their autonomy.

This Minnagara may be identified with the Patala of Alexander's expedition—the capital of the delta country. Vincent Smith locates it at Bahmanabad, 25° 50′ N., 68° 50′ E., about six miles west of the modern Mansuriyah. The site was discovered by M. Bellasis in 1854, and includes extensive prehistoric remains. The Indus delta has grown greatly since our author's time, and the courses of the Indus and all its tributaries have changed repeatedly. Vincent Smith says that the apex of the delta was probably about forty miles north of that place, approximately 26° 40′ N., 68° 30′ E. He cites numerous facts to prove that the coast-line has advanced anywhere from 20 to 40 miles since Alexander's time. The Rann of Cutch (Eirinon), now a salt marsh, he thinks was a broad open arm of the sea running to 25° N., with the eastern branch of the Indus emptying into it. Silt brought down by the river and formed into great bars washed southward by the violent tides, has now closed the mouth of the Rann almost entirely. The coast-line he thinks may have averaged 25° N. from Karachi to the Rann of Cutch.

Réclus (*Asia*, III, 142-5) says the Rann was probably open sea until about the 4th century, when a series of violent earthquakes elevated this whole region considerably. He reports ruins at Nagar Parkar, at the northeast corner, indicating a large sea-port trade there.

These changes may have been one cause of the great migration from this region to Java in the 6th and 7th centuries A. D.

38. **Parthian princes.**—The reference to the rule of "Parthian princes" over the "metropolis of Scythia" is very interesting. The first horde from Central Asia to overrun the Pamirs was the Saka, fleeing before the Yueh-chi. They settled in the Cabul valley, Seistan (Sakastene), and the lower Indus. By about 120 B. C. their leader Manes had established a kingdom at Cabul, subject to Parthia; his line was known as the "Indo-Parthian," but his race was, roughly speaking, "Scythian." Gradually the Yueh-chi pursued the Saka, first conquering Greek Bactria (they are referred to in this text, § 47, as the "very warlike nation of the Bactrians," living in the interior). Their king, Kadphises I, conquered Cashmere and the upper Indus; his son, Kadphises II, who acceded about 85 A. D., after a disastrous defeat at Kuché by the pursuer of the Yueh-chi, the Chinese conquering general Pan-Chao—about 90 A. D.—directed his armies southward and rapidly overran the Panjab and the lower Indus; and then reached the upper Ganges and interior points like Indore.

Both races were called by the Sanscrit "Min" or Scyths; the Periplus shows the Indo-Parthians ruling in the "metropolis of Scythia," then at the apex of the Indus delta; showing their power in the Kabul valley to have been broken already by the Yueh-chi or "Kushan" dynasty, but their subsequent complete conquest by the Yueh-chi had not yet been consummated.

The political conditions described in the Periplus were probably those that followed the death of Gondophares, the last powerful Indo-Parthian ruler in the Panjāb. This is supposed to have occurred about 51 A. D. After some years of anarchy and civil war, the Saka power was again consolidated under two lines of rulers; the "Northern Satraps" from the Indus to the Jumna, and the "Western Satraps" in Kāthiāwār, Gujarāt and Mālwā. Both these dynasties were at first tributary, and later subject to the Kushan power.

More distant southern raiding by the Indo-Parthians led to the "Pallava" dynasties along the west coast, which after a couple of centuries succeeded in gaining control of much of Southern India. These princes were thought by Fabricius to be the ones referred to in § 52 as ruling in Calliena, near Bombay.

39. **Figured linens.**—The text is *polymita.* Pliny (VIII, 74) says: "Babylon was very famous for making embroidery in different colors, and hence stuffs of this kind have obtained the name of Babylonian. The method of weaving cloth with more than two threads was invented at Alexandria; these cloths are called *polymita;* it was in Gaul that they were first divided into chequers."

Martial's epigram, "Cubicularia polymita" (XIV, 150) indicates that the Egyptian tissue was formed in a loom, like tapestry, and that the Babylonian was embroidered with the needle.

39. **Topaz.** The text is *chrysolithos.* This stone, according to Pliny, came from Aethiopia (Abyssinia) and islands in the Red Sea; and he adds that the best sort came from India. Here is a confusion between two kinds of stone; the Red Sea gem being the true topaz and the Indian either chrysolite or yellow sapphire. The knowledge of the Romans in regard to precious stones was vague, and we are apt to be led astray by assuming that because we have borrowed the Greek or Latin name we have applied it to the same stone.

The *chrysolithos* mentioned in the text was almost certainly our topaz, which was produced in abundance in the Red Sea islands, being an important item in the east-bound exports of Egypt, under the Ptolemies and Rome.

Strabo says: (XVI, iv, 6) "After Berenice is the island Ophiodes. It was cleared of the serpents by the king, on account of the topazes found there. . . . A body of men was appointed and maintained by the kings of Egypt to guard and maintain the place where these stones were found, and superintend the collection of them."

It is remarkable that the Periplus does not mention emeralds also as an export from Berenice to India. There was a large production from mines in the hills just west of our author's home. They may have fetched better prices in Rome than in India, where they would have had to compete with the native beryls.

For a description of these mines, as well as of the present appearance of the site of Berenice, see Bent, *Southern Arabia*, 291-7.

39. **Coral.** See also §§ 28 and 49. This was the red coral of the Western Mediterranean, which was one of the principal assets of the Roman Empire in its trade with the East. Pliny observes with some surprise (XXXII, 11) that coral was as highly prized in India as were pearls at Rome. The Gauls formerly ornamented their swords, shields and helmets with coral, but after the Indian trade was opened and its export value increased, it became extremely scarce with them.

Tavernier (*Travels in India*, II, xxiii) found the same conditions in his time: "Although coral does not rank among precious stones in Europe, it is nevertheless held in high esteem in the other quarters of the globe, and it is one of the most beautiful of nature's productions, so that there are some nations who prefer it to precious stones."

Ball, in his notes on Tavernier (II, 136), ascribes the preference for coral to "the way its tints adapt themselves to set off a dark skin, and also look well with a white garment."

It was also valued for its supposed sacred properties, and the belief in its uses as a charm continued through the Middle Ages, and even to the present day in Italy, where it is worn as a protection against the evil eye.

The principal red coral fisheries, then as now, were in Sicily, Sardinia and Corsica, near Naples, Leghorn and Genoa, in Catalonia, the Balearic Islands and the coasts of Tunis, Algeria and Morocco. Tavernier describes the method of fishing by "swabs"—crossed rafters, weighted, and bound with twisted hemp, which were let down and entangled amongst the coral on the rocky bottom, breaking more than they caught. For a fuller description, see *Encyclopædia Britannica*, art. "Coral."

Red coral is *Corallium rubrum*, family *Gorgonidæ*.

There was black coral in abundance in the Red Sea, and others along the Arabian coast, but these were not prized so highly. See Haeckel, *Arabische Korallen*.

39. **Costus.**—This is the cut root of *Saussurea lappa*, order *Compositæ*, a tall perennial, growing on the open slopes of the vale of Kashmir, and other high valleys of that region, at elevations of 8,000

to 13,000 feet. In the Roman Empire it was used as a culinary spice, also as a perfume, entering into many of the ointments, though in less quantity than pepper and cinnamon. The Revised Version gives it as a marginal reading for Exodus XXX, 24, in place of cassia, as one of the ingredients of the anointing oil of the Hebrew priests.

The root was dug up and cut into small pieces, and shipped to both Rome and China. Vincent describes the root as being the size of a finger; a yellowish woody part within a whitish bark. The cortex is brittle, warm, bitterish, and aromatic, of an agreeable smell, resembling orris.

Chishull (*Antiq. Asiat.*, 71) notes that the gifts from Seleucus Callinicus to the Milesians included frankincense, 10 talents; myrrh, 1 talent; cassia, 2 pounds; cinnamon, 2 pounds; costus, 1 pound.

By the Romans costus was often called simply *radix*, the root, as distinguished from nard, which was called *folium*, the leaf. The price in Rome is stated by Pliny (XII, 25) to have been 5 denarii per pound.

In modern Kashmir the collection of costus is a State monopoly, the product being sent to Calcutta and Bombay, for shipment to China and Red Sea ports. In China it is used in perfumes and as incense. In Kashmir it is used by shawl merchants to protect their fabrics from moths.

The word *costus* is from the Sanscrit *kushtha*, "standing in the earth."

See Watt, *op. cit.*, 980; Lassen, *op. cit.*, I, 287-8.

39. **Lycium.**—This was derived from varieties of the barberry growing in the Himalayas, at elevations of 6,000 to 10,000 feet. *Berberis lycium*, also *B. aristata*, *B. asiatica*, *B. vulgaris*, order *Berberidaceæ*.

From the roots and stems a yellow dye was prepared; while from the stem, fruit and root-bark was made an astringent medicine, the preparation of which is described by Pliny (XXIV, 77). "The branches and roots, which are intensely bitter, are pounded and then boiled for three days in a copper vessel; the woody parts then removed, and the decoction boiled again to the thickness of honey. It is mixed with various bitter extracts, and with a murca of olive oil, and ox-gall. The froth of this decoction is used as an ingredient in compositions for the eyes, and the other part as a face cosmetic, and for the cure of corroding sores, fluxes, and suppurations, for diseases of the throat and gums, for coughs, and locally for dressing open wounds." Many empty lycium pots have been found in the ruins of Herculaneum and Pompeii. (See also Watt, *op. cit.*, 130.)

39. **Nard** (the root, from the lowlands, as distinguished from spikenard, the leaf or flower, from the mountains, a totally different species). This is the root of the ginger-grass, *Cymbopogon schœnanthus*, order *Gramineæ*, native in the Western Panjab, India, Beluchistan and Persia, and the allied species, *C. jwarancusa*, native more to the east and south. It is closely allied to the Ceylon citronella, *C. nardus*.

From the root of this grass was derived an oil which was used in Roman commerce medicinally and as a perfume, and as an astringent in ointments.

This is no doubt the nard found by the army of Alexander on its homeward march, in the country of the Gedrosians, of which Arrian says (*Anabasis*, VI, 22): "This desert produces many odoriferous roots of nard, which the Phœnicians gathered; but much of it was trampled down by the army, and a sweet perfume was diffused far and wide over the land by the trampling; so great was the abundance of it."

39. **Turquoise.**—The text has *callean* stone, which seems the same as Pliny's *callaina* (XXXVII, 33), a stone that came from "the countries lying back of India," or more definitely, Khorassan. His description of the stone itself identifies it with our turquoise, which occurs abundantly in volcanic rocks intruding into sedimentary rocks in that district. The finest stones came from the mines near Maaden, about 48 miles north of Nishapur (the Nisæa of Alexander, 36° 30′ N., 58° 50′ E.). A natural trade-route from this locality would have been down the Kabul river, thence by the Indus to its mouth, where the author of the Periplus found the stones offered for sale.

(See also Heyd, *Commerce du Levant au Moyen Age*, II, 653; Ritter, *Erdkunde*, 325-330; Yule's Marco Polo, Cordier's ed., I, 92; Goodchild, *Precious Stones*, 284; Tavernier, *Travels in India*, II, xix: "Turquoise is only found in Persia . . . in two mines, one near Nishapur, the other five days' journey from it;" Lansdell, *Russian Central-Asia*, 515.)

39. **Lapis lazuli.**—The word in the text is *sappheiros*, and a natural inclination would be to assume this to be the same as our sapphire, which is also a product of India; but according to Pliny (XXXVII, 39) the stone known to the Romans as sapphire was an opaque blue stone with golden spots, which came from Media, that is, in a general way, from the country we call Persia. It was not suited for engraving because it was intersected with hard crystalline particles. This can be nothing but our lapis lazuli, which has been in demand from a very early time for ornament and also as a pigment, ultra-

marine, which was so extensively used by the Egyptians in their public buildings. Our sapphire seems to have been rather a product of southern India and Ceylon, and would hardly have been exported from the Indus valley.

Dionysius Periegetes refers to the "underlying rocks which gave birth to the beauteous tablets of the golden hued and azure sapphire stone which they detach from the parent rock," which seems to indicate lapis lazuli rather than our sapphire.

Goodchild (*Precious Stones*, p. 240), also thinks that this stone was almost certainly the sapphire of Theophrastus and other ancient writers. He says, "It has been known from very remote times, being much used by the Egyptians, and to a lesser extent by the Assyrians. Epiphanius, Bishop of Salamis, says the Tables of the Law given to Moses were inscribed on lapis lazuli. The Romans used it to some extent as a material for engraving on."

Lassen is of the same opinion. Beckmann (*Hist. Inv.*, 1, 467) writing in the 18th century, says that the real lapis lazuli came from Bokhara, particularly at Kalab and Badakshan; that it was sent thence to India, and from India to Europe. Some came also through Russia via Orenburg, but less than formerly. (The first route corresponds with the Periplus.) "I consider it as the sapphire of the ancients"—quoting Pliny, Isidori *Orig.* XVI, 9; Theophrast. *de Lapid.*; § 43; Dioscorides, V, 157; Dionys., *Orb. Desc.*, V, 1105; Epiphanius *de xii gemmis*, § 5; Marbodeus *de Lapidibus*, 55.

Tavernier, (*Travels in India*, II, xxv) speaks of a "mountain beyond Kashmir producing lapis," which Ball (*Economic Geology of India*, 529) locates near Firgámu in Badakshan, 36° 10′ N., 71° W. For a fuller description see Holdich, *Gates of India*, 426, 507.

Ultramarine was probably not the *cæruleum* of the Romans, which was rather copper ochre. Their blue glass was rather cobalt.

39. **Seric skins.**—Pliny (XXXIV, 41) says, "of all the different kinds of iron, the palm of excellence is awarded to that which is made by the Seres, who send it to us with their tissues and skins; next to which, in quality, is the Parthian iron." And again (XXXVII, 77) "the most valuable products furnished by the coverings of animals are the skins which the Seres dye."

These passages are sufficient answer to those who have doubted this statement in the Periplus. (Vincent, II, 390; Müller I, 288, opposed to whom see Fabricius, p. 151.) There is no more reason why furs should not have been sent overland across Asia in the 1st century than in the 16th to the 19th, when the trade was most important. Consider, for instance, the difficulty even to-day, in getting Russian sables to market, and how much easier to get the various wild animal skins from Tibet and Turkestan to the Indus mouth!

As to the "most excellent iron of the Seres" mentioned by Pliny, it is open to question whether this was not Indian steel, more correctly described in the Periplus as coming from the Gulf of Cambay to the Somali coast and Egypt. It was produced in Haidarábád, a short distance north of Golconda, and was shipped to the Panjab and Persia to be made into steel; the famous Damascus blades of the middle ages being derived mainly from this source. (Tavernier, *Travels*, Ball's ed., I, 157.) See also under § 6.

39. **Cloth.**—It is uncertain whether this should be connected with the following item, yarn, both being silk, or whether it is a separate item. If the latter, as seems probable, it would be muslin, as noted under §38—the *sindôn* of the Greeks, long a staple product of the Panjab and Sind.

39. **Silk yarn.**—According to the Periplus, the Roman traders found silk at the mouths of the Indus and Ganges, at the Gulf of Cambay, and in Travancore, whither it had been brought by various routes from N. W. China.

The principal highway for silk, at this time as well as later, was through Turkestan and Parthia. As the demand in Mediterranean countries grew more insistent, the restrictions of the Parthian government became more severe, and quarrels over the silk trade were at the root of more than one war between Rome and Parthia, or later between the Byzantine Empire and Sassanian Persia. This effort of Constantinople to reach China direct, without dependence on Mesopotamia, led to alliances with Abyssinia, for the sea trade, and with the Turks, for a route north of the Caspian; but no permanent result was reached until the 6th century, when a couple of Christian monks under Justinian succeeded in bringing back from China the jealously-guarded silk-worm's eggs, from which the silk culture was introduced into Greece, and imports from the East diminished.

At the time of the Periplus, Rome and Parthia being at war, the sea-route was the only one open to the Roman silk traders.

See also under §§ 49, 56 and 64.

39. **Indigo,** a dye produced from *Indigofera tinctoria*, Linn., order *Leguminosæ;* and allied species, of which about 25 exist in Western India alone, and about 300 in other tropical regions. Concerning the modern production see Watt (*op. cit.*, 664). It was valued in Western Asia, Egypt, and the Mediterranean countries as a dye and a medicine. Pliny says (XXXV, 25-7):

"We have indicum, a substance imported from India, with the composition of which I am unacquainted. When broken small it is of a black appearance, but when diluted it exhibits a wondrous combination of purple and deep azure. There is another kind of it which floats in the caldrons in the purple dye-houses, and is the scum of the purple dye. . . . If used as a medicine, indicum acts as a sedative for ague and other shivering fits and desiccates sores."

Marco Polo says (III, xxii) "it is made of a certain herb which is gathered, and (after the roots have been removed) is put into great vessels upon which they pour water and lave it until the whole of the plant is decomposed. They then put this liquid in the sun, which is tremendously hot there, so that it boils and coagulates, and becomes such as we see it. They then divide it into pieces of four ounces each, and in that form it is exported to our ports."

40. **The Gulf of Eirinon** is the strange expanse now known as the Rinn or Rann (Wilderness) of Cutch, the name coming from the crescent-shaped rocky island bordering it on the south. It is a uniform saline plain about 140 miles long, and reaching 60 miles from shore to shore; and in the dry season (of the N. E. monsoon) it is dry and firm, 10 to 20 inches above sea-level. It opens seaward by a narrow channel, and west of Cutch the northern Rann communicates through a second channel with the Rann, which is connected with the low-lying coast of the Gulf of Cutch. In the rainy season (of the S. W. monsoon) the sea is driven through these channels by the wind, and the rain descending from the hills also flows into it, forming a sheet of stagnant water about 3 feet deep. But the ground is so level that the Rann is never deep enough to stop the camel caravans, which cross it at all seasons, traveling by night, to avoid the terrible heat and refraction, and the illusions of the mirages which constantly hover over the Rann. The guidance of stars and compass is preferred.

This saline plain was certainly at one time flooded by the sea, as shown by the abundance of salt and by the remains of vessels dug up near the neighboring villages. Old harbor works are observed near Nagar Parkar, on the eastern side of the Rann. Within historical times it was probably the scene of an active sea-trade; even in modern times the port of Mandavi, on the southern coast of Cutch, carries on a direct trade with Zanzibar, in small vessels averaging 50 tons, of less than 10 feet draught.

We are here again reminded of the ancient Turanian (Accadian-Dravidian) sea trade, which must have centered in these bays.

The whole area was probably raised by some great earthquake.

The upheaval is too regular to have occurred by ordinary causes. At the time of the Periplus it seems to have been open water, although shoal, with a clear opening into the ocean below the Indus delta, and with a branch of the Indus running into it. Now the Indus delta is pushed very much farther south, and the scour of the tides has carried its alluvium along the coast, almost blocking up the Rann; while the branch that watered it no longer flows in that direction.

One is led to surmise that the great migration from Cutch and Gujarat to Java, which occurred in the 6th and 7th centuries, and which led to the establishment of Buddhist kingdoms there (surviving in the tremendous temples of Boroboedor and Brambanan) may have been due even more to this cause than to the invasion of hostile Aryan tribes from the upper Indus. The conversion of a navigable bay into a salt desert, and the diversion of the rivers that watered it, must have spelled ruin and starvation to multitudes of its agricultural and seafaring inhabitants, who would have been forced to migrate on a scale unusual in history.

Geological considerations tend to confirm the tradition, otherwise unsupported by historic evidence, that the Indus was formerly deflected by the Rohri Hills directly into the Rann of Cutch, where it was joined by the river which was supposed to have formed a continuation of the Sutlej and Sarasvati through the now dried-up Hakra (Wahind) canal. During exceptional floods the waters of the Indus still overflow into the eastern desert and even into the Rann. Other channels traversing the desert farther south still attest the incessant shifting of the main stream in its search for the most favorable seaward outlet. According to Burns, a branch of the Indus known as the Purana, or "Ancient," still flowed in 1672 about 120 miles east of the present mouth.

The constant shiftings of the river-bed toward the west have rendered the eastern regions continually more arid, and have changed many river-channels into salt-pits. In the year 1909 a city of 25,000 inhabitants, Dera Ghazi Khan, was almost annihilated by the Indus.

The name Eirinon, Rinn or Rann is from the Sanscrit *aranya* or *irina*, a waste or swamp.

40. **The Gulf of Baraca** is the modern Gulf of Cutch. Whether the name survives in the modern Dwarka (22° 22′ N., 69° 5′ E.), is uncertain. It seems to be the same as *Bahlika*, which is associated with Surāshtra in the *Mahābhārata*, the *Rāmāyana* and the *Vishnu Purāna*.

41. **Ariaca.**—This word in the text is very uncertain. Lassen thinks that the name is properly the Sanscrit *Latica* (pronounced *Larica*)

and included the land on both sides of the Gulf of Cambay. Ptolemy also gives the name *Larica*. An inscription of Asoka mentions *Latica*. The earliest form seems to have been *Rāstika* or *Rāshtrika*, "belonging to the kingdom." This word appears also in *Syrastrene*. The Prakrit form of this word *Rāshtra* survives also in the modern Marātha (*Mahārāshtra*). (Lassen, I, 108.) Another explanation derives Ariaca from *Aparāntikā*, an old name for the western seaboard.

(Pandit Bhagvānlāl Indraji, in *Indian Antiquary*, VII, 259-263.)

According to Réclus (*Asia*, III, 165) both Cutch and Kāthiāwār (Baraca and Syrastrene) were originally islands. This whole area has been raised in historical times. The land connecting Kāthiāwār with the mainland is not over 50 feet above sea-level and is full of marine remains.

Its position seaward made it early a centre of trade, and a great mixture of races—also an asylum for refugees, political and religious.

41. **Nambanus.**—The text is *Mambarus*. This is probably the same as the Saka ruler Nahapāna. See under § 52.

41. **Abiria.**—This is the native *Abhira*, which Lassen (I, 538-9), argues must have been the Biblical Ophir. In the account of the Ophir trade given in I Kings, IX, 26-28; I Kings, X, 11; II Chronicles VIII, 17, and IX, 10, the products mentioned are gold, sandalwood(?), precious stones, ivory, silver, apes and peacocks. The word translated ape, Lassen remarks, is *kophi*, not a Hebrew word, but derived from the Sanscrit word *kapi*. The word for ivory is noted under § 49. The word for peacock, *tukhi-im*, is the Sanscrit *sikhi*, called in Malabar, *togei*.

Sandalwood, Lassen thinks, was the *almug* or *algum*, which he derives from the Sanscrit *valgu*, Malabar *valgum*. Lassen also refers to the Indian city Sophir (the Suppara of § 52).

But the location of Ophir in India is impossible. The land of Abhira, the modern Gujarāt, is and was purely an agricultural country. dealing in none of the products mentioned, and is at the northern end of India's west coast, not the southern, from which these products came. Later scholarship is sufficiently sure in locating Ophir on the Arabian coast of the Persian Gulf, but the Indian names for the products mentioned proved clearly enough that it was a trading center dealing with India, even if the land itself was not Indian.

The name, too, has a suggestive similarity. Just as we have Cutch, Kachh, Khuzistan=Kassites, and "wretched Cush," so Abhira, Apir, Ophir suggest the same Dravidian-Accadian activity between India, the Persian Gulf, and Africa, which later gave way to a Semitic, native Arabian activity. This would have been a couple of thousand years before Solomon's day.

41. **Syrastrene.**—Sanscrit, *Surāshtra;* the modern Kāthiāwār. The name survives in the modern Surat, which owes its name to Arabic domination. At the time of the Periplus this peninsula, together with the opposite coast of Cutch and Cambay, was subject to the Saka or Indo-Parthian dynasties.

41. **A fertile country.**—Gujarāt is still one of the richest regions in India, its prosperity being largely due to the 60 seaports fringing its coast-lines and to the fertility of its deep black soil, which is particularly adapted to the cultivation of cotton. Horses, cattle, sheep and grain are exported in large numbers to Bombay and other parts of India.

41. **Rice.**—*Oryza*, Linn., order *Gramineæ.* The species now most generally cultivated is *Oryza sativa.* There are various wild varieties, one of importance being *Oryza coarctata* (Roxb.) or *O. triticoides,* which was native in the Indus and Ganges valleys, and also apparently in Mesopotamia (see Watt, *op. cit.*, 823-5). This wild variety resembles wheat and seems to have been mistaken for it by Strabo and some of the Greek writers on India.

*Oryza sativa,* the cultivated form, is native in India, Burma, and Southern China. It is the principal food of Asia, and doubtless was so at the time of the Periplus, when it was exported to Arabia and East Africa. It was cultivated in China, according to Stanislas Julien, as early as 2800 B. C., and probably somewhat later in India. Watt thinks the cultivation began rather in Turkestan, whence it spread to China, India and Persia in the order named, the changing climate also forcing its wild habitat southwards. He thinks that coincides with the region through which the Dravidian invaders passed until they culminated in the Tamil civilization. He also cautions against the tempting derivation of the Greek word *oryza* and the Arabic *al-ruzz* (from which the modern *rice, riso, riz, arroz,* etc.), from the Tamil *arisi,* thinking that they are rather from the old Persian *virinzi* (Sanscrit *vrihi*), indicating an early connection before migrations had radiated from Central Asia.

41. **Sesame oil,** expressed from the seeds of *Sesamum Indicum,* D. C., order *Pedalineæ*; an annual plant cultivated throughout the tropical and subtropical regions of the globe for the oil obtained from the seed. Originally, perhaps, it was a native of Africa, but was regularly cultivated in India long before it reached the Mediterranean countries. At the time of the Periplus it is safe to assume that sesame

was an important crop throughout India and the warmer parts of Central Asia. Our author shows us that the oil was exported from the Gulf of Cambay to both Arabia and Africa, whence doubtless it was reshipped to the Roman world.

According to the statistics given by Watt (*op. cit.*, 982) the area under cultivation in India in 1904-5 was over 4,000,000 acres, of which about 700,000 was in the Cambay states.

In modern India the oil is largely used for culinary purposes, in anointing the body, in soap manufacture, and as a lamp-oil. It is also used as an adulterant of *ghi* or clarified butter.

It is a yellow oil, without smell, and not liable to become rancid. In many properties it closely resembles olive oil, and is similarly used where the olive oil is not cultivated. It is extracted by simple expression in mills. Strabo (XVI, i, 20) refers to the ancient custom in Mesopotamia of anointing the body with sesame oil.

41. **Clarified Butter.**—The text is *boutyron* (see also under § 14). This is not fresh butter made from cream, but rather the Indian *ghi*, an oil reduced from butter. Fabricius says that it could not have been transported from India to Africa under the tropical sun, and would read *bosmoros*, an Indian grain; but *ghi* stands long journeys to-day and might very likely have been in demand in the 1st century on the African coast, which produced no oil except from the cocoanut palm. According to Watt (*op. cit.*, 478) *ghi* is an oil decanted after heating the butter about twelve hours, during which the moisture is driven off and the residue (casein, etc.) is deposited as a sediment. The butter thus loses about 25 per cent of its bulk. It is made from buffalo's milk rather than cow's.

*Ghi* is mentioned in some of the most ancient of the Hindu classics.

If carefully enclosed in leather skins or earthen pots, while still hot, it may be preserved for many years without requiring the aid of salt or other preservatives. Fryer, in 1672-81, speaks of tanks of *ghi* in the Deccan, 400 years old, of great value medicinally, and high price.

This word *boutyron* has been variously emended by the commentators, all of whom had fresh butter in mind, although Lassen should have been familiar with the durability of clarified butter, and with the probability of its export from the rich agricultural region of Gujarat.

Lassen, Oppert and others, following a mention of *boutyros* by Theophrastus, identify it with asafœtida, by way of the Sanscrit *bhutari* ("the enemy of evil spirits"). But asafœtida was a product of Afghanistan and would have been brought to the Indus mouth rather than to Barygaza. While Theophrastus may have referred to it as *boutyros*, the Romans knew it more intimately as *laser*, which is the word that the author of the Periplus would probably have used. It entered into Roman medicine as a remedy for fevers and tropical digestive disorders. (Pliny, XIX, 15).

Fabricius needlessly alters the text to read *bosmoros*, a grain, which he does not identify. McCrindle suggests wild barley or millet. The following passages from Strabo throw some light on that question:

He says (XV, ii, 13) "By the vapors which ascend from so many rivers, and by the Etesian winds, India, as Eratosthenes states, is watered by the summer rains, and the level country is inundated. During the rainy season, flax and millet, as well as sesamum, rice and bosmoros are sown; and in the winter season, wheat, barley, pulse, and other esculents with which we are unacquainted." And again:

(XV, ii, 18) "Onesicritus says of bosmoros that it is a smaller grain than wheat, and is grown in countries between rivers. It is roasted after being threshed out, and the men are bound by oath not to take it away before it has been roasted, to prevent the seed from being exported."

The treasuring of this *bosmoros* and the prejudice against its exportation indicate the native millet, which was regarded as particularly pure, and was the grain most used for temple-offerings.

Other grains which might suggest themselves, are the African millets, *Holcus sorghum* (Hindu *juár*) or Kaffir corn (see Pliny, XVIII, 10, for description of its remarkable size and prolific increase) and *Pennisetum typhoideum* (Hindu, *bájra*) or spiked millet. Both are important crops in modern India, but were probably brought from Africa more recently than the date of the Periplus, and being native in Somaliland, would not be probable articles of import there.

Wild barley, suggested by McCrindle, was also native in Egypt and Somaliland, and therefore not likely to have been imported.

Another possible grain is the Indus valley wild rice, *Oryza coarctata* (Hindu, *barirdhan*), which has been confused with wheat. See Watt, p. 823.

The common millet, *Panicum miliaceum*, while grown in India, was native in Egypt and the Mediterranean countries.

Altogether the *bosmoroi* of Strabo was most probably "Poor man's millet," *Panicum Crus-galli;* which is extensively cultivated to-day in China and Japan as well as India. The native name given it in Bengal, *bura shama*, might readily be Hellenized into *bosmoros*.

According to Watt (*op. cit.*, 843) *Panicum Crus-galli*, order *Gramineæ*, is a large, coarse plant, preferring wet ground, such as borders of ponds and banks of streams. It is extensively cultivated as a rainy-season crop over most of India—on the Himalayas to 6500 feet. It thrives on light sandy soils and is often cultivated when the rains are over, on the banks of rich silt deposited by rivers. The yield is fifty fold in good soil. It is the quickest-growing millet, harvested sometimes in six weeks, and is consumed chiefly by the poorer classes, for whom it is useful because it ripens early and affords a cheap article of food before *bâjra* and the other millets.

41. **Cotton and the Indian cloths.**—These were the *monachê, molochinê*, and *sagmatogênê* of §§ 6 and 14. The account given by Tavernier throws some light on the earlier production. He says (*op. cit.*, II, xii) "White cotton cloths come to Renonsari (near Surat) and Broach, where they have the means of bleaching them in large fields, on account of the quantity of lemons growing in the neighborhood. . . . The cloths are 21 cubits long when crude, but only 20 cubits when bleached. There are both broad and narrow kinds. The broad are 1⅓ cubit wide, and the piece is 20 cubits long." And again: "The cotton cloths to be dyed red, blue, or black, are taken uncolored to Agra and Ahmadābād, because these two towns are near the place where the indigo is made, which is used in dyeing. The cheaper kinds are exported to the coast of Melinde (the Azania of the Periplus), and they constitute the principal trade done by the Governor of Mozambique, who sells them to the Kaffirs to carry into the country of the Abyssins and the kingdom of Saba, because these people, not using soap, need only rinse out these cloths."

Vincent's translation of *sagmatogênê* by "stuffing," that is, unspun cotton, is supported by Tavernier, who says "the unspun cottons from Gujarāt do not go to Europe, being too bulky and of too small value, and they are only exported to the Red Sea, Hormus, and Bassora."

Marco Polo (III, 26) says of this locality: "They have also a great deal of cotton. Their cotton trees are of very great size, growing six paces high, and attaining to an age of 20 years. (*Gossypium arboreum.*) It is to be observed, however, that, when the trees are so old as that, the cotton is not good to spin, but only to quilt or stuff beds withal. Up to the age of 12 years, indeed, the trees give good spinning cotton, but from that age to 20 years the produce is inferior."

Pliny also (XII, 21) quotes from Theophrastus a description of the tree cotton, contrasting it with silk: "trees that bear wool, but of a different nature from those of the Seres; as in these trees the leaves produce nothing at all, and indeed might very readily be taken for those of the vine, were it not that they are of smaller size. They bear a kind of gourd, about the size of a quince, which when ripe bursts asunder and discloses a ball of down, from which a costly kind of linen cloth is made."

41. **Minnagara.**—This capital was identified by Müller with the modern Indore, but according to Vincent Smith (*op. cit.*, 192-3) may be the ancient town of Madhyamikā or Nāgarī, one of the oldest sites in India, of which the ruins still exist, about eleven miles north of Chitōr (24° 53′ N., 74° 39′ E.).

McCrindle and Fabricius prefer, but quite conjecturally, to place it in Kāthiāwār; but the text indicates the mainland in observing that from Minnagara cotton cloth was "brought down," by river presumably, to Barygaza.

The name Minnagara means "City of the Min," which was the Hindu name for the Saka invaders.

41. **Barygaza.**—This is the modern Broach (21° 42′ N., 72° 59′E.). The Greek name is from the Prakrit *Bharukacha*, supposed to be a corruption of *Bhrigukachha*, "the plain of Bhrigu," who was a local hero. Here is at least a suggestion of Dravidian connection with the Brahui of Gedrosia, their hero Braho and their *Kach* place-names.

The district of Barygaza was an important part of the empire of Chandragupta Maurya, who is said to have resided at Suklatirtha. After the collapse of his dynasty it fell into the hands of the Saka princes, who were in power at the time of the Periplus.

41. **Signs of the Expedition of Alexander.**—The Greek army reached Jhelum (32° 56′ N., 73° 47′ E.) on the river of the same name. Somewhat above that place, on the opposite side of the river, Vincent Smith locates the field of his battle with Porus. (*Early History of India*, 71-8.) Alexander then penetrated to Gurdaspur, on the Sutlej river, about 50 miles N. E. from Amritsar. Here he began his retreat. The author of the Periplus is mistaken in supposing that the Macedonians got beyond the Indus region, and is probably quoting what was told him by some trader at Barygaza, who would hardly have distinguished Alexander from Asoka. Under the caste system the traders were not concerned with the religious or political activities of the country, and those concerned with foreign trade were often, as now, mere outcasts; while even had they been informed, they would have been quite equal to attributing anything, for the moment, to Alexander, out of deference to their Greek customers, who were far more interested in his exploits than any Hindu could be.

41. **The promontory of Papica** is Goaphat, or Gopinath Point.

42. **Another gulf.**—This is the Gulf of Cambay.

42. **Bæones** is Piram Island opposite the mouth of the Narbada (21° 36′ N., 72° 21′ E.), as shown on the following map. Diu Island, the modern Portuguese possession, preferred by Vincent, does not conform to the sailing-course of the Periplus, as shown by Müller (I, 290.)

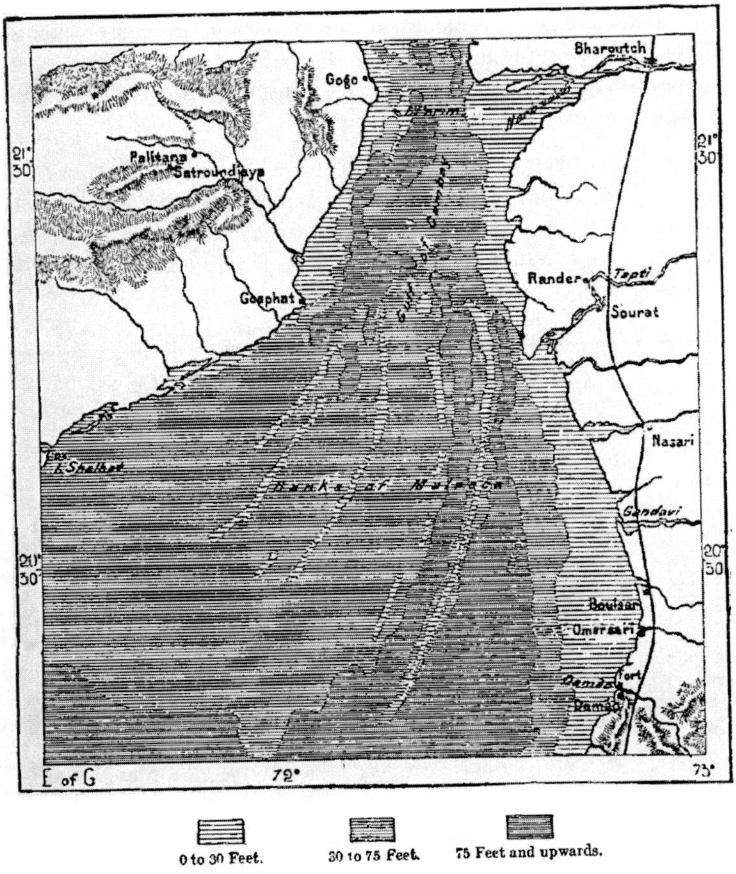


According to the *Imperial Gazetteer*, XX, 149-150, it is a reef of rock partly covered by brown sand, and is surrounded by rocky reefs rising to the surface from a depth of 60 to 70 feet. To avoid the tide-currents, chopping sea and sunken reefs, boats have still to follow the course toward the Narbada, as described in the Periplus.

42. **The great river Mais** is the modern Mahi, emptying into the head of the gulf, at the city of Cambay. (22° 18′ N., 72° 40′ E.)

42. **The river Nammadus**—Hindu, Narmada—is the modern Narbada or Nerbudda.

43. **Hard to navigate.**—The sketch-map on the preceding page, from Réclus, *Asia*, Vol. III, illustrates the difficulties.

Herone shoal is no doubt the long bar at the eastern side of the gulf, and Cammoni would be at the end of the promontory that lies to the N. W. of the mouth of the Tapti River, the entrance to the prosperous mediæval port of Surat. This is, perhaps, the same as the Camanes of Ptolemy.

44. **Trappaga and Cotymba.**—The first word Lassen derives (II, 539) from *trapâka*, a type of fishing boat mentioned by other travellers to this region. The second suggests the modern *kotia*, a craft from these waters found by Burton in the Somaliland ports (*First Footsteps*, 408).

Fishing-boats entering Bombay Harbor

44. **Anchorages and basins.**—The maintenance of this regular service of pilotage, under which incoming vessels were met at least 100 miles from Barygaza, indicates an active and regular commerce, such as our author describes. The use of "stations" in the river is still necessary here, and in other rivers such as those of Burma, where modern sailing traffic is more active.

45. **Very great tides.**—The vivid description of the tidal bore, in this and the following paragraph, is certainly the result of personal experience. To a merchant familiar with the all but tideless waters of the Red Sea, it must indeed have been a wonder of nature. The same thing occurs in many places where a strong tide is forced into a narrow, shallow and curving estuary, as in Burma, the Bay of Fundy, the Bay of Panama, and elsewhere. According to the *Imperial Gazetteer of India*, IX, 297, high spring tides in the Gulf of Cambay rise and fall as much as 33 feet, and run at a velocity of 6 to 7 knots an hour. Ordinary tides reach 25 feet, at 4½ to 6 knots. The inevitable damage to shipping, under such difficulties, was the cause of the desertion of the Cambay ports for Surat and, more recently, Bombay.

46. **The sea rushing in with a hoarse roar.**

———"Through hoarse roar never remitting,
Along the midnight edge by those milk-white combs careering."
Walt Whitman: *Patrolling Barnegat.*

47. **Arattii.**—This is a Prakrit form of the Sanscrit *Arāshtra*, who were a people of the Panjāb; in fact the name *Arātta* is often synonymous with the Panjāb in Hindu literature.

47. **Arachosii.**—This people occupied the country around the modern Kandahar (31° 27′ N., 65° 43′ E.). McCrindle (*Ancient India*, 88) says "Arachosia extended westward beyond the meridian of Kandahar, and was skirted on the east by the river Indus. On the north it stretched to the western section of the Hindu Kush and on the south to Gedrosia. The province was rich and populous, and the fact that it was traversed by one of the main routes by which Persia communicated with India added greatly to its importance."

47. **Gandaræi.**—(Sanscrit, *Gāndhāra.*) This people dwelt on both sides of the Cabul River, above its junction with the Indus; the modern Peshāwar district. In earlier times they extended east of the Indus, where their eastern capital was located—*Takshasilā*, a large and prosperous city, called by the Greeks *Taxila*.

(See also Holdich, *Gates of India*, 99, 114, 179, 185; Vincent Smith, *Early History*, 32, 43, 50, 52, 54; Foucher, *Notes sur la géographie ancienne du Gāndhāra.*)

The trade-route briefly referred to in the mention of Gāndhāra and Pushkalāvatī was that leading to Bactria, whence it branched westward to the Caspian and the Euphrates, and eastward through Turkestan to China, the "Land of This" of § 64.

47. **Poclais.**—(Sanscrit, *Pushkarāvatī*, or *Pushkalāvatī*, "abound-

ing in lotuses." Prakrit, *Pukkalaoti*, whence the *Peucelaotis* of Arrian.) This was the western capital of Gāndhāra (*cf.* Strabo, XV, 26-8; Arrian, *Anabasis*, IV, xxii; *Indica*, IV; Lassen, II, 858), the modern Chārsadda, 17 miles N. E. of Peshāwar, on the Suwāt River.

47. **Bucephalus Alexandria.**—This is identified by Vincent Smith (*op. cit.*, 62) with the modern town of Jhelum. (See under § 41.) Its position is marked by an extensive mound west of the present settlement. The mound is known as *Pindi*, "the town," and yields large ancient bricks and numerous Græco-Bactrian coins. Its position at a ferry on the high-road from the west to the Indian interior gave it great commercial importance.

47. **Warlike nation of the Bactrians.**—This passage, with its reference to Græco-Bactrian coins current in Barygaza, presents a view of Indian history which does not appear in any other contemporary work. The sequence of events in Bactria during the four centuries between Alexander and the Periplus, which is fully set forth by Vincent Smith (*op. cit.*, IX, X) is summarized as follows:

The Empire of Alexander was broken up at his death and the whole Eastern section from Syria to India fell to Seleucus, one of his generals. The Indian conquests were lost immediately, but the intervening country remained under Greek control for nearly 100 years under Antiochus Theos. The two northeastern provinces of Parthia and Bactria revolted. The Parthians, an Asiatic race akin to the Turks, set up for themselves, and built up a military power which later absorbed the country beyond the Euphrates. The Bactrian country, which was then populous and productive, remained under the government of Greek princes, and its independence was finally recognized in 208 B. C. The Greek monarchs in Bactria immediately set about enlarging their domains by striving to gain an outlet to the sea through the Indus Valley. In 190 B. C. Demetrius conquered the whole Indus Valley and that part of Afghanistan lying around the modern Cabul.

During his absence in India a relative, Eucratides, revolted and Demetrius returned home but his name does not reappear. From 160 to 156 there seems to have been anarchy in Bactria which ended in the assassination of Eucratides by his son Apollodotus, whose reign seems to have been very short.

In the years 155-153 a Greek King Menander, apparently a brother of Apollodotus, whose capital was Cabul, annexed the entire Indus Valley, the peninsula of Surāshtra (Syrastrene) and other territories on the western coast; occupied Mathurā; besieged Madhyamikā (now Nāgari near Chitōr), and threatened the capital, Pātaliputra, which is the modern Patna. Menander had to retire, however, to Bactria. He is supposed to have been a convert to Buddhism, and has been immortalized under the name of Milinda in a celebrated dialogue entitled *The Questions of Milinda*, which is one of the most noted books in Buddhist literature.

Heliocles, son of Eucratides, seems to have been the last Greek king to rule north of the Hindu Kush Mountains.

This phase of Asiatic history is reflected by the mention of the Greek coinage of Apollodotus and Menander, current in Barygaza at the time of the Periplus. The coins must have been over 200 years old, and the preservation of small silver coins in commercial use for that length of time is remarkable.

To understand the 'very warlike nation of the Bactrians' which our author mentions as 'living in the interior under their own king,' one must go to the history of central Asia. Chinese annals mention that in the year 165 B. C., a nomadic Turki tribe in northwestern China and owing allegiance to the Chinese emperors, known as the Yueh-chi, were driven out of their territory by the Hiongnu or Tartars, and migrated westward. This displaced numerous savage tribes in central Asia, who in turn moved westward; and thus the great waves of migration were begun which inundated Europe for centuries, overwhelmed the Roman Empire, and long threatened to extinguish white civilization.

The Yueh-chi in their westward movement drove out a tribe known as the Saka, who had lived between the Chu and Jaxartes rivers. These tribes in the years 140-130 poured into Bactria, overwhelmed the Greek Kingdom there and continued into the country known as Seistan, then called, from its conquerors, Sakastene. Another branch of the Saka horde settled in Taxila in the Panjāb and Mathura on the Jumna, where Saka princes ruled for more than a century under the Parthian power. These Saka tribes seem to have been originally connected with the Parthians. Another section of the Sakas at a later date pushed on southward and occupied the peninsula of Surāshtra, founding a Saka dynasty which lasted for centuries. This country is referred to by the author of the Periplus in § 38 as "subject to Parthian princes who were constantly driving each other out."

The Sakas of India seem to have been subject to the Parthians, and Indo-Parthian princes appear at Cabul and in the Panjāb about 120 B. C. There is a long line of Parthian princes recorded as ruling in Cabul; among them Gondophares, who acceded in 21 A. D. and reigned in Cabul and the Panjāb for thirty years. This is the same prince who is mentioned in the apocryphal 'Acts of St. Thomas,' which, although not composed until the third century A. D., reflects the prominence with which his name was regarded in the history of the time.

The Indo-Parthian princes were gradually driven southward by the advancing Yueh-chi, who had expelled the last of them from the Panjāb before the end of the first century A. D.—that is, at the time of this work.

The Yueh-chi, whose westward migration started all this trouble, had settled in Bactria north of the Oxus River about 70 B. C. The scattered tribes were gradually brought together under a central power, and their wandering habits were changed for agriculture and industry; so that when the Yueh-chi nation was unified under Kadphises I, who began to rule in 45 A. D., it represented a different people from the savages who had overwhelmed the Greek Kingdom of Bactria. Kadphises reigned over Bokhara and Afghanistan for 40 years, and was succeeded by his son Kadphises II, who extended his conquests into India.

The Chinese emperors had never abandoned their assertion of sovereignty over the Yueh-chi. An embassy was sent from China to the Oxus River in the years 125-115 B. C. to try to persuade the Yueh-chi to return to China, but the mission was unsuccessful, and subsequent revolutions kept Chinese interest at home between 100 B. C. and 70 A. D.

A Tartar army under the Chinese General Pan Chao reasserted Chinese supremacy over all of Central Asia, extending its conquests as far as the Caspian Sea. Thus, with the submission of Khotan and Kashgar to Chinese armies in 73 A. D., the route south of the Central Asian desert was thrown open to commerce from end to end. With the reduction of Kuché and Kharachar in 94 A. D., the route north of the desert was also thrown open, and for the first time regular commerce between East and West was made possible.

It should be borne in mind that this route was still policed by savage tribes only nominally subject to the Chinese Empire, and while communication was opened up immediately, trade was not carried on in large volume until the time of the Roman Emperor Marcus Aurelius, 100 years later.

Kadphises II, ruler of the Yueh-chi, who had in the meantime extended his conquest into India but not yet as far as the Indus delta, sent an army of 70,000 cavalry against the Chinese General Pan Chao, and was totally defeated near Kashgar; and was obliged for some years to send tribute to China.

About 95 A. D. he began his further conquests of India, and his kingdom reached as far as Benares and Ghazipur on the Ganges River.

The Yueh-chi opened up the commerce between India and the Roman Empire. Here, as in Central Asia, the trade had been merely incidental and subject to depredations of numerous savage tribes. The Parthians had done what they could to control and organize it and to levy tribute on the Roman merchants, but they had not controlled it to the eastward. The existence of unified power in the Indus Valley and Afghanistan made possible a regular trade from the Ganges to the Euphrates. The rapid growth of such trade is indicated by the coinage of the Yueh-chi Kings in India. Kadphises I struck coins in bronze only, which were imitated from those of Augustus. Kadphises II imitated the gold coins of the Roman Empire, which were then pouring into India in a steady stream. In Southern India, where there was an active Roman maritime trade, there was no native gold coinage, the Roman being sufficient.

It is probable that the Indian embassy, which offered its congratulations in Rome to the Emperor Trajan, was dispatched by Kadphises II, to announce his conquest of Northwestern India.

47. **Alexander penetrated to the Ganges.**—This is, of course, quite untrue, the Panjāb having been the turning-point of his expedition. The great mass of India was entirely unaffected by his invasion, except as it led to the subsequent centralization of power under Chandragupta Maurya. Our author is confusing Alexander with Menander.

"The East bowed low before the blast
In patient, deep disdain;
She let the legions thunder past,
And plunged in thought again."

Matthew Arnold: *Obermann.*

48. **Ozene.**—This is the modern Ujjain, 23° 11′ N., 75° 47′ E., the chief city of Mālwā. The Sanscrit form is *Ujjayinī*, "victorious." The Prakrit is *Ujjenī*, from which the Greek is derived.

Ujjain is one of the seven sacred cities of India, not yielding even to Benares. In Hindu legend it was here that the elbow of Satī fell, on the dismemberment of her body by Siva. The river Sipra, on which it is located, is also sacred. The place was important under the earliest Aryan settlements in Mālwā. In early times it was known as Avantī, a kingdom which is described in Buddhist literature as one of the four great powers of India. As Ujjeni it is very prominent in Buddhist records, having been the birthplace of Kachāna, one of

Sākyamuni's greatest disciples. Here was a Buddhist monastery known as the Southern Mount, while it was the principal stage on the route from the Deccan to Srāvastī, then the capital of the great kingdom of Kosala. Here also in his younger days Asoka, later emperor, and the greatest patron of Buddhism, was stationed as viceroy of the western provinces of the Maurya Empire. This was the custom also in several subsequent dynasties, on both sides of the Vindhyas, for the heir-apparent to act as viceroy in the western provinces.

Ujjeni was the Greenwich of India, the first meridian of longitude of its geographers. By its location it was a trade center for all produce imported at Barygaza, whence distribution was made to the Ganges kingdoms. At the time of the Periplus it was no longer a capital, the royal seat being at "Minnagara." The Maurya empire had broken up, and in the anarchy following the irruptions in the northwest, its western provinces of Surāshtra and Mālwā had been raided by Saka freebooters, who finally established themselves in power as the "Western Satraps," or Kshatrapa dynasty. For a generation or so before the formal proclamation of the dynasty the invaders' stronghold was their capital. After their claims were recognized they probably ruled from Ujjeni, which Ptolemy describes as the capital of *Tiastenos* or Chashtana, the Kshatrapa ruler of his time. It remained, apparently, in Saka hands until about the 5th century A. D., when it reverted to Brahman power under the Gupta Empire; this expulsion of the "misbelieving foreigners" giving rise to the tradition of Vikramāditya of Ujjain, the King Arthur of India, at whose court the "nine gems," the brightest geniuses of India, were supposed to have flourished.

(See *Imperial Gazetteer*, VIII, 279-280; XXIV, 112-114; Lassen, I, 116.)

48. **Spikenard**: *Nardostachys jatamansi*, order *Valerianaceæ*. A perennial herb of the alpine Himalaya, which extends eastward from Garhwal and ascends to 17,000 feet in Sikkim. "The drug consists of a portion of the rhizome, about as thick as the little finger, surmounted by a bundle of reddish-brown fibers, the remains of the radical leaves. It is aromatic and bitter, and yields on distillation an essential oil. In India it is largely used as an aromatic adjunct in the preparation of medicinal oils, and is popularly believed to increase the growth and blackness of the hair." (Watt, *op. cit.*, 792.)

According to Pliny (XII, 26), "Leaf nard varies in price according to the size; for that which is known by the name of hadrosphærum, consisting of the larger leaves, sells at 40 denarii per pound. When the leaves are smaller, it is called mesosphærum, and is sold at 60. But that which is considered the most valuable of all, is known as microsphærum, and consists of the very smallest of the leaves; it sells at 75 denarii per pound. All these varieties of nard have an agreeable odor, but it is most powerful when fresh. If the nard is old when gathered that which is of a black color is considered the best."

Pliny observes that leaf nard, or spikenard, held the first place in Rome among the ointments of his day. Compare Mark XIV, 3-5, which tells of the "alabaster box of ointment of spikenard very precious," valued at more than 300 denarii.

See under § 24: also, for further references, Lassen, I, 288-9.

48. **Caspapyra.**—This is the Greek form of the Sanscrit *Kāsyapapura*, "city of the Kāsyapa." The same word survives in the modern Kashmīr, which is from the Sanscrit *Kāsyapamata* (pronounced *pamara*), and meaning "home of the Kāsyapa" (one of the 'previous Buddhas.') According to the division of the Greek geographers, Gāndhāra was the country below Cabul, while Kāsyapamata was the adjoining district in India proper. (See Lassen, I, 142; II, 631.)

It was from a town named Caspapyra, that Scylax of Caryanda began his voyage of discovery at the command of the Persian king Darius. The story is given by Herodotus (IV, 44). He refers to the place as being "in the Pactyan land," and Hecatæus calls it "a city of the Gandaræans." It could not have been far above the modern Attock (33° 53′ N., 72° 15′ E.). Vincent Smith (*Early History*, 32) doubts the connection of the name with Kashmīr; but while outside the present limits of that district, it is not impossible that its earlier extension was wider. The fact that the Periplus distinguishes it from Gāndhāra points in that direction.

48. **Paropanisus** was the name given the mountain-range now called Hindu Kush. It was made the boundary between the empire of Seleucus, Alexander's successor, and that of Chandragupta Maurya, by a treaty ratified in 303 B. C.; by which the newly-established Indian empire received the provinces of the Paropanisadæ, Aria, Arachosia and Gedrosia. "The first Indian emperor, more than two thousand years ago, thus entered into possession of 'that scientific frontier' sighed for in vain by his English successors, and never held in its entirety even by the Mogul monarchs of the 16th and 17th centuries." (Vincent Smith, *Early History*, 113; also 132-4; Strabo, XV, i, 10 and ii, 9; Plutarch, *Alexander*, lxii; Justin, XV, 4; Pliny, VI, 20; Arrian, *Anabasis*, V, 5; *Indica*, II. See also Holdich, *Gates of India*.)

48. **The Cabolitic country** is, of course, the modern Cabul valley, above the Khyber Pass; being within the present limits of Afghanistan.

48. **Scythia.**—See under § 41. This was the region which was subject to the Parthian princes, weak successors of Gondophares, whose reign had ended about 51 A. D.

49. **Lead.**—Pliny (XXXIV, 47-50) distinguishes between black lead and white lead; the former being our lead, the latter tin (see also under § 7). White lead he says came from Lusitania and Galicia, doubting its reported origin in "islands of the Atlantic," and its transportation in "boats made of osiers, covered with hides."

Black lead, he says, came from Cantabria in Spain, and his description suggests galena, or sulphide of lead and silver. It came also from Britain, and from Lusitania—where the Santarensian mine was farmed at an annual rental of 250,000 denarii.

Lead was used in the form of pipes and sheets, and had many medicinal uses, being used in calcined form, made into tablets in the same way as antimony (see under this §), or mixed with grease and wine. It was used as an astringent and repressive, and for cicatrization; in the treatment of ulcers, burns, etc., and in eye preparations; while thin plates of lead worn next the body were supposed to have a cooling and beneficial effect.

As an import at Barygaza lead was required largely for the coinage of the Saka dominions.

49. **Bright-colored girdles.**—These were probably for the Bhīls, a Dravidian hill-tribe, who worked the carnelian mines then as now. The modern Coorgs, a related tribe, still wear a distinctive "girdle-scarf" which is now made at Sirangala. (*Imp. Gaz.*, VIII, 101-4; IX, 36.)

49. **Sweet clover.**—This is *Trifolium melilotus*, order *Leguminosæ*, the "melilote" of the Greeks and Romans, used for making chaplets and perfumes, and medicinally. Pliny (XXI, 29) says the best sorts were from Campania in Italy, Cape Sunium in Greece, also from Chalcidice and Crete; native always in rugged and wild localities. "The name *sertula*, garland, which it bears sufficiently proves that this plant was formerly much used in the composition of chaplets. The smell, as well as the flower, closely resembles that of saffron, though the stem itself is white; the shorter and more fleshy the leaves, the more highly it is esteemed." And again (XXI, 87), "the melilote applied with the yolk of an egg, or else linseed, effects the cure of diseases of the eyes. It assuages pains, too, in the jaws and head,

applied with rose oil; and employed with raisin wine, it is good for pains in the ears, and all kinds of swellings or eruptions on the hands. A decoction of it in wine, or else the plant itself beaten up raw, is good for pains in the stomach."

Concerning the use of chaplets in the Roman world, Pliny gives many details (XXI, 1-10). The chaplet was a crown of honor given the victors in the sacred games. Originally laurel and other tree foliage was used; flowers were added by the painter Pausias, at Sicyon, about 380 B. C. Then came the "Egyptian chaplet" of ivy, narcissus, and pomegranate blossoms, and then a durable article of thin laminæ of horn, and of leaves of gold, silver, or tinsel, plain or embossed.

Chaplets were won by personal prowess in the games, or by that of slaves or horses entered by the winner, and gave the victor "the right, for himself and for his parents, after death, to be crowned without fail, while the body was laid out in the house, and on its being carried to the tomb. On other occasions, chaplets were not indiscriminately worn."

The use of chaplets by those not entitled to them was forbidden by law, and Pliny cites several cases of punishment for the offence.

Chaplets were used also in honor of the gods, the Lares, the sepulchres and the Manes; this custom still surviving in the laying of immortelles on tombs of departed friends.

> "Atque aliquis senior veteres veneratus amores,
> Annua constructo serta dabit tumulo."
>
> —Tibullus, II, 4.

For such uses the plaited chaplet, the rose chaplet, and various devices embroidered by hand, came into use, and Pliny notes that in his time there was a demand for chaplets imported from India, made of nard leaves on fabrics, "or else of silk of many colors steeped in unguents. Such is the pitch to which the luxuriousness of our women has at last arrived!"

It would seem as if this sweet clover might also be intended for the manufacture of chaplets for re-exportation to Rome.

49. **Realgar.**—The text is *sandarakê.* This is the red sulphide of arsenic. It was principally from Persia and Carmania, and reached India from various Persian Gulf ports. In modern times both realgar and orpiment are produced in large quantities in Burma and China, where it is not impossible that production existed at the time of the Periplus.

Pliny (XXXIV, 55) says "the redder it is the more pure and friable, and the more powerful its odor the better it is in quality. It is detergent, astringent, heating, and corrosive, but it is most remarkable for its antiseptic properties." Dioscorides (V, 122) says it was burned with resin and the smoke inhaled through a tube, as a remedy for coughs, asthma, or bronchitis. Theophrastus also describes its properties.

The Greek word survives in the modern gum sandarac from *Callitris quadrivalvis*, order *Coniferæ*, produced in Algeria and Morocco; but this was not its meaning in classical times. The word is of eastern origin, referring apparently to the color, and was extended from ore to gum because of appearance, reversing the process in the case of cinnabar (§ 30).

The wood in this sandarac tree was much valued by the Greeks and Romans for furniture, being, perhaps, the "thyine wood" of Revelation XVIII, 12.

Tavernier also (II, xii) found "vermillion" brought by the Dutch to trade for pepper.

49. **Antimony.**—The text is *stimmi.* This was the sulphide ore, stibnite. It was made into ointments and eye-tinctures, both in India and Egypt. The ore came from Eastern Arabia and Carmania, and is mentioned in an Egyptian inscription in the tomb of Khnumhotep II, at Benihasan (under Sesostris II, 1900 B. C.), being brought by "Asiatics of the desert."

Pliny (XXXIII, 33-4) describes it as found in silver mines, "a stone made of concrete froth, white and shining . . . being possessed of astringent and refrigerative properties; its principal use, in medicine, being for the eyes." Pounded with frankincense and gum, it was valued as a cure for various eye irritations, and mixed with grease, as a cure for burns. But its main use was for dilating the pupils and for painting the eyebrows. Omphale, the Lydian queen who captivated Hercules, is represented by the poet Ion as using *stimmi* in her toilet; Jezebel, in II Kings, IX, 30, probably used it when she "painted her face and tired her head;" while it is the chief ingredient in the *kohl* used by women in modern Egypt and Persia.

Pliny and Dioscorides (V, 99) agree in their description of its preparation. It was enclosed in dough or cow-dung, burned in a furnace, quenched with milk or wine, and beaten with rain-water in a mortar. This being decanted from time to time, the finest powder was allowed to settle, dried under linen, and divided into tablets.

49. **Gold and silver coin.**—The Roman *aureus* and *denarius* were current throughout Western India, and strongly influenced the Kushan and Kshatrapa coinages. See under § 56; also Rapson, *Indian Coins*.

The profit on the exchange was due to the superiority of the Roman coinage to that of India, which latter was still crude, of base metal (bronze or lead), for which even the bullion, (copper, tin and lead), was imported.

49. **Ivory.**—For references see Lassen, I, 311-315. The original word is *ibha*, "elephant." From this came the word used in I Kings, X, 22, *shen habbin*, "elephant's teeth," which the Hebrews shortened to *shen*, "tooth," which is the word used in Amos, III, 15; Cant. V, 14. In ancient Egypt this word *ibha* became *abu*, whence the Roman and Etruscan *ebur* for ivory. The Greek *elephas*, or rather the root form *elephantos*, applied first to the ivory and later to the animal, was the Arabic article *el* and the Sanscrit *ibhadanta*, "elephant's teeth."

49. **Agate and carnelian.**—See also under § 6. The text is *onychinê lithia kai mourrhinê*.

According to Watt (*op. cit.*, 561), the murrhine vases and other articles which were so highly prized in Mediterranean countries, were largely of agate, carnelian and the like, and came from the Gulf of Cambay, which was the chief market for that Indian industry.

The stone is from the amygdaloidal flows of the Deccan trap, chiefly from the State of Rajpipla. The most important place at which agates are now cut is Cambay, but the industry exists also at Jabbalpur and elsewhere within reach of the Deccan trap. They are much used for ornamental and decorative purposes, being made into brooches, rings, seals, cups, etc.

While collecting the pebbles the miners divide them into two primary classes—those that are not improved by burning, and those that are. Of the former there are three—onyx, cat's eye, and a yellow half-clear pebble called *rori*. All other stones are baked to bring out their color. During the hot season, generally in March and April, the stones are spread in the sun in an open field. Then, in May, a trench, two feet deep by three wide, is dug round the field. The pebbles are gathered into earthen pots, which, with their mouths down and a hole broken in their bottoms, are set in a row in the trench. Round the pots, goat or cow-dung cakes are piled, and the whole kept burning from sunset to sunrise. The pots are then taken out, the stones examined, and the good ones stowed in bags. About the end of May the bags are carried to the Narbada and floated to Broach (Barygaza).

By this treatment the light browns brighten into white, and the darker shades into chestnut. Of yellows, maize becomes rosy, orange deepens into red, and an intermediate shade becomes a pinkish purple.

Pebbles in which cloudy browns and yellows were first mixed are now marked by clear bands of white and red. The hue of the red carnelian varies from the palest flesh to the deepest blood-red. The best are of a deep, clear, and even red color. The larger and thicker the stone, the more it is esteemed. White carnelians are scarce, and when of large size and good quality are much esteemed.

This burning of agates is fully described by Barbosa in 1517, and seems to be of very ancient date. It was then, as now, chiefly the industry of the Bhīls, an ancient Dravidian tribe which may formerly have possessed the Cambay coast, but had been driven to the hills by later invaders. It is this product, in all probability, which is the "onyx stone" of Genesis II, 12, which reached the ancient world through the "land of Havilah" on the Persian Gulf.

Pliny (XXXVII, 7, 8) says that murrhine was first known to the Romans after the conquests of Pompey the Great in Asia; that it was fabulously dear, T. Petronius having broken one of Nero's basins valued at 300,000 sesterces, while Nero himself paid 1,000,000 sesterces for a single cup. Pliny attributes the vessels to Parthia and Carmania. They were of moderate size only, seldom as large as a drinking-cup, supposed to be of a moist substance, solidified by heat under ground; shining rather than brilliant; having a great variety of colors, with wreathed veins, presenting shades of purple and white, with fiery red between. Others were quite opaque. They occasionally contained crystals, and depressed spots that looked like warts. They were said to have an agreeable taste and smell.

While Pliny's description is not very definite, it suggests agate more than any other substance, and the reference to Parthia and Carmania rather than to the Gulf of Cambay means that until the Romans discovered the sea-route to India they were dependent on the Parthian trade-routes for their Eastern treasures, and had only such information, often misleading, as the Parthians offered them.

49. **Silk cloth.**—See under §§ 49 and 64.

49. **Mallow cloth.**—See also under § 6. This was a coarse fabric, like the native cloth made by the East African negroes, which is imitated by the modern blue drill. It was dyed with the flowers of *Hibiscus Rosa-Sinensis*, order *Malvaceæ*, a shrub which is native throughout India and China. See Watt, p. 629.

49. **Long pepper:** *Piper longum*, Linn., order *Piperaceæ*. Watt (p. 891), says it is a perennial shrub, native of the hotter parts of India from Nepāl eastward to Assam, the Khasia hills and Bengal, westward to Bombay, and southward to Travancore and Ceylon. The Sanscrit name *pippali* was originally given to this plant, and only

within comparatively recent times was transferred to black pepper. Long pepper is mentioned by Pliny (XII, 7) as well as the Periplus.

The fruit is gathered when green, and is preserved by drying in the sun. The dried unripe fruit and the root have long been used in medicine.

50. **Dachinabades.**—This is the Sanscrit *dakshināpathas*, "the way toward the south;" Prakrit *dakkhinābadha*: the modern Deccan.

50. **Many populous nations.**—An interesting account is given by T. C. Evans, *Greek and Roman India*, in the *Anglo-American Magazine* for 1901, pp. 294-306. His conclusion is that "the Greek invader found there an ancient and highly organized society, differing little in its usages and modes of living from those which exist at the present time; and although there are no means of verifying the conjecture, it is not unlikely that the population of the peninsula was as great in that period as in our own." If this view is correct, India was the most populous region of the world at the time of the Periplus, as it was the most cultivated, the most active industrially and commercially, the richest in natural resources and production, the most highly organized socially, the most wretched in the poverty of its teeming millions, and the least powerful politically.

The great powers of India were the Kushan in the far northwest, the Saka in the Cambay country, the remains of the Maurya in the Ganges watershed, the Andhra in the Deccan, and the Chēra, Pāndya and Chola in the South. The economic status of the country made it impossible that any one of these should possess political force commensurate with its population, resources and industries. It was made up of village communities, which recognized the military power only so far as they were compelled to do so; and they were relatively unconcerned in dynastic changes, except to note the change in their oppressors.

For a contemporary account of the nations of India, see Pliny, VI, 21-3.

51. **Pæthana:** Sanscrit, *Pratisthāna*. This is the modern Paithān, on the Godāverī River (19° 28′ N., 75° 24′ E.).

According to the *Imperial Gazetteer* (XIX, 317), Paithān is one of the oldest cities in the Deccan. Asoka sent missionaries to the *Petēnikas*, and inscriptions of the 2d century B. C. in the Pitalkhara caves refer to the king and merchants of Pratisthāna. Ptolemy mentions it as the capital of Pulumāyi II, the Andhra king (138-170 A.D.); but it was probably the capital of the western provinces, the seat of the Andhra monarchs having been in the eastern part of the kingdom, at *Dhānyakataka*, the modern Dhāranikotta, on the Kistna river just above Amarāvati (16° 34′ N., 80° 22′ E.).

According to the Periplus, Paithān was an important center of the textile industry. To-day it retains a considerable manufacture of cotton and silk. Almost all traces of the ancient city are said to have disappeared.

51. **Tagara.**—The Sanscrit name had the same form, appearing in several records between the 6th and 10th centuries A. D. The place is identified by Fleet with the modern Tēr (Thair) (18° 19′ N., 76° 9′ E.), being a contraction of *Tayara*, the *g* and *y* being frequently interchanged. It is about 95 miles southeast of Paithān, and agrees substantially with the distance and direction given in the text. From Broach to Paithān the actual distance, by road, is about 240 miles, and from Paithān to Tēr 104 miles, being 20 and 9 days' journey of 12 miles, respectively. There are said to be some very interesting remains of the ancient city.

As pointed out by Campbell, the "merchandise from the regions along the sea-coast" was not from the west coast, but from the Bay of Bengal; and Fleet traces briefly the routes—the first starting at Masulipatam (16° 11′ N., 81° 8′ E.), and the second from Vinukonda (16° 3′ N., 79° 44′ E.), joining about 25 miles southeast of Haidarābād, and proceeding through Tēr, Paithān, and Daulatābād, to Mārkinda (in the Ajanta Hills). Here the main difficulties began, through the Western Ghāts, over the 100 miles to Broach.

This was the great highway of the Andhra kingdom, and its natural terminus was at Calliena in Bombay Harbor, as suggested in § 52. The obstruction of that port by the Saka power in Gujarāt forced the tedious overland extension of the route, through the mountains, to Barygaza.

(See J. F. Fleet, *Tagara: Tēr*, in *Journal of the Royal Asiatic Society*, 1901, pp. 537-552; Sir James Campbell, in *Gazetteer of the Bombay Presidency*, xvi, 181; H. Cousens, *Archæological Survey of India, Annual Report*, 1902-3, p. 195; *Imperial Gazetteer*, II, 82; xxiii, 284.)

51. **Country without roads.**—Tavernier says of the Deccan (I, xi) "wheel carriages do not travel, the roads being too much interrupted by high mountains, tanks, and rivers, and there being many narrow and difficult passes. It is with the greatest difficulty that one takes a small cart. I was obliged to take mine to pieces frequently in order to pass bad places. There are no wagons, and you only see oxen and pack-horses for the conveyance of men, and for the transport of goods and merchandise. But in default of chariots, you have the convenience of much larger palanquins than in the rest of India; for one is carried much more easily, more quickly, and at less cost."

52. **Suppara.**—This is the modern Sopāra (19° 25′ N., 72° 41′ E.), a few miles north of Bombay. It is said to have been the capital of the Konkan between 500 B. C. and 1300 A. D. It appears in the *Mahābhārata* as Shurpāraka, as a very holy place. Some Buddhist writings assert that Gautama Buddha, in a former birth, was Bodhisattva of Sopāra. See *Imp. Gaz.*, XXIII, 87.

52. **Calliena.**—This is the modern Kalyāna (19° 14′ N., 73° 10′ E.), on the eastern shore of the harbor of Bombay. It was the principal port of the Andhra kingdom during the periods when it held the west coast. According to Lassen, the name was also applied to the strip of coast on either side of the harbor, roughly between 18° and 20° N.

Cosmas Indicopleustes, in the 6th century A. D., found it one of the five chief marts of Western India, the capital of the powerful Chālukya kings, with a trade in brass, blackwood logs, and articles of clothing. See *Imp. Gaz.*, XIV, 322.

The word *kalyāna* means "blest," and is at least reminiscent of similar names on the western shores of the Erythræan Sea.

52. **The elder Saraganus; Sandares;** to which should be added **Nambanus** of § 41. (The text has *Sandanes* and *Mambarus.*) Here are three important references, both for fixing the date of the Periplus and for throwing light on a dark period of Indian history.

The great empire of the Mauryas went to pieces in the 2d century B. C., leaving as its strongest successor its Dravidian element, the Andhra country in the Deccan, which comprised the valleys of the Godāverī and Kistna; the Telugu peoples, roughly the modern Nizam's dominions. In the south the other Dravidian kingdoms, the Tamil-speaking Cholas, Pāndyas and Chēras, retained their independence as before. North of the Vindhyas there was anarchy. The Bengal states had resumed their local governments, while the West and Northwest had succumbed to the Asiatic invaders, the Saka and Kushan tribes. The western coast below the Vindhyas was a bone of contention between the Saka commanders and the Andhra monarchs, who maintained the feud for at least a century, with varying success.

The provinces of Surāshtra, Gujarāt and Mālwā, after years of warfare, were incorporated under a stable government by the Western Kshatrapa, or Saka Satraps, who subsequently defeated the Andhras and annexed the Konkan coast. This is thought to have been the origin of the Saka era, dating from 78 A. D., still largely used in India. A half-century later the Andhras under Vilivāyakura II, or Gautamīputra Sātakarni, reconquered the coast-land, only to lose it to the

Satraps after another generation. From the Saka era of 78 A. D. for 46 years, there are coins of a monarch named Nahapāna, by whom the line of the Satraps was established. This is thought to be the same as the *Mambarus* of § 41, whose name should be written Nambanus.

The Andhra kings are enumerated in the Purānas, which, together with the coinage, afford almost the only information concerning them. A dynastic name, borne by many of these monarchs, was Sātakarni, and this is supposed to be the *Saraganus* of § 52 (probably Arishta Sātakarni, who reigned about 44-69 A. D.); while *Sandanes* is probably the same as Sundara Sātakarni, whose short reign of a year, succeeded by another of six months, is affirmed by at least two of the Purānas. The reign of this Sundara (the text should be altered to Sandares) is fixed by Vincent Smith and others at 83-4 A. D.

From these facts it has been supposed that the Periplus itself must be dated in the same year, 83-4 A. D., but this does not necessarily follow. Its date is considered in the introduction, pp. 7-15, and upon ample evidence—Roman, Arabian, and Parthian—is fixed at 60 A. D.

If Nambanus of § 41 is the same as Nahapāna, it must yet be shown that he is the same as the great satrap whose victories over the Andhras and conquest of the Konkan are cited as one of the numerous events thought to be commemorated by the Saka era of 78 A. D. At least one predecessor, formerly thought to be identical with that Nahapāna, has now been distinguished under the name of Bhumaka, and the materials are not yet at hand for affirming, or denying, the possibility of others, in the so-called Kshaharāta line which preceded the achievements of the Satraps.

And if Sandares of § 52 is the same as Sundara Sātakarni, there is a great difficulty in the way of identifying the Periplus with the single year of his reign. Calliena, his own port, he must be supposed to have closed, in order that its foreign trade might be diverted to Barygaza, the port of his Saka rival and bitter enemy! He, the Andhra monarch, must have done this, for the port was still "in his possession;" not, be it observed, in that of the Satraps. The Konkans were still nominally, though evidently not effectually, an Andhra dependency.

The inference is unmistakable that the Periplus is describing a state of things prior to the recognition of the Kshatrapa power and its annexation of the Andhra coast; prior, that is, to the Saka era of 78 A. D. It describes clearly enough an Andhra port, still subject to the Andhra kingdom, but harried and dominated, "obstructed" as the text has it, by the powerful navy of its northern enemy, while that enemy was still struggling to obtain possession.

What, then, of Nahapāna and Sundara? The doubt as to the indivisibility of the former has already been suggested; as to the latter, the shortness of his own reign and those of his successor and his immediate predecessors, and the length of that of his predecessor Arishta (25 years) indicate for him a long period of waiting as one of the royal heirs; which, according to the Andhra custom, was spent, at least in part, as viceroy at the western capital, Paithān. Here he exercised all the functions of a monarch, and his would be the name to appear on all proclamations issued on the western coast. "Since it came into the possession of Sandares" indicates, therefore, a date toward the end of the reign of Arishta Sātakarni, who is referred to as "the elder Saraganus," and who, it may be inferred, had been, as viceroy at Paithān, a more powerful ruler than the youthful Sandares, now struggling against greater odds to maintain the Andhra power on that coast.

Between Arishta and Sundara the Vāyu and Matsya Purānas are agreed in placing three other monarchs: Hāla (with whose name the adoption of Sanscrit as the literary language of Northern India is so closely associated), who reigned 5 years; Mandalaka, 5 years; Purindrasena, 5 years. Then came Sundara, 1 year, and Chakora, 6 months, followed by Siva Sātakarni, 28 years. These five short reigns, coming between two long ones, seem to suggest a quick succession of weak and impractical sons of a strong monarch, followed in their turn by another long reign of sterner purpose; a succession of events like the reigns of the sons of Henry II. and Catherine de Medici in France. This would account for the condition described to the author of the Periplus by some acquaintance at Barygaza: "When the old king Saraganus (now ruling at Dhānyakataka) was viceroy at Pæthana, he made Calliena an active port; now that he is on the throne and his sons have tried their hand at the viceroy's post one after the other, in the intervals of their literary and artistic pursuits, and it has finally been turned over to young Sandares, it has been an easy matter for our Saka general to send down his ships and stop its trade." Had the story been written in 83 A. D., the informant would have said, "our satrap has annexed that country to his own dominions, and closed its ports."

The same explanation is perfectly feasible for Nahapāna, who is known to have been governor in Surāshtra before he was satrap at Ujjeni. But as the great satrap lived until the Saka year 46, or 124 A. D., it is more probable that one of that name in 60 A. D. was his predecessor.

There are other explanations of these three names. Fabricius alters both Mambarus and Sandanes to *Sanabares*, supposing him to have been an Indo-Parthian successor to Gondophares; McCrindle thinks Sandanes was a tribe-name, and refers to the *Ariakê Sadinôn* of Ptolemy. But neither supposition is convincing.

The explanation based on the Puranic lists and the coinage has inherent probability, and is confirmed by the description of political conditions in § 52 of the Periplus, if that be applied to the reign of the Andhra king Arishta Sātakarni (44-69 A. D.), through the medium of his heir-presumptive Sundara, ruling as viceroy at Paithān, and displaying in the Konkans the only show of Andhra authority which would have come under the observation of a Græco-Roman merchant and shipmaster.

(See A.-M. Boyer, *Nahapāna et l'ère Çaka*, in *Journal Asiatique*, July-Aug., 1897, pp. 120-151; an excellent paper, in which the only matter for criticism is that the inscriptions of the Nabatæan Malichas should be thought less trustworthy than the chronology of the Abyssinian Chronicles, compiled much later.—C. R. Wilson, *Proposed identification of the name of an Andhra king in the Periplus*, in *Journal of the Asiatic Society of Bengal*, June, 1904; with which the foregoing suggestions are in accord, except as to their sequel.—Vincent Smith, *Andhra History and Coinage*, in *Zeitschrift der Deutschen Morgenländischen Gesellschaft*, Sept., 1903.—Pandit Bhagvānlāl Indraji, *The Western Kshatrapas*, in *Journal of the Royal Asiatic Society*, 1890, pp. 639-662. —E. J. Rapson, *The Coinage of the Mahākshatrapas and Kshatrapas*, J. R. A. S., 1899, 357-404; same author, *Ancient India*, in Numismatic Supplement, J. A. S. B., 1904, p. 227. Col. J. Biddulph, in a note to Mr. Rapson's first article, observes that our knowledge of the Satraps is derived solely from their coins, of which the former are undated; that each ruler puts his father's name on his coins as well as his own; that the dates overlap frequently; and that of the two titles, Mahākshatrapa indicates the monarch, and Kshatrapa the heir-apparent.—Vincent Smith, *Catalogue of the Coins in the Indian Museum, Calcutta*; also Chronology of Andhra Dynasty, in his *Early History*, p. 190.—E. J. Rapson, *Coins of the Andhra Dynasty, the Western Kshatrapas*, etc., British Museum. See also Cunningham, *Book of Indian Eras*; Duff, *The Chronology of India from the Earliest Times to the Beginning of the 16th Century.*)

53. **Semylla.**—This is the *Symulla* of Ptolemy, the *Chimolo* of Yuan Chwang, the *Saimur* of the early Mohammedan travellers; the modern Chaul (18° 34′ N., 72° 55′ E.), about 25 miles south of Bombay. The ancient Hindu name was *Champāvati*, and was con-

nected with the reign of Krīshna in Gujarāt. (See McCrindle, *Ancient India*, 161; *Imp. Gaz.*, X, 184; Müller, I, 295.)

53. **Mandagora.**—This is probably the modern Bānkot (17° 59′ N., 73° 3′ E.) at the mouth of the Sāvitri River. The port is closed during the S. W. monsoon. It is now a fishing village of no importance, but in former times it was a great center for the trade in teak and blackwood, and for shipbuilding. (See *Imp. Gaz.*, VI, 383; Müller, I, 295.) The name suggests the Sanscrit *Mandara-giri*. (In Ptolemy the positions of this and the following port are reversed.)

53. **Palæpatmæ.**—This is probably the modern Dābhol (17° 35′ N., 73° 10′ E.), the name being from the Sanscrit *Dābhileshwar*, a name of Siva. It is of considerable historical importance, being the principal port of the South Konkan. From the 14th to the 16th centuries it had an extensive trade with the Persian Gulf and Red Sea ports. Here is the underground temple of Chandikābai, dating from the 6th century. (*Imp. Gaz.*, XI, 100.)

The name *Palæpatmæ* is probably the Sanscrit *Pāripatana*—the suffix meaning "town," while *Pāri* was a general term applying to the Western Vindhya mountains and the coast south of them. (Nundo Lal Dey, *Geographical Dictionary of Ancient and Mediæval India*, p. 68.)

53. **Melizigara.**—This is placed by Müller and McCrindle at the modern Jaigarh (17° 17′ N., 72° 13′ E.), formerly a port of some size, but now little more than a fishing-village. It is not impossible that it may be the modern Rājāpur (16° 34′ N., 73° 31′ E.), which lies at the head of a tidal creek, and is the only port on this Ratnāgiri coast to which Arab boats still trade direct, though vessels of any size cannot approach within three miles of the old stone quay. (See *Imp. Gaz.*, XIII, 379; XXI, 66.)

This is the *Sigerus* of Pliny—the *Melizēgyris* of Ptolemy.

The name seems to suggest the Sanscrit *Malaya-giri*, "Malaya hills," a name which covered the southern part of the Western Ghāts. The same name appears in the *Malē* of Cosmas and our Malabar.

53. **Byzantium.**—This is evidently a corruption. Lassen (III, 6) assumes it to have been a colony of Byzantine Greeks, but there is not the slightest evidence of the existence of such a colony. It is probably the modern Vizadrog (Sanscrit, *Vijayadurga;* 16° 33′ N., 73° 20′ E.), described as being one of the best harbors on the western coast. (*Imp. Gaz.*, XXIV, 310; so Vincent, Müller and McCrindle.)

53. **Togarum.**—This is probably the modern Devgarh (16° 23′ N., 73° 22′ E.) described as "a safe and beautiful landlocked

harbor, at all times perfectly smooth. The average depth of water is 18 feet. The entrance, only 3 cables in width, lies close to the fort point." (*Imp. Gaz.*, XI, 275; so Vincent, Müller and McCrindle.)

53. **Aurannoboas.**—The text has initial *T* instead of *A*, no doubt a corruption. McCrindle places it at the modern Mālvan (16° 3′ N., 73° 28′ E.). It is a place of considerable importance, good iron ore being found in the neighborhood. To the Marāthās an island in the harbor is Sivājī's cenotaph, and his image is worshipped in the chief shrine. (See *Imp. Gaz.*, XVII, 96.)·

The name Mālvan is a contraction of *Mahā-lavana*, "salt marsh," and the Greek *Aurannoboas* is perhaps intended for the Sanscrit *Aranya-vaha*, which would have a similar meaning.

53. **Islands of the Sesecrienæ.**—These are probably the Vengurla Rocks (15° 53′ N., 70° 27′ E.), a group of rocky islets some 3 miles in length and 9 miles out from the modern town of Vengurla, which was a port of considerable importance during the Dutch occupation in the 17th century. (*Imp. Gaz.*, XXIV, 307.)

53. **Island of the Aegidii.**—This is perhaps the island of Goa (15° 20′ N., 74° 0′ E.), the present Portuguese possession. It is of historical importance, having been settled by Aryans at an early date, and appearing in the Puranas. (*Imp. Gaz.*, XII, 251; so Müller and McCrindle.) The *Imperial Gazetteer*, following Yule, prefers to identify it with Anjidiv (14° 45′ N., 74° 10′ E.); but the location is less satisfactory unless we assume the order in the text to be wrong, and to refer to the grouping of this and the following island on either side of the Kārwār point.

53. **Island of the Cænitæ.**—This is probably the Oyster Rocks (14° 49′ N., 74° 4′ E.), a cluster of islands west of, and facing, the roadstead of Kārwār.

53. **Chersonesus.**—Greek, "peninsula." This answers for the projecting point at the modern Kārwār (14° 49′ N., 74° 8′ E.), from early times a trade center for the North Kanara, and an active port as late as the 16th century, exporting fine muslins from Hubli and elsewhere in the interior, also pepper, cardamoms, cassia, and coarse blue *dungari* cloth. (*Imp. Gaz.*, XV, 65.)

53. **Pirates.**—Marco Polo (III, xxv), says of this coast, "there go forth every year more than a hundred corsair vessels on cruise. These pirates take with them their wives and children, and stay out the whole summer. Their method is to join in fleets of 20 or 30 of these pirate vessels together, and then they form what they call a sea cordon, that is, they drop off till there is an interval of 5 or 6

miles between ship and ship, so that they cover something like a hundred miles of sea, and no merchant ship can escape them. For when any one corsair sights a vessel a signal is made by fire or smoke, and then the whole of them make for this, and seize the merchants and plunder them. After they have plundered them they let them go, saying, 'Go along with you and get more gain, and that mayhap will fall to us also!' But now the merchants are aware of this, and go so well manned and armed, and with such great ships, that they don't fear the corsairs. Still mishaps do befall them at times." In this same vicinity, Yule observes, Ibn Batuta fell into the pirates' hands, and was stripped to the drawers. The northern part of Malabar, Kanara, and the Southern Konkan, were a nest of pirates from a very ancient date until well into the 19th century, when their occupation was destroyed by the British arms.

Marco Polo says (III, xxiv) of the kingdom of Ely (near Mangalore), "if any ship enters their estuary and anchors there, having been bound for some other port, they seize her and plunder the cargo. For they say, 'You were bound for somewhere else, and 'tis God has sent you hither to us, so we have right to all your goods.' And they think it is no sin to act thus. And this naughty custom prevails all over the provinces of India, to wit, that if a ship be driven by stress of weather into some other port than that to which it was bound, it was sure to be plundered. But if a ship came bound originally to the place they receive it with all honor and give it due protection."

In 1673, Yule notes, Sivājī replied to the pleadings of an English embassy, that it was "against the laws of Conchon" (Ptolemy's Pirate Coast!) "to restore any ship or goods that were driven ashore."

Abd-er-Razzak notes the same practices at Calicut.

53. **White Island.**—This is probably the modern Pigeon Island (14° 1′ N., 74° 16′ E.), also known as Nitrān. It lies about 10 miles off the coast, about 300 feet high, and is visible for 25 miles. It abounds in white coral and lime. (*Imp. Gaz.*, XX, 136.)

This is probably the same as the *Nitrias* of Pliny (VI, 26), the stronghold of the pirates, who threatened the Roman merchants; and may be the *Nitra* of Ptolemy.

53. **Naura and Tyndis, the first markets of Damirica.** It seems clear that a long stretch of coast on either side of the modern Goa was given a wide berth by foreign merchant-ships because of the piratical habits of its people, and because it produced no cargo of which they were in search.

Like the following ports, Muziris and Nelcynda, these two have been placed too far north by most of the commentators. The inference from the few words in the Periplus is that the South Konkan and Kanara districts were those more particularly infested by pirates. These may be identified with the Satiya kingdom of Asoka's inscriptions. The Tamil ports, strictly speaking, lay within the region where the Malayālam language is now spoken, that is, within the modern districts of Malabar, Cochin, and Travancore. The Tulu, Kanarese and Telugu districts seem to be within our author's *Dachinabades* rather than his *Damirica*. These four ports probably lay respectively within the four districts into which the Portuguese and Dutch found the Kerala kingdom divided: Cannanore, Calicut, Cochin and Travancore; of which the last-named, at the time of the Periplus, was held by the Pāndya kingdom.

The four Tamil states, Chola, Pāndya, Kerala, and Satiya, are all named in the 2d Rock Edict of Asoka. (Vincent Smith, *Asoka*, p. 115). Mr. Smith thinks (*Early History*, pp. 164, 340-1) that Kerala did not extend north of the Chandragiri river (12° 36′ N.).

Naura being then in North Malabar, may be identified with the modern Cannanore (11° 52′ N., 75° 22′ E.). The latter place is known to have been an active port in the days of the Roman trade, and has yielded one of the most important finds in India of Roman coins, of the reigns of Tiberius, Claudius and Nero.

It seems clear that the identification of this place with the modern Honāvar (14° 17′ N., 74° 27′ E.), while a tempting one, owing to the similarity of names, is not in accord with the facts. Honāvar lies rather within the strip of coast which was in dispute between the Andhra and Saka dynasties, as well as the petty Maurya and Pallava princes; while from similarity of name the modern Cannanore would answer equally well.

The location of Tyndis, of the Chēra kingdom, depends on that of Muziris. It is described as "a village in plain sight on the shore," and may be identified with the modern Ponnāni (10° 48′ N., 75° 56′ E.). This place lying at the mouth of the river of the same name, which drains a rich section of the western mountains known as the Anaimalai Hills, would have been a natural terminus for the pepper produced there, as well as for the beryls of the Coimbatore district. This Ponnāni river, according to the *Imperial Gazetteer* (XX, 164), unlike nearly all others on the west coast, is navigable for small vessels for some distance inland.

Dr. Burnell prefers Kadalundi near Beypore (11° 11′ N., 75° 49′ E.) on the north bank of the river of the same name, which is also navigable to the foot of the mountains, and carries down large quantities of timber. (*Imp. Gaz.*, VIII, 17.) But the distance of 500 stadia between Tyndis and Muziris indicates Ponnāni.

53. **Damirica.**—The text has *Limyrikê*, which previous editions have retained. That name does not appear in India, or in other Roman accounts of it, and it is clearly a corruption caused by the scribe's confusing the Greek *D* and *L*. The name appears in its correct form in the XIIth segment of the Peutinger Tables, almost contemporary with the Periplus, and in Ptolemy as *Dimirikê;* and there seems no good reason for perpetuating the mistake.

Damirica means the "country of the Tamils," that is, the Southern Dravidians as they existed in the first century, including particularly the Chēra, Pāndya and Chola kingdoms; known in their own records as *Drāvida-dēsam*.

53. **Muziris.**—The location of this port was fixed by Burnell, Caldwell and Yule at *Muyiri-kotta*, which as Kodungalur or Cranganore (10° 14′ N., 76° 11′ E.), was an important port in mediæval times. Their argument was based on the 7000 stadia named in the text as the distance between Barygaza and Damirica.

Vincent Smith (*Early History* 340-1) is confident that Muziris and Cranganore are the same. He says "The Kingdom of Satiyaputra must have adjoined Keralaputra; and since the Chandragiri river has always been regarded as the northern boundary of that province, the Satiyaputra Kingdom should probably be identified with that portion of the Konkans—or lowlands between the Western Ghāts and the sea—where the Tulu language is spoken, and of which Mangalore is the center. The name of Kerala is still well remembered and there is no doubt that the Kingdom so called was equivalent to the Southern Konkans or Malabar coast. The ancient capital was Vanji, also named Karuvūr, the *Karoura* of Ptolemy, situated close to Cranganore; which represents Muziris, the port for the pepper trade, mentioned by Pliny and the author of the Periplus at the end of the first century A. D." Vanji, according to the *Imperial Gazetteer* (XX, 21), must be placed at the modern Parūr or Paravūr (10° 10′ N., 76° 15′ E.), where the Periyār River empties into the Cochin back-waters. Parūr is still a busy trading center, as well as the headquarters of the district. While now in the district of Travancore, it formerly belonged to Cochin,—that is, to Chēra or Kerala. It is said to comprise almost all the Jews in Travancore; and the settlement may date from the end of the first century, when it is known that there was a considerable Jewish migration to Southern India.

The earlier identification of Muziris and Nelcynda placed them at Mangalore and Nīleshwar (12° 52′ N., 74° 51′ E., and 12° 16′

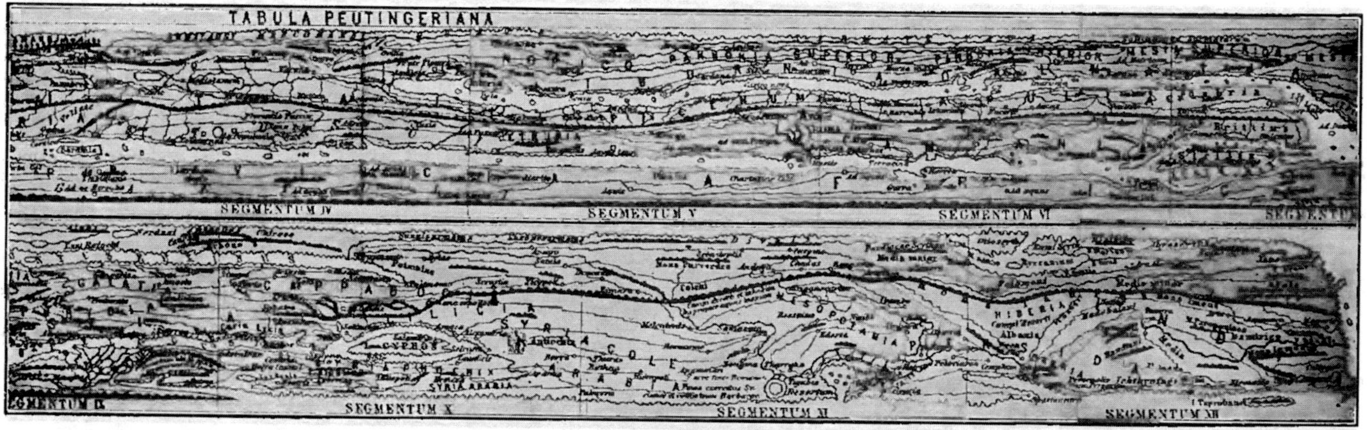


Portion of the Peutinger Tables, from Justus Perthes, *Atlas Antiquus.*

N., 75° 8′ E.). This conflicts with nearly all that we know of the geography and politics of the Tamil kingdoms, and is entirely impossible for Nelcynda. This port, according to the Periplus, belonged to the Pāndyan kingdom, which certainly never extended so far north.

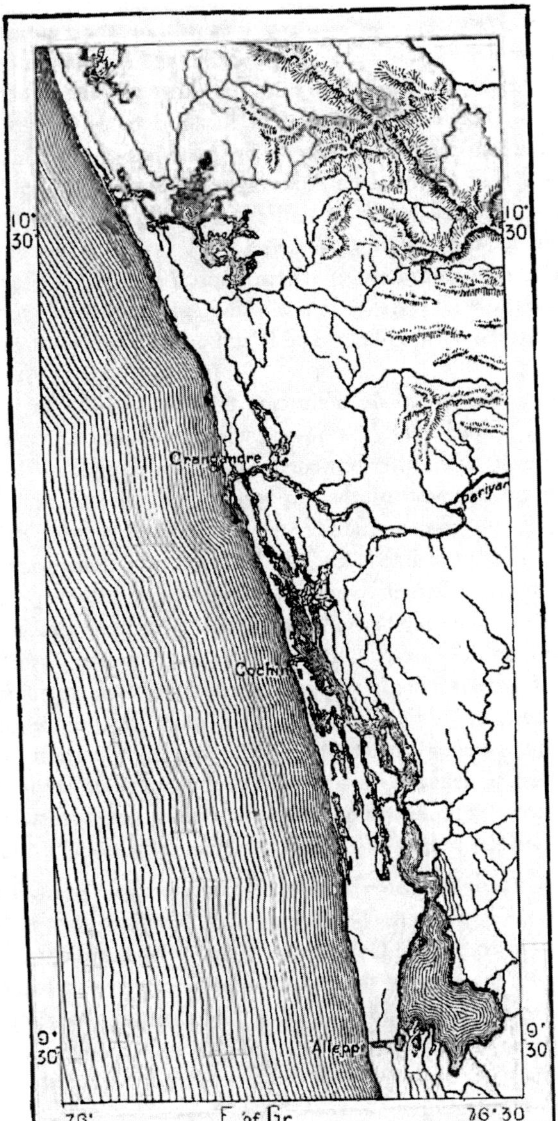


The Cochin Backwaters: from Réclus, *Asia*, Vol. III.

The text tells us that Muziris was distant from Tyndis, "by river and sea, 500 stadia," and Nelcynda from Muziris, "by river and sea, 500 stadia." This can hardly refer to anything but the Cochin backwaters.

53. **Nelcynda.**—This port is called *the city of the Neacyndi*, by Pliny; *Melkynda* by Ptolemy; *Nincylda* by the Peutinger Tables, *Cyncilim* by Friar Odoric, and *Nilcinna* by the Geographer of Ravenna. It was probably in the backwaters, or thoroughfares, behind Cochin (9° 58′ N., 76° 14′ E.), the exact location being uncertain because of the frequent shifting of river-beds, sand-bars and islands; but certainly very near the modern Kottayam (9° 36′ N., 76° 31′ E.), which is exactly 500 stadia, or 50 miles, from Cranganore. Kottayam, according to the *Imperial Gazetteer* (XVI, 7), is a center of the Syrian Christian community, whose church here is one of the most ancient on the west coast. It is also the natural terminus for the trade-routes from the Pīrmed hills, and is still a trade-center of considerable importance.

The name *Nelcynda*, Fabricius thinks (p. 160), is the Sanscrit *Nīlakantha*, "blue neck," a name of Siva. Caldwell, however, prefers *Melkynda*, which he translates "Western Kingdom."

A good account of the topography of the coasts of India is given by J. A. Bains (*Mill's International Geography*, 1907 ed., p. 469). "The coast-line is singularly devoid of indentations, except at the mouths of the larger rivers and toward the northern portion of the west coast. The only harbors except for light-draft vessels, are found a little way up the deltas of the chief rivers, or where, as at Bombay, a group of islands affords adequate shelter from the open sea. The eastern coast, in particular, is provided with little more than a few imperfectly protected roadsteads. The southern portion of the west coast is distinguished by a series of back-waters, or lagoons, parallel with the coast, and affording a safe and convenient waterway for small vessels when the season of high winds makes the ocean unnavigable."

54. **Cerobothra.**—This is a transliteration of *Chēraputra* or *Keralaputra*, the western Tamil kingdom, which in its greatest extension reached from Cape Comorin to Kārwār Point, nearly 7 degrees of latitude. At the time of the Periplus the northern part had separated, while the southern end had passed to its neighbor, the Pāndyan kingdom; leaving Kerala nearly coterminous with modern Malabar and Cochin districts. The capital was at Karūr, or Parūr, opposite Muziris or Cranganore.

Chēraputra is "son of Chēra," one of the legendary three brothers who founded the Dravidian power in South India.

Pliny's use of the word as the name of a king was incorrect; it applies to the country, and is also a dynastic name or royal title.

The Chēra backwaters seem to be referred to by Pliny in a debated passage on the trade of Ceylon with the "Seres" (VI, 22): "their accounts agreed with the reports of our own merchants, who tell us that the wares which they deposit near those brought for sale by the Seres, on the further bank of a river in their country, are removed by them if they are satisfied with the exchange."

Here *Seres* must be read as meaning Chēra, the *Ch* and *S* being interchanged, just as the neighboring Chola kingdom is always *Soli* in Sinhalese records.

It is quite possible that Chēra is also meant by Pliny's *Seres* of XXXIV, 41, who sent the best iron to Rome; this being a product of Haidarābād, and referred to in § 6 of the Periplus, as shipped from India to Adulis. See also under Sarapis, p. 146.

The "silent trade," noted by Fa-Hien in Ceylon itself, is referred to under § 65, and again by Pliny (VI, 20), Pausanias (III, xii, 3), and Cosmas Indicopleustes (book II).

For further references to Chēra and the other Tamil states growing out of the original establishment at Korkai, see Vincent Smith, *Early History*, Chap. xvi;—Caldwell, *Grammar of the Dravidian Languages*, introduction; also *History of Tinnevelly*;—Burnell, *South Indian Palæography*;—Shanguni Menon, *History of Travancore*;—Francis Day, *The Land of the Permauls*;—J. B. Pandian, *Indian Village Folk*;—Sir Walter Elliot, *Coins of Southern India*;—Foulkes, *The Civilization of the Dakhan down to the 6th century B. C.*, in *Indian Antiquary*, 1879, pp. 1-10;—K. P. Padmanabha Menon, *Notes on Malabar and its place-names*, in *Indian Antiquary*, Aug., 1902;—Wilson, *The Pāndyas*, in *Journal of the Royal Asiatic Society*, iii, 199;—Dawson, *The Chēras*, in J. R. A. S., viii, 1;—Sewell, *Lists of Inscriptions, and Sketch of the Dynasties of Southern India*, in the *Archæological Survey*, Madras, 1884;—F. Kielhorn, *Dates of Chola and Pāndya Kings*, in *Epigraphia Indica*, Vols. IV-VIII, inclusive;—*Imperial Gazetteer*, Vol. II, Chaps. i, iii, iv, v, ix;—Bühler, *Indische Palæographie*, and generally, his *Grundriss der Indo-Arischen Philologie und Altertumskunde*;—Fleet, *The Dynasties of the Kanarese Districts*, and Bhandarkar, *Early History of the Dekkan*, in *Gazetteer of the Bombay Presidency*, I, ii;—Loventhal, *Coins of Tinnevelly*;—Hultzsch, *South Indian Inscriptions*.

54. **Abounds in ships.**—In these protected thoroughfares flourished a sea-trade, largely in native Dravidian craft, which was of early creation and of great influence in the interchange of ideas as well as commodities, not only in South India, but in the Persian Gulf,

Merchant-ship of the 2d century, from a relief on a sarcophagus in the Lateran Museum.

and the coasts of Arabia and Africa, with which the trade was principally maintained. Both Buddhist and Brahman writings testify to its existence in the 5th century B. C.; but their evidence is late, as they are the product of the Northern Aryans, an inland race, who appeared in South India after its activities had been widely developed. Better evidence is given by the Dravidian alphabet, supposed to be from a Semitic (Himyaritic, or Phœnician) original, and to date from about 1000 B. C., whereas the Aryan, or Kharosthī, alphabet was formulated after the conquest, about 500 B. C. (R. Sewell, *Hindu Period of Southern India*, in *Imp. Gaz.*, II, 322.)

"Sent from Arabia and by the Greeks" were the ships found by our author in the Chēra backwaters. The text has *Ariaca*, but the error is obvious, as the articles of trade were from foreign, and not Hindu, sources. "No Aryan language had penetrated into these kingdoms, which lived their own life, completely secluded from Northern India, and in touch with the outer world only through the medium of maritime commerce, which had been conducted with safety from very early times. The pearls of the Gulf of Manār, the beryls of Coimbatore, and the pepper of Malabar were not to be had elsewhere, and were largely sought by foreign merchants, as early as the 7th or 8th century B. C." (Vincent Smith, *Early History*, 334.)

Benjamin of Tudela, in the 12th century, gives the following account of trade on this coast:

"Thence is seven days' journey to Khulam (Quilon) which is the beginning of the country of the Sun-worshippers. These are the sons of Cush, who read the stars and are all black in color. They are honest in commerce. When merchants come to them from distant lands and enter the harbour, three of the King's secretaries go down to them and record their names and then bring them before the King, whereupon the King makes himself responsible even for their property which they leave in the open unprotected. There is an official who sits in his office, and the owner of any lost property has only to describe it to him when he hands it back. This custom prevails in all that country. From Passover to New Year, that is all during the summer, no man can go out of his house because of the sun, for the heat in that country is intense, and from the third hour of the day onward, everybody remains in his house until evening. Then they go forth and kindle lights in all the market places and all the streets, and then do their work and business at night-time. For they have to turn night into day in consequence of the great heat of the sun. Pepper is found there. They plant the trees thereof in the fields, and each man of the city knows his own plantation. The trees are small and the pepper is as white as snow. And when they have collected it they place it in sauce-pans and pour boiling water over it, so that it may become strong. Then they take it out of the water and dry it in the sun, and it turns black. Cinnamon and ginger and many other kinds of spices are found in this land."

54. **Pandian kingdom.**—This was Pāndya, the southernmost, and traditionally the earliest, of the three Tamil states. Roughly it coincided with the modern districts of Tinnevelly and Madurā; at the time of the Periplus it extended beyound the Ghāts and included Travancore. The capital, originally at Korkai (the *Colchi* of § 59, which see) had been removed to Madurā (9° 55′ N., 78° 7′ E.).

Here too, as in the Chēra kingdom, the name is used for the country and as a dynastic title, not as the name of any king.

55. **Bacarē.**—(Ptolemy gives *Barkarē*, which is perhaps the preferable reading.) This place, distant 120 stadia from Nelcynda, at an inlet of the sea, can be no other than Porakād (9° 22′ N., 76° 22′ E.), for which it is a close transliteration; while the distance from Kottayam is exactly in accord with the text.

Porakād was once a notable port, but declined with the rise of Alleppey, built a few miles farther north after a canal had been cut through from sea to backwater and harbor works constructed. (*Imp. Gaz.*, XX, 188.) The Portuguese, and subsequently the Dutch, had settlements at Porakād. It is mentioned by Varthema (1503) as *Porcai*, and by Tavernier (1648) as *Porca*. The remains of a Portuguese fort and factory are now covered by the sea, being visible at low water. (Ball, in his edition of Tavernier, I, 241.)

Here also is the mouth of the Achenkoil river, which rises in the Ghāts near the Shencottah pass, the main highway between Travancore and Tinnevelly.

According to Menon (*Notes on Malabar and its place-names*), the settlements were nearly all east of the backwaters at the Christian era, and the present beaches existed only as tide-shoals. During the middle ages there was a period of elevation, which led to the formation of new islands, while floods from the mountains changed the courses of the rivers, and the location of the inlets. At present the tendency is toward subsidence, houses built at Cochin a century ago being now under water. About 800 B. C., according to local tradition, the sea reached the hills.

Megasthenes, in the 4th century B. C., mentioned as "on the sea-coast" the town of Tropina (Tripontari) now on the mainland side of the backwaters; Ptolemy's three shore towns between Muziris and *Barkarē* are likewise on the land side.

56. **Large ships.**—The increase in the size of shipping following the discovery of Hippalus is referred to also in § 10. Pliny speaks

of the same thing in describing the trade between Malabar and Ceylon. "The navigation," he says (VI, 24), "was formerly confined to vessels made of rushes, rigged in the manner familiar on the Nile. The vessels of recent times are built with prows at either end so that there may be no need of turning around while sailing in these channels, which are extremely narrow. The tonnage of the vessels is 3,000 amphoræ." (About 33 tons.)

By "double prows" Pliny probably means some such build and rig as shown in the accompanying illustration, which is typical of the Indian Ocean generally. Mast and sail can be reversed at will, so that the craft can be sailed in either direction.

56. **Pepper,** black and white.—*Piper nigrum,* Linn., order *Piperaceæ.* A perennial climber, wild in the forests of Travancore and Malabar, and extensively cultivated from very early times, in the hot, damp localities of Southern India.

Lassen (I, 278), notes that the Greek word *peperi,* Latin *piper,* simply repeats the Indian name *pippali.*

The antiquity of the trade in pepper is not so easily shown as that in other spices. There is no certain mention of it in the Egyptian inscriptions. In the Hebrew scriptures it is unknown, nor has it a place among the "mint and anise and cummin" of the Gospels. Herodotus has no bit of folklore to attach to it. Theophrastus, indeed, in the 4th century B. C., knows it as a medicine, and Dioscorides distinguishes between black, white and long pepper. The Sanscrit writers describe it as a medicine for fever and dyspepsia, used together with ginger and long pepper; these were their "three pungent substances." (*Mahāvagga,* VI, 19, 1; see also I-tsing, *Record of Buddhist Practices* [7th century A. D.], chap. xxviii; Takakusu's edition, p. 135.) The Romans had it after their conquests in Asia Minor, Syria and Egypt, and at once provided the greatest market for it. Egypt knew it, probably, through the sea-trade of the Ptolemies; Syria through the caravan-trade to Tyre from the Persian Gulf. There is some reason for supposing that pepper was the spice more especially in demand in Babylonia and the Persian Gulf trade generally, just as cinnamon was that more especially reserved for Egypt; and that the most active demand for it came with the extension of the Persian empire under Darius. The trade was by sea and not overland; Herodotus knows the Dravidians (III, 100) only as having "a complexion closely resembling the Aethiopians," and as being "situated very far from the Persians, toward the south, and never subject to Darius." It may also be surmised that a steady demand for pepper existed in China before it arose in Rome, and that this was one reason for the sailing of the junks to the Malabar coast in the 2d century B. C. and probably earlier. In Marco Polo's day the tonnage of the junks was calculated according to their capacity in baskets of pepper; and he found (II, lxxxii) "for one shipload of pepper that goes to Alexandria or elsewhere, destined for Christendom, there come a hundred such, aye and more too, to this haven of Zayton" (Chwan-chau, above Amoy).

The trade in pepper in the time of the Roman Empire brought the merchants unheard-of profits just as it did later the Genoese and Venetians. It was one of the most important articles of commerce between India and Rome, supplying perhaps three-quarters of the total bulk of the average westbound cargo.

The constant use of pepper in the most expensive Roman cookery is reflected by its price, quoted by Pliny (XII, 14) as 15 denarii, or about $2.55 per lb.

Among the offerings by the emperor Constantine to the church under St. Silvester, were costly vessels and fragrant gums and spices, including frankincense, nard, balsam, storax, myrrh, cinnamon, saffron and pepper.

That it continued in high esteem is shown by the terms offered by Alaric for raising the siege of Rome: "the immediate payment of 5,000 lbs. of gold, of 30,000 lbs. of silver, of 4,000 robes of silk, of 3,000 pcs. of fine scarlet cloth, and of 3,000 lbs. weight of pepper." (Gibbon, *Decline and Fall*, III, 271-2.)

Pliny, indeed, expresses surprise at the taste that brought it into so great favor (XII, 14): "It is quite surprising that the use of pepper has come so much into fashion, seeing that in other substances which we use, it is sometimes their sweetness, and sometimes their appearance that has attracted our notice; whereas, pepper has nothing in it that can plead as a recommendation to either fruit or berry, its only desirable quality being a certain pungency; and yet it is for this that we import it all the way from India! Who was the first to make trial of it as an article of food? And who, I wonder, was the man that was not content to prepare himself by hunger only for the satisfying of a greedy appetite?"

In mediæval Europe the trade was highly organized, the spice being handled especially by merchants called "pepperers;" and the prices quoted in Rogers' *History of Agriculture and Prices in England* show that in the years just prior to the Portuguese discovery of the Cape route, a pound of pepper brought two shillings, being four days' pay for a carpenter! Yet the people preferred it above all other spices; it was the first thing asked for by "Glutton" in *Piers Plowman* (V, 310-13):

"I haue gode ale, gossib," quod she· "glotown, wiltow assaye?"
"Hastow aughte in thi purs· any hote spices?"
"I haue peper and piones," quod she· "and a pounde of garlike,
A ferthyngworth of fenel-seed· for fastyngdayes."

Friar Odoric (Chap. iii) describes the pepper production of "Minibar" as follows: "the wood in which it grows containeth in circuit eighteen days' journey. And in the said wood or forest there are two cities, one called Flandrina, and the other Cyncilim" (probably Nelcynda). "In the aforesaid wood pepper is had after this manner: first it groweth in leaves like unto pot-herbs, which they plant near unto great trees as we do our vines, and they bring forth pepper in clusters, as our vines do yield grapes, but being ripe, they are of a green color, and are gathered as we gather grapes, and then the grains are laid in the sun to be dried, and being dried are put into earthen vessels; and thus is pepper made and kept. . . At the south end of the said forests stands the city of Polumbrum, which aboundeth with merchandise of all kinds." (The proper form would be Polumbum, the Latinized version of Polum or Kolum, the modern Quilon. *P* and *K* are interchanged here as in the case of Karūr, the modern Parūr.)

Tavernier found pepper sold principally at Tuticorin and Calicut. Some, however, came from Rājāpur on the Ratnāgiri coast. "The Dutch," he says (II, xii. Ball's ed.), "who purchase it from the *Malabaris* do not pay in cash for it, but exchange for it many kinds of merchandise, as cotton, opium, vermilion, and quicksilver, and it is this pepper which is exported to Europe. . . . 500 *livres* of it brings only 38 *reals*, but on the merchandise which they give in exchange they gain 100 per cent. One can get it for the equivalent in money of 28 or 30 *reals* cash, but to purchase it in that way would be much more costly than the Dutch method."

He mentions also (I, xvi) a large storehouse kept by the Portuguese at Cochin, called the "Pepper House."

See also Watt, 896-901;—Flückiger and Hanbury, *Pharmacographia*, p. 579;—*Encyclopædia Britannica*, article "Pepper;"—Brandis, *Indian Trees*;—Vignoli, *Liber Pontificalis*, Rome, 1724-55.

Odoric also describes a propitiation of the serpents guarding the pepper, similar to those of the frankincense and diamond; the story is better in the version of "Sir John Mandeville" (Chap. xviii): "In that country be many manner of serpents and of other vermin for the great heat of the country and of the pepper. And some men say, that when they will gather the pepper, they make fire, to burn about to make the serpents and the cockodrills to flee. But save their grace of all that say so. For if they burnt about the trees that bear, the pepper should be burnt, and it would dry up all the virtue, as of any other thing; and then they did themselves much harm, and they should never quench the fire. But thus they do: they anoint their hands and their feet with a juice made of snails and of other things made therefor, of the which the serpents and the venomous beasts hate and dread the savour; and that maketh them flee before them, because of the smell, and then they gather it surely enough."

This belief in the guarding of treasure, or of wealth-producing trees, or the habitation thereof, by spirits in the form of serpents, has already been noted as attaching to frankincense (§ 29), and will appear likewise with the diamond (§ 56). The supposed necessity of appeasing or else expelling the serpents by the use of other substances was held strongly in Rome itself. Pliny ascribes this power to galbanum, "a kind of giant fennel" (XII, 56). "If ignited in a pure state it has the property of driving away serpents by its smoke." And again (XXIV, 13), "the very touch of it, mingled with oil and spondylium, is sufficient to kill a serpent." So also Virgil (*Georgics*, III, 415):

> "Galbaneoque agitare graves nidore chelydros."

The frankincense gatherers depended on burning storax; see under § 29, pp. 131-2.

56. **Malabathrum.**—Heeren, Vincent and McCrindle translate this "betel," and thereby accuse the Periplus of a blunder in §§ 63 and 65, where the substance is described as coming from the Himalaya mountains. The translation rests on an assumption that the *petros* of the text in § 65 is the same as the Portuguese *betre* or *betle* meaning betel.

Watt (p. 891) says this latter is rather derived from a Malay word *vettila* or *vern-ila*, meaning "leaf," and it is very doubtful if the betel of modern times entered into international commerce in the Roman period.

The word *petros* is rather from the Sanscrit *patra*, "leaf," of the *tamala* tree which, as explained under §§ 10, 13 and 14, is a variety of cinnamon or laurel. The leaf exported from Southern India was also from *Cinnamomum iners*, and possibly from the *Cinnamomum zeylanicum* which in later times was cultivated in Ceylon and is one of the sources of our cinnamon. (See Tavernier, *Travels*, II, xii). The leaf coming from the Himalaya mountains was principally from the *Cinnamomum tamala*, which was native there. Pliny says that the *malabathrum* which entered so prominently into Roman perfumes should have a smell like nard, and other Roman writers seem to have confused it with the Ganges nard mentioned in § 63. (See also Lassen, I, 279-285; II, 555-561.)

Horace, (II, vii, 89), refers to it as follows:

———"Coronatus nitentes
Malobathro Syrio capillos."

Malabathrum and spikenard were the two most treasured ingredients of the ointments and perfumes of the Roman empire.

A curious trade condition is suggested by the fact that the Romans knew cinnamon and cassia only as coming from the Somali coast of Africa, while they knew the malabathrum as coming from various parts of India; and yet the malabathrum was, in at least one case, the leaf from the same tree that produced a variety of cinnamon. The Periplus in no place mentions the export of cinnamon from India, but in §§ 56 and 63 describes the export of *malabathrum*. This seems to indicate a trade monopoly of very ancient date and thorough enforcement, by which the bark only went for trade purposes to the African coast, while the leaf was an open article of trade to India.

Lindsay (*History of Merchant Shipping and Ancient Commerce*, I, 156-7), also remarks on this "striking instance of the secrecy with which the ancients conducted the more valuable portions of their trade." Herodotus, he thinks, "could only have obtained his information about cinnamon from the merchants who traded along the shores of Malabar . . . who kept the secret of its *provenance* as the Carthaginians kept that of British tin."

Another letter from Mr. R. E. Drake-Brockman, dated Berbera, April 27, 1910, gives further confirmation of the absence of the cinnamon species from the Somali peninsula. (See under § 13, p. 87).

"It is unlikely that the original inhabitants of this country knew anything of cinnamon until they had heard of its commercial value from the natives of India or Arabs, who have been known to the coastal people from the earliest times. These same traders, if they penetrated into the interior at all, which is extremely doubtful, would have hunted for anything of any commercial value, and if cinnamon had existed they would have continued to export it up to the present day as they do frankincense, myrrh and gum arabic. A point which is worthy of notice is that the Somalis have names for all the last three, whereas they have had to go to the Arabic language for their names for cinnamon. They know of two varieties, *koronfol* and *karfa*, both of which are imported.

"It is highly probable that both Strabo and Pliny were led to believe that the myrrh, frankincense, cinnamon and spices pouring into the kingdom of Aethiopia and upper Egypt all came from the same place. Possibly traders in Aethiopia obtained a better price for their myrrh and cinnamon if they stated the difficulties and dangers they experienced collecting it in the countries of the savage Gallas or their antecedents in the Horn of Africa.

"There can be no doubt that the natives of these regions have always been greatly feared by their less warlike neighbors. The Somalis and their antecedents have always been keen traders, and there can be little doubt that if cinnamon ever existed in these regions, the practice of collecting it would not have been dropped unless the species here collected was of a very inferior quality and gradually lost its marketable value."

---

Through the courtesy of the same gentleman in gathering specimens of the various aromatic gums of Somaliland, a more positive statement may be made than was possible under § 32, pp. 141-2, concerning the Egyptian frankincense trade, in determining the character of the trees depicted on the Punt reliefs at Deir el Bahri, a photograph of which was reproduced on page 120.

Professor Breasted in his *Ancient Records of Egypt* (II, 263-5), calls this tree *myrrh*, and translates it as myrrh wherever the records refer to it. In the publications of the Egypt Exploration Fund (*The Temple of Deir-el-Bahri*, III, 12), it is called *frankincense*, but is located in Somaliland in the neighborhood of Mosyllum, because of the supposed African appearance of the Punt people who appear elsewhere in the reliefs.

Specimens of true myrrh sent from Somaliland show clearly that no sculptor could have intended to depict by the rich foliage on the reliefs, the bare, thorny, trifoliate but almost leafless myrrh tree, nor yet the almost equally leafless varieties of Somaliland frankincense. This tree is clearly *Boswellia Carteri*, the frankincense of the rich plain of Dhofar in Southern Arabia. This is the only place producing frankincense where the trees can be cultivated on a fertile plain by the shore, in the midst of green fields and cattle. There is no place on the African coast which meets these conditions. Naville's objection that the natives are "not Arabs," *i. e.*, not Semitic, is really in favor of such a belief; they were the pre-Semitic, Cushite race whose dominions centered at Dhofar, and who are represented there by the modern Gara tribe. There can be no question that the trees in that relief are the frankincense of Dhofar, the "Sachalitic frankincense" of the Periplus, the modern *Shehri luban*.

To the possible objection that the Darror and Nogal valleys, in the southern part of the Somali peninsula, are fertile and might produce a better foliage than the northern coast, it may be said that the fertility stops far short of the east coast, which is absolutely desert; whereas the reliefs show a rich and fertile plain bordering the sea.

56. **A great quantity of coin.**—The drain of specie from Rome to the East has already been referred to under § 49, and is bitterly condemned by Pliny. "The subject," he says (VI, 26), "is one well worthy of our notice, seeing that in no year does India drain us of less than 550,000,000 *sesterces* ($22,000,000) giving back her own wares, which are sold among us at fully 100 times their first cost."

A generation before the Periplus, in 22 A. D., this was made the subject of a letter from the emperor Tiberius to the Roman Senate:

"If a reform is in truth intended, where must it begin? and how am I to restore the simplicity of ancient times? . . . How shall we reform the taste for dress? . . . How are we to deal with the peculiar articles of feminine vanity, and in particular with that rage for jewels and precious trinkets, which drains the empire of its wealth, and sends, in exchange for baubles, the money of the Commonwealth to foreign nations, and even to the enemies of Rome?" (Tacitus, *Annals*, iii, 53.)

This extravagant importation of luxuries from the East without adequate production of commodities to offer in exchange, was the main cause of the successive depreciation and degradation of the Roman currency, leading finally to its total repudiation. The monetary standard of Rome was established by accumulations of precious metal resulting from its wars. The sack of the rich city of Tarentum in 272 B. C., enabled Rome to change her coinage from copper to silver. After the destruction of Carthage and Corinth in 146 B. C., gold coinage came into general use, and through the wars of Cæsar gold became so plentiful that in 47 B. C. its ratio to silver was as 1 to 8.9, lower than ever before or since. Under Augustus the ratio was about 1 to 9.3, the *aureus* being worth 25 silver *denarii*. Under Claudius the sea-route to India was opened, after which came the reign of Nero, marked by every form of wastefulness and extravagance, during which the silver *denarius* fell from 1-84 to 1-96 pound of silver, an alloy of 20 per cent copper being added to it. Under Trajan the alloy reached 30 per cent, and under Septimius Severus 50 per cent. Finally, under Elagabalus, 218 A. D., the *denarius* had become wholly copper and was repudiated. Even the golden *aureus* was tampered with. Exported in large quantities to become the basis of exchange in India, the supply at home was exhausted. Under

Augustus the *aureus* weighed 1-40 of a pound of gold, and under Diocletian it weighed but 1-60. Under Constantine it fell to 1-72, when the coin was taken only by weight (Sabatier, *Monnaies Byzantines*, i, 51-2; Brooks Adams, *Law of Civilization and Decay*, 25-8). It was this steady loss of capital, to replace which no new wealth was produced, that led finally to the abandonment of Rome and to the transfer of the capital at the end of the 3d century to Nicomedia and soon afterward to Byzantium.

Coin of Nero commemorating the opening of the harbor-works at Ostia.

In the Madras Government Museum there is nearly a complete series of the coins of the Roman Emperors during the period of active trade with India, all of them excavated in southern India. A notable fact is that there are two distinct breaks in the series; which may of course be supplied by later discovery, but which seem to indicate a cessation of trade due to political turmoil in Rome. The coins of Tiberius, Caligula, Claudius and Nero are numerous. There are very few of Vespasian and Titus anywhere in India. Those of Domitian, Nerva, Trajan and Hadrian are frequent; then there comes another break lasting until the time of Commodus. This indication, so far as it has any value, points again to the dating of the Periplus during the reign of Nero rather than during those of Vespasian and Titus.

For a full account of Roman coins discovered in South India, see E. Thurston, Catalogue No. 2, Madras Government Museum, pp. 1-47.

56. **Crude glass.**—The origin of the glass industry in India is uncertain. According to Mitra, *Antiquities of Orissa*, I, 101, it was made in Ceylon in the 3d century B. C., and Pliny (XXXVI, 66) refers to the glass of India as superior to all others, because "made of pounded crystal." Mirrors, with a foil of lead and tin, were largely used there at the time of the Periplus, and Pliny indicates (XXXVII,

20) that "the people of India, by coloring crystal, have found a method of imitating various precious stones, beryls in particular." An early play, the *Mrichchhakatikā* or *Little Clay Cart*, gives a scene in a court of justice to this effect (Mitra, *op. cit.*, 100; see also A. W. Ryder's translation, Cambridge, 1905):

"Do you know these ornaments?"

"Have I not said? They may be different, though like; I cannot say more; they may be imitations by some skillful artist."

"It is true; provost, examine them; they may be different, though like; the dexterity of the artists is no doubt very great, and they readily fabricate imitations of ornaments they have once seen, in such a manner that the difference shall scarcely be discernible."

56. **Copper, tin, and lead.**—As at Barygaza, intended chiefly for the coinage. So Pliny (XXXIV, 17): "India has neither brass nor lead, but exchanges precious stones and pearls for them." The Indian coins were of lead, slightly alloyed with either copper or tin. (Sir Walter Elliot, *Coins of Southern India*, p. 22.)

Lead was used also, mixed with a little tin in thin sheets, as a foil for the manufacture of mirrors. (Mitra, *op. cit.*, p. 101.)

56. **Orpiment.**—This is the yellow sulphide of arsenic, appearing in the form of smooth shining scales, which have long been an article of export from the Persian Gulf to India.

Pliny (VI, 26) says, "Next to these is the nation of the Ori and then the Hyctanis (Rud Shur?) a river of Carmania, with an excellent harbor at its mouth, and producing gold; at this spot the writers state that for the first time they caught sight of the Great Bear. The star Arcturus too, they tell us, was not to be seen here every night, and never when it was seen, during the whole of it. Up to this spot extended the empire of the Achæmenidæ, and in these districts are to be found mines of copper, iron, arsenic, and red lead."

The principal use of orpiment was as a yellow pigment—*auri pigmentum*—making a durable mineral paint, as did realgar and lapis lazuli.

56. **Wheat for the sailors.**—Marco Polo also notes (III, xvii), "No wheat grows in this province, but rice only."

56. **Cottonara.**—Dr. Burnell derives this from *Kolatta-nādū*, which he identifies with North Malabar, of which Cannanore and Tellicherry are the centers. Dr. Buchanan prefers *Kadatta-nādū*, South Malabar, on either side of Calicut. In mediæval times the domain of the Rājās of *Kolatnād* included both. Bishop Caldwell, in his *Dravidian Grammar*, derives the name from Malayālam *kadatta*, transport or conveyance, and *nādū*, district. Menon (*Indian Antiquary*, Aug. 1902), suggests *kadal*, sea, or *kōdu*, mountain; and

*kōdu-nādū*, the hill-country back of the sea-coast, would accord with the facts while supporting the transliteration of the text. In any case the term does not seem to have been applied to an exact locality.

56. **Great quantities of fine pearls.**—These were from the fisheries of the Gulf of Manār, mentioned in § 59, and brought to be sold in the Chēra ports, the meeting-point of Eastern and Western trade.

56. **Silk cloth.**—From China, by way of Tibet and the Ganges. See under §§ 39, 49 and 64.

56. **Gangetic spikenard.**—See under § 63.

56. **Transparent stones.**—These were principally the beryls of the Coimbatore district, for which there was a constant demand in Rome, and which always found their principal foreign market in the Malabar ports. This localization of the gem trade continued until after the Portuguese period in India; the reason is stated by Tavernier (II, xxi):

"Goa was formerly the place where there was the largest trade in all Asia in diamonds, rubies, sapphires, topazes, and other stones. All the miners and merchants went there to sell the best which they had obtained at the mines, because they had there full liberty to sell, whereas, in their own country, if they showed anything to the kings and princes, they were compelled to sell at whatever price they pleased to fix. There was also at Goa a large trade in pearls, both of those which came from the island of Bahrein in the Persian Gulf, and those fished for in the Straits of Manār on the coast of the island of Ceylon."

India and Ceylon were preeminently the source of production of precious stones of all kinds, which were exported to every part of the civilized world. Watt (p. 556) classifies the production as follows:

1. The Beryl group, from the sea-green aquamarine to the white. (The *beryllium* of Pliny, XXXVII, 20.)
2. Diamond. (The *adamas* of Pliny, XXXVII, 15.)
3. Pearl.
4. Ruby. (The *carbunculus* of Pliny, XXXVII, 25.)
5. Sapphire, occurring in numerous colors, various blues, violet, yellow, green and white. Produced mainly on the Southern Malabar hills, now rarely found in India but more frequently in Ceylon. (The *hyacinthus* of Pliny, XXXVII, 41.)
6. Spinel. (Included among the 12 varieties of Pliny's *carbunculus*.)
7. Topaz. Watt doubts its production in India at any place, and the Periplus shows on the contrary that it was imported

from the Red Sea. (The *chrysolithos* of Pliny, XXXVII, 42.)

8. Turquoise. A product of Persia, not occurring in India but reaching the northwestern ports of trade. (The *callaina* of Pliny, XXXVII, 33.)
9. Garnet. Common in many parts of India; those of Rajputana being the best. (One of the 12 varieties, perhaps the *alabandic*, of Pliny's *carbunculus*.)
10. Jade and Jadeite; found mainly in Turkestan but also in upper Burma, while a serpentine from Afghanistan is often substituted. While not produced in India, these all find their way to Indian markets. The leading market is China.
11. Lapis Lazuli, or ultramarine; also from Persia. Largely used for decoration of all kinds and in demand in India, Egypt and the Mediterranean world from the earliest times. (The *sapphiros* of Pliny, XXXVII, 39.)
12. Quartzose, including
    a. Rock crystals, white and colored, which the Romans do not seem to have distinguished from more precious stones. (The *crystal* of Pliny, XXXVII, 9-10.)
    b. Agate, carnelian, bloodstone, chrysoprase, jasper, chalcedony, cat's eye, onyx, opal, etc. (*Achates*, *murrhine*; *sarda*; *heliotropium*; *chrysoprasus*; *iaspis*, *carchedonia*; *sardonyx*; *astrobolos*; *onyx*; *opal* (Pliny, XXXVII.)
13. Tourmalines, varying from black through red, dark blue, olive green, and white, the red varieties being commonest in India. (The *lychnis* of Pliny, XXXVII, 29.)

For further discussion of the deposits and trade, see Lassen, I, 229-43; Tavernier, II.

"Beryls," says Pliny (XXXVII, 20), "are produced in India, and are rarely to be found elsewhere. The lapidaries cut all beryls of a hexagonal form, because the color, which is deadened by a dull uniformity of the surface, is heightened by the reflection from the angles. If they are cut in any other way, these stones have no brilliancy whatever." (The crystals are naturally hexahedral.) "The most esteemed beryls are those which in color resemble the pure green of the sea. . . . The people of India are marvelously fond of beryls of an elongated form, and say that these are the only precious stones they prefer wearing without the addition of gold."

In the *Mrichchhakatikā*, an early Sanscrit play, there is a scene which includes a row of jewelers' shops, "where skillful artists are examining pearls, topazes, sapphires, beryls, rubies, lapis lazuli, coral and other jewels; some set rubies in gold; some work with gold ornaments on colored thread, some string pearls, some grind the lapis lazuli, some pierce shells, and some cut coral." (Mitra, *op. cit.*, p. 100.)

56. **Diamonds.**—The text is *adamas*. Some commentators, notably Dana, have doubted whether the Romans ever knew the true diamond. There can be no doubt that Pliny in his description (XXXVII, 15) includes under *adamas* other substances, probably quartz, iron ore, emery, etc., but he also says that the diamond possessed the greatest value, not only among the precious stones, but of all human possessions; and as Watt says (p. 556), India was long the only source of diamonds known to European nations.

Garcia de Orta (1563), mentions various Eastern diamond mines, such as those of "Bisnager" (Vijayanagar) and the "Decam" (Deccan). Ball, in his translation of Tavernier's *Travels*, gives full particulars of all the Indian sources of diamonds (II, 450-461). Tavernier was a diamond merchant and the first European (1676) to examine critically the diamonds and court jewels of India.

The principal districts were,

(1) Southern Group:—districts of Kadapa, Bellary, Karnúl, Kistnā, Godāverī, (Golconda, etc.);

(2) Middle Group:—Mahānadī valley, districts of Sambalpur, Chanda;

(3) Northern Group:—Vindhyan conglomerates near Panna (still worked).

Pliny (XXXVII, 15) describes the Indian *adamas* as "found, not in a stratum of gold, but in a substance of a kindred nature to crystal; which it closely resembles in its transparency and its highly polished hexangular and hexahedral forms." (The true form of the diamond is octahedral.) "In shape it is turbinated, running to a point at either extremity, and closely resembling, marvelous to think of, two cones united at the base. In size, too, it is as large even as a hazel-nut."

The Romans seem to have had no knowledge of diamond-cutting. Pliny goes on to say that "its hardness is beyond all expression, while at the same time it quite sets fire at defiance; owing to which indomitable powers it has received the name which it derives from the Greek." (*a* privative, and *damaō*, "to subdue.")

After his description of the hardness of the diamond, Pliny observes, "this indomitable power, which sets at naught the two most violent agents in nature, fire, namely, and iron, is made to yield before the blood of a he-goat. The blood, however, must be fresh and warm; the stone, too, must be well steeped in it."

Ball (Tavernier, *Travels*, II, 460-1), quotes a story from Nicol Conti (15th century) about Indian diamonds obtainable only by flinging pieces of meat on the mountain,'' where the diamonds could not be collected owing to the number of serpents. The pieces of meat with diamonds sticking to them were then carried to their nests by birds of prey, from whence they were recovered by diamond seekers. . . . This myth is founded on the very common practice in India on the opening of a mine, to offer up cattle to propitiate the evil spirits who are supposed to guard treasures—these being represented by the myth. At such sacrifices birds of prey assemble to pick up what they can;'' which is the foundation for the remainder of the story.

Here we have a striking similarity to the beliefs connected with the gathering of frankincense, as outlined under § 29, and pepper (§ 56).

The *Thousand Nights and One Night* gives substantially the same story (dxliv-v; Sinbad the Sailor, 2d voyage), while sufficiently identifying the stone:

"Walking along the valley I found that its soil was of diamond, the stone wherewith they pierce jewels and precious stones and porcelain and onyx, for that it is a hard dense stone, whereon neither iron nor steel hath effect, neither can we cut off aught therefrom nor break it, save by means of the leadstone.''

Marco Polo (III, xix) records more definitely this ancient belief:

"Moreover in those mountains great serpents are rife to a marvelous degree, besides other vermin, and this owing to the great heat. The serpents are also the most venomous in existence, insomuch that any one going to that region runs fearful peril; for many have been destroyed by these evil reptiles.

"Now among these mountains there are certain great and deep valleys, to the bottom of which there is no access. Wherefore the men who go in search of the diamonds take with them pieces of flesh, as lean as they can get, and these they cast into the bottom of a valley. Now there are numbers of white eagles that haunt those mountains and feed upon the serpents. When the eagles see the meat thrown down they pounce upon it and carry it up to some rocky hill-top where they begin to rend it. But there are men on the watch, and as soon as they see that the eagles have settled they raise a loud shouting to drive them away. And when the eagles are thus frightened away the men recover the pieces of meat, and find them full of diamonds which have stuck to the meat down in the bottom. For the abundance of diamonds down there in the depth of the valley is astonishing, but nobody can get them; and if one could it would be only to be incontinently devoured by the serpents which are so rife there."

The part played by the eagles is that of other sacred birds, for the defence and profit of man. Compare the bird Jatāyu, who gave his life in defence of Sītā against the Raksha Rāvana, in the *Rāmāyana;* the ibis at Buto who defended Egypt against the frankincense-serpents, (p. 132), and the eagles who fought the dragons. (Virgil, *Aeneid,* XI, 755; Pliny, X, 5.)

Connected with these beliefs was that in the efficacy of the diamond in warding off from the wearer all sorts of evils. "Sir John Mandeville" (*Travels,* XVII), recounts it for his day, and it may still be observed.

"He that beareth the diamond upon him, it giveth him hardiness and manhood, and it keepeth the limbs of his body whole. It giveth him victory of his enemies in plea and in war, if his cause be rightful. . . . And if any cursed witch or enchanter should bewitch him, all that sorrow and mischance shall turn to himself through virtue of that stone. And no wild beast dare assail the man that beareth it on him. And it healeth him that is lunatic, and them that the fiend pursueth or travaileth. And if venom or poison be brought in presence of the diamond, anon it beginneth to wax moist and for to sweat. . . Nathles it befalleth often time that the good diamond loseth his virtue by sin, and for incontinence of him that beareth it. And then it is needful to make it to recover his virtue again, or else it is of little value."

56. **Sapphires.**—The text is *hyakinthos,* which has been translated as jacinth, ruby and amethyst. Jacinth is a product of Africa rather than India. Rubies are from Burma and probably never came in great quantities from India. Pliny says that the hyacinth resembles the amethyst, but draws a distinction between them. Pliny probably had in mind a violet sapphire, and his word really might be translated as meaning all tints of sapphire from blue to purple.

Dionysius Periegetes refers to the "lovely land of the Indians where the complexions of the dwellers are dark, their limbs exquisitely sleek and smooth, and the hair of their heads surpassing smooth and dark blue like the hyacinth." (McCrindle, *Ancient India,* p. 188.)

W. Goodchild (*Precious Stones,* p. 183), also thinks that the sapphire was the *hyacinthus* of Pliny, and says that the principal source of sapphires in that part of the world was in the watered gravels of Southern Ceylon, which were derived from watered crystaline rocks; and at the time of the Periplus the natural market would have been on the Malabar coast. The ruby, which is practically of the same chemical composition, being of the corundum group, was found in the same place as the sapphire in Ceylon, and was probably classified by Pliny under the *carbunculus* (XXXVII, 25). Both rubies and sapphires are found in much greater quantities in Burma and Siam, but at the time of the Periplus these deposits were probably unknown to western commerce.

56. **Tortoise-shell from Chryse.**—Fabricius objects to this reading, and alters it to "that found along the coast;" but it is probable that the text gives a correct reference to the active trade of Eastern shipping in South Indian ports; which is, indeed, specifically mentioned in §§ 60 and 63. Marco Polo notes particularly the ships "from the great province of Manzi," and says (III, xxv) that the ships from Malabar to Aden and Egypt "are not one to ten of those that go to the eastward; a very notable fact."

To assume that conditions were the same at the time of the Periplus would be to go beyond the evidence; yet the records of the Chinese themselves point strongly to the existence of an active sea-trade at that time, certainly to Malacca, and less frequently, perhaps, to India and beyond.

With this item ends the list of articles traded in by the author of the Periplus. It is interesting to compare it with the letter from the Zamorin of Calicut to the King of Portugal, carried by Vasco da Gama on his return from India fourteen centuries later: "In my kingdom there is abundance of cinnamon, cloves, ginger, pepper, and precious stones. What I seek from thy country is gold, silver, coral, and scarlet."

57. **Hippalus first discovered.**—The discovery of Hippalus, which may be placed at about 45 A. D. (see p. 8), opened a new ocean to Roman shipping; but it is probable that Arabian and Dravidian craft had frequented that ocean for many centuries, and inconceivable that they should not have made use of the periodic changes of the monsoons, by far the most notable feature of their climate. The evidence of both countries indicates, on the contrary, that they steered boldly out of sight of land, before records were written to tell of it

Mr. Kennedy in an article in the *Journal of the Royal Asiatic Society*, 1898, (pp. 248-287) also thinks that the monsoons were understood before the time of Hippalus, but doubts the beginning of any regular sea-trade before the beginning of the 7th century B. C., ascribing all such trade to the activities of Nabonidus, in whose time ships were known to have come to Babylon from India and even from China. Following this reign he thinks sea-trade between India and

Babylon flourished for a couple of centuries, being mainly Dravidian but partly Aryan, and leading to the settlement of Indian traders in Arabia, East Africa, Babylonia and China. He minimizes the importance of the early Egyptian trading-voyages, considering them purely local, while the numerous references to articles and routes of early trade in the Hebrew scriptures he passes by with the assertion that they are due to the revision following the return of Ezra.

But whatever may have been Ezra's revision of the Hebrew books, substantially the same articles of trade are described in the records of Egypt at corresponding dates, and they indicate a trade in articles of Indian origin to the Somali coast and overland to the Nile, centuries before Ezra's day. (See also under §§ 6, 10, 11, and 12.)

Such opinions presume a continuous trading-journey without exchange of cargoes at common meeting-points. But primitive trade passes from tribe to tribe and port to port. At the time of the Periplus cargoes changed hands in Malacca, Malabar, Somaliland, South Arabia, Adulis and Berenice. The custom is stated in detail in the Deir el Bahri reliefs describing Queen Hatshepsut's expedition of 1500 B. C., where Amon-Re tells the queen,

"No one trod the incense-terraces, which the people knew not; they were heard of from mouth to mouth by hearsay of the ancestors. The marvels brought thence under thy fathers, the Kings of Lower Egypt, *were brought from one to another*, and since the time of the ancestors of the Kings of Upper Egypt, who were of old, *as a return for many payments.*" (Breasted, *Ancient Records*, II, 287).

It was the particular achievement of the Egyptian Punt expeditions that they traced the treasured articles to their source and freed the land from the heavy charge of those "many payments." Likewise Hippalus must be remembered, not for a discovery new to the world, but for freeing the Roman Empire from Arabian monopoly of the Eastern trade by tracing it to its source. Beyond India no lasting discovery was made. Ptolemy, indeed, knew of Cattigara through the account given by Marinus of Tyre; but such voyages were exceptional, and the majority of the Chinese ships stopped at Malacca, while the Malay *colandia* carried the trade to Malabar. It remained for the Arabs to complete the "through line" by opening direct communication under the Bagdad Caliphate, between the ends of the earth, Lisbon and Canton.

Prof. T. W. Rhys Davids, in the *Journal of the Royal Asiatic Society*, 1899, p. 432, quotes an interesting Buddhist passage referring to early sea-trade as follows:

"In the Dialogues of the Buddha is a passage in the Kevaddha Sutta of Digha—5th cent. B. C. The Buddha says:

"Long ago ocean-going merchants were wont to plunge forth upon the sea, on board a ship, taking with them a shore-sighting bird. When the ship was out of sight of land they would set the shore-sighting bird free. And it would go to the East and to the South and to the West and to the North, and to the intermediate points, and rise aloft. If on the horizon it caught sight of land, thither it would go, but if not it would come back to the ship again. Just so, brother," etc.

Cosmas Indicopleustes found this same custom in Ceylon in the 6th century A. D., merchants depending on shore-sighting birds instead of observations of the sun or stars.

There are similar passages in the oldest of the Vedas (see Gibson's *Rig Veda*, Vol. I):

"Varuna, who knows the path of the birds flying through the air, he, abiding in the ocean, knows also the course of ships."

"May Ushas dawn today, the excitress of chariots which are harnessed at her coming, as those who are desirous of wealth send ships to sea."

"Do thou, Agni, whose countenance is turned to all sides, send off our adversaries, as if in a ship to the opposite shore. Do thou convey us in a ship across the sea for our welfare." (A remarkable prayer for safe conduct at sea.)

Kālidāsa, in the *Sakuntalā*, gives the story of the merchant Dhanavriddhi, whose immense wealth devolved to the king on the former's perishing at sea and leaving no heirs behind him.

The *Hitopadesa* describes a ship as a necessary requisite for a man to traverse the ocean, and a story is given of a certain merchant, "who, after having been twelve years on his voyage, at last returned home with a cargo of precious stones."

The Institutes of Manu include rules for the guidance of maritime commerce.

The passages quoted above indicate a well-developed and not a primitive trade. The sea-trade was principally of Dravidian development, while both the Vedas and the Buddhist writings are of Aryan origin, and refer to things new to their race but old in the world.

(See also Bühler, *Indische Studien*, in *Sitzungsberichte der Kais. Akad. d. Wissenschaften*, Vienna, 1895, No. 3, pp. 81-2; *Indian Palæography*, § 5; Foulke, in *Indian Antiquary*, XVI, 7; Lassen, III, 3.)

More significant is the Phœnician origin of the Dravidian alphabet, long before the Aryan invasion of southern India; while a passage in the *Rāmāyana* suggests the ships of those whom the invaders contemptuously called "monkeys." When Rāma was dispatching his messengers to the four winds in search of Sītā, it was the maligned Hanumān who "flew" across the Gulf of Manār to Ceylon and discovered her. Who can doubt that the wings he used were sails, or that the Dravidians ferried across to Ceylon a force of Aryan landsmen, who later turned and crushed them under the caste-system and established the dynasties of *Drāvida-desam?* Stern must have been the subjection that brought them to worship one of their own race under the guise of a monkey, and to carry the cult of the monkey-god Hanumān in their own ships to the vales of Oman, where monkeys are unknown and where it has outlived the memory of its founders, to the confusion of the modern observer. (Gen. S. B. Miles, in *Geographical Journal,* VII, 336.)

Significant also is the fact that Lieutenant Speke, when planning his discovery of the source of the Nile, secured his best information from a map reconstructed out of the *Purānas.* (*Journal,* pp. 27, 77, 216; Wilford, in *Asiatic Researches,* III). It traced the course of the river, the "Great Krishna," through *Cusha-dvîpa,* from a great lake in *Chandristhān,* "Country of the Moon," which it gave the correct position in relation to the Zanzibar islands. The name was from the native *Unya-muézi,* having the same meaning; and the map correctly mentioned another native name, *Amara,* applied to the district bordering Lake Victoria Nyanza.

"All our previous information," says Speke, "concerning the hydrography of these regions, originated with the ancient Hindus, who told it to the priests of the Nile; and all those busy Egyptian geographers, who disseminated *their* knowledge with a view to be famous for *their* long-sightedness, in solving the mystery which enshrouded the source of their holy river, were so many hypothetical humbugs. 'The Hindu traders had a firm basis to stand upon through their intercourse with the Abyssinians." (See § 14.)

Altogether it must be supposed that the navigation of the Indian Ocean began from the Persian Gulf and Arabia; that Western India claimed its share at an early date; and that this community of interest long excluded their customers of the Mediterranean world, from whose standpoint Hippalus was quite as great a discoverer as if he had really been

——"the first that ever burst
Into that silent sea."

57. **Throw the Ship's head.**—The text is *trachēlizontes,* which is a wrestlers' term meaning literally "throwing by the neck."

Stern of a Burmese rice-boat, showing method of steering, identical with the Egyptian and Roman rudders at the time of the Periplus.

The word has led to much unnecessary confusion in the translation of this passage. Our author is describing a sailing-course which is obvious by referring to the map. The straight course before the trade-wind, from Hisn Ghorab to the Gulf of Cambay or the mouth of the Indus, would carry a vessel along the Arabian shore as far as Ras Fartak, beyond which the coast gradually recedes, so that the vessel would stand out to sea without changing its course. A vessel bound for the Malabar ports and sailing before the wind, with the type of rigging then in use, would have required steering off her course the whole time, thus describing a wide curve before making the Indian coast. Boats were not handled as easily then as now on a beam wind. The quarter-rudder required a constant pull on the tiller by the hands of the steersman.

57. **The same course.**—Pliny's account of the voyage to India (VI, 26), which has been cited by most commentators on the Periplus, is appended for comparison. It will be seen that while it agrees with the Periplus in many points, particularly in its description of Arabia, its description of the Indian coast is not altogether the same:

"In later times it has been considered a well-ascertained fact that the voyage from Syagrus, the Promontory of Arabia, to Patala, reckoned at thirteen hundred and thirty-five miles, can be performed most advantageously with the aid of a westerly wind, which is there known by the name of Hippalus.

"The age that followed pointed out a shorter route, and a safer one to those who might happen to sail from the same promontory for Sigerus, a port in India; and for a long time this route was followed, until at last a still shorter cut was discovered by a merchant, and the thirst for gain brought India even still nearer to us. At the present day voyages are made to India every year; and companies of archers are carried on board the vessels, as those seas are greatly infested with pirates.

"It will not be amiss too, on the present occasion, to set forth the whole of the route from Egypt, which has been stated to us of late, upon information on which reliance may be placed, and is here published for the first time. The subject is one well worthy of our notice, seeing that in no year does India drain our empire of less than five hundred and fifty millions of sesterces, giving back her own wares in exchange, which are sold among us at fully one hundred times their prime cost.

"Two miles distant from Alexandria is the town of Juliopolis. The distance thence to Coptos, up the Nile, is three hundred and eight miles; the voyage is performed, when the Etesian winds are blowing, in twelve days. From Coptos the journey is made with the aid of camels, stations being arranged at intervals for the supply of fresh water. The first of these stations is called Hydreuma (watering-place), and is distant twenty-two miles; the second is situate on a mountain, at a distance of one day's journey from the last; the third is at a second Hydreuma distant from Coptos ninety-five miles; the fourth is on a mountain; the next to that is another Hydreuma, that of Apollo, and is distant from Coptos one hundred and eighty-four miles; after which, there is another on a mountain. There is then another station at a place called the New Hydreuma, distant from Coptos two hundred and thirty miles; and next to it there is another, called the Old Hydreuma, or the Troglodytic, where a detachment is always on guard, with a caravansary that affords lodging for two thousand persons. This last is distant from the New Hydreuma seven miles. After leaving it we come to the city of Berenice, situate upon a harbor of the Red Sea and distant from Coptos two hundred and fifty-seven miles. The greater part of this distance is generally travelled by night, on account of the extreme heat, the days being spent at the stations; in consequence of which it takes twelve days to perform the whole journey from Coptos to Berenice.

"Passengers generally set sail at midsummer, before the rising of the Dog-star, or else immediately after, and in about thirty days arrive at Ocelis in Arabia, or else at Cana, in the region which bears frankincense. There is also a third port of Arabia, Muza by name; it is not, however, used by persons on their passage to India, as only those touch at it who deal in incense and the perfumes of Arabia. More in the interior there is a city; the residence of the king there is called Sapphar, and there is another city known by the name of Save. To those who are bound for India, Ocelis is the best place for embarcation. If the wind, called Hippalus, happens to be blowing, it is possible to arrive in forty days at the nearest mart in India, Muziris by name. This, however, is not a very desirable place for disembarcation, on account of the pirates which frequent its vicinity, where they occupy a place called Nitrias; nor, in fact, is it very rich in articles of merchandise. Besides, the roadstead for shipping is a considerable distance from the shore, and the cargoes have to be conveyed in boats, either for loading or discharging. At the moment that I am writing these pages, the name of the king of this place is Cælobothras. Another port, and a much more convenient one, is that which lies in the territory of the people called Neacyndi, Barace by name. Here king Pandion used to reign, dwelling at a considerable distance from the mart in the interior, at a city known as Modiera. The district from which pepper is carried down to Barace in boats hollowed out of a single tree (see illustration on p. 212), is known as Cottonara. None of these names of nations, ports, and cities are to be found in any of the former writers, from which circumstance it would appear that the localities have since changed their names. Travellers set sail from India on their return to Europe, at the beginning of the Egyptian month of Tybis, which is our December, or at all events before the sixth day of the Egyptian month Mechir, the same as our Ides of January; if they do this they can go and return in the same year. They set sail from India with a south-east wind, and upon entering the Red Sea, catch the south-west or south."

58. **Dark Red Mountain.**—The text is *Pyrrhon.* There can be no doubt that it refers to the "Red Bluffs," a series of high sandstone and laterite headlands, which abut on the coast at Varkkallai (8° 42′ N.), and again below Anjengo (8° 40′ N., 76° 45′ E.). These are the "Warkalli Beds" of the Indian geologists, and have recently been pierced by a canal to complete the backwater communication between Tirūr and Trivandrum, nearly 200 miles. (*Imperial Gazetteer*, XXIV, 300.)

Beyond this point we must assume that the author of the Periplus did not go. The remainder of his work, usually referred to as the "sequel," represents what he learned by inquiring of acquaintances at Nelcynda or Bacarē, and set down in writing toward lightening the darkness of Mediterranean ideas concerning all matters oriental.

58. **Paralia.**—According to Caldwell (*Dravidian Grammar*, 56), this is a translation of the Tamil *Karei*, "coast;" according to Burnell and Yule, it is *Purali*, an ancient local name for Travancore. This is supported by Gundert in his *Malayālam Dictionary*, and by the Malayālam translation of the *Rāmāyana*. The Rājā's titles still include that of *Puralīsan*, "Lord of Purali." The native name for this country in general was *Malayālam*, from *mala*, mountain, and *ālam*, depth; the land at the foot of the mountains,—Piedmont.

Paralia, to the author of the Periplus, is the coast-line below the Travancore backwaters, around Cape Comorin, and as far as Adam's Bridge: comprised within the modern districts of Travancore and Tinnevelly.

58. **Balita.**—This is probably the modern Varkkallai (8° 42′ N., 76° 43′ E.). It was formerly the southern end of the long line of backwaters, and a place of considerable commercial importance. By cutting through a bluff the backwaters have recently been connected with others leading as far as Trivandrum, which is now the chief port

of the district. At Varkkallai is the celebrated temple of Janārdan, an *avatār* of Vishnu, visited by pilgrims from all parts of India; while numerous mineral springs in the vicinity make it a favorite health resort. (*Imp. Gaz.*, XXIV, 300.)

58. **Comari.**—This is Cape Comorin, the southern extremity of the Indian peninsula (8° 5′ N., 77° 33′ E.). The name is the Tamil form of the Sanscrit *Kumārī*, virgin, which was applied to the goddess Durgā, or Pārvatī, the consort of Siva.

Yule observes (Marco Polo, II, 882-3) that the monthly bathing in her honor is still continued; and according to the *Imperial Gazetteer* (X, 376), it is "one of the most important places of pilgrimage in Southern India."

In the first century of the Christian era Rome, Parthia, India, and China were the four great powers of the world, of which the first and last were advancing, the others passing through political transformation. Of the world's religions, the Buddhist, as Edmunds has well said (*Buddhist and Christian Gospels*, 3d ed., Tokyo, 1905, p. 23), "was the most powerful on the planet." But it was no longer the Buddhism of the Emperor Asoka. The disintegration of the Maurya Empire had been followed by the rise of the Indo-Scythian power in the northwest, and of the Andhra in the Deccan. Both these were Buddhist, the Scythian Kanishka in the following century being the second great exponent of that faith; but the ways of the barbarian were not those of the Hindu, the two chief Buddhist powers were at war, and in 126 A. D., when the Andhra king Vilivāyakura II, or Gautamīputra Sātakarni conquered, the queen-mother Balasrī set up a memorial at Kārlī telling how he "destroyed the Sakas, Yavanas, and Pahlavas . . . properly expended the taxes which he levied in accordance with the sacred law . . . and prevented the mixing of the four castes." (Vincent Smith, *Early History*, 188.) To the north the great missionary movement through Turkestan and China had only just begun, while the race-migrations from the Himalayas into Burma and Indo-China, which made of those kingdoms a bulwark of Buddhism in the middle ages, had not taken place. In Ceylon the native race, the Sinhalese, were heartily for the Law of Piety, as in Asoka's day; but opposed to them racially and in matters religious, were their neighbors and ancient enemies, the Southern Dravidians, with their Aryan dynasties and caste-systems, who had never embraced the Buddhist doctrine, and whose primitive nature-worship was included bodily within the cult of the Hindu gods. Siva especially, "the auspicious," Rudra of the *Vedas*; the god of the storm, the destroyer and reproducer, was the deity venerated by the

Dravidians, together with his consort or "energic principle," Durgā. (His symbol was the cobra, hers the lion, while their son was Ganesa, elephant-headed, the god of learning.) And as the southern kingdoms waxed strong, so their religion was pushed forward, steadily displacing Buddhism in its home-land as it in turn spread outward over the great continent of Asia; until the Deccan and Bengal returned to the earlier faith, while of the structure built up by Kanishka the White Huns had left but wreckage.

The religion of India as seen by the author of the Periplus was therefore twofold: at Barygaza under the Saka satraps, a heterodox Buddhism had supplanted the Law observed at Ujjenī and Pātaliputta under the Mauryas, and preached to the nations of the earth under Asoka in the third century B. C.; while the purer form still upheld by the Andhras could not be found at their western port, Calliena, which the Sakas had "obstructed." In the south the earlier faith was advancing, and in Nelcynda, where some acquaintance related to our author the things he set down about the eastern half of India, it was the great epics which supplied the information; the *Purānas*, the *Mahābhārata* and the *Rāmāyana*, which continued to uphold the "southern sisters" in the use of that visible altar-flame which those of the north had thought to replace by contemplation of the "inner light," but were learning anew their lesson from the *Katha Upanishad*: "that fire is day by day to be praised by men who wake, with the oblation."

Underlying the formal acceptance of the Brahman faith there still existed the earlier animism, the worship of spirits in the form of trees and serpents, with all the train of associated beliefs described in such works as Fergusson, *Tree and Serpent Worship*; Tylor, *Primitive Culture*; Frazer, *The Golden Bough*; W. Robertson Smith, *The Religion of the Semites*; Ernest Crawley, *The Tree of Life*. The identity of belief has been indicated by the legends attached to the most treasured articles of early trade. For international trade began largely on a religious basis, and was continued as a means of elaborating worship. And to the activity and persuasiveness of the commercial peoples may be attributed the wide acceptance of their assertions regarding the peculiar efficacy and sanctity of the spirits of their own sacred trees. There was no reason *per se* for the Egyptian faith in myrrh as a purifying and cleansing agent beyond the gum of their own trees, or for the trust of the Babylonians and Greeks in frankincense, or of the Romans in cinnamon, beyond their own pine-resin or the "golden bough" of their earlier faith; it was the result of the eclectic spirit which accepted that which was told them by strangers. The serpent-cult in Rome was no mere extravagance, but reflected the early faith in the existence of departed spirits in serpent form. The funeral of Sabina Poppæa, with its fabulous store of spices burned, was not mere show, but was intended to provide Nero's consort with a countless array of protecting spirits in the under-world.

This formless faith was the common property of those trading between east and west. Incorporated by Brahmanism, it persisted almost unmodified among the caste of those trading by sea, defiled beyond hope in Brahman eyes; it permeates the *Book of the Dead* and the Gilgamesh epic; it is the background of the Old Testament and the Koran, and it is still addressed to their *jinni* by those whom the Bents visited in Dhofar and Socotra, whose ancestors were among its earliest devotees and carried it to the ends of the earth.

59. **Colchi.**—This is the modern Kolkai (8° 40′ N., 78° 5′ E.). By tradition this was the earliest seat of Dravidian power in Southern India, where Chēra, Chōla and Pāndya, the legendary progenitors of the great dynasties, ruled in common before their dominions were separated. At the time of the Periplus it was one of the chief ports of the Pāndyan kingdom, being more accessible to the capital than Nelcynda. Owing to the deposit of silt by the Tāmraparni River the sea retired from Kolkai, and in mediæval times another nearby place, Kayal (the *Coil* of Marco Polo), became the port. At present the trade of this district passes through Tuticorin. (*Imp. Gaz.*, XV, 387; a good map is given in Yule's *Marco Polo*, Cordier's edition, II, 373-4.)

This is the country from which Hanumān, the monkey-god, made his leap across the sea from the Mahendragiri mountain to Ceylon, and so helped Rāma to the rescue of his consort Sītā from Rāvana, the demon king of Ceylon, as told in the *Rāmāyana;* and here was consequently a center of the worship of Hanumān, which was carried afar by the Dravidian sea-folk. In the rich Wadi Tyin in Oman, the trade of which passed through the port of Kalhat—that *Acila* of Pliny (VI, 32), "from which persons embarked for India," General Miles found a town Sibal, which, he observes, means "monkey," and was the name of a "famous pre-Islamic idol. No monkeys exist in Oman, but a temple stood here dedicated to that image." (*Geographical Journal*, VII, 522-537).

Two shrines of Hanumān are still venerated at Surat on the Cambay coast, which was also in constant communication with Arabia.

According to local tradition, this was the original capital of *Drāvida-dēsam*, and the birthplace of the dynasties ruling in Southern India at the time of the Periplus. This "dominion of the Pāndyas" was said to have been established by the descendants of Pāndu, who was the father of the Pāndava brothers, the heroes of the North Indian war recounted in the *Mahābhārata*. Whether the dynastic connection was real, or whether it was attached to the legend like Pushkalāvati and Takshasilā through Pushkala and Taksha, sons of Bhārata in the *Rāmāyana*, is less important than the obvious Aryan descent of the dynasty in this Dravidian land, and their rigid institution of the caste-system which still prevails here in a completeness long since outgrown in other parts of India. Those who would see in the northern spread of this dynasty a southern origin for the Dravidian race do not take into account the late origin of the dynasty, probably the 5th or 4th century B. C., and its alien character among a people already settled and developed.

Arrian (*Indica*, VIII) gives another version of the origin of this dynasty, from Pandæa, who, he says, was "the only daughter of Heracles, among many sons; the land where she was born, and over which she ruled, was named Pandæa after her." No worthy consort appearing, Heracles made her marriageable at the age of seven years, and married her himself, "that the family born from him and her might supply kings to the Indians."

The story is not accepted by Arrian in entire faith; he observes that the power exerted by Heracles in hastening the maturity of Pandæa might more naturally have been applied to the postponement of his own senility; but, as he says in another connection (XXXI), "I know, however, that it is a very difficult task for one who reads the ancient tales to prove that they are false."

In Greek literature concerning India, Heracles is usually identified with Vishnu, and Bacchus with Siva.

The dominion of the Pāndyas was divided among three reputed brothers, Chēra, Chōla and Pāndya, in which form it appears in Asoka's inscription of the 3d century B. C., and in the Periplus. The capital had been removed, as Pliny states, to Madura (9° 55′ N., 78° 7′ E.), which the *Rāmāyana* describes as a great city, its gates being of gold inlaid with gems.

The seceding kingdoms were larger and more powerful than the original, the most important being the Chōla, the "Coast Country" of § 59.

The dynastic succession of these kingdoms forms the longest unbroken chain in Indian history, covering a period of at least two thousand years.

(See *Imperial Gazetteer*, XVI, 389;—Vincent Smith, *Early History*, 341-7; and authorities quoted on p. 209.)

The Dravidians of Southern India were active traders and colonists in Ceylon, in opposition to the native Sinhalese, with whom they were in frequent conflict, and in spite of whom they had extended their power effectually over the northwestern coast of Ceylon, the region of the pearl-fisheries.

59. **Pearl-fisheries.**—These were, as at present, in the shallow waters of the Gulf of Manăr. (See under §§ 35, 36, and 56.)

Pliny (IX, 54-8) says that pearls came into general use in Rome after the surrender of Alexandria; but that they first began to be used about the time of Sylla.

"The first rank, and the very highest position among all valuables belongs to the pearl. . . . The most productive of pearls is the island of Taprobane.

"The origin and production of the shell-fish is not very different from that of the shell of the oyster. When the genial season of the year exercises its influence on the animal, it is said that, yawning, as it were, it opens its shell, and so receives a kind of dew, by means of which it becomes impregnated; and that at length it gives birth, after many struggles, to the burden of its shell, in the shape of pearls, which vary according to the quality of the dew. If this has been in a perfectly pure state when it flowed into the shell, then the pearl produced is white and brilliant, but if it was turbid, then the pearl is of a clouded color also; if the sky should happen to have been lowering when it was generated, the pearl will be of a pallid color; from all which it is quite evident that the quality of the pearl depends much more upon a calm state of the heavens than of the sea, and hence it is that it contracts a cloudy hue, or a limpid appearance, according to the degree of serenity of the sky in the morning. . . . It is wonderful that they should be influenced thus pleasurably by the state of the heavens, seeing that by the action of the sun the pearls are turned of a red color, and lose all their whiteness, just like the human body. Hence it is that those which keep their whiteness best are the deep-sea pearls, which lie at too great a depth to be reached by the sun's rays. I have seen pearls still adhering to the shell; for which reason the shells were used as boxes for ointments.

"The fish, as soon as it even perceives the hand, shuts its shell and covers up its treasures, being well aware that it is for them that it is sought; and if it happens to catch the hand it cuts it off with the sharp edge of the shell. . . . The greater part of these pearls are only to be found among rocks and crags, while, on the other hand, those that lie out in the deep sea are generally accompanied by sea-dogs. And yet, for all this, the women will not banish these gems from their ears!

"Our ladies glory in having pearls suspended from their fingers, or two or three of them dangling from their ears, delighted even with the rattling of the pearls as they knock against each other; and now, at the present day, the poorer classes are even affecting them, as people are in the habit of saying, that 'a pearl worn by a woman in public is as good as a lictor walking before her.' Nay, even more than this, they put them on their feet, and that, not only on the laces of their sandals but all over the shoes; it is not enough to wear pearls, but they must tread upon them, and walk with them under foot as well.

"I once saw Lollia Paulina, the wife of the Emperor Caius—it was not at any public festival, or any solemn ceremonial, but only at an ordinary betrothal entertainment—covered with emeralds and pearls, which shone in alternate layers upon her head, in her hair, in her wreaths, in her ears, upon her neck, in her bracelets, and on her fingers, and the value of which amounted in all to 40,000,000 sesterces; indeed she was prepared at once to prove the fact, by showing the receipts and acquittances. Nor were these any presents made by a prodigal potentate, but treasures which had descended to her from her grandfather, and obtained by the spoliation of the provinces. Such are the fruits of plunder and extortion! It was for this reason that M. Lollius was held so infamous all over the East for the presents which he extorted from the kings; the result of which was, that he was denied the friendship of Caius Cæsar, and took poison; and all this was done, I say, that his granddaughter might be seen, by by the glare of lamps, covered all over with jewels to the amount of forty millions of sesterces!"

Pliny then recounts the well-known story of Cleopatra's wager with Antony to serve him an entertainment costing ten millions of sesterces, and of her dissolving a great pearl in vinegar and swallowing it. The same thing had been done before, he says, in Rome, by Clodius, son of the tragic actor Aesopus, who served a meal in which each guest was given a pearl to swallow.

Of the pearl industry, Marco Polo says (III, xvi): "All round this gulf the water has a depth of not more than 10 or 12 fathoms, and in some places not more than 2 fathoms. The pearl-fishers take their vessels, great and small, and proceed into this gulf, where they stop from the beginning of April till the middle of May. . . . Of the produce they have first to pay the king, as his royalty, the tenth part. And they must also pay those men who charm the great fishes (sharks) to prevent them from injuring the divers whilst engaged in seeking pearls under water, one-twentieth part of all that they take. These fish-charmers are termed *Abraiaman* (Brahmans); and their charm holds good for that day only, for at night they dissolve the charm so that the fishes can work mischief at their will."

There can be little doubt that this kind of protection was sought by the divers at the time of the Periplus, and Yule observed it still in force, one of the "Brahmans" exercising this ancestral office being a Christian!

In the case of frankincense, pepper and diamonds, the guardian spirits took the form of serpents and were appeased or repelled by other spirits or by sacred birds. But sharks called for the visible aid of the priests. We may suppose the shark to have been a soulless and unimpressionable demon, or else that the industry dates from a time after the Aryan invasion of Southern India, so that the priestly caste could properly decline to stand aside for the benefit of the serpent-cults that had preceded them.

59. **Coast country.**—This country, different from, and beyond, the Pāndyan kingdom, is the third of the Dravidian states, the Chōla kingdom; at the time of the Periplus, as it states, the largest, richest, and most prosperous of the three. "Coast Country" is from the native name, "Chōla coast," *Chōla-māndalam*, from which the Portuguese derived our modern word *Coromandel.* By the Saracens it was given another name, *Maabar*, not to he confused with Malabar; the meaning being "ferrying-place," and referring to the shipping-trade for Malacca and the Far East. By the Ceylonese it was called *Soli*, which name they applied to both Chōla and Pāndya, even though their relations with Madura were more important. The boundaries were, roughly, from the Penner River on the north (emptying into the Bay of Bengal at 14° 40′ N.), and on the south the Valiyar River (10° 3′ N.), or even the Vaigai (9° 20′ N.). During the mediæval period the Chōla kingdom conquered and absorbed its progenitor, the Pāndyan, and they are still classified together in the modern "Carnatic."

The pearl-fisheries belonging to this kingdom, the product of which was sold only at the capital, Uraiyūr, were those of the Palk Strait, north of Adam's Bridge, as distinguished from those of the Gulf of Manār, which belonged to the Pāndyan kingdom, and were administered from Madura.

59. **Argaru.**—This is nearly a correct transliteration of *Uraiyūr* ("city of habitation"), the ancient capital of the Chōla kingdom, now part of Trichinopoly (10° 49′ N., 78° 42′ E.).

Previous identifications of this name have failed to take into account the fact that it was inland, and in a different country from the Pāndyan kingdom.

The capital grew up around a fortress built on the summit of the Rock of Trichinopoly, which rises abruptly out of the plain to a height of 340 feet above the old city, which nestles picturesquely at its foot. "The view from the frowning heights of the rock is very grand. Little is now left of the old fortifications but the citadel and a pagoda-like temple. A covered passage hewn out of the rock leads to them." (Furneaux, *India*, p. 430.)

After the destruction of Uraiyūr about the 7th century A. D., the capital was removed to Malaikurram, the modern Kumbakonam (10° 58′ N., 79° 22′ E.), which still retains traces of its former grandeur; and after other changes to Tanjore (10° 47′ N., 79° 8′ E.). (Sir Walter Elliot, *Coins of Southern India*, 130; Vincent Smith, *Early History*, 164, 342.)

59. **Argaritic muslins.**—The textile industry of both Trichinopoly (or Uraiyūr) and Tanjore has been famous from early times. There can be little doubt that some of the finest fabrics that reached the Roman world came from this kingdom of Chōla. From this part of India, in the middle ages, came those gold-threaded embroideries which were in such demand in the Saracen markets.

60. **Ships from the north**—that is, from the Ganges and Bengal. Kālidāsa, in the *Raghuvamsa*, tells of a tour of conquest of India, made by Raghu, the great-grandfather of Rāma; starting from Ayodhyā (the modern Oudh) he went eastward to the ocean, "having conquered the Bangālis, who trusted in their ships." (Foulkes, in *Indian Antiquary*, 1879, pp. 1-10.)

60. **Camara.**—Ptolemy mentions a *Chabēris emporion*, at one of the mouths of the Kāverī River; probably both this and the *Camara* of the Periplus were nearly, if not quite, identical with the modern Kārikāl (10° 55′ N., 79° 50′ E.).

60. **Poduca.**—This is probably intended for *Puduchchēri*, "new town," the modern Pondicherry (11° 56′ N., 79° 49′ E.). So Bohlen, Ritter, Benfey, Müller, McCrindle and Fabricius; Yule, following Lassen, prefers Pulikat (13° 25′ N., 80° 19′ E.).

60. **Sopatma.**—This is probably *Su-patana*, "fair town," and may be identified with the modern Madras (13° 4′ N., 80° 15′ E.).

Lassen (II, 542) doubts the possibility of identifying either Camara or Sopatma; and there is no evidence that Pondicherry existed at the time of the Periplus. The location of all three ports can be no more than conjectural.

60. **Ships of the country: Sangara.**—The first were, no doubt, the craft made of hollowed logs with plank sides and outriggers, such as are still used in South India and Ceylon (pictured on p. 212); the larger type, *sangāra*, were probably made of two such canoes joined together by a deck-platform admitting of a fair-sized deck-house. Dr. Taylor (*Journal of the Asiatic Society of Bengal*, Jan., 1847, pp. 1-78), says that the name *jangār* is still used on the Malabar coast for these double canoes. Caldwell gives the forms *changādam* in Malayālam; *jangāla* in Tulu; and *samghādam* in Sanscrit, "a raft." Benfey (art. on *India* in Ersch & Gruber's *Encyklopädie*, 307) derives it from the Sanscrit *sangāra*, meaning "trade;" Lassen, however (II, 543), doubts the application of the word to shipping, and Heeren (*Ideen über die Politik*, etc., I, iii, 361) ascribes the word to a Malay original. This is quite possible, as the type itself is Malay, and found throughout the archipelago.

Modern double canoe with deck-structure, of the *sangāra* type; in general use in South India, Ceylon, and the Eastern Archipelago.

The comparatively large size of the shipping on the Coromandel coast is indicated also by the Andhra coinage, on which a frequent symbol is a ship with two masts, apparently of considerable tonnage.

"The maritime traffic, to which the ship type bears witness, is also attested by the large numbers of Roman coins which are found on the Coromandel Coast." (E. J. Rapson, *Coins of the Andhra Dynasty*, lxxxii).

### Early South Indian Coins

(re-drawn and restored from Elliot, *Coins of Southern India*)

Plate I, fig. 38 Plate II, fig. 45

Kurumbar or Pallava coin of the Coromandel coast; showing a two-masted ship like the modern coasting vessel or *d'honi*.

Andhra coin, showing a two-masted ship, presenting details like those of the Gujarāti ship at Boroboedor, and the Persian ship at Ajanta.

The shipping of the Andhra and Pallava coins doubtless survives in the modern "masula boats" at Madras:

"The harbor (of Madras) can never be a harbor of refuge, and all that the works will secure is immunity for landing and shipping operations from the tremendous surf which is so general along the whole of the Coromandel coast. Passenger traffic from the shore to the vessels is carried on by jolly-boats from the pier, or masulah boats from the shore. These latter are relics of a bygone day, when Madras was an open roadstead and when landing through the surf by any form of jolly-boat was a matter extremely difficult, if not impossible. These masulah boats are flat-bottomed barges constructed of planks sewn together with rope of cocoanut fibre, caulked with oakum, and are able to withstand better than far more solidly built craft the shock of being landed on the sandy beach from the crest of a seething breaker." (Furneaux, *India*, 254.)

Similar in a general way to the Andhra coin-symbol is the Gujarāti ship carved in bas-relief on the frieze of the Buddhist temple at Boroboedor in Java. While dating from about 600 A. D., this vessel was probably not different from those of the 1st century, while the short broad sail with double yards is identical with those of the Egyptian Punt Expedition of the 15th century B. C.

Gujarāti ship of about 600 A. D.; from the Boroboedor frieze. Ships of this type were doubtless included among the *trappaga* and *cotymba* of § 44, which piloted merchants into Barygaza.

"In the year 525 (Saka era, = 603 A. D.), it being foretold to a king of Gujarāt that his country would decay and go to ruin, he resolved to send his son to Java. He embarked with about 5000 followers in 6 large and about 100 small vessels, and after a voyage of four months reached an island they supposed to be Java; but finding themselves mistaken, re-embarked, and finally settled at Matarem, in the center of the island they were seeking. . . . The prince now found that men alone were wanting to make a great and flourishing state. He accordingly applied to Gujarāt for assistance, when his father, delighted at his success, sent him a reinforcement of 2000 people. . . . From this period Java was known and celebrated as a kingdom; an extensive commerce was carried on with Gujarāt and other countries, and the bay of Matarem was filled with adventurers from all parts." (Sir Stamford Raffles, *History of Java*, II, 87 ff.)

60. **Colandia:**—This name seems to be of Malay origin, and perhaps means no more than "ship." *Koleh panjail*, "sailing ship," is the name for the fast fishermen entered in modern Singapore regattas. (Pritchett, *Sketches of Shipping and Craft*, 166.)

The text is *kolandiophonta*, generally supposed to be corrupt, the *onta* being the present participle of "to be." But Rājendralāla Mitra (*Antiquities of Orissa*, I, 115) derives the word from the Sanscrit *kolāntarapota*, "ships for going to foreign shores."

Burmese *laung-zât*, (without rigging); a carvel-built vessel on the same lines as the dug-out *laung-gô* for river use. The larger type, in general use on the Chindwin River, shows Chinese influence, although the lines are those of ancient Egypt. This type displays the stern-cabins differently arranged from those in the higher-built Chinese junk. See also Chatterton, *Sailing Ships*, 7, 31.

The *colandia* which made the voyage to Chryse and were of great size, must have been similar to the Chinese junks or the Burmese *laung-zât, kattu* or Chindwin traders. The sea-trade of the Gulf of Tonkin was of very early date. Chinese annals mention voyages to Malacca prior to the Christian era, and probably as early as the 12th century B. C. This region, known to the Chinese as *Yüé-cháng*, was independent until the extension of the Chinese boundaries under the Han dynasty (2d century B. C.). The compass, or "south-pointing chariot," was known in the 11th century B. C., but, as indicated by Hirth (*Ancient History of China*, pp. 126-136), was probably used mainly for geomancy until applied to navigation by Persians and Arabs visiting China in the 6th and 7th centuries A. D. The Chinese themselves steered by the stars and the sun, and by observing the nature of the sea-bottom.

Model of an early type of Chinese junk, showing the individual cabins in the stern-structure, each occupied by a merchant with his stock of goods, as told by Marco Polo; from the serial collection of models of commercial shipping, exhibited in the Commercial Museum, Philadelphia.

The Arabian geographer Mas'udi mentions Chinese junks which came to Bassora in his time, and in the cave-paintings at Ajanta, commemorative of the visit of a Persian embassy in the early 7th century, a ship is shown which, if not a junk, is manifestly influenced by that type of vessel. (See Torr, *Ancient Ships*, plate VII, fig. 40.)

Marco Polo (Book III, Chap. I) gives a detailed description of the junks of that day: (Yule's edition II, 249-51.)

"The ships in which merchants go to and fro amongst the Isles of India, are of fir timber. They have but one deck, though each of them contains some 50 or 60 cabins, wherein the merchants abide greatly at their ease, every man having one to himself. The ship hath but one rudder, but it hath four masts; and sometimes they have two additional masts, which they ship and unship at pleasure. . . .

"The larger of their vessels have some thirteen compartments or severances in the interior, made with planking strongly framed, in case mayhap the ship should spring aleak. . .

"The fastenings are all of good iron nails and the sides are double, one plank laid over the other, and caulked outside and in . . . with lime and chopped hemp, kneaded together with wood-oil.

"Each of their great ships requires at least 200 mariners, some of them 300. They are indeed of great size, for one ship shall carry 5000 or 6000 baskets of pepper; and they used formerly to be larger than they are now. And when there is no wind they use sweeps, so big that to pull them requires four mariners to each. . . . Every great ship has certain large barks or tenders attached to it; these are large enough to carry 1000 baskets of pepper, and carry 50 or 60 mariners apiece; some of them 80 or 100." So Fa-Hien left Ceylon in "a large merchantman, on board of which there were more than 200 men, and to which was attached, by a rope, a smaller vessel, as a provision against damage or injury to the large one from the perils of the navigation." (*Travels*, chap. xi.) And landing from this vessel in *Java-dvīpa*, where he spent five months, he "again embarked in another large merchantman, which also had on board more than 200 men. They carried provisions for 50 days."

(See Yule's *Marco Polo*, II, 252-3, for description of junks in other mediæval writers; also, for a full account of Burmese ship-building, primitive and modern, Ferrars, *Burma*, 132-8.)

60. **Imported . . everything.**—Yule, in his *Marco Polo* (II, 333), quotes from the Arab geographer Wassáf: "Maabar extends in length from Quilon to Nellore, nearly 300 parasangs along the sea-coast. The curiosities of Chín and Máchín, and the beautiful products of Hind and Sind, laden on large ships which they call *Junks*, sailing like mountains with the wings of the wind on the surface of the water, are always arriving there. The wealth of the Isles of the

Persian Gulf in particular, and in part the beauty and adornment of other countries, from Irak and Khurásán as far as Rúm and Europe, are derived from Maabar, which is so situated as to be the key of Hind."

Marco himself (III, xx) calls Chōla "the kingdom of Maabar called Soli, which is the best and noblest province in India, and where the best pearls are found."

Friar Odoric (chap. iv) says of this kingdom: "The king of the said region is most rich in gold, silver and precious stones, and and there be the fairest unions (pearls) in all the world."

61. **Palæsimundu.**—This is the modern Ceylon. According to Lassen (I, 201) this word is the Sanscrit *Pālisīmanta*, "abode of the law of piety;" that is, the *Dharma* of Gautama Buddha. The distinction is of interest; "by the ancients" it was called *Taprobanē*, which is the Sanscrit *Tāmraparnī*, the name given to it in the *Rāmāyana*. The knowledge concerning Ceylon which reached the west through Onesicritus, Eratosthenes and Strabo, was of the island before its conversion to Buddhism under the missionary zeal of Asoka. Our author speaks of it in the time of its greatest devotion to the new religion, which its neighbors the Dravidian kingdoms of Southern India never fully accepted.

According to McCrindle (*Ancient India*, 20, 160), the name *Taprobanē*, or *Tāmraparnī*, was given by Vijaya, who led the first Indian colony into the island, and applied to the place where he first landed. The name means "copper-colored;" compare *Tāmra-lipti*, the sea-port town at the mouth of the Ganges. The Pāli form, *Tambapanni*, appears in the inscription of Asoka at Girnār. Another Brahmanical name, *Dvīpa Rāvana*, "island of Rāvana," (the demon-king, kidnapper of Sītā in the *Rāmāyana*), is thought by some to be the origin of *Taprobanē*.

Ptolemy notes that the *ancient* name was *Simundu* (mistaking the first two syllables of our author's word Palæsimundu for the Greek *palai*), but in his own time *Salikē*, the country of the Salæ. Cosmas Indicopleustes called it *Sielediba*; which, as McCrindle notes, is through the Pāli the true Sanscrit name for the island: *Sinhala-dvīpa*, "island of the lions," or lion-like men-heroes. "To this source may be traced its other names, Serendib, Sylan, and Ceylon."

Pliny knows the name *Palæsimundus* (VI, 24) but applies it to a city "adjoining the harbor that lies facing the south," and calls it "the most famous city in the island, the king's place of residence, containing a population of 200,000." But there is no harbor on the south coast of Ceylon, and Pliny seems to be confusing his city and harbor with the actual position of the island in relation to the ancient harbor, now lost, at Cape Comorin.

In the *Rāmāyana* the Sinhalese are referred to as *rakshas* and *nagas*, demons and spirits, not human because racially opposed to the Aryan invaders. So Fa-Hien describes them in an interesting passage relating to their trade (*Travels*, chap. xxxviii): "the country originally had no human inhabitants, but was occupied only by spirits and *nagas*, with which merchants of various countries carried on a trade. When trafficking was taking place, the spirits did not show themselves. They simply set forth their precious things with labels of the price attached to them; while the merchants made their purchases according to the price; and took the things away." And he found in the capital city "many Vaisya clans and Sabæan merchants, whose houses are stately and beautiful."

Cosmas Indicopleustes (*Christian Topography*, book XI), tells of Ceylon and its trade in the 6th century A. D.; his account amplifies what is said in the Periplus, and a translation is appended for comparison:

"This is the great island of the ocean, situated in the Indian Sea; which is called by the Indians Sielediba, by the Greeks Taprobanê, where the hyacinthus stone is found; and it lies beyond the pepper country. It has other small islands scattered around it in great number; of which some have fresh water, and cocoanut palms. They are very close to one another. But that great island, so its inhabitants say, is 300 leagues in length, and in breadth about 90 miles. Two kings reign in the island, hostile to each other; of whom one has the region of the hyacinthus, and the other the rest of the island, in which is the market-town and port. It is frequented by a great press of merchants from far countries. In that island is established the Church of Christ, of the sect of the Persians, and there is a presbyter sent from Persia, and a deacon, and the whole service of the church. But the natives, and the kings, are of other faiths. Many temples are to be seen in this island; on the top of one of them, they say, is a hyacinthus, in full view, sparkling and very great, like a great spinning-top; and it shines brightly, sending out fiery rays almost like the sun itself, a marvellous sight. From all parts of India, Persia and Aethiopia come a multitude of ships to this island, which is placed as it were midway between all lands; and it sends ships likewise hither and thither in all directions.

"From the inner regions, that is, from Tzinista and from the other market-towns, are brought silk cloth, aloe-wood, cloves, and sandalwood, and other products according to the place; and it forwards them to those of the outside, that is, to Malē, in which pepper grows; to Calliana, where brass is found, and sesamin wood, and various kinds of cloth (for it, too, is a great market-town); and to Sindu, where the castor musk is found, and spikenard; and to Persia, to the country of the Homerites, and Adulis; and in return it receives other things from all these places, which it transmits to the inner regions, with its own products likewise. Now Sindu is the beginning of India; for the river Indus, which empties into the Persian Gulf, separates Persia from India. These are the best-known market-towns of India: Sindu, Orrhotha, Calliana, Sibor, and Malē which has five ports to which pepper is brought; Parti, Mangarouth, Salopatana, Nalopatana, Pudapatana. And then, at a distance of about five days and nights from the mainland, out in the ocean, is Sielediba, that is, Taprobanē. Then again, on the mainland, is a market-town, Marallo, shipping conch-shells; and there is Kaber, shipping alabandenum, and then the country from which cloves are shipped; and then Tzinista, which sends silk cloth; within which there is no other land, for the ocean encircles it on the east.

"And so this island Sielediba, placed in the midst of India, which produces the hyacinthus, receives goods from all markets and ships to all, being itself a very great market. And there came thither on matters of trade one from our own parts, named Sopater, who died about 35 years ago. And his business took him to the island of Taprobanē, where it happened that a vessel arrived at the same time from Persia, and there landed together those from Adulis, among whom was Sopater, and those from Persia, among whom was an ambassador of the Persians. And so, as the custom was, the captains and tax-collectors receiving them, brought them before the king. And being admitted into the presence of the king, after they had offered the proper homage, he bade them be seated. And then he asked them: "How goes it with your countries, and how with your trade and commerce?" "Excellently well," they said. Replying, the king asked, "Who, of your kings, is the greatest and most powerful?" Without delay the Persian answered: "Ours is the most powerful, the greatest and the richest; he is the king of kings; and he has power to do whatever he wills." But Sopater was silent. Then said the king, "You, Roman, have you nothing to say?" And Sopater replied, "What have I to say, when this man says such things? If you wish to learn the truth, you have both kings here; examine them, and you will see which one is the most magnificent and the most powerful." But the king was amazed at this speech, and said, "How have I both kings here?" And he answered, "You have the money of both; you have the gold coin of the one king, and the drachma of the other, that is, the milliarense; compare the images of both, and you will see the truth." And he, approving and assenting, bade that both be produced. . Now the gold coin was fine, bright, and well-shaped; for thus are the best exported thither; and the milliarense was of silver and I need hardly say, not to be compared with the gold coin. The king looked at both obverse and reverse, and then at the other; and held forth the gold coin with admiration, saying, "Truly the Romans are magnificent and powerful and wise." And he commanded that Sopater should be treated with honor; that he should be seated upon an elephant, and led around the whole city with drums, and acclaimed. This Sopater told me, and those also from Adulis, who voyaged with him to that island. And when these things happened, so they say, the Persian was greatly ashamed."

61. **Almost touches Azania.**—Our author's ideas of the world in general are similar to those of Pomponius Mela, with whom he was nearly contemporary; whose map (reproduced on p. 100) retains the old idea of a balancing southern "continent of the Antichthones," with the eastern end of which he identifies Taprobanē. The Periplus does not indicate quite that extent for Ceylon, but exaggerates its size tenfold. The confusion may have been partly due to the grandiloquent descriptions left by the Ceylonese embassy which visited the Emperor Augustus. (See Bunbury, *History of Ancient Geography*, Vol. II.)

62. **Masalia.**—This is the *Maisolia* of Ptolemy, who has a river *Maisolos*, probably the Kistnā. In Sanscrit, as McCrindle shows, the name is *Mausala*, which survives in *Machhlipatana*, the modern Masulipatam (16° 11′ N., 81° 8′ E.), until the construction of the Bombay railway the chief port of entry for the Deccan. At the date of the Periplus it was, no doubt, the greatest market of the Andhra kingdom. Tavernier found it (I, xi) "the best anchorage in the Bay of Bengal, and the only place from which vessels sail for Pegu, Siam, Arakan, Bengal, Cochinchina, Mecca, and Hormus, as also for the islands of Madagascar, Sumatra, and the Manillas."

The text notes the great quantity of cotton cloth made there. In Tavernier's time it was especially noted for its painted, or pencilled, chintzes (II, xii) "called *calmendar*, that is to say, made with a brush." He contrasted these fine hand-painted fabrics with the coarse printed goods from Bengal. The supply, he observes, was never equal to the demand.

See also *Imperial Gazetteer*, XVII, 215.

The difficulties of travel through the Andhra kingdom are noted under § 50. Fa-Hien also found the kingdom of Dakshina "out of the way and perilous to traverse. There are difficulties in connection with the roads; but those who know how to manage such difficulties and wish to proceed should bring with them money and various articles and give them to the king. He will send men to escort them. These will, at different stages, pass them over to others, who will show them the shortest routes." (*Travels*, xxxv.)

62. **Dosarene.**—This is the Sanscrit *Dasarna*, the modern Orissa, the "Holy Land of India." The name appears in the *Vishnu Purāna* and the *Rāmāyana*, as a populous and powerful country. Ptolemy mentions also a river *Dosarōn*, the modern Mahānadi. The ivory from this region has long been famous. It is mentioned both in the *Mahābhārata* and the *Vishnu Purāna*, as the most acceptable offering which the "king of the Odras" could take to the Pāndu sovereign. (See also Mitra, *Antiquities of Orissa*, I, 6.)

62. **Cirrhadæ.**—This was a Bhota tribe, whose descendants, still known as *Kirāta*, live in the Morung, west of Sikkim. They are of Turanian race, with marked Mongolian features as described; and were formerly independent and powerful, having provided a dynasty of considerable duration in Nepāl. Their location is not on the sea, as indicated by the text, but in the valleys of the Himalayas; we need only omit the words "the course trending," easily inserted by a scribe, to make our author's information correct. The *Mahābhārata* locates them on the Brahmaputra.

Lassen (I, 441-450) fully describes the Bhota race, whose name survives in the modern Bhutān. They were allied to the Tibetans, and inhabited much of Bengal at the time of the Aryan migration. Lassen names ten different tribes, one being the Kirāta. Their native capital was at Mokwanpur in Eastern Nepāl. They were a warlike, uncultivated, polygamous race, whose native animism yielded imperfectly to Brahman or Buddhist teaching, and whose neglect of religious rites caused the Brahman Hindus to reduce them to the rank of Sudras. Hence the contemptuous description of their Mongolian faces as "noseless." Pliny calls them *Scyrites* (VII, 2), and says "they have merely holes in their heads instead of nostrils, and flexible feet, like the body of a serpent." Ptolemy calls their country *Kirrhadia*.

The Kirāta were under-sized, and by the Aryan Hindus were called "pigmies." In the Brahman mythology there was a bird of Vishnu, called Garuḍa, who was a special enemy of the Kirāta, and

Lassen (II, 657) thinks this story the original of the battle between pigmies and cranes, in Hesiod and other Greek writers.

Megasthenes relates the story in some detail, and is reproved by Strabo (XV, i, 57): "he then deviates into fables, and says that there are men of five, and even three spans in height, some of whom are without nostrils, with only two breathing orifices above the mouth. Those of three spans in height wage war with the cranes (described by Homer) and with the partridges, which are as large as geese; these people collect and destroy the eggs of the cranes which lay their eggs there; and nowhere else are the eggs or the young cranes to be found; frequently a crane escapes from this country with a brazen point of a weapon in its body, wounded by these people."

This tribe is especially referred to in one of the *Kāvyas*, called *Kirātārjunīya*, which recounts the combat, first mentioned in the *Mahābhārata*, between Siva in the guise of a Kirāta, or mountaineer, and Arjuna.

62. **Bargysi.**—These are the *Bhargas* of the *Vishnu Purāna*, there mentioned as neighbors of the Kirāta, and doubtless of like race. (Taylor, *Remarks on the Sequel to the Periplus*, in *Journal of the Asiatic Society of Bengal*, Jan. 1847.)

62. **Horse-faces and Long-faces.**—This is no invention of our author, but was no doubt told him by some friend at Nelcynda, who spoke by his book—the Sanscrit writings. The Aryans professed the greatest contempt for the Tibeto-Burman races at their eastern frontier, and their references to them are full of exaggeration and fable. The *Vara Sanhita Purāna* mentions a people "in the mountains east of India," that is, in the hills on the Assam-Burma frontier, called *Asvavadana*, "horse-faced."

(Taylor, *op. cit.*; so Wilford in *Asiatic Researches*, VIII and IX.)

62. **Said to be Cannibals.**—Herodotus notices such a custom among the "other Indians, living to the east, who are nomads and eat raw flesh, who are called Padæans." (III, 99.) "When any one of the community is sick, whether it be a woman or a man, if it be a man the men who are his nearest connections put him to death, alleging that if he wasted by disease his flesh would be spoiled; but if he denies that he is sick, they, not agreeing with him, kill and feast upon him. And if a woman be sick, in like manner the women who are most intimate with her do the same as the men. And whoever reaches old age, they sacrifice and feast upon; but few among them attain this state, for before that they put to death every one that falls into any distemper."

So Tibullus (IV, i, 45), "Ultima vicinus Phoebo tenet Arva Padæus;" and Strabo (XV, i, 56), quoting Megasthenes' account of Indian mountaineers "who eat the bodies of their relatives."

The same practices were said by Dr. Taylor to be followed a couple of generations ago by the Kukis, or Kuki Chin, a Tibeto-Burman tribe in the Chin Hills between Assam and Burma; the sick and aged were killed and eaten because of the belief that by such means their souls remained in the tribe, and were preserved from the agonies of transmigration into the bodies of animals.

The name of "Padæans" is probably meant for *Purushada*, under which they appear in the *Vara Sanhita Purāna*.

63. **Ganges.**—The name is applied in the same paragraph to district, river and town. By the district is meant Bengal; by the river, more especially the Hughli estuary, but east of Gangā-Sāgar island and not west of it, as at present. This, until about the 15th century, was the largest mouth of the Ganges; the Hughli river and Sāgar island were the sacred places, and still retain their sanctity. This ancient mouth, the Adi Gangā, silted up, and the river constantly tending eastward, finally joined its main channel to that of the Brahmaputra, emptying into the Meghna estuary as at present (*Imp. Gaz.*, XII, 133-4). By the town of Ganges is probably meant Tāmra-lipti, the modern Tamluk (22° 18′ N., 87° 56′ E.), which gave its name to the Tāmra-parnī river in the Pāndya kingdom, and to the island of Ceylon. This was the sea-port of Bengal in the Post-Vedic and Buddhist periods, being frequently mentioned in the great epics. It was the port of the "Bangālis, who trusted in their ships," who were conquered by the hero of Kālidāsa's *Raghuvamsa*. Here it was that Fa-Hien sojourned two years, after which he embarked in "a large merchant vessel, and went floating over the sea to the southwest . . . to the country of Singhala."

This identification, which is supported by many scholars, seems preferable to that of Fergusson and Dr. Taylor, who would place Tāmra-lipti at the modern Sonārgāon (23° 40′ N., 90° 36′ E.), the ancient Suvarnagrāma, the chief port of Eastern Bengal under the Gupta Empire and in the middle ages. Near here was Vikramapura, the modern Bikrampur, one of the capitals of Chandragupta Vikramāditya. But its importance does not seem to date from so early a period as that of the Periplus; while it is more likely that the name of Ganges would have been localized on the sacred, and at that time the principal, estuary.

Strabo has been accused of ignorance for remarking (XV, i, 13) that the Ganges "discharges its waters by a single mouth." But his information probably reflects the esteem in which that mouth was held, as well as its predominant size, in his time

63. **Malabathrum.**—This was from the Eastern Himalayas, the greatest source of supply, as noted under § 65. Ptolemy, also, says "the best malabathrum is produced in the country of the Cirrhadæ."

63. **Gangetic spikenard.**—This was probably the true spikenard, from the Himalayas, noted under § 49, and valued sufficiently to be shipped in considerable quantity to Nelcynda, where the Romans found it (§ 56).

Pliny describes another kind from the Ganges (XII, 26) which "is altogether condemned, as being good for nothing; it bears the name of *ozænitis*, and emits a fetid odor." This, as Watt remarks (pp. 451, 462, 792), was a variety of *Cymbopogon* or *Andropogon*, allied to the "nard root" of § 39; probably *Cymbopogon jwarancusa*. These species, the lemon-grass, ginger-grass, citronella, etc., all yield aromatic oils, and until recently have been much confused.

Pliny confuses this grass also with malabathrum, which, he remarks (XII, 59), "is said to grow in the marshes like the lentil."

63. **Pearls.**—These were not of the best quality; as Dr. Taylor remarks, those of the Ganges streams are inferior, being small, often irregular, and usually reddish.

63. **Muslins of the finest sort, called Gangetic.**—These are the muslins of the Dacca district, the most delicate of all the fabrics of India, an ancient test of which was for the piece to be drawn through a finger-ring. *Ventus textilis*, or *nebula*, were names under which the Romans knew of them. They are mentioned in the Institutes of Manu, in a way to show the organization of the industry: "let a weaver who has received 10 *palas* of cotton thread give them back increased to eleven, by the rice-water and the like used in weaving; he who does otherwise shall pay a fine of 10 *panas*."

Tavernier tells of a Persian ambassador who took his sovereign, on returning home, "a cocoanut of the size of an ostrich's egg, enriched with precious stones; and when it was opened a turban was drawn from it 60 cubits in length, and of a muslin so fine that you would scarcely know that you had it in your hand."

The history of cotton spinning in India goes back to remote antiquity, being associated with the Vedic gods or goddesses who are described and pictured as wearing woven garments. The patterns of such garments, showing great skill in both woven and tinted design, are abundantly reproduced from early temples in Mitra (*Antiquities of*

*Orissa,* Vol. II), from whence it appears certain that the cotton textile industry at the time of the Christian era was far in advance of that of any of the western countries.

While cotton may possibly have been spun first in Turkestan, it seems more likely that it has always been native in the Indian peninsula and that the Aryan invaders found the cultivation and industry both well established. The early *Vedas,* for example, referred principally to woolen cloth of various kinds, some doubtless of fine quality, such as are still made in Kashmir. In the *Rig Veda* the material used in clothing is not specified.

The *Mahābhārata*—in the *Sabha Parva*—enumerates presents brought to Yudhisthira:

Cloths and skins; the former of wool and embroidered with gold, shawls and brocades; the latter marten and weasel; blankets of various manufacture by the Abhiras of Gujarāt; cloths not of cotton, but of sheep or goat wool, or of thread spun by worms (silk?), or of *patta* fibres and linen, or woven, by Scythians, Turkharas and Kankas; housings for elephants, by princes of the Eastern tribes, lower Bengal, Midnapur and Ganjam; fine muslin from people of Carnatic and Mysore.

The *Rāmāyana* mentions silken, woolen and cotton stuffs of various kinds. The trousseau of Sītā consisted of "woolen stuffs, furs, precious stones, fine silk, vestments of divers colors, princely ornaments, and sumptuous carriages of every kind."

Heeren supposes the woolen stuffs to have been Cashmere shawls. Rāmānuja mentions a stuff from Nepāl.

The change of custom as the Aryans penetrated into the hot climate of the Ganges Valley is shown in the Laws of Manu, which prohibited Brahmans the use of wool.

Aside from the priestly caste, however, fine fabrics of all kinds were in use. In an early play, the *Mrichchhakatikā,* the buffoon inquires: "who is that gentleman dressed in silken raiment, glittering with rich ornaments, and rolling about as if his limbs were out of joint?" (Act IV, Sc. II).

There can be little doubt that the fine muslins of Eastern Bengal known under such names as "Textile Breeze", "Evening Dew", or "Running Water" were made there before the Aryan invasion. Spinning and weaving, of course, were both by hand, and although this industry was renewed by the cottons from Manchester and the starting of mills about Bombay, this superlatively fine yarn is still produced in some quantities. In 1888 the spinners who supplied the finest quality were said to be reduced to two elderly women in the village of Dhamrai, about 20 miles north of Dacca, but it was thought that the industry might be revived with any revival of the demand for this fine fabric.

An incredible amount of patience and skill were required in this industry. One way of testing the fineness of the fabric, often described by mediæval and earlier travelers, was to pass a whole piece of 20 yards long and 1 yard wide through an ordinary finger-ring. The best test, however, was by the weight in proportion to size and number of threads. It is said that 200 years ago a piece of muslin 15 yards long by 1 yard wide could be made so fine as to weigh only 900 grains, or a little over 1-10 of a pound. In 1840 a piece of the same dimensions and texture could not be made finer than 1,600 grains and was valued at about $50. A piece of this muslin 10 yards long by 1 yard wide could not be woven in less than five months, and the work could only be carried on in the rainy season when the moisture in the air would prevent the thread from breaking.

At several places in northwestern India fine muslins were produced, but nowhere of quality equal to those of Bengal. These also were shipped westward, appearing in the Periplus as exports at the mouth of the Indus and at the Gulf of Cambay. The change from hand spinning and weaving to power looms and spindles was not gradual as in Europe, but was due to the direct importation of European fabrics, so that a few months sufficed to destroy the earlier industry and to lay the way for the modern textile mills of India.

(See Henry Lee, *The Vegetable Lamb of Tartary*. J. H. Furneaux, *India:* Bombay, 1899; chap. iii. T. N. Mukharji, *Art Manufactures of India.* Also, *The Cotton Plant,* published by the U. S. Department of Agriculture, 1896.)

63. **Gold mines.**—This was probably the gold of the Chota Nagpur plateau, located from 75 to 150 miles west of the Ganges mouth. The rivers flowing north and east of these highlands have long produced alluvial gold in considerable quantities. The river Sōn, which formerly flowed into the Ganges at the site of the ancient capital *Pātaliputra,* the modern Patna, was called by the classical writers *Erannoboas,* from the Sanscrit *hiranya-vaha,* "carrying gold." (McCrindle, *Ancient India,* p. 43; *cf.* the Aurannoboas of § 53.)

There was also a substantial supply from Tibet, which produced the famous "ant-gold" mentioned by all the classical writers from Herodotus to Pliny. As Ball pointed out (*Journal of the Royal Irish Academy,* June, 1884), the "ant-gold" was a Sanscrit name for the small fragments of alluvial gold; this name was passed on, being applied to the dogs of the Tibetan miners, which were also referred to as griffins. The "horn of the gold-digging ant," mentioned by Pliny as preserved in the temple of Hercules at Erythræ, was a gold-miner's pick-axe, made of a wild sheep's horn mounted on a handle. (See Herodotus III, 102-5; Arrian, *Anabasis* V, 4-7; Strabo, XV, i, 44; Pliny, XI, 36; McCrindle, *Ancient India*, 51.)

Gold was also brought into India through the Tipperah country about 60 miles east of the Ganges delta; coming chiefly from the river-washings of Assam and northern Burma.

Tavernier notes (III, xvi) that it was of poor quality, like the silk of that country, and that both were sent overland to China in exchange for silver.

In Assam, Ball notes, it was formerly the custom for the rulers to require their subjects to wash for gold a certain number of days every year, while regular gold-washers were taxed.

Tipperah merchants trading in Dacca, according to Tavernier (III, xv), took back "coral, yellow amber, tortoise-shell bracelets, and others of sea shells, with numerous round and square pieces of the size of our 15 *sol* coins, which are also of the same tortoise-shell and sea-shells."

The Assam washings are, however, of substantial yield, as Tavernier himself states (III, xvii). See also Ball, *Economic Geology of India*, p. 231, and the *Alamgir nama* of Muhammad Kazim (1663), in the *Indian Antiquary*, July, 1887.

The coin called *caltis* is thought by Benfey to be the Sanscrit *kalita*, "numbered." There was, however, a South Indian coin called *kali* (Elliot, *op. cit.*, 137), while Vincent, quoting Stuckius, mentions one of Bengal called *kallais*. Wilford (*Asiatic Researches*, V, 269), preferred the refined gold called *canden*.

Pliny mentions gold on the Malabar coast (coming from the mines of Mysore); but, as Watt observes (p. 565), gold has always been mainly an article of import in India.

63. **Chryse Island** (the "golden").—There can be little doubt that by this was meant the Malacca peninsula, known to Ptolemy as the *Aurea Chersonesus*, although the location "just opposite the Ganges" disposes of a long voyage in rather summary fashion. Immense gold mines of ancient date have been discovered in the Malayan State of Pahang, north of Malacca, and these are probably the ones which gave the name of "golden" to the peninsula. It is known from Chinese records that ships from that country made the journey to Malacca as early as the 4th century B. C., and perhaps as early as the 12th; while the legend of Buddha's visit to Cambodia is at least

suggestive of the great influence exercised from India over all Indo-China.

H. C. Clifford (*Further India*, N. Y., 1904, pp. 6-7) gives an excellent account of the hazy, yet vaguely correct, ideas of the Romans in the 1st and 2d centuries concerning the Far East. "Of Chryse, the golden, Pliny has nothing to tell us, and the author of the Periplus tells us only that it was situated opposite to the Ganges. He speaks, however, of Thina, the land of silk, situated 'where the seacoast ends externally,' whence we may gather that Chryse was conceived by him as an island lying not only to the east of the Ganges, but also to the southward of the Chinese Empire. This indicates a distinct advance in knowledge, for the isle of Chryse, albeit still enveloped in a golden haze, was to the author of the Periplus a real country, and no mere mythical fairyland. Rumors must have reached him concerning it, on which he believed he could rely; and this would tend to prove that the sea-route to China via the Straits of Malacca, even though it was not yet in general use, was no longer unknown to the mariners of the east. We know that less than a century later the sailor Alexander, from whom Marinus of Tyre derived the knowledge subsequently utilized by Ptolemy, himself sailed to the Malay peninsula, and beyond, and it may safely be concluded that the feasibility of this southeastern passage had become known to the seafarers of China long before an adventurer from the west was enabled to test the fact of its existence through the means of an actual voyage." And as illustrating the state of knowledge in the Roman world in the 1st century, Mr. Clifford aptly cites Josephus (*Antiquities of the Jews*, VIII, 2) who recounts the Ophir voyages of Solomon, venturing some curious identifications: "At Ezion-Geber, a bay of Egypt on the Erythræan Sea, the king constructed a number of ships. The port is now named Berenice(!), and is near the city of Elan, formerly deemed to be in the Hebrew jurisdiction. King Hiram greatly assisted King Solomon in preparing his navy, sending him mariners and pilots, who conducted Solomon's officers to the land *that of old was called Ophir, but now the Aurea Chersonesus*, which belongs to India, to fetch gold."

It is uncertain what knowledge Pliny had of Further India. His account of Eastern Asia (VI, 20) professes to begin with the "Scythian Ocean,"—that is, the Arctic—and after some names of doubtful origin he mentions "the Promontory of Chryse . . . and the nation of the Attacori on the gulf of that name, a people protected by their sunny hills from all noxious blasts . . . and in the interior the Caseri, a people of India, who look toward the Scythians, and eat human flesh. Here are also numerous wandering nomad tribes of India."

The numerous migrations from India into Indo-China, both before and after the Christian era, give ample ground for the belief that the ports of South India and Ceylon were in truth, as the Periplus states, the center of an active trade with the Far East, employing larger ships, and in greater number, than those coming from Egypt.

The great migration from Gujarāt to Java in the 6th century A. D., and the resulting Hindu kingdoms, have already been referred to, and their greatest monuments remain to us in the tremendous Buddhist temples of Boroboedor and Brambanan. If Clifford's belief is correct, the ruins at Angkor-Wat in Cambodia are no less distinctively of ancient Hindu origin. Of these he quotes François Garnier: "Perhaps never, in any place, has a more imposing mass of stone been raised with more art and science. If we wonder at the Pyramids as a gigantic achievement of human strength and patience, then to a strength and patience no whit less here we must add genius!"

64. **A Land called This.**—This can hardly be other than the great western state of China, Ts'in, and "the city called Thinæ" (meant, probably, as the genitive of This), was its capital, Hién-yang, later known as Si-gnan-fu, on the Wei river not far above its confluence with the Hoang-ho, in the present province of Shen-si. This state of Ts'in was for centuries the most powerful of the Chinese states, and a constant menace to the imperial power. The Chóu dynasty, which ruled from 867 to 255 B. C., found itself harassed in the west by the Tartar tribes, and in the east by rebellious subjects, the states of Weï, Han, Chau, Ts'i and Ch'u. Very early in the dynasty, perhaps in the 8th century B. C., a portion of their sovereign rights were resigned to the prince of Ts'in, in consideration of his undertaking the defence of the frontier against the Tartars. This policy naturally profited Ts'in more than the empire, and the princes of Ts'in, as the annals put it, "like wolves or tigers wished to draw all the other princes into their claws, so that they might devour them." The power of Ts'in grew until it overbalanced the confederation of eastern states, and the imperial power itself. As Tartar territory was conquered it was incorporated into the Ts'in dominions, and finally a Ts'in prince became Emperor of China in 255 B. C. The greatest of the Ts'in monarchs, Ts'in Chi Hwangti, who ruled from 221 to 209 B. C., is one of the brighest names in Chinese history. It was he who began the Great Wall, and who pushed the Chinese frontier across the Gobi desert, making Hami, under the Tian-Shan mountains, his outpost, and thus preparing the way for direct communication with Bactria. Regular caravan travel between China and Bactria is said to have begun in 188 B. C.

But the success of Ts'in had brought its own reaction. It was itself so much a Tartar state that it could not control all China, and it gave way to the Han dynasty. The political importance of the state was emphasized, however, by the first Han emperor, Kaotsou, who removed his capital from Loyang in Honan to Hién-Yang or Singanfu in Shensi, the ancient Ts'in capital, and in order to make that western location more accessible to the rest of the empire, built a great high-road from Loyang to Singanfu, which is still in use.

Buddhist pilgrim in northwestern China: from a 6-ft. panel in the Commercial Museum, Philadelphia, 1128 times enlarged from a portion of a film exposed by Bailey Willis, Carnegie Institution, Washington.

The Han dynasty soon lost its outposts beyond the wall, and made no effort to recover them until the reign of Kwang Vouti, 25-58 A. D., who made China a military power and conquered Anam, and by his policy toward the Yueh-chi reasserted sovereignty over Turkestan. His son, Mingti, began the aggressive westward policy which led to the great conquests of the General Pan-chao, who led his army of Chinese and Tartars as far as the Caspian, and who defeated near Khotan the Yueh-chi king Kadphises, then established in upper India. It was in this region that Buddhism seems first to have reached China, rather than through Tibet or Burma, and from this time China was always more or less directly in communication with Western Asia.

(See Hirth, *Ancient History of China;*—Richard, *Comprehensive Geography of the Chinese Empire;*—Douglas, *China;*—Boulger, *History of China;*—E. H. Parker, *China;*—H. B. Morse, *The Trade and Administration of the Chinese Empire.*)

64. **Raw silk and silk yarn and silk cloth.**—See also under §§ 39, 49 and 56. This is the earliest correct statement of the source of silk and of the routes by which it reached the world's markets.

Silk is the cocoon-secretion of the mulberry-leaf moth, *Bombyx mori*, family *Bombycidæ*, order *Lepidoptera;* native, apparently, and first cultivated, in the warm-temperate climate of northwestern China.

Chinese legends mention the making of musical instruments of wood, with silk threads, under the emperor Fu-hi, (29th century B. C.), while the rearing of the worms and the invention of reel, loom, etc., are ascribed to Leï-tsu, known as the "Lady of Si-ling," wife of the emperor Huang-ti (27th century B. C.). Cloth was woven of silk, embroidered by the empress, and those of the higher classes were enabled to discard skins as wearing apparel. Soon other textile materials were discovered, and dyeing introduced; so that rank and position were for the first time indicated by the man's outward appearance.

In the *Chóu-li*, dating from the 11th century B. C., it appears that the Chinese government supervised the production of silk in every detail, and that specialties of design, ornament, and embroidery, were already monopolized in different families. The same book describes the provinces of China: King-chóu, the modern Hu-nan, had a trade in cinnabar, ivory, and skins; Yu-chóu, next on the north and reaching the Yellow River, traded in bamboos, varnish, silk and hemp; while the northernmost, Ping-chóu (the modern Shan-si) was noted especially for cotton and silk textures. It was this province which was most in contact with the nomad tribes of Central Asia, through whose hands silk first reached the western nations.

(Hirth, *Ancient History of China*, 9, 22-3, 117, 121-2).

The antiquity of the silk industry in India is uncertain, but the weight of evidence seems to be in favor of its importation from China, by way of the Brahmaputra valley, Assam and Eastern Bengal, early in the Christian era; while the cultivation of native varieties, not feeding on mulberry leaves—the *Saturnidæ*, including *Antheræa paphia* (the modern tasar silk); *Antheræa assama* (feeding on laurel species principally), and *Attacus ricini* (feeding on the castor-oil plant) were probably all stimulated by the value of the *Bombyx* silk.

(See Watt, pp. 992-1026; *Cambridge Natural History*, VI, 375.)

The trade in silk yarn and silk cloth existed in Northern India soon after the Aryan invasion. Silk is mentioned several times, as gifts from foreign countries, in the *Mahābhārata*, the *Rāmāyana*, and the Institutes of Manu; and it may be assumed that some trade at least went farther west. The Egyptian records do not mention it prior to the Persian conquest, and it was, no doubt, through the empires of Darius and Xerxes that it first reached the Mediterranean world.

The Hebrew scriptures contain at least two references to silk: the *dmeshek* of Amos III, 12 seems to be the Arabic *dimaks*, English *damask*, a silken fabric; while *meshi* in Ezekiel XVI, 10 seems to mean a silken gauze. Isaiah also (XLIX, 12) mentions the *Sinim* in a manner indicating extreme distance.

It has been supposed that the Greeks learned of silk through Alexander's expedition, but it probably reached them previously through Persia. Aristotle (*Hist. Anim.*, V, xix, 11) gives a reasonably correct account: "It is a great worm which has horns and so differs from others. At its first metamorphosis it produces a caterpillar, then a bombylius, and lastly a chrysalis—all these changes taking place within six months. From this animal women separate and reel off the cocoons and afterwards spin them. It is said that this was first spun in the island of Cos by Pamphile, daughter of Plates." This indicates a steady importation of raw silk on bobbins before Aristotle's time. The fabric he mentions was the famous *Coa vestis*, or transparent gauze (woven also at Tyre and elsewhere in Syria), which came into favor in the time of Cæsar and Augustus. Pliny mentions Pamphile of Cos, "who discovered the art of unwinding the silk" (from the bobbins, not from the cocoons) "and spinning a tissue therefrom; indeed, she ought not to be deprived of the glory of having discovered the art of making garments which, while they cover a woman, at the same time reveal her naked charms." (XI, 26).

He refers to the same fabric in VI, 20, where he speaks of "the Seres, so famous for the wool that is found in their forests. After steeping it in water, they comb off a soft down that adheres to the leaves; and then to the females of our part of the world they give the twofold task of unraveling their textures, and of weaving the threads afresh. So manifold is the labor, and so distant are the regions which are thus ransacked to supply a dress through which our ladies may in public display their charms." Compare Lucan, *Pharsalia*, X, 141, who describes Cleopatra, "her white breasts resplendent through the Sidonian fabric, which, wrought in close texture by the skill of the Seres, the needle of the workman of the Nile has separated, and has loosened the warp by stretching out the web."

Silk fabrics of this kind were much affected by men also during the reign of Augustus, but the fashion was considered effeminate, and early in the reign of Tiberius the Roman Senate enacted a law "that men should not defile themselves by wearing garments of silk." (Tacitus, *Annals*, II, 33.) The cost was enormously high; from an account of the Emperor Aurelian we learn that silk was worth its weight in gold, and that he neither used it himself nor allowed his wife to possess a garment of it, thereby setting an example against the luxurious tastes that were draining the empire of its resources.

Pliny includes it in his list of the "most valuable productions" (XXXVII, 67); "the most costly things that are gathered from trees are nard and Seric tissues."

Pliny (XXI, 8) speaks of other uses for silk: "Luxury arose at last to such a pitch that a chaplet was held in no esteem at all if it did not consist entirely of leaves sewn together with the needle. More recently again they have been imported from India, or from nations beyond the countries of India. But it is looked upon as the most refined of all, to present chaplets made of nard leaves, or else of silk of many colors steeped in unguents. Such is the pitch to which the luxuriousness of our women has at last arrived!"

Among both Greek and Roman writers there was some confusion between cotton and silk, both being called "tree wool;" and Fabricius, in his translation of the Periplus, omits silk altogether, considering raw material, yarn and cloth alike to be Turkestan cotton. But although these accounts err in some details, Pliny is sufficiently correct in his description of cotton. He distinguishes the wool-bearing trees of the Seres from those of the Indians (XIV, 4), and describes the cotton shrub, with its "fruit resembling a bearded nut, containing on the inside a silky down, which is spun into threads; the tissue made from which is superior to all others in whiteness and softness" (XIX, 2), while his account of the silkworm is at least within sight of the trutl although not so near it as Aristotle's:

"At first they assume the appearance of small butterflies wi naked bodies, but soon after, being unable to endure the cold, th throw out bristly hairs, and assume quite a thick coat against the wint by rubbing off the down that covers the leaves, by the aid of tl roughness of their feet. This they compress into balls by carding with their claws, and then draw it out and hang it between tl branches of the trees, making it fine by combing it out as it were; la of all, they take and roll it round their body, thus forming a nest i which they are enveloped. It is in this state that they are take after which they are placed in earthen vessels in a warm place, ai fed upon bran. A peculiar sort of down soon shoots forth upon tl body, on being clothed with which they are sent to work upon anoth task. The cocoons which they have begun to form are rendered so and pliable by the aid of water, and are then drawn out into threa by means of a spindle made of a reed. Nor, in fact, have the m even felt ashamed to make use of garments formed of this materi in consequence of their extreme lightness in summer; for so great have manners degenerated in our own day that so far from wearing cuirass, a garment even is found to be too heavy."

(See also Lassen, I, 317-322; III, 25; Yates, *Textrinum A tiquorum.*)

The reeling of silk from the cocoons was confused into a com ing of down from the leaves, which had also a basis of truth, but w the cause of the confusion with cotton. Compare Virgil, *Georgi* II, 121;—"Velleraque ut foliis depectant tenuia Seres."

Pliny finally distinguishes between the two fibers in referring Arabian cotton (XII, 21): "trees that bear wool, but of a differe nature from those of the Seres; as in these trees the *leaves* produ nothing at all, and indeed might very readily be taken for those of tl vine."

The word "silk" is from a Mongolian original, *sirkek*, meani silk; Korean *sir*, Chinese *ssi*. Hence the Greek *sēr*, Latin *sericu* From this word the name *Seres* was applied to the peoples throu whose hands the product came; by which must be understood, n the Chinese themselves, but rather the Turkish or Tibetan interme aries. That the word was loosely extended to cover most of Easte Asia is undeniable; but Ptolemy distinguishes the *Sinæ*, Isaiah tl *Sinim*, while the Periplus gives nearly the correct form, *This*, f China proper.

Pliny has a curious mixture of Seres and Cirrhadæ in his *Scyri*

(VII, 2), whose flat-nosed Mongolian faces he describes as having "merely holes in their faces instead of nostrils," and whom he connects with an allied race, the Astomi, "a people who have no mouths, who live on the eastern side of India, near the source of the Ganges; their bodies are rough and hairy, and they cover themselves with a down plucked from the leaves of trees." Here he shows some knowledge of the silk trade through Assam.

Ammianus Marcellinus (XXIII, vi) has more knowledge of the Seres:

64. "Beyond the districts of the two Scythias, on the eastern side, is a ring of mountains which surround Serica, a country considerable both for its extent and the fertility of its soil. This tribe on their western side border on the Scythians, on the north and the east they look toward snowy deserts; toward the south they extend as far as India and the Ganges. . . .

67. "The Seres themselves live quietly, always avoiding arms and battles; and as ease is pleasant to moderate and quiet men, they give trouble to none of their neighbors. Their climate is agreeable and healthy; the sky serene, the breezes gentle and delicious. They have numbers of shining groves, the trees of which through continued watering produce a crop like the fleece of a sheep, which the natives make into a delicate wool, and spin into a kind of fine cloth, formerly confined to the use of the nobles, but now procurable by the lowest of the people without distinction.

68. "The natives themselves are the most frugal of men, cultivating a peaceful life, and shunning the society of other men. And when strangers cross their river to buy their cloth, or any other of their merchandise, they interchange no conversation, but settle the price of the articles wanted by nods and signs; and they are so modest that, while selling their own produce, they never buy any foreign wares."

But to the Græco-Roman world the Seres were a people as ubiquitous as the subjects of Prester John in the middle ages. The Chēras of Malabar (*Seri* in Sinhalese mouths; see p. 209), and even Ausar and Masira in Southern Arabia (see p. 140) were identified with them.

Concerning the long struggles of the emperors at Constantinople with the Sassanid monarchs in Persia, over the ever-increasing silk-trade, culminating in the romantic success of the Christian monks who succeeded in bringing the jealously-guarded eggs to Justinian, hidden in a bamboo cane, thereby laying the foundation of the silk-culture of Greece and the Levant, see Beazley, *Dawn of Modern*

*Geography*, Vol. I;—Heyd, *Histoire du Commerce du Levant au Moyen Age*;—D'Anville, *Recherches géographiques et historiques sur la Sérique des anciens* (1768) in *Mémoires de l'Académie Royale des Inscriptions et Belles-Lettres*, xxxii, 573-603;—Reinaud, *Relations politiques et commerciales de l'Empire Romain avec l'Asie Orientale pendant les cinq premiers siècles de l'ère chrétienne.*

See also Richthofen, *China*, I, chap. x;—Stein, *Sand-buried Ruins of Khotan*;—Götz, *Verkehrswege im Dienste des Welthandels*, 496-511;—Speck, *Handelsgeschichte des Altertums*, I;—Letourneau, *L'Evolution du Commerce*;—Noël, *Histoire du Commerce du Monde*, I;—Lindsay, *History of Merchant Shipping and Ancient Commerce*, I;—Mayr, *Lehrbuch der Handelsgeschichte*, I, § 16;—Tozer, *A History of Ancient Geography*, 281;—Bunbury, *History of Ancient Geography*, I, 565; II, 166, 658;—Edmunds, *Buddhist and Christian Gospels*, 4th ed., introduction.

64. **Through Bactria to Barygaza.**—The overland travel from the Yellow River to Bactra, first instituted, possibly, early in the 2d century B. C. and then obstructed for nearly two centuries, followed two routes. The earlier, and to the Chinese the most important because it led to the Khotan jade-field, was the *Nan-lu* or "southern way," the stages of which may be traced on the map as follows:

Singanfu, Lanchowfu, Kanchow, Yümenhsien, Ansichow, Lop Nor to Tsiemo (the *Asmiræa* of the Greeks) where the routes divided. The *Nan-lu* followed south of the Tarim River to Khotan and Yarkand, thence over the Pamirs and westward to the Oxus and Bactra. This was the earliest route opened by the Chinese army under Pan Chao, being cleared in 74 A. D. The second route, the *Péi-lu* or "northern way," followed the same course from Singanfu to Tsiemo, thence north of the Tarim through Kuché and Aksu to Kashgar, and over the tremendous heights of the Terek to the Jaxartes and Samarcand. Thence a route led southward to Bactra, while another led southwestward more directly to Antiochia Margiana (Merv.) This second route was opened by Pan Chao in 94 A. D.

A variant of the *Péi-lu* led from Yümenhsien to Hami, Turfan and Kharachar, meeting the above route at Kuché; this was preferable in some respects, being close to the mountains, but was subjected to constant attacks by the savage Tartar tribes, Hami especially being a storm-center in the Chinese annals, and an important outpost for the defence of the main route. Another variant led from Turfan through the Tian-shan to Urumtsi and Kuldja, thence by the Ili River and north of the mountains to Tashkend, Bokhara and Merv. This did not become important until later.

The general topography of these Turkestan routes is shown by a passage from the Han Annals quoted by Richthofen (*China*, I, 460) from Stanislaus Julien (*Notices sur les pays et les peuples etrangers, tirées des géographes et des historiens chinois*, in *Journal Asiatique*, Ser. IV, Vol. VIII, 1846, pp. 228-252), as follows:

"*Hsi-yü* is bounded on the east by the barriers of *Yümen-kwan* and *Yang-kwan*, and on the west by the *Tsung-ling* (Pamirs). But the *Tsung-ling* is the trunk from which the great mountain-ranges branch out, which enclose the district on the north and the south, and these same ranges bound the districts of *Nan-lu* and *Péi-lu* on the south and north." And again: "The land along the *Nan-shan* (Kuen-lun) is called *Nan-tau*, and that along the *Péi-shan* (Tian-shan) is called *Péi-tau*. Both these provinces lie to the south of *Péi-shan*. . . . *Hsi-yü* extends 6000 *li* from east to west, and 1000 *li* from south to north."

That is, Tibet and Sungaria had no part in the transcontinental silk-trade in Roman times.

This Central Asian trade-route was first comprehensively described by Marinus of Tyre, some two generations later than the Periplus. His account is preserved by Ptolemy, and is said to be based on the notes of a Macedonian silk-merchant named Maës, whose Roman name was Titianus; who did not perform the whole journey, but repeats what he learned of Turkestan from his "agents" or trading associates whom he met at the Pamirs. The route, he says, began at the Bay of Issus in Cilicia, crossed Mesopotamia, Assyria and Media, to Ecbatana and the Caspian Pass; through Parthia and Hyrcania, to Antiochia Margiana (Merv); thence through Aria into Bactria. Thence the route passed through the mountainous country of the Cōmēdi, and through the territory of the Sacæ to the "Stone Tower," the station of those merchants who trade with the Seres (Tashkurghan, in Sarikol, on the upper Yarkand River in the Chinese Pamirs; a fortified town built on a great rocky crag that rises from the Taghdumbash valley, at the convergence of routes from the Oxus, the Indus and the Yarkand. See Stein, *op. cit.*, 67-8.) Thence to the Casii (Kashgar) and through the country of the Thaguri, until after a seven-months' journey from the "Stone Tower" the merchants arrived at "Sera Metropolis," the "City called Thinæ" of the Periplus.

By too literal an application of this "seven-months' journey" both Marinus and Ptolemy were led into grave error as to the longitudinal extension of Asia; but the evidence of direct trade between Rome and China is remarkable.

The first part of the route was minutely described before our author's time, in the *Mansiones Parthicæ* of Isidorus of Charax Spasiṇi.

This route of Maës the Macedonian followed very nearly the same direction as the Chinese *Nan-lu*, after leaving Bactra, crossing the Pamirs diagonally to Kashgar, on the *Pei-lu*, but then turning southward through Yarkand to Khotan, and in passing "Thagura" took a more southerly, and also a more direct route than the *Nan-lu* itself, which it joined half-way between Lop Nor and the Bulunzir (the "river of the Hiong-nu"); east of which all three routes were identical as far as Singanfu.

(See map to face p. 500, Vol. I, of Richthofen's *China;*—Stieler's *Hand-Atlas*, maps 61-2;—Stanford, *Atlas of the Chinese Empire*, plates 12, 13, 19, 21;—Lansdell, *Chinese Central Asia*, Vol. II;—Stein, *op. cit.*, chap. v. and map.)

At Bactra this overland trade-route branched again, following westward through the Parthian highlands to the Euphrates, or southward to Bamian, the Cabul valley, the Khyber Pass and the Indus. From Taxila the highway of the Maurya dynasty led through the Panjāb to the capital at Palibothra, with a branch from Mathurā southward to Ozene and the Deccan. The route down the Indus to its mouth was less important owing to the character of the tribes living on the lower reaches. This is indicated by the text, which says far more of the products carried by the overland route to Barygaza than of those coming to *Barbaricum*.

Yet a part of the Chinese trade was, apparently, localized at the mouth of the Indus. While the valuable silk cloth went to Barygaza, the yarn, or thread, went to *Barbaricum*, where it was exchanged for a product always more highly valued in China than in India—namely, frankincense; the white incense, or *shehri luban*, which Marco Polo still found in extensive use in China under the name of "milk perfume." This is not listed in the Periplus among the imports at other Indian ports, and evidently found its way up the Indus to Peucelaotis and Bactra, and thence to China. The silk yarn, in return, went to Arabia, where it was used in making the embroidered and silk-shot fabrics for which Arabia and Syria were so famous in the Roman market.

---

Concerning the frankincense of the Deir-el-Bahri reliefs Mr. R. E. Drake-Brockman writes again from Bulhar, Sept. 18, 1910, that the cattle shown in those reliefs are not the humped cattle peculiar to

Somaliland (and likewise to much of East Africa, Madagascar and Western India) but the ordinary type, without humps; which are bred in Southern Arabia and Socotra.

"The cattle of these regions and in fact the whole of Gallaland and Southern Abyssinia are all the humped variety. I have travelled fairly extensively in these regions and have never seen the non-humped breed, and very much doubt if they ever existed in these dried-up parts, as the hump is to these cattle what the camel's hump is to the camel, a sort of storehouse. Besides this, cattle are rare in Somaliland proper, and it is improbable if they ever existed in greater numbers or were exported."

Vase of black pottery ornamented with figures of humped cattle. From the Madagascar collection in the Commercial Museum, Philadelphia.

This is one more proof that the Punt Expedition did not make its terminus on the Somali coast, but must have gone to the Plain of Dhofar, or possibly to the south side of Socotra, which was a dependency of Dhofar. The localization of the island *Pa-anch* of the XIIIth dynasty tale, and the incense-land *Panchaia* of Virgil, in

Socotra, makes that an interesting possibility; but altogether the scene on the reliefs is more strongly suggestive of Dhofar, the *Sachalites* of the Periplus. (See also pp. 120, 141-2, and 218.)

---

See Ptolemy, I, 11-12, VI, 13;—De Guignes, *Sur les liaisons et le commerce des Romains avec les Tartares et les Chinois:* in *Mémoires de l'Académie Royale des Inscriptions et Belles-Lettres*, Vol. xxxii (1798) pp. 355-69;—Rémusat, *Remarques sur l'extension de l'Empire Chinois du côté de l'occident* (1825);—Lassen, I, 13-14, II, 519-660;—Yule, *Cathay and the Way Thither;*—Stein, *Sand-Buried Ruins of Khotan;*—Gen. M. R. Haig, *The Indus Delta Country*;—Richthofen, *China*, Vol. I;—Vincent, II, 573-618;—Merzbacher, *The Central Tian-Shan Mountains*;—Bonin, *Grandes voies commerciales de l'Asie Centrale;*—Manifold, *Recent Exploration and Economic Development in Central and Western China* (with map) in *Geographical Journal*, xxiii, 281-312, Mar. 1904;—Geil, *The Great Wall of China;*—Keane, *Asia*, I, chap. v. Col. M. S. Bell, in *Proceedings of the Royal Geographical Society*, 1890, describes his journey of 1887 along the entire Central Asian trade-route between Kashgar and Peking.

64. **To Damirica by way of the Ganges.**—This was the route across the Tibetan plateau, starting in the same direction as the Turkestan routes, from Singanfu to Lanchowfu; branching here, it led to Siningfu, thence to Koko Nor, and southwestward, by Lhasa and the Chumbi Vale to Sikkim and the Ganges. The route from Lhasa by the lower Brahmaputra was little used, owing to the savage tribes inhabiting it. There were numerous other passages into India; as, for instance, a frequented route by the Arun River through Nepāl to the Ganges, or by following the upper Brahmaputra to the sacred peak of Kailās and the source of the Sutlej, or continuing through Gartok to the upper Indus. But natural conditions, as stated in § 66 of the Periplus itself, made these routes through Western Tibet almost impracticable for commerce.

This was the route which later became the great highway of Buddhist pilgrim-travel between Mongolia and Lhasa. It is best described by one of the few white men who have ever traversed it: Huc, *Recollections of a Journey through Tartary, Thibet and China during 1844-46.*

The Chinese Buddhist monk Fa-Hien spent two years in "the country of Tamalipti, the capital of which is a seaport . . . after this he embarked in a large merchant-vessel, and went floating over the sea to the southwest. It was the beginning of winter and the wind was favorable; and after fourteen days, sailing day and night, they came to the country of Singhala." (*Travels*, chap. xxxvii.)

"To Damirica" came the eastern shipping, according to the text; that is, the Chēra backwaters were a meeting-point for the trade from the China Sea to the Gulf of Suez. Our author did not meet these vessels at Nelcynda, because the same monsoon that brought them would have taken him away.

Marco Polo tells us something of this trade in his day (III, xxv): "There is in this kingdom of Melibar a great quantity of pepper, and ginger, and cinnamon, and turbit, and of nuts of India. They also manufacture very delicate and beautiful buckrams. The ships that come from the east bring coffee in ballast. They also bring hither cloths of silk and gold, and sendels; also gold and silver, cloves and spikenard, and other fine spices."

See Holdich, *Tibet the Mysterious*;—Rockhill, *The Land of the Lamas*;—Sven Hedin, *Central Asia and Tibet*;—Waddell, *Lhasa and its Mysteries*; Younghusband, *The Geographical Results of the Tibet Mission*, in *Geographical Journal*, xxv, 1905;—Crosby, *Tibet and Turkestan*; Candler, *The Unveiling of Lhasa*;—Landon, *Lhasa*, and *The Opening of Tibet*;—Sarat Chandra Das, *Journey to Lhasa and Central Tibet*;—Littledale, *A Journey across Tibet*;—Deasy, *In Tibet and Chinese Turkestan*;—Carey, *Adventures in Tibet*;—Sandberg, *The Exploration of Tibet*;—Tsybikoff, *Lhasa and Central Tibet* (Smithsonian Report, 1903);—Prjevalski, *Mongolia, the Tangut Country, and the Solitudes of Northern Tibet*;—Sherring, *Western Tibet and the British Borderland.*

64. **Few men come from there, and seldom.**—Until the subjugation of Turkestan by China, travel and trade overland were naturally hazardous. The routes through Tibet and upper Burma were never so actively used as those leading through the Pamirs. For this, racial and topographical reasons were alike responsible.

See Lassen, I, 167-9;—Kemp, *The Face of China*; also, for a most useful and detailed account of a recent journey along the little-travelled Burmese route, R. F. Johnston, *From Peking to Mandalay.* Another theory, outlined by Kingsmill (*The Mantse and the Golden Chersonese*, and *Ancient Tibet and its Frontagers*, in *Journal of the Royal Asiatic Society*, China Branch, xxxv and xxxvii), and Terrien de Lacouperie (in his introduction to Colquhoun's *Among the Shans*), locates this entire traffic in upper Burma; identifying Thinæ with *Theinni*, the Burmese form of Hsen-wi, or the Northern Shans, and with *Tien*, the name given by Marco Polo to the Chinese province of Yunnan. (See also Rocher, *La Province Chinoise de Yunnan.*) But whatever may be the relation of Ptolemy's *Sinæ* and Cosmas' *Tzinista* to Burma, it may be asserted that the Thinæ of the Periplus had nothing to do with that region. Silk was brought thence overland "through Bactria to Barygaza," that is, by the Turkestan route. Why ignore the ancient center of the silk industry, Singanfu, to find a fancied similarity of name in a locality never important in silk production, separated

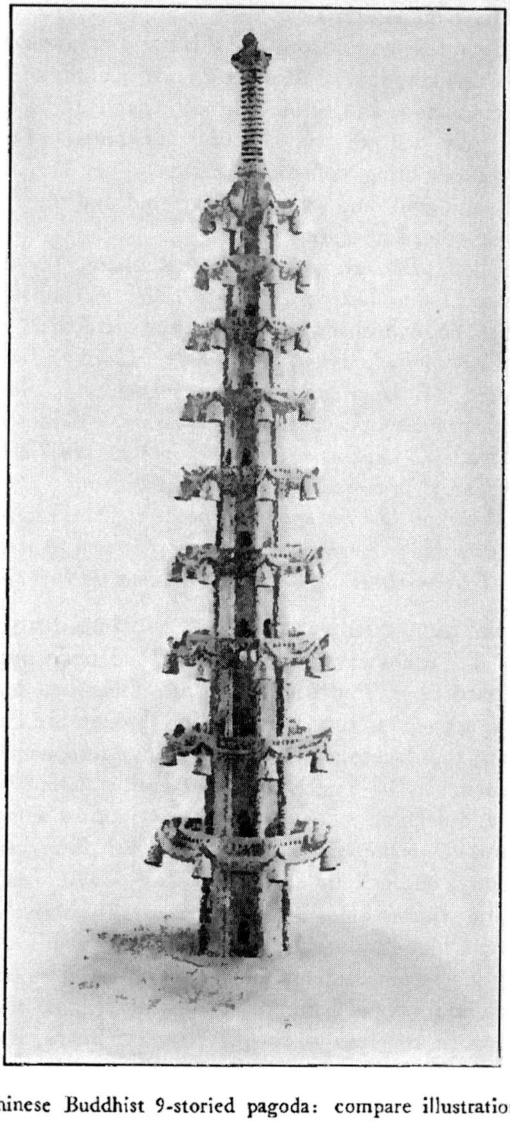

Early Chinese Buddhist 9-storied pagoda: compare illustrations of Hindu and Abyssinian types, on pp. 64-5. From a model exhibited in the Commercial Museum, Philadelphia.

from the silk-route by 1000 miles of the most difficult travelling in Asia, and not certainly settled by Shan tribes until some centuries later than the Periplus? The theory is manifestly impracticable.

With the rise of the Kushan dynasty in the northwest, and their relations towards their former home on the Chinese border, it was natural that communication by the Turkestan routes should increase. While the military successes of China did not begin until 73 A. D., it is known that the Chinese Emperor Ming-ti (who ruled from 58 to 75) introduced Buddhism into China by the invitation of two Indian Sramanas, Kāsyapa Mātanga and Bhārana, who arrived in 67 A. D. (Takakusu, Introduction to his edition of I-tsing, p. xvii.) Before such an invitation there must have been considerable activity on the part of missionaries, then as now the forerunners of commerce.

The text seems to be describing conditions prior to the journey of the Sramanas in 67 A. D.

As contrasting with the knowledge, or lack of it, which the Romans displayed concerning China, the following account of Roman Syria, particularly the district of Antioch, taken from Chinese annals of almost the same date as the Periplus, is of interest. (Quoted from Hirth, *China and the Roman Orient.)*:

## ANNALS OF THE HAN DYNASTY OF CHINA

### CHAPTER 88

*(Section "Hou-han-shu," partly written during the 5th century A. D., and embracing the period A. D. 25 to 220)*

The first detailed account of the Roman empire contained in the Chinese annals: this account describing Roman Syria and its capital Antioch, and being based on the report of the Ambassador Kan Ying, A. D. 97

(1) The country of *Ta-ts'in* is also called *Lichien* (Li-kin) and, as being situated on the western part of the sea, *Hai-hsi-kuo*, (*i. e.* "country of the western part of the sea"). (2) Its territory amounts to several thousand *li*; (3) it contains over four hundred cities, (4) and of dependent states there are several times ten. (5) The defences of cities are made of stone. (6) The postal stations and milestones on the roads are covered with plaster. (7) There are pine and cypress trees and all kinds of other trees and plants. (8) The people are much bent on agriculture and practice the planting of trees and the rearing of silk-worms. (9) They cut the hair of their heads, (10) wear embroidered clothing, (11) and drive in small carriages covered with white canopies; (12) when going in or out they beat drums, and hoist flags, banners, and pennants. (13) The precincts of the walled cities in which they live measure over a hundred *li* in

circumference. (14) In the city there are five palaces, ten *li* distant from each other. (15) In the palace buildings they use crystal to make pillars; vessels used in taking meals are also made. (16) The king goes to one palace a day to hear cases. After five days he has completed his round. (17) As a rule, they let a man with a bag follow the king's carriage Those who have some matter to submit, throw a petition into the bag. When the king arrives at the palace he examines into the rights and wrongs of the matter. (18) The official documents are under the control of thirty-six *chiang* (generals?) who conjointly discuss government affairs. (19) Their kings are not permanent rulers, but they appoint men of merit. (20) When a severe calamity visits the country, or untimely rain-storms, the king is deposed and replaced by another. The one relieved from his duties submits to his degradation without a murmur. (21) The inhabitants of that country are tall and well-proportioned, somewhat like the Chinese, whence they are called *Ta-ts'in*. (22) The country contains much gold, silver, and rare precious stones, especially the "jewel that shines at night," the "moonshine pearl," the *hsieh-chi-hsi*, corals, amber, glass, *lang-kan* (a kind of coral), *chu-tan* (cinnabar?), green jadestone (*ching-pi*), gold-embroidered rugs and thin silk-cloth of various colors. (23) They make gold-colored cloth and asbestos cloth. (25) They further have "fine cloth," also called *Shui-yang-ts'ui*, (*i. e.* down of the water-sheep); it is made from the cocoons of wild silk-worms. (25) They collect all kinds of fragrant substances, the juice of which they boil into *su-ho* (storax). (26) All the rare gems of other foreign countries come from there. (27) They make coins of gold and silver. Ten units of silver are worth one of gold. (28) They traffic by sea with *An-hsi* (Parthia) and *T'ien-chu* (India), the profit of which trade is ten-fold. (29) They are honest in their transactions and there are no double prices. (30) Cereals are always cheap. The budget is based on a well-filled treasury. (31) When the embassies of neighboring countries come to their frontier, they are driven by post to the capital, and on arrival, are presented with golden money. (32) Their kings always desired to send embassies to China, but the *An-hsi* (Parthians) wished to carry on trade with them in Chinese silks, and it is for this reason that they were cut off from communication. (33) This lasted till the ninth year of the Yen-hsi period during the emperor Huan-ti's reign (= A. D. 166) when the king of *Ta-ts'in*, *An-tun* (Marcus Aurelius Antoninus) sent an embassy who, from the frontier of *Jih-nan* (Anam) offered ivory, rhinoceros horns, and tortoise shell. From that time dates the (direct) intercourse with this country. The list of their tribute contained no jewels whatever, which fact throws doubt on the tradition. (34) It is said by some that in the west of this country there is the *Jo-shai* ("weak water") and the *Liu-sha* ("flying sands, desert") near the residence of the *Hsi-wang-mu* ("mother of the western king"), where the sun sets. (35) The *Ch'ien-han-shu* says "from *T'iao-chih* west, going over 200 days, one is near the place where the sun sets;" this does not agree with the present book. (36) Former embassies from China all returned from *Wu-i;* there were none who came as far as *T'iao-chih.* (37) It is further said that, coming from the land-road of *An-hsi* (Parthia), you make a round at sea and, taking a northern turn, come out from the western part of the sea, whence you proceed to *Ta-ts'in.* (38) The country is densely populated; every ten *li* (of a road) are marked by a *t'ing;* thirty *li* by a *chih* (resting-place). (39) One is not alarmed by robbers, but the road becomes unsafe by fierce tigers and lions who will attack passengers, and unless these be traveling in caravans of a hundred men or more, or be protected by military equipment, they may be devoured by these beasts. (40) They also say there is a flying bridge (*fei-chiao*) of several hundred *li*, by which one may cross to the countries north of the sea. (41) The articles made of rare precious stones produced in this country are sham curiosities and mostly not genuine, whence they are not (here) mentioned.

64. **Under the Lesser Bear**—meaning far to the north (of the Himalayas). No part of China is actually so far north as to have Ursa Minor in the zenith; this would require it to be within the Arctic Circle.

64. **Empty into the Ocean.**—This was the belief of most of the Greek and Roman geographers. See p. 100, where the map according to Pomponius Mela shows the Caspian directly connected with the Arctic Ocean, and Lake Mæotis connected by means of the Tanais, or Don, river. So Strabo (XI, vi, 1): "The Caspian is a bay extending from the ocean to the south. At its commencement it is very narrow; as it advances further inward, and particularly toward the extremity, it widens. . . . Eratosthenes says that the navigation of this sea was known to the Greeks; that the part of the voyage along the coast of the Albanians and the Gadusii comprised 5400 stadia; and the part along the country of the Anariaci, Mardi, and Hyrcani, as far as the mouth of the river Oxus, 4800 stadia, and thence to the Jaxartes, 2400 stadia." This passage, often ridiculed, is rather an indication of the strong probability that the Caspian and Aral Seas were joined together until after the Christian era, so that the Amu and Syr were in truth accessible to the Greek adven-

turers from Colchis, crossing from the Euxine Sea. As to Lake Mæotis (the Sea of Azov) Strabo says (XI, i, 5): "Asia has a kind of peninsular form, surrounded on the west by the river Tanais and the Palus Mæotis as far as the Cimmerian Bosphorus, and that part of the coast of the Euxine which terminates at Colchis; on the north by the Ocean, as far as the mouth of the Caspian Sea; on the east by the same sea, as far as the confines of Armenia."

These errors were corrected by Ptolemy, but subsequently revived. See Tozer, *History of Ancient Geography*, 345, 367;—Huntington, *The Pulse of Asia*;—Mackinder, *The Geographical Pivot of History*, in *Geographical Journal*, xxiii, 422-437, April, 1904;—Kropotkin, *The Desiccation of Eurasia*, *ibid.*, June, 1904.

In this group of modern Tibetans may be found all the types mentioned in the closing paragraphs of the Periplus: "the men with flattened noses," the "Horse-faces" and the "Long-faces," of § 62, and the "men with short, thick bodies and broad, flat faces" of § 65.

65. **Besatæ.**—These were another Tibeto-Burman tribe, allied to the Cirrhadæ, and to the modern Kuki-Chin, Naga and Garo

tribes. Ptolemy places them east of the Ganges, and corroborates the Periplus as to their personal appearance. Lassen (III, 38) identifies the name with the Sanscrit *vaishāda*, "wretchedly stupid," and says they were a tribe of Sikkim. Our author locates them "on the borders of the Land of This," indicating that Tibet was then subject to China. The location of their annual fair must have been near the modern Gangtok (27° 20′ N., 88° 38′ E.) above which the Cho-La or the Jelap-La Pass leads to Chumbi on the Tibetan side of the frontier, from which the overland route mentioned in § 64 led across the table-land to Koko Nor, Siningfu and Singanfu. Other passes through Nepāl are possible, particularly that by the Arun River, but the route through Sikkim involves the least deviation from the direct line from Koko Nor to the Ganges; while from Gyangste to the source of the Arun a pass must be scaled higher by 3000 feet than Jelap-La. (See Freshfield, *The Roads to Tibet*, in *Geographical Journal*, xxiii, Jan. and March, 1904; and *The Highest Mountain in the World*, *ibid.*, xxi, March, 1903;—O'Connor, *Routes in Sikkim*;—Louis, *Gates of Tibet.*)

Pseudo-Callisthenes (III, 8) refers to the *Bisadæ* "who gather a leaf. They are a feeble folk, of very diminutive stature, and live in caves among the rocks. They understand how to climb precipices through their intimate knowledge of the country and are thus able to gather the leaf. They are small men of stunted growth, with big heads of hair which is straight and not cut." (McCrindle, *Ancient India*, p. 180.)

Fergusson (*History of Indian Architecture*, I, 13) says: "The Tibetans are a fragment of a great primitive population that occupied both the northern and southern slopes of the Himalayas at some very remote prehistoric time. They were worshippers of trees and serpents; and they, and their descendants and connections, in Bengal, Ceylon, Tibet, Burma, Siam and China, have been the bulwark of Buddhism. In India the Dravidians resisted Buddhism on the south, and a revival of Aryanism abolished it in the north."

65. **Feast for several days.**—This description of a tribal festival and market resembles many accounts of other primitive peoples. Compare the following from Herodotus (IV, 196):

"The Carthaginians further say that beyond the Pillars of Hercules there is a region of Libya, and men who inhabit it; when they arrive among these people and have unloaded their merchandise, they set it in order on the shore, go on board their ships, and make a great smoke; that the inhabitants, seeing the smoke, come down to the sea, and then deposit gold in exchange for the merchandise, and withdraw to some distance from the merchandise; that the Carthaginians then, going ashore, examine the gold, and if the quantity seems sufficient for the merchandise, they take it up and sail away; but if it is not sufficient, they go on board their ships again and wait; the natives

On a modern trade-route through the mountains of Sikkim. The shoulder-baskets and covers of matting are easily distinguishable.

then approach and deposit more gold, until they have satisfied them; neither party ever wrongs the other; for they do not touch the gold before it is made adequate to the value of the merchandise, nor do the natives touch the merchandise before the other party has taken the gold."

Pomponius Mela (III, viii, 60) seems also to speak of the silent trade of the Himalayas; Ammianus Marcellinus, in the passage already quoted, tells of such a custom at Tashkurghan, the "Stone Tower" of the Pamirs, where silk passed from Eastern hands to Western; while Fa-Hien, describing a similar custom in Ceylon, ascribes it to the "spirits and nagas," the tutelary guardians of the precious articles of trade. (*Travels*, chap. xxxviii.)

65. **Great packs and baskets.**—The same thing is in constant use today in this region, being the regular burden of the coolies of Nepāl and Sikkim.

65. **Petri.**—Our author is misled by a fancied resemblance to the Greek *petros*, fiber; the word is the Sanscrit *patra*, leaf. Otherwise the description of the preparation of the *tamala* leaves is correct, being corroborated throughout by Pliny.

65. **Malabathrum.**—The *Cinnamomum tamala* is native in this part of the Himalayas, being one of the principal trees.

So Marco Polo (II, xlvi), in his account of *Tebet:* "It contains in several quarters rivers and lakes, in which gold-dust is found in great abundance. Cinnamon also grows there in great plenty. Coral is in great demand in this country and fetches a high price, for they delight to hang it round the necks of their women and of their idols." (See pp. 82-4, 87, 89, 216-18, 256.)

66. **Influence of the gods.**—This is still the geography of Brahman writings. Like Tavernier in the 17th century, who summarized the *Rāmāyana* in his *Travels*, so this merchant of Berenice in the 1st century came under the spell of the great epics of India, as he sojourned among

> "the sister nations three,
> Cholas, Cheras, and the Pandyas dwelling by the southern sea."

The region beyond Sikkim, "impassable by reason of its great cold," and including the mightiest peaks of the Himalayas, was within the sphere of the *Kurukshetra* of the later *Vedas*, the *Brāhmanas*, and the *Mahābhārata*, the home-land of the Brahman faith; with the greatest of all mountains, Everest, is associated the name of Gauri-sankar, a name of Siva and Durgā; in the western curve of the great chain is the sacred peak of Kailās, the Olympus of the Hindu gods, the axis of the universe and the way to heaven; while the ending of the Periplus is that of the Sītā-quest in the *Rāmāyana:*

> **"Halt not till you reach the country where the northern Kurus rest,**
> **Utmost confines of the wide earth, home of Gods and Spirits blest!"**

# ARTICLES OF TRADE MENTIONED IN THE PERIPLUS

*Enumerated according to the ports*

**Red Sea Coast.**

PTOLEMAIS.

*(Exports)*

Tortoise-shell
Ivory.

ADULIS.

*(Imports)*

Undressed cloth from Egypt
Robes from Arsinoe
Cloaks of poor quality, dyed
Double-fringed linen mantles
Flint glass, in many forms
Murrhine (glass imitation made in Diospolis)
Brass (for ornament and in cut pieces as coin)
Sheets of soft copper (for cooking-utensils, and bracelets and anklets)
Iron (for spears)
Axes, adzes and swords
Copper drinking-cups, round and large
Coin, a little
Wine of Laodicea and Italy
Olive oil
Presents for the king: gold and silver plate, military cloaks, thin coats of skin
Indian iron and steel (from Ariaca)
Indian cotton cloth (the broad *monachē*), also the *sagmatogēnē*, perhaps raw cotton
Girdles
Coats of skin
Mallow-colored cloth
Muslins
Lac.

*(Exports)*

Ivory
Tortoise-shell
Rhinoceros-horn.

**Horn of Africa** (The "far-side" coast).

AVALITES.

*(Imports)*

Flint glass, assorted
Juice of sour grapes from Diospolis
Dressed cloth, assorted
Wheat
Wine
Tin.

*(Exports* partly to Ocelis and Muza)

Ivory
Tortoise-shell
Myrrh (better than the rest).

MALAO.

*(Imports)*

The things already mentioned. Also
Tunics
Cloaks from Arsinoe, dressed and dyed
Drinking cups
Sheets of soft copper
Iron
Gold and silver coin.

*(Exports)*

Myrrh
Frankincense (the far-side)
Cinnamon (the harder)
*Duaca* (var. of frankincense)
Indian copal
*Macir* (medicinal bark from Malabar)

(These exports going to Arabia)

Slaves, rarely.

MUNDUS.

*(Imports)*

The things already mentioned.

*(Exports)*

The things already mentioned; also

*Mocrotu* (var. of frankincense).

MOSYLLUM.

(*Imports*)

The things already mentioned; also

Silver plate

Iron, very little

Glass.

(*Exports*)

Cinnamon, in great quantity

Fragrant gums and spices

Tortoise-shell

*Mocrotu* incense

Frankincense (the far-side)

Ivory

Myrrh.

ELEPHANT RIVER.

(*Exports*)

Frankincense (the best far-side)

MARKET OF SPICES (Cape Guardafui).

(*Imports*)

The things already mentioned.

(*Exports*)

Cinnamon (varieties, *gizir*, *asypha*, *arebo*, *magla*, *moto*)

Frankincense.

OPONE.

(*Imports*)

The things already mentioned.

(*Exports*)

Cinnamon (the better sort, *arebo* and *moto*, in great quantity)

Slaves of the better sort, for Egypt, in increasing numbers

Tortoise-shell, good quality, in great quantity

(Goods brought in Indian ships to this and the preceding far-side ports)!

Wheat

Rice

Clarified butter

Sesame oil

Cotton cloth (the *monachē*, also *sagmatogēnē*)

Girdles

Honey from the reed called *sacchari*.

**East Africa.**

RHAPTA, MENUTHIAS, &c.

(*Imports*, chiefly in Arabian ships)

Lances made at Muza

Hatchets, daggers and awls

Glass, various kinds

Wine, a little

Wheat, for free distribution to the savages.

(*Exports*)

Ivory (in great quantity, but inferior to that of Adulis)

Rhinoceros-horn

Tortoise-shell (the best after that from India)

Palm-oil, a little.

**Arabia.**

MUZA.

(*Imports*)

Purple cloths, fine and coarse

Clothing in Arabian styles, with sleeves; (plain, ordinary, embroidered, or interwoven with gold)

Saffron

Sweet-rush

Muslins

Cloaks

Blankets, plain and in the local fashion

Sashes of different colors

Fragrant ointments

Wine and wheat (not much, the country producing both)

Presents to the King and Chief: horses, sumpter-mules, vessels of gold and polished silver, finely woven clothing, copper vessels.

(*Exports*, the products of the country)

Myrrh, selected

Myrrh, the Gebanite-Minæan *stacte*

Alabaster

All the things already mentioned from Avalites and the far-side coast.

CANA (which has trade with Egypt, the far-side coast, India and the Persian Gulf).

(*Imports*)

Wheat and wine; a little, as at Muza

Clothing in the Arabian style, poor quality

Copper

Tin

Coral

Storax

Other things such as go to Muza

Presents for the king: wrought gold and silver plate, horses, images, thin clothing of fine quality.

(*Exports*, the native produce)

Frankincense

Aloes

The rest of the things mentioned from the other ports.

DIOSCORIDA ISLAND.

(*Exports*)

Tortoise-shell, various kinds

Indian cinnabar (dragon's blood).

(*Imports*, brought by merchants from Muza and by chance calls of ships returning from India)

Rice

Wheat

Indian cloth

Female slaves, a few

MOSCHA.

(*Imports*)

Cloth

Wheat

Sesame oil.

(*Exports*)

Frankincense.

SARAPIS ISLAND.

(*Exports*, to Cana, at regular intervals)

Tortoise-shell.

**Persian Gulf.**

OMMANA AND APOLOGUS.

(*Imports*)

Copper

Sandalwood

Teakwood timbers

Blackwood logs (from India)

Ebony logs " "

Frankincense (from Cana to Ommana).

(*Exports*)

Sewed boats called *madarata* (from Ommana to South Arabia)

Pearls, inferior to the Indian

Purple

Clothing, after the fashion of the place

Wine

Dates, in great quantity

Gold

Slaves (to both India and S. Arabia)

**Makran Coast.**

ORÆA.

(*Exports*)

Wheat

Wine

Rice

Dates

Bdellium.

**Indo-Scythia.**

BARBARICUM (at mouth of Indus river).

(*Imports*)

Thin clothing, in large quantity, some spurious

Figured linens

Topaz

Coral

Storax

Frankincense

Vessels of glass

Silver and gold plate

Wine, a little.

(*Exports*)

Costus

Bdellium

Lycium

Nard

Turquoise

Lapis lazuli

Seric skins

Cotton cloth

Silk yarn

Indigo.

**India** (the kingdom of Nambanus).

BARYGAZA.

(*Imports*)

- Wine: Italian preferred, also Laodicean and Arabian
- Copper
- Tin
- Lead
- Coral
- Topaz
- Thin clothing and inferior sorts of all kinds
- Bright-colored girdles a cubit wide
- Storax
- Sweet clover
- Flint glass
- Realgar
- Antimony
- Gold and silver coin (yielding a profit on the exchange)
- Ointments, not costly, a little
- Presents for the King: Costly vessels of silver, singing boys, beautiful maidens for the harem, fine wines, thin clothing of the finest weaves, the choicest ointments.

(*Exports*)

- Spikenard (coming through Scythia, also through Poclais, from Caspapyra, Paropanisus and Cabolitis)
- Costus
- Bdellium
- Ivory
- Agate and carnelian (onyx and murrhine)
- Lycium
- Cotton cloth of all kinds (muslins and ordinary)
- Silk cloth
- Mallow-cloth
- Yarn
- Long pepper
- Other things coming from the various ports.

**India** (Chēra and Pāndya kingdoms).

MUZIRIS, NELCYNDA AND BACARE; (to which large ships come for pepper and malabathrum).

(*Imports*)

- Coin, in great quantity
- Topaz
- Thin clothing, not much
- Figured linens
- Antimony
- Coral
- Crude glass
- Copper
- Tin
- Lead
- Wine, not much, but as much as at Barygaza
- Realgar
- Orpiment
- Wheat (for the sailors, the country not producing it).

(*Exports*)

- Pepper, produced in Cottorara
- Fine pearls in great quantity
- Ivory
- Silk cloth
- Spikenard from the Ganges
- Malabathrum from the interior
- Transparent stones of all kinds
- Diamonds
- Sapphires
- Tortoise-shell, from Chryse and from near-by islands

**India** (Chōla kingdom)

ARGARU (inland)

(*Exports*)

- Pearls
- Muslins (named from the place)

**India** (East Coast).

CAMARA, PODUCA AND SOPATMA (where ships come from the west coast, also from the Ganges and Chryse).

(*Imports*)

- Everything made in Damirica and the neighboring countries and most of what comes from Egypt.

**Ceylon.**

PALÆSIMUNDU, FORMERLY CALLED TAPROBANE.

(*Exports*)

Pearls
Transparent stones
Muslins
Tortoise-shell.

**India** (East Coast, farther north)

MASALIA.

(*Exports*)

Muslins, in great quantity.

DOSARENE.

(*Exports*)

Ivory.

**India** (Ganges delta).

GANGES.

(*Exports*)

Malabathrum
Gangetic spikenard
Pearls
Muslins of the finest sort, called Gangetic.

(The place has a gold coin called *caltis*).

**Malacca.**

CHRYSE ISLAND.

(*Exports*)

Tortoise-shell, the best of all.

**China.**

THINÆ.

(Difficult of access; few men come from there, and seldom)

(*Exports*, overland through Bactria to Barygaza, also by way of the Ganges to Damirica)

Raw silk
Silk yarn
Silk cloth.

**Himalaya mountains.**

THE BESATÆ.

(*Exports*)

Malabathrum; in three forms, the large-ball, the medium-ball, and the small-ball.

# ARTICLES SUBJECT TO DUTY AT ALEXANDRIA

## FROM THE RESCRIPT CONCERNING EASTERN TRADE IN THE DIGEST OF THE ROMAN LAW, XXXIX, XV, 5, 7.

*Classified as follows:*

(1) *Precious stones, etc.*
- Diamond (*adamas*)
- Alabanda
- Beryl
- Ceraunium
- Alabaster (onyx arabicus)
- Lapis lazuli
- Sardonyx
- Emerald
- Sapphire
- Garnet (alabanda)
- Pearls and pearl shell
- Tortoise shell
- Ivory.

(2) *Vegetable products valued for their fragrance: as incense, perfume, or medicine.*
- Aloe
- Amomum
- Galbanum
- Ginger
- Incense gums
- Gum dammar
- Cardamom
- Caryophyllon
- Cassia
- Cinnamon
- Xylo-cassia
- Costus
- Asafœtida
- Frankincense, Arabian and African
- Malabathrum
- Sugar
- Myrrh
- Spikenard
- Nard
- Pepper
- Sarcogalla
- Stacte
- Agallochum.

(3) *Dyes.*
- Lac
- Fucus (rock lichen or orchil).

(4) *Textile.*
- Byssus (flax cloth?)
- Muslins
- Cotton cloth
- Wool (Tibetan?)
- Capilli Indici(?)
- Silk, yarn and cloth.

(5) *Metal*
- Indian steel (Haidarábád).

(6) *Animal.*
- Tigers
- Leopards
- Panthers
- Lions and lionesses
- Babylonian skins.

(7) *Human*
- Eunuchs.

# DATE OF THE PERIPLUS, AS DETERMINED BY VARIOUS COMMENTATORS

The dates assigned fall into three groups. The first, which dates the Periplus before Pliny, assumes the trade to have been that which existed under Nero, and includes the possibility that Pliny quoted from or summarized the Periplus in his description of Arabia Felix. The latest date possible under these suppositions is the end of the reign of Malichas, whose inscriptions indicate that he ruled between 40 and 70 A. D.

The second group depends on the identification of Zoscales with Za Hakale in the Abyssinian Chronicle, whose dates were given by Henry Salt as 76 to 89 A. D. The dependence placed on these two dates, on which Salt himself cast doubt, is surprising in view of the fact that he antedated two kings in the list (El Abreha and El Atzbeha) more than 100 years, to bring them within the reigns of the Roman emperors Constantine and Constantius, who are known to have had relations with them; and if so great a liberty can be taken with the monarchs of the fourth century, it seems reasonable to suppose that one of the first century may be a score of years out of his proper order. The supposed confirmation of these dates by mention of contemporary Indian rulers points to an earlier date during the period of their viceroyalties rather than of their reigns.

The third group of identifications depends on the reference in tne text to the "emperors," assuming this to be a time when there were two Roman emperors reigning jointly. This assumption is entirely unnecessary.

First group:

"In the middle of the first century after Christ, nearly contemporary with Pliny."

Salmasius, *Exercitationes Plinianæ*, 835.

"A little earlier than Pliny."

Mannert, *Geographie der Griechen und Römer aus ihren Schriften dargestellt*, Nürnberg, 1799, I, 131.

"Soon after Claudius; about the tenth year of Nero" (which would be 63 A. D.).

Vincent, II, 59.

"Under Claudius or a little later."

Ukert, *Geographie der Griechen und Römer*, Weimar, 1816, I, i, 209.

"60 A. D."

Benfey, article *Indien* in Ersch and Grüber's *Encyklopädie*, Sect. II, Vol. 7, p. 90: Leipzig, 1840.

Lassen, *Indische Alterthumskunde*, II, 538; III, 3.

"Unquestionably before Pliny's Natural History."

Schwanbeck, in *Rheinischen Museum*, VII, 338.

"A little earlier than Pliny, who seems to quote from it; that is, prior to 77 A. D."

Dillmann, in *Berichte der K. Preuss. Akad. der Wissenschaften*, 1879, pp. 413-429.

"Nearly contemporary with Pliny, written before the dedication of the Natural History in 77 A. D."

Fabricius, p. 27.

"56-67 A. D."

Glaser, in *Ausland*, München, 1891, pp. 45-6.

*Skizze der Geschichte und Geographie Arabiens*, II, 164.

"Next before Pliny."

Robertson, *Disquisition on Ancient India.*

"60-63 A. D."

Watt, *Commercial Products of India*, p. 371, etc.

"56-71 A. D., as shown by Glaser."

"Before 77 A. D."

Speck, *Handelsgeschichte des Altertums*, I, 35; III, 2b., 919.

"During the reign of Malik III, King of the Nabatæans, 40-70 A. D."

Vogüé, *Syrie Centrale:* Inscriptions Sémitiques, p. 107. (Paris, 1869.)

"During the reign of Kariba-îl Watar Juhan'im, the Homerite King, about 40-70 A. D."

Glaser, *Die Abessinier in Arabien und Africa*, pp. 37-8.

"During the reign of Ilî-azzu Jalît, King of the Hadramaut, about 25-65 A. D."

Glaser, *Die Abessinier*, etc., p. 34.

"The author made his voyages at various times between 65 and 75 or 80 A. D. The work was *written* in the last quarter of the first century A. D."

Haig, *The Indus Delta Country*, 28.

SECOND GROUP:

"80-89 A. D."

C. Müller, *Geographi Græci Minores*, I, xcvi; depending on the doubtful dates given Za Hakale by Henry Salt, in his rearrangement of the Abyssinian Chronicle in 1812.

"75 A. D."

Bunsen, *de Azania commentatio philologica*, Bonn, 1852.

"80-85 A. D."

Vivien de Saint Martin, *Histoire de la Géographie et des découvertes géographiques, 1873*; also *Le Nord de l' Afrique dans l' antiquité grecque et romaine.*

"77-89 A. D., as shown by Müller."

Bunbury, *History of Ancient Geography*, II, 445; London, 1883.

"About 10 years after Pliny's death" (which occurred in 79 A. D.)

Tozer, *History of Ancient Geography*, p. 274: Cambridge, 1897.

"About 90 A. D." (referring to Nahapāna, the Nambanus of § 41),

A.-M. Boyer, in *Journal Asiatique*, Paris, July-Aug., 1897, pp. 120-151.

"83-84 A. D." (referring to Sundara Sātakarni, the Sandares of § 52).

C. R. Wilson, in *Journal of the Asiatic Society of Bengal*, June, 1904.

"Between 77 and 105 A. D."

Vincent Smith, *Early History of India*, p. 371, etc.

"Between 80 and 89 A. D."

McCrindle, in *Indian Antiquary*, VIII, 108-151.

"About 85 A. D."

J. F. Fleet, article *Epigraphy*, in *Imperial Gazetteer of India*, new edition, II, 76.

THIRD GROUP.

The following belong to the curiosities of criticism, all being based on the "emperors" of § 23:

"In the 2d century A. D., later than 161, under Marcus Aurelius and Lucius Verus."

Dodwell, in Hudson's *Geographiæ Veteris Scriptores*, pp. 85-105.

Heeren, *De Inaia Romanis cognita*, in *Commentationes societatis regiæ scientiarum.* Göttingen, 1793, XI, 101.

"Apparently of the 1st, or at latest of the 2d century A. D."

Heeren, *Ideen über die Politik, den Verkehr und den Handel der vornehmsten Völker der alten Welt.* Göttingen, 1824, I, iii, 316.

"A ship's log of the 2d century A. D."

Bohlen, *Das alte Indien, mit besonderer Rücksicht auf Aegypten.* Königsberg, 1830, I, 71.

"A merchant of Alexandria who lived in the first half of the 2d century A. D."

Külb, *Länder- und Völkerkunde in Biographien*, Berlin, 1846, I, 245.

"Of the 2d century A. D."

Ritter, *Geschichte der Erdkunde und der Entdeckungen*, Berlin, 1861, p. 124; also *Erdkunde Asiens*, IV, 1.

"Of the 1st or, rather, the following century."

Ritter, *Erdkunde Asiens*, VIII, 1.

"Of the 3d century."

Letronne, *Christianisme de Nubie*, 47.

"200-217 A. D."

Letronne, in *Nouveau Recueil de l'Académie des Inscriptions*, IX, 173.

Alex. v. Humboldt, *Kritischen Untersuchungen*, I, 315. *Kosmos*, II, 458.

Forbiger, *Handbuche der alten Geographe aus den Quellen bearbeitet*, Leipzig, 1842, I, 442.

"246-247 A. D., under the emperor Philip and his son."

Reinaud, in *Journal Asiatique*, series V, vol. 18, Paris, 1861, p. 226.

Reinaud, *Mémoires de l'Académie des Inscriptions et belles lettres*, vol. xxiv, pp. 227-278 (1864).

O. Peschel, *Geschichte der Erdkunde*, München, 1865.

These views are vigorously combated by

O. Blau, in *Zeitschrift der Deutschen Morgenländischen Gesellschaft*, xxii, 656.

A. Weber, *Indische Streife*, II, 266 (1869).

Vivien de Saint Martin, *Le Nord de l'Afrique dans l'antiquité grecque et romaine*, 1863, p. 197.

Dillmann, *loc. cit.*, pp. 414-428.

## RULERS MENTIONED IN THE PERIPLUS

§ 5. Zoscales, king of the people called Axumites.

(Dates fixed by Salt in 1804 as 76-89 A. D.; his conclusions, depending on an arbitrary arrangement of the Abyssinian Chronicle, as he said himself, are "not to be depended upon;" a more probable period for this reign would be 59-72 A. D.)

§ 19. Malichas, king of the Nabatæans.

(Mentioned also by Josephus, *Bell. Iud.*, III, 4, 2. Inscriptions cited by Vogüé fix his dates as 40-70 A. D.)

§ 23. Charibael, king of the Homerites and Sabaites.

(Inscriptions cited by Glaser fix his reign about 40-70 A. D.)

§ 23. The Emperors.

(Probably Claudius and Nero, 41-54 and 54-68 respectively.)

§ 27. Eleazus, king of the Frankincense Country.

(Inscriptions cited by Glaser fix his reign about 25-65 A. D.)

§ 38. Parthian princes at war with each other.

(Probably within the decade following the death of Gondophares, which occurred 51 A. D.)

§ 41. Nambanus, king of Ariaca.

(Perhaps Nahapāna, the Saka satrap—or a predecessor of that name—but *before* the victories which led to the establishment of the Saka era of 78 A. D.)

§ 52. The elder Saraganus, who had previously governed Calliena.

(Probably Arishta Sātakarni, then the Andhra king, who ruled about 44-69 A. D.; whose court was held at his eastern capital, Dhānyakataka, so that to the author of the Periplus, landing on the west coast, he was no more than a name, and the visible authority was vested in the western viceroy.)

§ 52. Sandares, who possessed Calliena.

(Probably Sundara Sātakarni—who ruled as Andhra king in 83-4 A. D.—but *before* his accession to the throne, while as one of the heirs presumptive he was acting as viceroy at Pæthana, toward the end of the reign of Arishta Sātakarni, the "elder Saraganus.")

# INDEX

References to the text are in **bold-faced type**; to the notes in light-faced

MAP TO ILLUSTRATE THE PERIPLUS MARIS ERYTHRAEI
60 A.D.

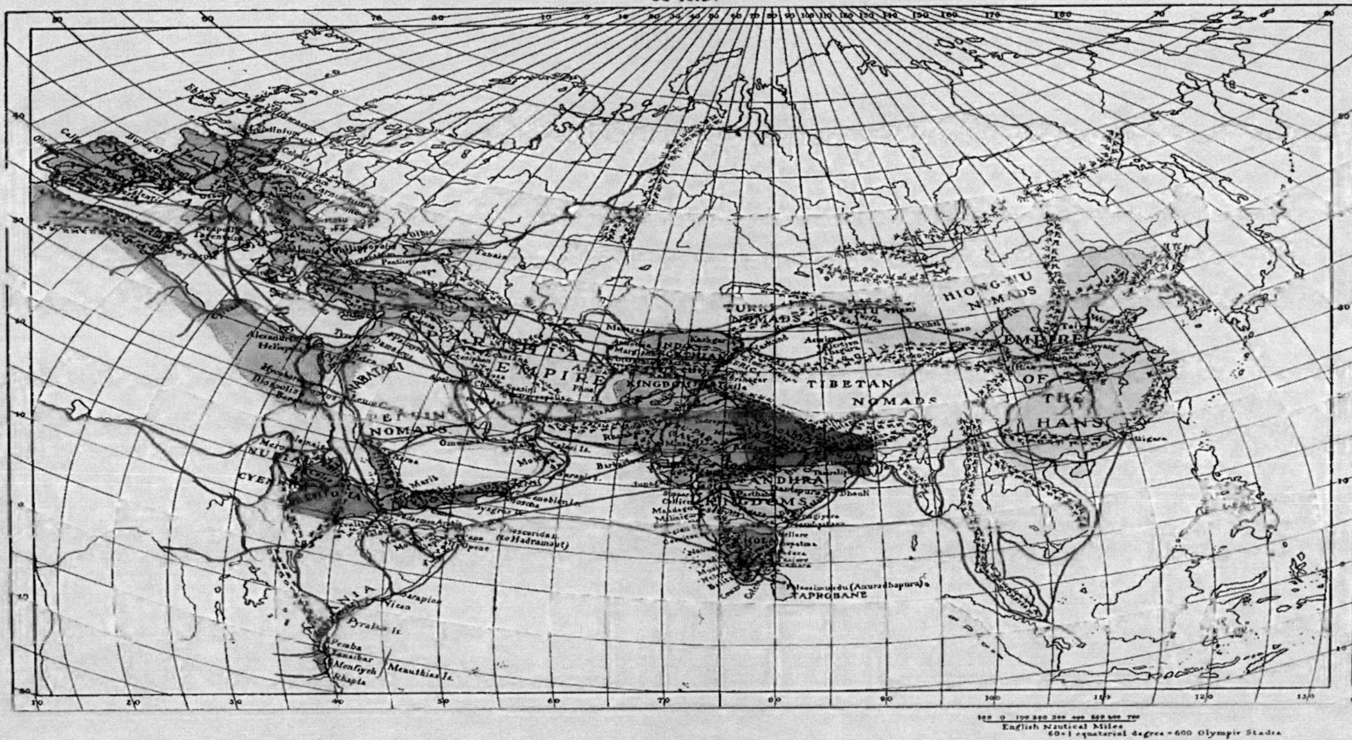